Heaven on Earth

The Gifts of Christ in the Divine Service

Heaven on Earth

The Gifts of Christ in the Divine Service

Arthur A. Just Jr.
Director of Deaconess Program

CONCORDIA PUBLISHING HOUSE · SAINT LOUIS

Published 2008 Concordia Publishing House
3558 S. Jefferson Ave., St. Louis, MO 63118-3968
1-800-325-3040 • www.cph.org

Manufactured in the United States of America

Library of Congress Cataloging-in-Publication Data

Just, Arthur A., 1953-

Heaven on earth : the blessings of God in the divine service / Arthur A. Just.

p. cm.

Includes bibliographical references.

ISBN 978-0-7586-0671-6

1. Public worship--Lutheran Church--History. 2. Lutheran Church--Liturgy--History. 3. Lutheran Church--Doctrines--History. I. Title.

BX8067.A1J87 2008

264'.041--dc22

2007047132

1 2 3 4 5 6 7 8 9 10 17 16 15 14 13 12 11 10 09 08

Contents

Preface

Since studying New Testament and liturgical texts at Yale Divinity School, my pastoral and academic vocation has been focused on matters liturgical, even though I consider myself, first and foremost, a student of the New Testament. Aidan Kavanagh, one of the most influential liturgists of the late twentieth century, was a profound influence on my understanding and appreciation of Christian liturgy, and he encouraged me to pursue my own Lutheran tradition. My parish experience coincided with the publication of *Lutheran Worship* in 1982. The call to teach New Testament homiletics and liturgics at Concordia Theological Seminary, Forth Wayne, Indiana, occurred as the worship wars in our Church body commenced. With the advent of alternative liturgical forms outside the Lutheran tradition being used in our Church, I found myself addressing clergy and laity on the treasures of historic Lutheran liturgy.

Further study in the New Testament at the University of Durham on "Table Fellowship and Eschatology at Emmaus" attempted to combine New Testament and liturgical interests by investigating the liturgical structures of table fellowship in the Emmaus narrative and Luke's Gospel. Throughout my career, requests for articles on worship kept coming, for example, "Liturgical Renewal in the Parish" in *Lutheran Worship: History and Practice* (Concordia Publishing House, 1993), and even the Lukan commentary for Concordia Publishing House addressed the Gospel as a catechetical and liturgical document.

At the request of the Indiana District Board of Worship of the The Lutheran Church—Missouri Synod, we produced the video *Lutheran Liturgy: Yesterday, Today, and Forever* (1999). This coincided with our work on *Lutheran Service Book*, and it was a privilege to serve as chairman of the lectionary committee and as a member of the steering committee. Through the generous support of Pr. John Fiene and the saints at Advent Lutheran Church in Zionsville, Indiana, as well as people such as Elaine Graff, who produced the video, and Ken Ring of Lutheran Visuals, who distributed it, we were able to offer the Church an accessible entrance into the treasures of our liturgical life as Lutherans. Most of us were surprised at the positive response of our Church to this twelve-part series on the the liturgy, particularly the desire for a book that covered in more depth the topics of the video. Concordia Theological Seminary graciously granted me a sabbatical in the spring/summer of 2003 to work on the manuscript for *Heaven on Earth*, and Thrivent Financial for Lutherans provided some financial support.

Teaching, speaking, and writing about matters liturgical is my hobby, and after the liturgy video, I was ready to focus on the New Testament. But then along came the inception of the Good Shepherd Institute in 1999, and my appointment as dean of Kramer Chapel in 2000. The publication of papers from the Good Shepherd Institute conferences created annual opportunities to reflect on liturgical topics. No matter how hard I tried to move away from matters liturgical, the liturgy kept finding its way back to me. Ironically, this book appears after my tenure as dean of the chapel. What a great joy and privilege to serve alongside Cantors Resch and Hildebrand, two of the finest churchmen I know, in forming the worship life of our campus. Serving as dean of Kramer Chapel has been the highlight of my years at the seminary, but I could not be more pleased to give way to my good friend and colleague, Dr. Paul Grime, who brings fresh leadership to the worship life of our seminary after his extraordinary work on *Lutheran Service Book*.

Sections of *Heaven on Earth* may sound familiar to some, for it pulls together in one place everything I have written on the liturgy. I am grateful to CPH for allowing me to republish in modified form some of the material from the commentary, as well as the Good Shepherd Institute for material from our monograph series.

Many thanks also to Scot Kinnaman and the editorial staff at CPH for their marvelous work, and to Deaconess Sara Bielby, who read the first draft from the perspective of the person in the pew, offering many fine suggestions to make this even more accessible to a wider audience.

This book sets before pastors, church workers, and laypeople the liturgical and theological treasures of our Lutheran heritage as we rejoice together that, in Christ, heaven is on earth.

All Saints' 2007

Introduction
The Historic Liturgy

We are in the midst of an identity crisis. Our culture bombards us with unrealistic images of what "normal" human beings should be like. No one is immune to this identity crisis, not even Christians. And this is a great tragedy, for we know that our life is defined by Jesus Christ, our Creator and our Redeemer. Our identity is in conformity to His holy life. So why are we struggling to understand who we are?

Telling the World Its Story

Each and every one of us has a story to tell about our lives. My story begins with my grandmother, the daughter of a Lutheran pastor. Before she passed away at the age of 95, she told her grandchildren and great-grandchildren her story. Her story and the story of the Church were inseparably intertwined. How different from our time! I have since wondered how I would tell the story of my life to my grandchildren or how my children would tell it to theirs. The world has become so complicated, it appears as if the world has lost its story. And to lose one's story is to lose one's identity.

Until modern times, it was commonly accepted that the Creator told the world its story, which was synonymous with the Holy Scriptures. However, in this postmodern and post-Christian society, the world has lost its connection to the Bible, the story of our faith. Questions about where we come from, where we are going, and how we are to live along the way are no longer formed by the "realistic narrative" of the Bible.[1] In fact, in past centuries one sign of a well-educated and well-rounded individual was familiarity with Scripture. Unfortunately, the world no longer knows the biblical narrative and therefore does not order its life according to the themes of that story. In previous generations, the Church could assume that those in the pews not only had a working knowledge of the Bible but also that Holy Scripture shaped the narrative of their lives. Sadly, this is no longer the case. If individuals no longer know the basics concerning the origin of this world and of human beings, the promises of God for our physical and spiritual welfare, and the history of God's chosen people throughout time, how can they be expected to know that Christ Jesus has come to make them His own?

Perhaps there is confusion about our identity in Christ because we no longer know where it is that we see Jesus. Our self-centered culture persuades us that the only place to find Jesus is in our hearts, that is, in our emotions and feelings. But when Scripture speaks of the heart, it means the very core of the human being, the very place in us where Christ dwells. Our identity is in the person of Jesus. We see Jesus where He has promised to be for us and for our salvation—in His Word, in Baptism, and in the Lord's Supper.

It would be simple to assign our loss of identity to busy schedules or to the lack of Christian education or to the lack of church attendance, and these certainly are contributing factors. Perhaps the larger problem is that we do not see Christ as the center of our story. We do not see Christ as the center of the liturgy, the place where His story—the story of the world—is told. Such a towering assertion goes against the grain of our postmodern sensibilities and expectations. Yet the history of the Church testifies that, for centuries, our brothers and sisters in Christ invited those who did not share our faith to come to the Divine Service, where they then heard the salvation story in its entirety through the rhythm of the liturgy. In our worship, Christ, the author of life, is present, telling that story through the words of the prophets and apostles and serving as host of a heavenly feast where the world's story is given its heavenly reality.

The Liturgy

The story told in the Divine Service is about the real world in which we live. This real world was created by God as good and right, but became terribly wrong. Our sins are evidence that this world has been infected with a virus from which we cannot escape. Everyone is able to see this evidence, especially in those who suffer physical, emotional, and physical pain from the consequences of sin, or in those broken by violence and tragedy, by sickness and death. Only God is able to make right what has gone wrong. He loved us so much that He was willing to send His Son from heaven into our world in order to bear all our burdens—even to the point of death.

Hanging on a cross, Jesus shows the Father's mercy for us. His death makes right what had gone wrong, releasing our fallen world from its captivity to darkness and death. His suffering and death was traded for our life. Jesus the Creator entered our creation as a creature for one purpose: to make all things new. From the moment of His conception and incarnation, the world has never been the same. Jesus came to live among us to show how God first intended us to live when He created us in His own image. That is why Jesus' journey took Him from heaven to this world and ultimately to the cross. Jesus experienced the full tragedy of our fallen humanity, becoming sin for us, so that He might reverse sin's curse and make right what had gone wrong. Jesus entered into this messy world of our making in order to be faithful even unto death and restore our flesh to God's image, making us whole. The empty tomb testifies that death could not hold Him. He has been raised from the dead. As those who have received the benefits of Christ's suffering and death, we also will not have to experience eternal death. We, too, will be raised from the dead to live with Him forever in heaven.

The world can never return to the state it was before Jesus entered our cosmos in human flesh. God be praised! Therefore, the world's story cannot be told without Jesus' conception, birth, life, death, and resurrection at the center of that story. Now and forever the world and its story are marked by His incarnation. As we confess in the Apostles' Creed, the very same flesh-and-blood Jesus who was "born of the Virgin Mary, suffered under Pontius Pilate, was crucified, died and was buried, on the third day rose again from the dead, ascended into heaven, and sits at the right hand of the Father" continues to be present in His Church *in the Church's worship.* Jesus Christ, crucified and risen, is now present among us in the preaching of the Gospel and the sacramental life of the Church. In order to tell the world its story, we must enter into the mysteries of Jesus' real presence and realize that Jesus, God-and-man, continues to be present among us in His flesh, telling us the story of a world made new in Him.

Journeying with Christ to Jerusalem

For Christians, life is a pilgrimage from Baptism to death, which is the entrance into eternity. When Christians put on Christ in Baptism, we begin our journey to a destination of full communion with Christ in heaven. In the baptismal font, Christ's story becomes our story. As we journey through life, we live under the cross where, through daily repentance and forgiveness, we die and rise with Christ in our baptismal lives. We are continually living in

Christ as we hear His Holy Word and feed upon His holy food, which will sustain us on the way. In Word and Sacrament, we hear the story of the world. That story is not some inert fact. The very telling of the world's story in Word and Sacrament brings us right into the story and changes us. Our pilgrimage leads us inevitably to our physical death, which is an entrance to full communion with Christ in His heavenly home. The goal of the journey is to live in Christ's presence forever and to feast at His table for eternity. The Christian pilgrimage is an incarnational life in Christ because from the moment we are baptized we are joined to Him and to His life, for He dwells in us and we dwell in Him.

As we journey from Baptism to death, we are accompanied by the song of the Church. Our response to God's story is sung through liturgical hymns. The liturgy takes us on a journey with Jesus from His birth at Christmas as we sing the Gloria in Excelsis, the hymn of the angels, to His death in Jerusalem as we sing about the Lamb of God who takes away the sin of the world. We also travel with Jesus during the Church Year that begins with the celebration of His birth in Bethlehem, climaxes at Easter with His death and resurrection, and continues at Pentecost with the ongoing life in Christ as the Church, the Body of Christ. To live as a Christian in the world is to be united to Jesus Christ, the source of all life, who cleanses us from our sins to make us a fit dwelling for His presence.

In order to tell the world its story, we must proclaim that in our liturgy of Word and Sacrament the Creator of all things unites us to Himself for eternity. This life of communion with Jesus begins at the font and is sustained by Word and Sacrament every Sunday. His suffering and resurrected flesh restores our impure and unclean flesh to wholeness and wellness. Every baptismal font reminds us that we are washed from our uncleanness and have been given a new identity that defines our life by Christ's life—a life of forgiveness. Every pulpit reminds us that Christ manifests Himself in the Divine Service as He speaks to us about our new life in Him—a life of freedom from bondage. And every altar reminds us that our story is one of suffering and sacrifice, but that the story ends with resurrection and new life delivered to us in the body and blood of our Lord.

Confident Liturgy for a World that Has Lost Its Story

This book does not intend to *impose* some law of worship on the Church, but rather to *propose* a more excellent way (1 Corinthians 12:31) to tell the story of real life in Christ—the way of the historic liturgy that has been used by countless Christians for almost fourteen hundred years, perhaps even longer. This is how the Church has survived persecution, heresy, wars, famine, and plague. It had a place to retreat and to engage in a confident expression of the story of the world. When it seemed as if the world might be coming to an end, or even worse, as if the world was losing its story, the Church regrouped to the measured cadences of the biblical story told through the historic liturgy. When things looked as if they could not get much worse, the Church entered into the safe haven of the historic liturgy, where through Kyrie and Gloria, through Sanctus and Agnus Dei, it proclaimed to a world in chaos the story of God's redeeming love.

Confident liturgy is the more excellent way of worshiping, the way of our grandmothers and great-grandmothers, stretching all the way back into the New Testament and even beyond that into the Old Testament. This book does not propose that we return to some supposed golden age and reenact a liturgy of a bygone era, but rather that we learn from the past as it is now embraced by our own present-day worship.

> How best to do this we may learn from his Word and from the way his Word has prompted his worship through the centuries. We are heirs of an astonishingly rich tradition. Each generation receives from those who went before and, in making that tradition of the Divine Service its own, adds what best may serve in its own day—the living heritage and something new.[2]

A living heritage and something new is what I propose, for this wonderful way of describing the vibrancy of good liturgical worship is at the heart of a confident liturgy.

Recovering Our Liturgical Roots

In this book we will journey into the history of Jewish and Christian worship in order to discover our liturgical origins. This journey will put us in touch with countless saints whose identity was shaped by entering into the presence of Christ to receive from Him what only He can give—a life that is defined by His presence and His gifts of forgiveness, life, and salvation.

We will discover who we are as worshiping Christians by investigating how Jesus worshiped. Jesus sought His Father's presence in the temple in Jerusalem where God's glory dwelt in the Holy of Holies. Jesus traveled to Jerusalem many times to His Father's house to hear the Word of God with other Jews. He heard the Word of God every Sabbath of His life in the synagogue. During His ministry He was invited to read and preach the Word of God. For Jesus, God's Word was God's food, and to hear the Word of God was to be nourished by God with food that lasts forever. Our hearing of the Word of God is structured in a very similar way to Jesus' hearing of that Word in the synagogue.

Jesus also celebrated the Passover, the most important feast of the Jews. And on the night in which He was betrayed, during a Passover meal where He served as host, Jesus instituted the Lord's Supper for us to commune with Him in a miraculous way to forgive us our sins and make us holy. In, with, and under bread and wine, we now eat and drink the very body and blood of Jesus Christ—the very body and blood that was crucified on the cross to cleanse us from our sins, the very body and blood that was raised on the third day to make right what had gone wrong. By our participation in this meal we are now joined to Christ's death and resurrection. By joining Himself to us in this sacred meal of holy food, we are now joined to all the saints who have died and risen in Christ. This communion of saints is where heaven and earth are joined together in Him. We are members of this eternal community, a community that even now participates in the heavenly things as a foretaste of the feast to come.

The Liturgy of Life

When Sunday comes to an end, the liturgy of the Church goes into the world with us through each unique vocation. We are Christ's people, standing in the midst of a broken world. As the baptized, we bear witness in our words and lives to the Christ who dwells in us. Our lives testify that Christ's presence in the world transforms the culture and makes it new. To live in Christ is to bear witness that Jesus Christ is present in our world in His gifts. Christ is present in the world through us, and He is present for the life of the world.

Many people today *want* to know how to be a Christian. What they are really asking is how to live like Christ. The response: "Be like Christ who lives in you!" But they will ask: "What does this mean?" The answer comes from Jesus' Sermon on the Plain (Luke 6): "Love your enemies, be merciful and compassionate, forgive, and do works of charity." But they will ask:

"How is this done?" The answer: "Come to church and receive the gifts of Christ's flesh in hearing the Gospel and feasting at His banquet. And then go. Go out into the world and be what you have become in Christ." This is life in Christ! This is how we continue to tell the world its story about real life in Christ through our lives! **This is the liturgy of life!**

In Christ Forever

What God said in the past, in Holy Scripture, is at the center of our worship. God uses the words He spoke through the prophets and the apostles as the means by which Christ comes to us in this *present* moment, *today*, *right now*. And God uses these same words to take us on a journey with Him through death and resurrection all the way to *heaven*. In Jesus Christ, yesterday and today are joined forever, and earth and heaven come together in one place. He is the Alpha and the Omega, the beginning and the end. He is the story.

1
The Theology of Worship

Our journey to recover our liturgical roots begins with understanding our distinct Lutheran theology of worship. What is God doing as we gather together around His Word and Sacraments? The structure of rite, space, and time in our worship will answer this question and be at the heart of our discussion.

Our distinct Lutheran theology of worship comes to us from the New Testament liturgical structures of Word and Sacrament. What Christian worship is could be described from either the perspective of the Christian assembly or from the perspective of God. In most descriptions of worship, one hears the Church's perspective, that is, the Church gathers to praise, give thanks, and glorify God because of faith that grasps hold of the gifts of God in Jesus Christ. *Worship* is an appropriate word to describe our response to God's gracious activity in Jesus Christ, for worship defines our perspective, what we do in view of what God has done. Worship, then, would describe our reverence and praise, our service and adoration.

However, this description of the Christian community's communal activity on Sunday goes against the grain of Lutheran confessional theology. Lutherans seldom begin theology from below, from man's perspective, but from above, from God's perspective. Martin Luther and the Reformation helped us to see that what is foremost in our worship is not our service and sacrifice to God but His service and sacrifice to us. The gifts of Jesus are hidden in the simple means of water and Word, bread and wine. We join a world outside ourselves by receiving gifts from heaven in the flesh of Jesus and submitting ourselves to the great mystery that heaven comes to earth through this bodily presence of our Savior. We sometimes think of heaven abstractly, as somewhere "up there," but heaven is wherever Jesus is. Because Jesus is present among us in the gifts of Word and Sacrament, then heaven itself is present among us. It is the world of "angels, archangels, and all the company of heaven."

This mystery of heaven on earth is a biblical theology of worship. God does not need our worship and praise and service. But we do need His service, His presence, and His gifts of forgiveness, life, and salvation. Whatever praise we give to God, whatever honor is due His name, is our response to God's service to us. What is this service that God gives? How does He serve us with His gifts? What are the gifts that He gives?

The Biblical Context of Lutheran Worship

What is significant in the worship of the Old and New Testaments, of Israel and the Church? Foremost would be the gathering around the presence of God, who offers Himself to His people. All the Old Testament saints gathered for worship to stand in the presence of God and to receive from God His Word, His direction, His guidance. God's presence was always tied to His saving intentions, for God was always present to save His people from their sins. The Israelite places of worship were houses of prayer for all the nations where they petitioned God on behalf of the world to "Hear us!" and to visit them with salvation.

Before the fall, the life of our first parents in the Garden of Eden was a life of worship. Adam and Eve were created to behold the glorious presence of their Creator in His creation and to worship Him. The essence of this worship is the response of the people of God to the presence of God, but the response is always dependent on the presence and on the blessings that proceed from that presence. When the virus of sin infected the world, our first parents were cast out of the garden. Their access to God would no longer be direct. The Old Testament is the account of God paving the way for the promised Messiah, who would reconcile the world to Himself and bring in a new creation. It's about access to God and His presence.

The entire Old Testament cultic system of sacrifices pointed forward to the sacrifice of the Messiah in a violent death for the sins of the world. The prophet Isaiah described it this way: "His appearance was so marred, beyond human semblance, and His form beyond that of the children of mankind—so shall He sprinkle many nations" (Isaiah 52:14–15). The elaborate Passover liturgy that marked the height of Israel's worship was molded by the presence of the One who would end death by the sacrifice of His very own Son for sin.

Israel's worship was centered in God's presence and therefore in God's holiness. This holy presence attracted the people of God because it was the source of their salvation, but it also repelled them because they knew how dangerous God's holy presence was for those who were not worthy to enter it. Moses understood the consequences: no one could look upon God without the risk of death. Moses could only approach God's presence in the burning bush with his face covered and sandals removed because he was standing on holy ground (Exodus 3:2–6). God's presence on Mount Sinai was so dangerous that He warned Moses, "Take care not to go up into the mountain or touch the edge of it. Whoever touches the mountain shall be put to death" (Exodus 19:12). Even the ark of the covenant as the place of God's presence was so powerful that it could strike down entire armies that looked upon it (1 Samuel 6:19). When David had the ark carried into the hill country of Judea and oxen bearing the ark stumbled, Uzzah, a son of Abinadab, was struck dead for reaching out and touching the ark, even though he intended to keep it from falling (2 Samuel 6:5–7).

God set apart one of the tribes of Israel, the Levites, to mediate God's presence for the people with rituals of cleansing that prepared them to enter God's presence worthily. This is why there are so many boundaries in the temple in Jerusalem, for one must be worthy to enter God's presence. Even in the New Testament, the presence of God through the words of the angel Gabriel caused Mary to be afraid (Luke 1:30), as Peter also was afraid to stand in Jesus' presence at the great catch of fish (Luke 5:8–10). Both the angel Gabriel and Jesus proclaimed words of absolution when they said, "Do not be afraid," for they were telling Mary and Peter that they were worthy to stand in God's presence without perishing. For both the Old and New Testaments, the words ring true: "It is a fearful thing to fall into the hands of the living God" (Hebrews 10:31).[1]

The presence in the world of the Word made flesh (John 1) marks the redemption of the world. With the incarnation, worship is no longer the people of God gathered in expectation and hope for the salvation soon to be revealed. Rather, worship is the celebration of the presence of salvation that has broken through in Jesus Christ and now permanently resides in the world. Salvation has come **now**—it is here **today**. The entire creation receives now the benefits of the new, greater, Second Adam who has come to re-create, renew, and redeem.

From the day of Pentecost, the apostles celebrated the presence of the crucified and risen Lord among them through their "teaching and fellowship, to the breaking of bread" (Acts 2:42). The Early Church was a eucharistic community gathered to commune with Jesus by hearing His Word and by receiving His body and blood. Although the Early Church expected the Lord to return at any time, they were, in fact, living in the presence of end-time blessings in their simple liturgy of Word and Sacrament. The same holds true for us today. If salvation is here because Jesus Christ is present in our worship forgiving sins, then the Lord may return today, tomorrow, or in fifty years. The time does not matter because we have now the blessings of the *not yet.* The blessings for which we wait are ours, even though those blessings have not yet come to us completely. These blessings we receive by faith through Word and Spirit. By faith we enter His presence as unworthy sinners confessing our sins, cleansed by His blood through the forgiveness of sins. By faith we receive the blessing of the **not yet** even **now** in our ears when we hear God's Word read and preached. By faith we receive these blessings in our mouths as we eat His body and drink His blood. By faith we are called to His Church where we are surrounded by His saints and receive Christ bodily in ear and mouth. This is participation in Christ's flesh in a sinful world where there is suffering, tragedy, and death. We are not fully home yet, for that will come only when we enter into full communion with Christ at death or at His coming again in glory.

Liturgy as Inaugurated Eschatology

What we are speaking about here is the *eschaton*, the end times. Eschatology is a way of describing what will happen when Jesus comes again in His glory. But eschatology is concerned with more than the second coming, it is also concerned about the last things, that is, what we will experience in heaven after the final judgment. The most significant "last thing" is full communion with Christ and the Holy Trinity, a communion that we now experience through our Baptism, through the hearing of His Word, and through His Holy Meal. The experience of the last things has already begun in our worship! This is what some call "inaugurated eschatology," the beginning of the last things and the end times.[2] We proclaim this belief in our liturgy of Word and Sacrament every time we sing "This Is the Feast": "For the Lamb who was slain has begun His reign. Alleluia" (*LSB*, p. 155).

Eschatology, therefore, is to speak about the person of Christ, whose presence according to His divine and human natures is ongoing in the Church's liturgy. It is to speak about Christ's Body, the Church—God's eschatological community, where Christ dwells by Word and Spirit. Wherever Christ is, there are the last things, the *eschaton*, so eschatology is about the Gospel and Sacraments as the means for Christ's presence. The liturgy is an eschatological moment because the end times are brought forward and made present by Christ's presence in His gifts of mercy and forgiveness. In the liturgy those end times are upon us now, even as we wait for Christ's return to judge the living and the dead. Eschatology declares that the final end of Christian existence is to be with Jesus Christ, our creator and re-creator, both now in liturgy and forever at the Lamb's high feast. To be with Christ forever is the goal of our pilgrimage, its end and its beginning. Eschatology is more than simply the end of all things—it is our return home to God in Christ to dwell in His presence at the ongoing feast.

Biblical Eschatology and Worship

Early Christians believed that Jesus, the crucified and ascended Lord, was present with them through Word and Sacrament. This biblical eschatology is missing in many discussions about worship and liturgy today. In our liturgy we join all saints in one worshiping assembly because there Jesus Christ is present both in heaven and on earth. The saints in heaven and the worshiping congregation on earth manifest their unity in the one liturgy. In the liturgy the Church tells the world that its story is an eternal one because the presence of Jesus Christ, the eternal One, now dwells in the world.

The liturgy places us on a historical and eschatological line through God's great, objective, cosmic act of justification in Jesus Christ. We now have the same status in the kingdom of God as both the prophets of old and the saints in glory. We are surrounded by a cloud of witnesses who have gone before us, and, with Christians everywhere, we rejoice in their presence. They are standing with us and joining their voices with ours in one glorious liturgy. The song of heaven is "Holy, holy, holy, is the Lord God Almighty, who was and is and is to come!" (Revelation 4:8). The song of the Lamb is "Worthy are You to take the scroll and to open its seals, for You were slain, and by Your blood You ransomed people for God from every tribe and language and people and nation, and You have made them a kingdom and priests to our God, and they shall reign on the earth" (Revelation 5:9–10).

Inaugurated eschatology, then, heightens the anticipation of the consummation in Christ's second coming. Following the New Testament pattern, worship is decidedly communal—not individualistic as is so much worship today. Individualism has become a core value of today's culture. The biblical culture of Jesus and the apostles would have had trouble recognizing their faith wrapped in the garb of our modern individualism. At the time of our Lord, a person's identity came not from within, by what a person felt about oneself or one's deeds or accomplishments. Rather, a person's identity came from the outside, by the community. First-century Christians would not know where to begin with the individualistic worship of our world with its focus on our response to God, on our praise and thanksgiving, and not on the gifts given and received by the community of believers—the Body of Christ, His Church. In fact, when Paul addressed Christians in the congregations he founded, he seldom addressed individuals but rather spoke to communities whose identities came from their common confession of Christ crucified, Christ risen from the dead. The communal character of our worship is not merely restricted to those in the congregation whom we see. Wherever Christ is bodily present in Word and Sacrament, there also are all the saints who have died and risen in Christ. They join us in our worship.

Liturgy

At its most basic definition, liturgy is what Jesus does for His people when He gathers them together. The word *liturgy* also describes what God's people do when they gather on Sunday around Word and Sacrament. But today, when people hear the word *liturgy*, there seems to be some confusion as to its true definition. Many might think of the hymnal they use as "the liturgy." Although worship resources contain liturgical texts that assist us in our worship, they are not "the liturgy."

For the Life of the World

The word *liturgy* has undergone many changes in meaning over the last two thousand years. Today's tendency is to dismiss this word as an accurate description of Christian worship because it seems to describe worship from man's perspective. But this does not reflect the original meaning of the word for the early Christian communities. Our understanding of liturgy has been influenced by the later medieval notion of "the work of the people," but this is a misrepresentation of its original intent. *Liturgy* is taken from the Greek word *leitourgia*, which Christians borrowed from Roman culture to describe their worship. Philip Melanchthon describes *leitourgia* well: "To the Greeks it meant public burdens, such as tribute, the expense of equipping a fleet, or similar things" (Apology of the Augsburg Confession XXIV 81).[3] What is often overlooked in this discussion is that the tax/obligation/responsibility that a Roman citizen owed was for the sake of the empire. The Roman citizen did not pay this tax for himself, but for the good of the Roman community. Only secondarily was this tax a subjective act, that is, if he did not pay, the "Roman IRS" would be after him. No, primarily it was an objective act performed as a faithful Roman citizen.

On account of this notion of tax for the sake of the empire, early Christians adopted the word *leitourgia* to describe their worship. Typical of things borrowed from paganism, the word was Christianized. Early Christians kept the objective character of the word, that is, what Romans citizens gave for the sake of the empire, and translated it into the broader sense of what God the Father was doing in sending His Son to give up His life **for the life of the world**, or for the life of all creation, which is what "the world" implied.

The One who is working in the liturgy is God, and He is working "for the life of the world" (John 6:33). It is God who serves His people with gifts that come from the gracious presence of His Son. The Father's liturgy is eschatological—He sent the Son to His creation to bring in a new creation. Christ comes not as a leader but as a servant at a table He prepares in the midst of His enemies. Nothing new is made when Jesus visits His creation, but all things are made new. He takes what is broken and makes it whole; He frees the captives, gives sight to the blind, releases those who are oppressed, and forgives the sins of all. Jesus was sent into this world by the Father. His sacrificial death gave up His life for the life of the world. The Son's liturgy is to free the world from the bondage of its fallenness through His bloody death—to take into His own flesh our sin, our sickness, and our death, so that when He was lifted up on that cross, the new creation He brought meant the end of bondage and the beginning of a new, liberated cosmos that waits for full release at the second coming.

Gottesdienst: Divine Service Where God Gives Us His Gifts

Lutherans, like the early Christians, believe that Christ is bodily present through Word and Sacrament, offering His people the gifts of heaven. The liturgy is, first and foremost, the activity of God who is serving us with the gifts. But it is also the Christian assembly whose right and privilege it is to stand in God's presence and receive His gifts for the sake of the world. Christians are agents of God in the world, for no one else in the world could do this service! And as Christians respond to the Word and Sacraments, they respond in Christ, that is, their songs of praise, their prayers, and their confession of faith are not their own, but they are from the Christ who is in them, responding back to the Father through Him. And so both the gifts given and the gifts responded to are in Christ.

Here we see the origin of Luther's word for worship, *Gottesdienst*—God serving the world with His gifts of forgiveness, life, and salvation through Word and Sacrament. The liturgy is the context in which God acts to save His people and in which God's people respond. First, they receive the gifts God pours upon the world through the Christian liturgy; then, as representatives of the world, they respond to the gifts in acts of worship. The liturgy is where God is present in Christ to save us from sin, death, and the devil. This definition of liturgy may well have been endorsed by Luther, whose sole principle in renewing the liturgy was justification by grace through faith.[4]

Luther's reforms could also be described by the criteria of faith and love. Here again are expressed the two different perspectives on worship. When described in terms of justification, it is from God's perspective, what God has done for the world in Jesus Christ, His objective acts that are present and proclaimed in the liturgy. The supreme expression of justification is in the liturgy. If our liturgies are to be Lutheran, they must be understood in the context of justification and justification in the context of the liturgy. God's solution to the fallenness of creation is now present in the Christian assembly. The end is here and celebrated because Christ, the heavenly Bridegroom, is present offering the gifts of the wedding feast for His Bride, the Church, through His teaching at the table and His presence in the meal. God proclaims to the world that the kingdom of God in Jesus Christ is present among us through Word and Sacrament.

Faith Receives

It is also possible to view the liturgy as our response to the objective act of justification that is present and proclaimed in the liturgy. By faith, one speaks of the passive act of standing in the presence of God and receiving His gifts through the justifying act of Christ's presence. We bring nothing to the liturgy; we simply respond in Spirit-produced faith to God's gift of salvation. This is God's liturgy, His act, His expression of who He is and what He has done for the world in Christ, and we are incorporated by Him into His liturgy. This is what we really mean by the word *worship*—the supreme act of faith that responds to God's justifying act and saving gifts. And in this act God gives us the faith to worship Him. The Apology of the Augsburg Confession describes liturgy in this way:

> Faith is the divine service (*latreia*) that receives the benefits offered by God. The righteousness of the Law is the divine service (*latreia*) that offers to God our merits. God wants to be worshiped through faith so that we receive from Him those things He promises and offers. (Apology of the Augsburg Confession IV 49)

This is how God wants to be known and worshiped, that we accept His blessings and "receive them because of His mercy, not because of our merits" (Apology of the Augsburg Confession IV 60).

Love Responds

By love, one speaks of our active response that flows from the faith that passively receives the gifts of life and salvation. We express this love in many ways: We confess before God our many sins. We sing those glorious, liturgical hymns of praise the Church has sung for almost fourteen hundred years to show our thanksgiving for the salvation that God gives us in Word and Sacrament. We respond in prayer, first with the Lord's Prayer, the perfect petitionary prayer that Jesus gave us to pray, and then with all other prayers of thanksgiving and petition in which we either thank God for salvation in Jesus Christ or we petition God to sustain us in the burdens of this life so that we might not lose faith. All liturgical prayer is salvific in its content, that is, it either thanks God for salvation or petitions God to keep on saving, forming a continuous cycle. Liturgical prayer is the faithful response of God's people to God's love in Jesus Christ in which they petition God to help them accept by faith the life He has given them.

So far this response of love has been love to God expressed in confession, thanksgiving, praise, and prayer. For Luther, this fulfills the First Table of the Law, to love the Lord our God with all our heart, soul, and mind. Thus our first and primary response of love in the liturgy is toward God.

The second expression of love in the liturgy fulfills the Second Table of the Law, to love our neighbor as ourselves. Our confession of sins, thanksgiving, praise, and prayer also fit under this category, for in these things we by faith join ourselves with the community of saints in confessing the sins of thought, word, and deed we have committed against our neighbor, in thanking God for salvation, and in praising Him for His great acts of mercy toward us. In our prayers, we pray as community for our neighbor in all his needs, that he might continue in faith no matter what affliction or calamity may overcome him.

In the early Christian communities, the prayers of dismissal were a high point of the liturgy when, after the Service of the Word, those not worthy to partake of the Eucharist were dismissed from the community with prayer, particularly the catechumens. Following the prayers of dismissal, the faithful who would partake of the Sacrament exchanged the kiss of peace, a full-bodied kiss on the mouth, men to men and women to women. This was an outward sign of the love and reconciliation that now existed among the faithful before the Liturgy of the Sacrament, a kiss the faithful were able to give because of the freedom of the Gospel. This was not a cultural phenomenon but an anti-cultural one that the Christians shared because of their reconciliation in Christ. The kiss of peace was the supreme expression of love for the neighbor of faith as the worshiping community prepared to give thanks to the giver of eternal gifts.

Loving Our Neighbor Who Knows Not Christ

How can the Christian community demonstrate its love for neighbors who do not know the gifts of God? Here is where evangelism and missions are properly placed, not as the essence of the Church, but as what the Church does. Our greatest act of love to our unbelieving neighbors is to bring them into the liturgical assembly to receive the gifts of salvation. The Great Commission is an act of love, inspired by faith that receives the gifts in the liturgy, to go out to the highways and byways and bring our lost neighbors into the liturgy so they may behold the presence of Jesus Christ and receive the gifts of the Gospel proclaimed in the Service of the Word. In the prayers of the Church, we pray for the world and its needs, that all people may join us in faith and eventually in the reception of the Supper.

However, our neighbors who do not know Christ cannot join us in the reception of the Sacrament until they first believe and are catechized to be prepared to receive Christ in Baptism and in the Eucharist. Catechesis teaches table etiquette, that is, how one stands in the presence of God to receive His mercy and forgiveness in a manner that is reverent and faithful to that presence. Throughout the history of the Church, this catechesis took time, as it was not always easy for people who lived in darkness and the shadow of death to learn how to live in the light of Christ and His forgiveness. The things of this world were sometimes difficult to give up, and the Gospel was painful as they were called to separate from their sinful ways, which often meant leaving behind their families and friends and becoming outcasts in the world in which they used to live.

It takes time to teach our neighbors who do not know Christ how to hear the Word and respond to the Word that prepares them to recline with the saints at the feast of the Lord's Supper spread before them. This table is not intended for neighbors who do not know Christ. It is for the baptized who were cleansed at the baptismal font and who love the Host of the table with their heart, soul, and mind, and who by faith fully understand what sitting at table with the Host in His kingdom means. Our neighbors who do not know Christ must first come to know Him by sitting at His feet and hearing His Word proclaimed and interpreted by one who has been called to stand in Christ's stead and by His command. Teaching table etiquette is one of the great ways in which we show our neighbors that we love them so much that we do not want them to be harmed by coming into Christ's presence unworthy or unprepared. For if they come to the presence of Christ and are unclean, that is, if they have not been cleansed by the blood of the Lamb through the waters of Holy Baptism, they will only experience condemnation for rejecting the forgiveness of sins by Jesus.

Therefore, our worship must immediately proclaim to our unbelieving neighbors that something is happening in the liturgy that happens nowhere else in all of creation. God, who is everywhere, chooses to locate Himself in the liturgy in Word and Sacraments. Here is God's divine normality—here is the center of the universe—the King reigning over His kingdom, the Creator re-creating His creation, the Bridegroom presiding at His wedding feast offering the food and drink of heaven. Our neighbor from the highways and byways must see that no more important business is being carried out in the world than the business transacted in the liturgy proclaimed for the life of the world. If our liturgy does not express this, then we cannot expect our visiting neighbors to return to our liturgy. If they do not see a world made new in Jesus Christ in the gifts of salvation, then they will not desire to enter into catechesis that prepares them to receive the justifying gifts of Christ in Baptism and to celebrate a world made new in Christ in the Eucharist.

Our unbelieving neighbors must also see in us Christ's love and mercy as we leave the sanctuary and go out in the world as bearers of His forgiveness and compassion. Many unbelievers entered the Church in the early days because they could see how Christians loved one another, and how that love spilled over to them. Serving our neighbors in love in the various vocations God has placed us demonstrates what we call "the liturgy of life" where Christ is present in the world in us, in our love and mercy. Lutherans have always understood such service to be *diakonia*, concrete acts of mercy as expressions of Christ's love in us spent out through us in love to our neighbor. Lutheran liturgy has always assumed that Christ's gifts received in the Divine Service would be extended to our neighbors in need. Luther's Post-Communion Collect petitions the Father: "We implore You that of Your mercy You would strengthen us through the same in faith toward You and in fervent love toward one another" (*LSB*, p. 201). Luther's hymn "O Lord, We Praise Thee" expresses this in beautiful poetic speech: "May God bestow on us His grace and favor / That we follow Christ our Savior / And live together here in love and union / Nor despise this blest Communion" (*LSB* 617:3).[5]

The Way of Prayer, the Way of Belief

Lex Orandi, Lex Credendi

Prosper of Aquitaine, a lay monk and disciple of Augustine, first coined the phrase *lex orandi, lex credendi* (fully, *legem credendi lex statuat supplicandi*), that is, "the law of worshiping founds the law of believing" (he is believed to have written this between AD 435 and AD 442). This maxim maintains that since the time of the apostles, liturgy has been the primary way the Church has handed down the faith to future generations. The liturgy and hymnody of a congregation shape the faith of the people more than anything else. The Church's belief and confession may be observed from her liturgy, hymns, preaching, and catechesis, not convention resolutions. The Church's belief and confession are inseparable from her liturgical life. For 1,500 years liturgy was not in written form in the hands of lay people. Liturgical changes evolved imperceptibly over a long period of time from within the congregation. With the invention of the Gutenberg press, however, liturgy became a physical text that could be edited or rewritten or even frozen in time, and this radical development has been taken to new levels in recent years with the advent of desktop publishing.

Prosper of Aquitaine's maxim bantered about in liturgical circles today needs to be fully discussed so that both those who study the liturgy and those who use that liturgy may be reconciled in their goals and the approaches to accomplish those goals. Recent tradition has in effect reversed that maxim to read: "the law of believing founds the law of worshiping." We need to recognize that if we want right teaching (*orthodidaskalia*) to be a leaven in our churches, then right worship (*orthodoxia*) must prevail and help to form true doctrine. If this does not happen, we will continue to experience warped worship and with it warped doctrine. Only with knowledge of Scripture and a clear head about liturgical tradition will we be able to approximate orthodoxy in the true sense of the word. Our "right worship," our "authentic orthodoxy" will be right for us because we are continually "rehearsing the faith of the fathers and then drawing its implications for today and tomorrow, playing the melody of theology and then developing variations on its ancient themes."[6]

Watchwords for Today: Reverence and Fidelity

Thus, the watchwords for the Church must be **reverence**, not relevance, **fidelity**, not innovation.[7] This will necessarily involve understanding biblical theology, Christology, ecclesiology, eschatology, liturgical tradition, and the Reformation. For some lay people, these may be heady, seemingly irrelevant topics, let alone incomprehensible words. But when we are at worship, regardless of whether we can pronounce the words and articulate the concepts, we are engaging in all those heady topics and more. Our Lutheran theology is deep and our heritage is rich. We have access to that theology and that heritage through the Lutheran liturgy. The liturgy shapes a worshiping community, giving it a Lutheran ethos.

Lutheran Liturgy Creates Its Own Culture

There is a common assumption today that the liturgy must reflect the language and the ethos of the current culture. If this is true, then liturgies will veer toward the pop culture in which we live. These culturally devised liturgies are at times exciting and entertaining, but are not transcultural. At most, they will give only immediate satisfaction. These liturgies then become just another expression of the culture's malaise, a feel-good, shallow, artificially uplifting sentimentality.

Furthermore, focusing on the centrality of the worshiper's experience in contemporary liturgies runs contrary to our Lutheran understanding of the hiddenness of the Kingdom in the world in which we live. The Church's liturgy is a humble expression and demonstration of the nature of the Kingdom. No matter how difficult our hymns, how untrained our organist, how weak our singing, God is present in our liturgy, offering His gifts of salvation. We dare not be seduced into thinking that the Kingdom comes by our own relevant production and performance. We must always maintain that the Kingdom is hidden under the humble means of God's proclamation of the new era of salvation in Jesus Christ through simple words, simple water, simple bread, and wine. This is why our liturgies are sacramental and why they give what we need the most: the forgiving mercy of God in Christ through which we are cleansed and made worthy to stand in His presence and receive His gifts. Believing that God is sacramentally present in our ancient but enduring liturgy is at the center of our understanding of God's revelation of Himself in Jesus Christ and His salvation of the world through suffering and sacrifice. The liturgical structures of Word and Sacrament transcend all cultures and create our Lutheran theology of worship.

Lutheran worship is its own culture, distinct from both the pop culture of secular society and the worship that characterizes most evangelical denominations in our country today. The Lutheran Church must develop and maintain its own cultural language that reflects the values and structures of Scripture, not of the current culture. And this language can be shaped only by a biblical theology that affirms Christ's work of making right what has gone wrong in declaring us righteous and offering this righteousness to us through His bodily presence in our worship in Word and Sacrament. Our belief that Jesus Christ is present in worship binds our Church together as a community, confessing one Lord, one faith, one Baptism, one God and Father of us all. This community is the Body of Christ, the Church. One day, the liturgical problems will no longer exist for the Church, for we will worship the Lamb in His kingdom that has no end. For now, however, we must constantly remember that we have now the one God who is sacramentally present among us as Savior and who continually invites us to the ongoing feast.

2

The Structure of the Historic Liturgy

The terms *liturgy* and *Divine Service* have been bantered about for the past twenty years or so. As we look closer at the structure of the liturgy and the Divine Service, it is important to state this fact: both the Liturgy of Word and Sacrament and the Divine Service are the same thing. Therefore, the blessing delivered in the Divine Service can rightly be attributed to the liturgy: Christ is present bodily. Thus we can rightly say that in the Divine Service Christ is present bodily. To speak of Christ's bodily presence is to speak of the gifts that come from His presence. No one describes these gifts better than Martin Luther. In his Small Catechism response to the question "What is the benefit of this eating and drinking?", he describes the gifts that come from Christ's body and blood in the Sacrament of the Altar as "forgiveness of sins, life, and salvation. . . . For where there is forgiveness of sins, there is also life and salvation" (SC, "The Sacrament of the Altar," p. 31). The reason people come to the liturgy/Divine Service is to receive these gifts. They come to be freed of their sins, released from the guilt and shame under which they labor and struggle. They come to join their life to the life of the Son of God, a life that began in the waters of Holy Baptism, continues at the table of His body and blood, and will be consummated at the marriage feast of heaven. They come to be saved, rescued from enemies they know and fear, and enemies they know not.

However, where did the liturgy come from? This is not always easy to answer. The Church's confession concerning God's action in the liturgy influences everything that will be presented here regarding the structure of the historic liturgy, particularly its origins. Most major liturgical changes are instituted for theological reasons. God's action in worship is the foundation for the structure of the liturgy.

On the day of Pentecost, when the Holy Spirit came down upon the disciples, He did not bring with Him the structure of the historic Church liturgy. Early Christians worshiped the way they knew best—like Jews who had been transformed into a new people by the death, resurrection, and ascension of Jesus Christ. We must never forget that early Christians were Jewish Christians, and that our Lord worshiped like a Jew, for He was the Jewish Messiah for the whole world who brought about in His own life, death, and resurrection a new kingdom called the Christian Church.

THE STRUCTURE OF RITE—
THE LORD'S WORD AND THE LORD'S SUPPER

There are three different structures in the worship life of the Christian Church. The first is the order (structure) of the Church's rite of Word and Sacrament. The *rite* is nothing more than the order of service, the way in which it flows. The structure of the rite grows as the life of the Church grows. The early Christian order of service was very simple, but as the Church grew in numbers and influence through different historical circumstances, the order of service developed into a larger rite through which the gifts of Christ's bodily presence were given to the people of God. Below is a diagram of the historic liturgy of Word and Sacrament as it has been handed down to us today.

Entrance	WORD	Preparation	SACRAMENT	Distribution
Confession & Absolution	Old Testament Gradual	Offering Offertory	Preface Proper Preface	AGNUS DEI (7th Century)
Introit	Epistle Alleluia		SANCTUS (3rd Century)	Canticle
KYRIE (5th Century)	GOSPEL Sermon		Prayer	Collect
HYMN OF PRAISE Gloria in Excelsis (6th Century) This Is the Feast (20th Century)	CREED (11th Century)		Lord's Prayer	Benediction
	Prayers for the Faithful		WORDS OF INSTITUTION Peace of the Lord	
Collect				

The gifts of Word and Sacrament come to us through the historic liturgy of the Church, represented above with an order inherited by Martin Luther from the ancient Church and continued today in our Divine Service. The two squares represent the two structures of the Divine Service from the time of Jesus: Word and Sacrament. The pattern of Christ's presence in Word and Sacrament is a continuing table fellowship with God that reaches back into the Old Testament and looks ahead to the marriage feast of the Lamb in heaven. If one traces the liturgical structures of Word and Sacrament through the history of the liturgy, these structures are stable cornerstones during each era.

The three circles correspond to the times of movement in the liturgy, the only significant additions to the historic liturgy of the Early Church. These additions are the ordinaries, the great liturgical hymns of praise located around the structures of Word and Sacrament. The Kyrie (Luke 18) and Gloria in Excelsis (Luke 2) precede the Liturgy of the Word and the Creed follows it. The Sanctus (Isaiah 6) precedes the Words of Institution, and the Agnus Dei (John 1) is the first hymn to accompany the distribution.[1] The ordinaries first appeared in the Divine Service to accompany the three new structures of liturgy (entrance, preparation for the Lord's Supper, and distribution of the Sacrament) that required physical movement in the huge basilicas of the Constantinian era.[2] Psalmody and liturgical hymns accompany movement in the Church's liturgy, whether that movement involves the entrance of the clergy and their attendants (circle #1), the entrance of the bread and wine into the sanctuary for the Eucharist (circle #2), or the distribution of the Sacrament (circle #3). This combination of Word and Sacrament with the ordinaries make up what is commonly called "the historic liturgy of the Church" that was fully in place by the seventh century.

The structures of both Word and Sacrament and the ordinaries are based in Scripture. The historic liturgy is transcendent and transcultural because of its biblical foundation. It is clean, elegant, and simple.

Liturgy and Ritual

The structure of the historic liturgy is a ritual. Unfortunately, in some circles today the word *ritual* has negative connotations. Most of us could not survive in this world without rituals. Some are short-term that get us through the day; others mark significant events in our personal lives or in our corporate lives as Church or nation. In every culture, people develop public rituals that identify what is important to them. For centuries, the great public rituals of the Western world were the majestic liturgies of the Roman Catholic Church. This is still true in countries such as Spain, Italy, and many countries in Central and South America. In the United States, the great rituals of our society are sporting events, marked by pageantry and ceremony. Everyone has a part to play, from the announcers to the cheerleaders to the band, not to mention the coaches, players, and spectators. People are bound together by the ritual events of the game as they participate with enthusiasm in the same patterns time after time. Whether they realize it or not, the ritual of the game is a significant reason why they come, and the satisfaction they experience is as much from participating in the ritual as it is in the outcome of the game.

Functional Definition

What, then, is ritual? Here is a functional definition:
Ritual is:

1. a pattern of formal, repetitive behavior
2. that communicates meaning symbolically
3. both verbally and non-verbally,
4. which is necessary for group relationships to operate
5. in order that the group may stick together and thus survive.[3]

Applying this to a sporting event, it is clear that a pattern of formal, repetitive behavior occurs in every competition. Although there is great variety in the game itself, there is a formal structure to the event that is repeated every contest. It is a scripted event, from the band to the cheerleaders, the national anthem, the introduction of the players, and the four quarters of the game. During time-outs everyone sticks to the script, such as the cheerleaders taking a moment to encourage their fans. Without the patterns of the formal, repetitive behavior, there would be utter chaos, and no one would have any fun. But within the structure of the ritual there is opportunity for great joy that results from the surprise we experience when things happen that we did not expect. This surprise is only possible if there is a pattern of formal, repetitive behavior.

Ritual communicates meaning, and this meaning is most effective when it occurs symbolically. Anthropologists make a distinction between signs and symbols. A sign conveys a single meaning, like a stop sign. When one arrives at an intersection with a stop sign, one does not ask, "What does this mean?" There is only one meaning: stop. Symbols, however, are more ambiguous. There are layers of meaning in symbols that give one room to enter into the full significance of the symbol. These meanings are not contradictory, but they are complex. For example, what might the meaning be of an altar parament that displays a lamb with a staff and a cut in its side from which flows blood that empties itself in a cup? It is a symbol of the Lamb who was slain and raised again, the Lamb who conquers through death and gives us life through the blood we receive in the cup of the Lord's Supper. These meanings are complementary, not contradictory. As we contemplate that symbol, there is room for us to roam as we enter its more complex world and meditate on the richness of its meaning. This symbol does not produce a one-word meaning, but encourages us to contemplate the layers of meaning embedded in the symbol. The singing of the national anthem before a sporting event evokes similar complex interpretations, from pride in our nation to the respect for the colors to humility in the face of over two hundred years of democracy to excitement as it marks the beginning of play.

All symbolic communication is open to interpretation. Both the image of the lamb on the altar parament and the American flag at a sporting event are examples of non-verbal communication. As any married couple will confirm, non-verbal communication is sometimes more important than verbal communication. "I love you" is a powerful statement, but even more powerful are the tangible expressions of that love, the simple acts of kindness that communicate love in ways no words could do.

But we are a people of language, and words matter, especially in the Church. So much of our language is also symbolic, as even the three words "I love you" attest, for in those words one expresses not simply the emotional feeling for that person, but a sacrificial love that reflects Christ's love for the Church as He willing gave up His life for her. This kind of love is almost impossible to put into words, but through a long marriage of joys and sorrows, husbands and wives show that kind of love to one another through mercy and forgiveness as they live under the Gospel. The Scriptures and liturgy are especially rich in images and metaphors that communicate meaning symbolically. Jesus used symbolic language when describing Himself as the Good Shepherd or as the vine. John the Baptist's declaration that Jesus is the "Lamb of God, who takes away the sin of the world" (John 1:29) is a symbolic statement. It means Jesus is both humble and meek, both slaughtered for sin and dispenser of forgiveness.

When the stadium is filled to capacity and the assembly of fans is ready to embark on the ritual, most know the meanings of the verbal and non-verbal symbols they will encounter in the game. They know what to expect, even if they do not know how the contest will turn out. They are a group, a community, and for them to operate as such they must have a pattern of formal, repetitive behavior that communicates meaning symbolically. As fans root for their team, they are bound together as comrades in the contest with the other team. Sometimes the cohesion of these groups becomes so strong that it leads to violent actions, as when fans express their disappointment after loss by turning over cars or tearing down goalposts.

Rituals cause communities to cohere as a group, and in many cases, that cohesion is the means by which the group is able to survive with its identity intact. There would still be chemistry class on Monday at the high school even without a game on Friday. Religious communities, however, depend on ritual not merely to establish identity but also to hand down faith to new hearers and succeeding generations.

The history of both Jews and Christians is marked by times of persecution when their liturgical rituals helped them survive as a community. In fact, the history of the Christian Church during times of persecution offers numerous examples of liturgical rites as a means of helping communities survive. During the scattering of Jews from Israel throughout world, a liturgical pattern developed in synagogues that preserved the Jewish faith when they were separated from the liturgical rites in the temple. After the Bolshevik Revolution, when Lutherans were sent to Siberia from St. Petersburg and Moscow, they maintained a Lutheran faith by preserving from memory the Lutheran liturgy and Luther's Small Catechism. According to the first missionaries who arrived in Siberia after the fall of the Soviet Union, many handwritten hymnals and catechisms were still extant after seventy years of use. The Lutheran tradition was handed down through these primitive means, and because of persecution, the contents of these catechetical and liturgical documents were precious. Under such circumstances, very little creative liturgy goes on, for what is most important is preserving the faith and handing it on to another generation.

Application of the Functional Definition

Our historic liturgy, which we call the Divine Service, is a pattern of formal, repetitive behavior. Those who feel that our historic liturgy is an impediment to missions and evangelism will point to the formal, repetitive aspect of our liturgy and describe it as a "dead ritual." But rituals themselves are neither dead nor alive. Those who participate in them make them appear as living, vital rituals or as dead ones. Said plainly, it is not the ritual that is dead; it is we who are dead.

People who have not been born from above (John 3:3) are not able to receive God's gifts because they have no life in them. Those who understand the historic liturgy and see that it is the means through which Christ's bodily presence comes to us with gifts of forgiveness, life, and salvation would never describe the historic liturgy as dead. God's Word and God's Holy Sacrament are not dead, but alive and able to transform sinners into saints, to make the dead alive because Christ, the living One, is bodily present through these means of grace. This is why it is so important for us to know the liturgy and to teach it to our children. Most Christians who understand their worship would never think of their worship as dead or consider departing from it. They know, like any good teacher does, that repetition is the key to solid learning. And as any good coach knows, to be able to perform in a given sport, it is necessary to practice over and over again. Likewise, in our worship, we repeat the same elements each Sunday to learn the posture of forgiveness in daily life. This posture is formed in us through hearing His Word read, preached, and celebrated in a sacrament of His body and blood, where God has bound Himself to be present with His gifts.

These two structures of the liturgy, Word and Sacrament, communicate meaning symbolically. This symbolism is important in that all liturgical language and action is open to interpretation by the community, and that interpretation is always centered in Christ and His bodily presence among us. The words of Jesus read in the Gospel make Him present in our assemblies, and the words of consecration at the Lord's Supper bring His body and blood to us in, with, and under bread and wine. Every word, action, or image used in our liturgical rituals must proclaim Christ and His saving presence among us. So when one looks at the altar, one sees a symbol that embodies Christ's sacrifice on Calvary for the sins of the world as it is now offered to us in bread and wine. When one looks at the baptismal font, one sees a symbol of rebirth and entrance into Christ's eternal flesh.

These powerful, stable images communicate that Baptism and the Lord's Supper are the initiating and sustaining cornerstones in the life of the Church. Without these marks of the Church and the profound, mysterious realities they communicate, the Church could not be what Christ called it to be. The historic liturgy is a pattern of formal, repetitive behavior that moves the community from font to altar as it journeys from Entrance Hymn to Benediction, pausing to confess sins, sing hymns, hear the Word of God read and preached, confess faith, pray, and then sup at His table on heavenly food. By this simple ritual of Word and Sacrament, with its surrounding structures of movement, communities are bound together as the Body of Christ, His Church.

For most of us in Western Christianity, our symbolic communication is restricted to language and does not take advantage of action and ceremony and image. The non-verbal communication can communicate in ways as powerful as verbal communication, especially for those who are challenged in their language abilities. To enter a church with a baptismal font in the narthex makes a statement about the identity of that community as one that is constituted by its union with Christ at the font. Looking down the aisle to the altar, one sees the goal of the community's journey is communion with this same Christ at a table prepared for a feast where heaven itself is present among us in bread and wine.

The weekly ritual of patterned, repetitive behavior in the Divine Service is the means God has given to make us His people, His coherent Body. This is how He comes to us for our salvation—this is how He comes to us bodily through Scripture and the Lord's Supper, giving His gifts. The history of the Church is the history of communities large and small, grand and humble, that survived empires and gross outbursts of persecution through the stable ritual of the historic liturgy. Survival is the key to the ritual, and the historic liturgy helps us survive in a world gone mad—to survive as Christians in a world that is hostile to Christ and His Gospel, and therefore to us.

Characteristics of Ritual[4]

Rituals do not analyze, they assume. Rituals do not hand out instruction manuals. When one engages in ritual, there should be very little explanation. Those who engage in the ritual know the ritual, and those who do not know it are taught the meaning of the ritual before engaging in it. When we analyze our rituals instead of simply doing them, we become untouched spectators instead of receivers of the Lord's actions. Once the Divine Service begins, we should have very few announcements or explanations, letting the service instead take us into its rhythms. This symphony of movement flows toward Jesus' clear voice in the Gospel and in the Words of Institution, the two climaxes of the liturgy.

Rituals do not discourse, they assert and proclaim. When we gather for worship, we do not discuss the Gospel and the mystery of Christ's bodily presence. We proclaim the Gospel by reading and hearing His Word. We participate in Christ's bodily presence by eating and drinking His body and blood. The Divine Service is not a lecture about Christ, the Gospel, and justification, but rather a series of actions that proclaim Christ, the Gospel, and justification to the hearer. Again, rituals do not explain in a didactic way, even though much may be learned during the ritual. The purpose of ritual is not to teach but to engage the participant in a ritual process. In rituals you do not explain, you just do; you experience rituals. You do not think about it, or even reflect on how you feel about it or how the ritual is affecting you. In the Divine Service you commune with Christ's bodily presence, and your sins are forgiven. You are joined to His life that has no end. You are saved from your enemies.

Rituals do not conceive, they perceive. Certainly "faith comes from hearing, and hearing through the word of Christ" (Romans 10:17), yet we are more than our ears and the liturgy is more than simple words, though words and hearing are the most important aspects of ritual. Our other senses give us access to meaning, deepening and broadening our ritual experience. For example, both music and scent can transport us to a different place or time. Both access memory in a way that words do not. Perception brings ambiguity, but the kind of delicious ambiguity that makes life worth living. Unfortunately, since the Enlightenment, our church buildings and their liturgies have become temples to the rational mind, and we have spurned the sensuousness of the ancient liturgies. When one enters the sacred space of the church, it should smell different, look different, and the sounds one hears should be unlike any other in the culture. Entering church, you enter into a foretaste of heaven, a space that has its own unique culture and its own distinctive story to tell. Your eyes, ears, nose, and mouth testify that you are able to see, hear, smell, and taste that the Lord is good. You enter into the presence of Jesus.

Rituals do not reflect reality, they enact reality. The Divine Service does not simply reflect what Christ is like, it enacts us in His flesh as His Word is **broken open** through preaching that reveals Christ to us as He was revealed to the Emmaus disciples in the breaking of the bread. To break open God's Word is to see Christ at its center, for as Jesus Himself tells the Emmaus disciples concerning the testimony of the Old Testament: "Was it not necessary that the Christ should suffer these things and enter into His glory?" (Luke 24:26). God's Word is first broken open for us in the Liturgy of the Word so that we might be prepared in the Holy Supper to eat His body broken in death and His blood poured out for the remission of sins. In the liturgy of Word and Sacrament you leave behind the world and all its cultural baggage, and only then do you begin to perceive through your rational mind and your senses that Christ is present bodily to give you the gifts of heaven.

Rituals are not a mirror to show us what reality might look like; *rituals are reality*, and by our participation in those rituals we enact reality. At the center of the Liturgy of the Lord's Supper is the cross, where we feast on the body and blood of our host. Think of the ambiguity of this act of participating in a banquet of joy in which the food is the One who sacrificed Himself in a humiliating, shameful, and scandalous death. It is hard to comprehend that through Christ's bodily presence, heaven itself is present with angels and archangels and all the company of heaven when we eat His body and drink His blood. What is it that we perceive here through our eyes, our ears, our nose, our mouths? Joy at our salvation at the heavenly feast? Horror that the violence of Calvary is in, with, and under what we consume into our bodies? Sadness that participating with us in Christ are all the saints who are no longer with us, including our closest relatives and friends? These are thoughts that ritual can evoke, and they are too big to be analyzed, discussed, categorized, and pared down to size.[5]

Liturgy: the Boundary between Heaven and Earth

The highest moments of ritual activity occur at the crossing of a boundary or a threshold from one life status to another—a "rite of passage." Crossing boundaries and thresholds in real life are often tenuous, anxious, even frightening experiences, as can be testified to by anyone who has entered a country where freedom does not have the same sway as it does in the United States and other Western countries. Going through customs and immigration may be a harrowing experience, especially coming out of that country. When boundaries or thresholds mark significant life changes, such as weddings, funerals, or even a presidential inauguration or a pastor's ordination, not only the main participants feel anxiety and fear, but everyone who participates in the rite of passage experiences some emotional response. These moments of passage are "in betwixt and in between" two different stages in life, marking the transition by what they say about this momentous event in the very ritual itself.

This is especially true when a pastor or deaconess visits the sick and the dying. These are heightened moments of great tension, filled with suffering, grief, and loss. When the news is bad and we are taxed beyond our means, the Lutheran liturgy, learned and held in the memory by a lifetime of worship, often is the only way we are able to survive the crippling emotions felt during these liminal moments. Here ritual becomes our great friend and support: the sign of the cross upon the forehead, the smell of anointing oil, familiar psalms and readings, the Liturgy of the Lord's Supper, the Lord's Prayer, the Aaronic Benediction—these rituals provide enormous comfort. One of the great challenges facing pastors and deaconesses is visiting those who are sick and dying and may not have access in their memory to these basic liturgical rites.

Returning to our functional definition of ritual as a pattern of formal, repetitive behavior, we observed that the final goal of ritual is survival. This is why, at moments of great change where emotions are charged and people are on edge, our natural tendency is to reach for a ritual to help us negotiate these significant boundaries. The liturgical traditions at these significant rites of passage proclaim repeatedly to the community its confession about how Christ has changed the way we look at such things as life and death. They proclaim the faith of the Church at these critical moments of life changes.

The most significant boundary we cross is the boundary between heaven and earth. This boundary is marked by the Divine Service, the appointed place where the now of our lives today comes together with the not yet of heaven to come in the bodily presence of Christ. This is truly a moment in which we are "in betwixt and in between" heaven and earth, as we move from our mundane lives of work and family into a space that is charged by the presence of the Creator, who comes to us in both His divine and human natures as the crucified and resurrected Lord. Heaven and earth were joined together in Jesus on the Mount of Transfiguration as His earthly disciples gathered alongside Moses and Elijah. In the same way, in Jesus heaven and earth are bridged by our liturgy.

> The liturgy bespeaks this reality of being "in betwixt and in between" heaven and earth from Invocation to Benediction. To begin with a trinitarian Invocation and sign of the cross is to proclaim the invasion of the Son into our space, where heavenly realities reign, though hidden in common flesh and blood. As pilgrims lining the royal highway, we petition the King who enters our midst bearing holy gifts, and we exclaim that every gift from the King is an expression of His mercy, for we are sinners who lift up our eyes in expectation of His compassion. Then, our voices united with angelic choirs, we proclaim that at His incar-

nation there is glory in the highest heavens and peace on earth. Through our trinitarian hymn we praise the ongoing visitation of the Lamb's holy presence for, as we sing in another paschal hymn, "the Lamb who was slain has begun His reign, Alleluia!"

This victory feast reaches its first peak as God's Word breaks open to reveal Christ, and we banquet on the living voice of God through prophet and apostle, a Word that creates what it says. This Word comes from the Word made flesh, a Word that has power to cast out demons, heal the sick, raise the dead, and release us from our sins. With the Old Testament saints, we acknowledge that God's Word is His food for hungry pilgrims who in Christ have journeyed through a baptism of His death and resurrection toward final destination of full communion with Him in heaven. "Today this Scripture has been fulfilled in your hearing" (Luke 4:21). From ear to mouth to eye, we hear and taste and see that the Lord is good, that the promise of heavenly gifts from the King is true, that He is merciful and His love does endure forever.

With cherubim and seraphim we join heavenly choirs singing "Holy, holy, holy Lord God of pow'r and might: Heaven and earth are full of Your glory. Hosanna. Hosanna. Hosanna in the highest. Blessed is He who comes in the name of the Lord" (*LSB* p. 161). Pilgrims first shouted these words to Jesus as they lined Jerusalem's entrance and strewed palms in His path, but in their giddy joy they knew not that they were preparing His funeral procession to the apocalyptic tree. "Sometimes they strew His way / And His sweet praises sing; Resounding all the day Hosannas to their King. Then 'Crucify!' / Is all their breath, / And for His death / They thirst and cry" (*LSB* 430:3). Pilgrims now, lining the aisle to Jerusalem new with table set for eucharistic feast, sing those same words, knowing that Jesus now comes as heavenly Lord to feed us holy food. Earth and heaven are joined together in peace as the King prepares to enter His kingdom. Prayer is offered, petitioning the Father: Thy kingdom come; give us today our daily bread; forgive us our trespasses.

And so our eyes are opened in the breaking of the bread, and our journey ends as we recline at His table where He offers us the best seat and the finest food, girding His loins for the

Paschal Feast and serving us as our liturgist. We have come home to be with God in the Father's house, a foretaste of our final homecoming at the Lamb's banquet in His kingdom that has no end. So we depart in peace as Simeon bids us do. Our eyes have seen His salvation, and His face shines upon us in one final Benediction. But our summons home in Christ has not ended, for by His Spirit His eschatological presence goes with us, and we now go out as messengers of His peace, greeting pilgrims on the way as heralds of the kingdom.

New millennia come and go, but the Church goes on and on celebrating the Creator's re-creating presence—in betwixt and in between heaven and earth—as she waits for His final return.

The Structure of Space—the Lord's House

In the first three hundred years of the Church's life Christians worshiped in homes, in small spaces. Luke and Acts provide most of the New Testament information about house churches. Jesus instituted what would become a natural pattern for early mission activity when He sent the Twelve (Luke 9:1–6) and the seventy(-two) (Luke 10:1–24) into various houses. Acts provides us with the most detailed descriptions of house worship,[6] and further evidence for them is scattered throughout the New Testament, particularly in the Pauline Epistles.[7] Jews also worshiped in houses during the first century, particularly on Friday night for the Sabbath evening Seder.[8] That house meal was the probable setting for much of Jesus' table fellowship during His ministry.[9] Pagans also had their house gods and house religions. It was natural, therefore, for both Jews and pagans to worship in houses, which is why Christians continued to use the house as a place for their liturgical assemblies. Even today in places such as China, the home is a natural place to begin a worshiping congregation.

Until the Edict of Constantine ensured tolerance for Christianity in AD 313, Christians worshiped primarily in houses. Only after Constantine was there a widespread construction of church buildings as we tend to think of them. Synagogues were used during the second period of evangelization and catechization (AD 30–46), and some were later converted into Christian churches during the end of the third century, but that seems to have been rather rare, and many were not much larger than a house church. The architectural movement for Christian liturgical space in the first three centuries was from a house church (the home of a Christian) to a "home" adapted into a church, and in some rare instances, to a much larger house church. In the first century, Christians worshiped in a house that still functioned as a home for a family, while in the second and third centuries Christians worshiped in a house that had been completely converted and remodeled into a liturgical space and was no longer in use as a home. These worshipers included cross-sections of society, both rich and poor, slave and free, with different occupations, lifestyles, and cultures.[10]

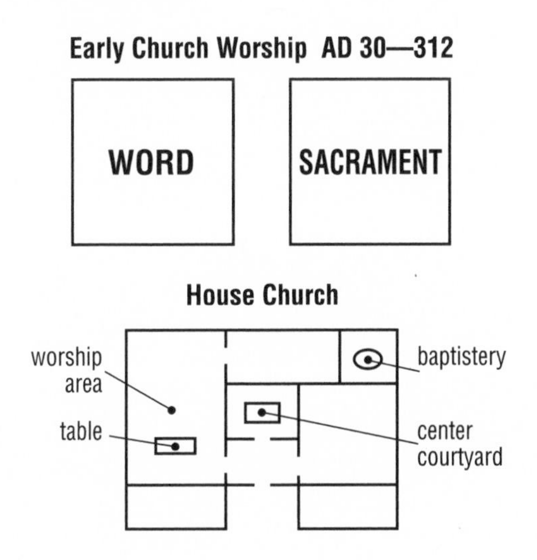

The general configuration of the church was consistent. One such house church discovered in Dura Europas, a Roman outpost on the Euphrates in Syria, dated ca. AD 241, included a place for Baptism. The basic configuration of these houses until the Edict of Constantine was rather uniform, reflecting a normal tenement house one would find in most Mediterranean cities. They were small in size; the church in Dura Europas measures about 16 x 40 feet. There was little movement in these spaces and therefore little ceremony. There would have been a table for the scrolls used in the Liturgy of the Word and for the bread and wine for the Liturgy of the Lord's Supper. Benches along the sides of the room may have been used for the infirm, the aged, and women with children. The space was simple, as was the liturgy used in this space. The diagram above indicates the liturgy with the two simple structures of "Word" and "Sacrament." It is in such a context that the Gospels were first read and heard, and this is the setting Luke and the other evangelists had in mind as they wrote the Gospels.[11]

One of the reasons the rite, that is, the liturgical form of words and actions, grew was because the structure of the space grew in which the rite was done. When the space grows, so does the liturgy. We will follow that growth through the development of rite and space together, for structures of rite and the structure of the space in which that rite occurs go hand in hand.

Liturgy and Architecture

As one discovers histories of the architecture of Christian churches and their shape, it becomes clear that there is no one ideal way to structure the space where Christ's presence is received with thanksgiving and praise. However, there are some general theological principles that help us understand how rite and space go hand in hand.

The space for worship must signal Christ's presence through Word and Supper, for at the heart of our faith is the incarnation of Jesus, who came from heaven to earth to enter our space and time and offer Himself up as a sacrifice for our sins. Our worship space must proclaim that Jesus continues to be present bodily in His Church, offering that very same body and blood sacrificed at Golgotha in consecrated bread and wine. His presence takes place through bodies washed at the baptismal font, ears filled with words of grace, and mouths that taste the heavenly food. Font, pulpit/lectern, and altar are the focal points in the worship space that bespeak Christ's presence in the Divine Service, as well as His presence in the community of the baptized who gather around these spaces to receive His gifts.

The Baptismal Font—The Space for Washing

Baptism is the sacrament by which we enter into Christ and His Church, and Christians have marked this reality by the baptismal font's location. We enter as the baptized, and the font's location in the narthex or in the beginning of the nave acknowledges that our identity begins in these sacred waters. However, few churches have a font at the entrance; more likely it is toward the front of the sanctuary, outside the altar rail. The guideline is that a physically, visibly central font reflects our baptismal theology. What joy and delight for the baptized to pass the font as they go to the altar! As one enters the sanctuary, to see the altar through the font is to see that our life is made and sustained by these two miracles of grace. At Baptism, we are born into a world that knows no end by our union with Christ in His death and resurrection; at the Lord's Supper, we feast upon His eternal body and blood as the means to nourish this new life in Christ.

The early Christians used the baptistery, located outside of the room or building where the assembly gathered for worship, as a primary place for Christian art and symbolism. Early baptisteries were constructed to look like a mausoleum, for Baptism is where one dies to the old, pagan world and rises to a new world in Christ and His Church. Because the earliest Christian buildings were inside the walls of the city, it would have struck the pagan world as odd to see a building shaped like a tomb inside the city walls. However, when one enters the Christian Church, one dies to the world and to the sinful flesh, burying it all with Christ in His tomb. For the Christian, death comes to an end in Baptism, for to be joined to Christ is to be joined to His everlasting life. This is also why baptismal fonts and the space in which they stood were eight-sided. The number eight was the number for eternity in the Old Testament (circumcised on the eighth day; cf. Leviticus 12:3) as well as the ancient world of the New Testament. Other symbolism that would have adorned the baptistery, including images of paradise to suggest that Baptism is when paradise is restored to us, and the font as a circle, suggesting eternity once again where there is no beginning and no end.

Baptistery at Pisa

As Paul proclaims in Romans 6, we are buried with Christ in Baptism, and immersion into the watery grave vividly declares this reality. This means that our fonts should not only be centrally located in our churches, but that they should be substantial in size and shape. Although the rite of Baptism requires simple water and the trinitarian formula through which the Holy Spirit works to bring new life, Christians have always honored this simple rite by adorning it with symbols and ceremonies. These ritual additions accent the theological depths of this cosmic act of moving a person from darkness to light, from Satan's kingdom into the kingdom of God.

Today's font should be substantial enough in size to be visible to all as the sacrament by which the Church makes new members. It should also be large enough to provide an opportunity for ample use of water. Baptism is first and foremost a washing away of sins through water and the Word. Immersion is an ancient and venerable practice, and though it is not feasible to hope that many congregations will immerse infants, not to mention adults, there is a movement within liturgical churches to provide congregations the use of more generous amounts of water in their baptismal rites to signify that Baptism is a bath in which the old Adam is drowned and the new Adam rises to a life that never ends.

The Pulpit and Lectern—The Space for Preaching and Hearing

The liturgy's sole purpose is to proclaim the presence of the Word made flesh through His Word read and preached. The Word comes to us in our ears through the voice of the pastor and the lectors, and so the most fundamental issue for the space reserved for reading and preaching is that this Word be heard by the community. The earliest catechumens were called "hearers of the Word" because they attended to God's Word in the Liturgy of the Word, which later became known as the "liturgy of the catechumens." The centrality of the Word in our Divine Service is accented by insuring that Christ's Word read and preached may be heard by all, and hearing is more important than the actual location.

This does not mean, however, that pulpit or lectern should be hidden or relegated to a space that is not easily seen by all or recognized for its centrality in the liturgy. In the ancient synagogues, the reading of the Word and its exposition was the means by which God was present, superseded only by His presence in the Most Holy Place of the temple. As a result, the two focal points in the synagogue accented God's saving presence: the seat of Moses was where the rabbi sat as teacher of the Torah (or Pentateuch, the first five books of the Old Testament), and the ark where the scrolls of the Scripture were placed. These two symbolic places reminded the people that the Word and the reader/preacher of the Word were the reasons why the people gathered for worship. In fact, the ark was the focal point because it pointed to the ark of the covenant in the temple where blood was poured and sins were washed away.[12]

So today, the place of reading is marked by what is read and the place of proclamation by the preacher whose voice brings us the life-giving Word. The Word must be heard, and there should be designated space for its reading and preaching.[13] Preachers who leave the pulpit and move around the sanctuary call attention to themselves instead of what they embody. Pastors stand in the stead and by the command of Christ, and Christ speaks through them. Their Word is not their own, but is founded on Christ's Word. This Word is embodied in both preacher and Book, and the Book needs a place to rest. It is fitting that the Scriptures are read from the Bible or the lectionary, not from bulletin inserts that are disposed of after the service. A book of the Gospels, used in festive processions for reading in the midst of the assembly, may be placed on the altar as Word and Sacrament are visibly joined. And so, the place of reading, as well as the books from which Scripture is read, are holy because Christ becomes present for us and for our salvation as the Word made flesh.[14]

The Altar: The Space for Feasting

On the night He was betrayed, Jesus instituted the Lord's Supper in the context of the Passover meal. We must never forget that the celebration of the Lord's Supper is first and foremost a meal where we feast upon the body and blood of our Lord in, with, and under bread and wine. The earliest celebrations of the Lord's Supper were in the context of a meal that followed the pattern of the Passover, and only when there were abuses of the meal, in places such as Corinth, did Christians cease to use the meal as the framework for their eucharistic celebrations. The place where the Lord's Supper was celebrated was first a table, for Lord's Supper is exactly that, a supper. Later during the Middle Ages did the Lord's Supper become for the Roman Church an unbloody sacrifice that required an altar from which to offer this sacrifice, a perspective on the Lord's Supper that was one of the reasons for Luther's call to reform the Church. Today, we commonly call the place for our eucharistic celebration an altar because Christ, our paschal sacrifice, is offered to us as gift from God in bread and wine. As some would say, it is Christ as sacrifice (noun) and not our sacrifice to God (verb) that distinguishes between the Lord's Supper as Christ's sacrifice given as gift or Christ sacrificed to appease God. When we gather around the table/altar, it is always to receive from God's hand His gift of the very body and blood of His Son, offered as a sacrifice for sin on Calvary. This gift has been the climactic moment in the Christian liturgy since the time of the apostles.

Therefore, the altar has always been the focal point of church architecture. As we enter the sanctuary, our eyes should immediately be led to the altar. Most churches are still constructed on the basilica model in which one enters through a narthex and sees at the end of a long aisle an altar, usually elevated at the east end of the church. There is great rationale for such arrangement of the space, though in recent years many have exchanged this traditional shape for such arrangements as church in the round, where the altar is centered in the church and the people surround it. As we shall describe in chapter 8, Christian life is a journey from font to heaven, and Christian churches built with a font in the narthex and an altar at the end of the long aisle enact this journey each Sunday as the baptized make their way from font to altar, to a foretaste of the heavenly banquet, to the new Jerusalem awaiting us as we commune in Christ with angels, archangels, and all the company of heaven.

> Each Sunday we cross the threshold from earth to heaven as we dip our fingers in the font at the narthex, making the sign of the cross that marks us as Christ's and recalling our entrance into His life that has no end. Then we proceed to the altar and the new Jerusalem, hearing Christ's words as we travel along the way, as He tells us the story of our family's travels from the Old Testament, Epistle, and Gospel lessons. We are surrounded by this great cloud of witnesses who rise up with us on hearing God's Word read and proclaimed and proceed with us to the feast of fat things,[15] the very food of the crucified and resurrected Savior. Moving from font to altar accompanied by God's Word is the rhythm of the life of the Christian who sees already now in his pilgrimage a preview of his final destination: Jerusalem the golden.

So the altar is the Church's Most Holy Place. It is the Holy of Holies, adorned with reverence, acknowledged by all for what it is—a foretaste of the feast to come. It is both table and altar, so those items used in feeding the people of God with holy food are necessary and proper. But all other unnecessary items, such as flowers and excessive candles, distract from the essential items. The Gospel book and the sacramental vessels are adornment enough. The altar must do what all sacred things do: not only invite people to come and feast but also caution them that they are entering holy ground. To capture this sense of accessibility and distance requires architectural imagination that is given to very few.

Recent attempts to pull altars from their mooring on walls and make them freestanding has potential to capture the table as hospitable and the altar as awesome. Pastors who preside at freestanding altars will be able to accent those things that are sacrificial, that is, where they stand in Christ with the people in praise and thanksgiving to God, and those things that are sacramental, that is, where they speak for Christ in His stead and by His command. The offertory marks the place where pastors move behind the altar to proclaim from preface to dismissal the Lord's gift of Himself in bread and wine. And if the distribution of the Lord's Supper to the worshipers reflects the hospitality of a God who invites us to dine with Him now and for eternity, then the table/altar becomes a place of feasting that has no end. Word and Supper are the feast of victory for our God. Alleluia!

Recent attempts to pull altars from their mooring on walls and make them freestanding has potential to capture the table as hospitable and the altar as awesome.

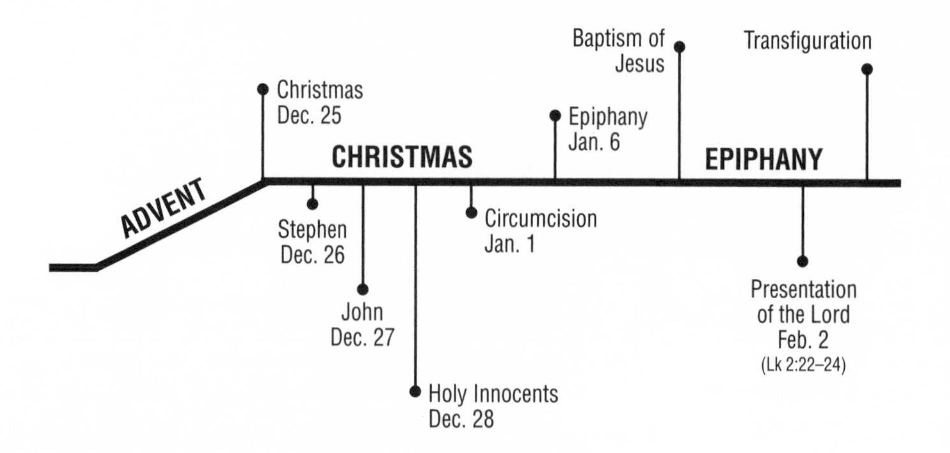

The Structure of Time—The Lord's Day

How do we as Christians structure our time in the Church? The early Christians had no Church Year as we know it today. The important day for Christians was Sunday, the Lord's Day. Sunday was considered by early Christians to be not only the first day of the week but also the eighth day. Christians understood that in the beginning God created the world in six days, then rested on the seventh, the Sabbath—the day of rest and worship in the Old Testament. But when Jesus came, the Lord of the Sabbath, He showed us in His resurrection that a new creation has dawned and as a result, a new day of worship. As you count the six days of creation and the seventh Sabbath day, the first day of the second week is really the eighth day. Baptismal fonts are eight-sided because eight represented eternity. Early Christians understood that in Baptism and on Sunday they entered into eternity because they entered into the presence of Christ, who is eternal. The structure of time is so important, we will discuss in chapter 7 the Christian concept of time that will focus on Sunday, the eighth day, the Church Year, and the Liturgy of the Hours, the way in which Christians marked the day with prayer.

These three structures of rite, space, and time were fundamental ways in which early Christians ordered their lives. And they are fundamental ways in which we order our lives today. The structure of rite is the way in which we come together to hear the Word of the Lord and receive the Lord's Supper, thereby receiving the gifts from Christ's bodily presence. The structure of space is where we gather together in the Lord's house as the Body of Christ to receive these gifts. And the structure of time, Sunday, the Lord's Day, is the

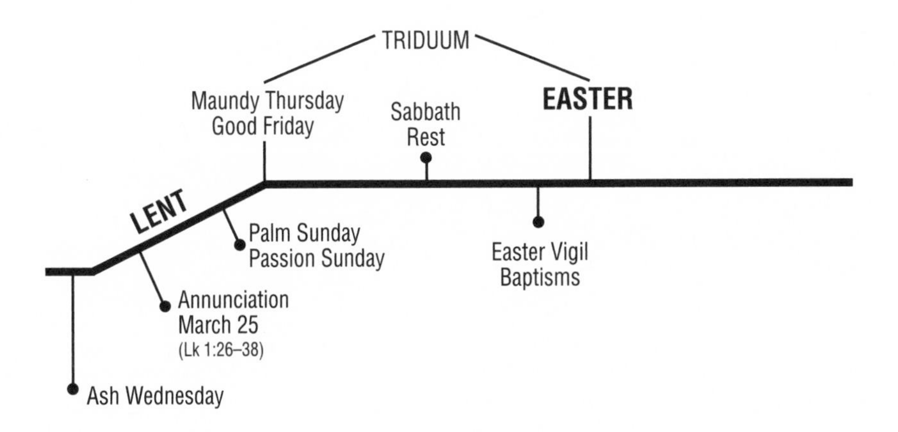

day in which we, as the Body of Christ, His Church, come together to receive the gifts that come to us in Word and Sacrament.

The Lord's Word and the Lord's Supper in the Lord's House on the Lord's Day—these three important structures are the way we continue with the Early Church to structure our life.

3

Jewish Origins of Christian Worship

The worship of early Christians was not prophetically delivered at Pentecost but developed from Jewish worship and the ministry of Jesus. It came about after a long and slow process of recognizing how the life, death, and resurrection of Jesus Christ had changed worship forever. The New Testament gives us the theology behind Christian worship while hinting at the forms. Christian worship is about Christ, therefore early Christians made use of whatever was available to accent that Christ was present among them bodily, offering His gifts of life, salvation, and the forgiveness of sins. They used the Old Testament worship they knew as Jews, Jesus' ministry of table fellowship with sinners, the New Testament writings, and the guidance of the apostles to create many of the worship forms that we still follow today.

Jesus' critique of Israel's religious life is really a comment on what comprises true worship, for reality must always be seen Christologically and defined by the God we worship. Jesus tangled with the Pharisees over the interpretation of Scripture. At stake was a foundational understanding of the Old Testament: was it principally Gospel or Law? Jesus knew the Old Testament taught the way of the Gospel, a Gospel of mercy and compassion, and not the way of the Law, which led to slavery and imprisonment. Jesus blasted the Pharisees for not recognizing the suffering and death of the Messiah at the center of everything. The failed interpretation prevented the Pharisees from entering the kingdom and, even worse, prevented others from entering (Luke 11:52).

For Jesus, the lens through which we must view reality is Him, as He told the Samaritan woman, "Those who worship [God] must worship in spirit and truth" (John 4:24). To worship "in spirit and truth" is to worship Christ, for wherever Jesus is there is His Spirit, and wherever the Spirit is there is Jesus, who is the way, the truth, and the life (John 14:6). Our Lord healed on the Sabbath and entered into a great controversy with the Pharisees over His willingness to do this. The Pharisees misunderstood the meaning of the Sabbath, and Jesus, as Lord of the Sabbath, healed on the Sabbath because He wanted everyone to see that eternal rest comes from the God who heals and makes things whole. Jesus was simply doing what the Lord does, bringing healing to the people of God.

Although Jesus was critical of such aspects of Israel's religious life, He never spoke against Israel's liturgical life. He submitted Himself to its rhythm as a faithful descendant of Abraham. Jesus was a faithful Jew who worshiped where Jews worshiped and participated fully in Jewish rites. When He cleansed the temple, it was the marketplace located in the Royal Portico (Stoa) on the southwest side of the Temple Mount, which is not part of the temple proper. Jesus never spoke against the Jewish rituals in the Holy Place or the Holy of Holies. He never criticized the Jewish liturgies in the synagogue or at the Passover. His disciples and other followers followed their Lord by their uncritical acceptance of Israel's liturgical life, and adapted Israel's worship to form the backbone of Christian worship.

Christian liturgy, therefore, grew out of Jewish worship rites. Understanding why we worship as we do requires that we recognize how Jesus and the disciples worshiped. We shall consider the basic ordering not only of worship but of Jewish life in general by means of the Seder that stands at the center of the structure of Jewish life. Then we shall consider the Passover, the places of Jewish worship, and the way Jews prayed as the basic unit of worship. In considering these Jewish origins, we shall reflect on how they influenced the development of Christian worship.

The Seder

One of the fundamental concepts in Jewish worship is the Seder. Most of us are familiar with this word from the Passover Seder that Jesus celebrated with His disciples throughout His ministry and that was also the context in which He instituted the Lord's Supper. The word *seder* itself simply means "order" or "structure." The Israelites used the word *seder* to refer to the way in which God ordered His creation. The beginning of Genesis is the story of God's seder of the creation in six days and resting on the Sabbath. The rest of Genesis records the seder of genealogies where, after the fall, God planted in the loins of Israel the seed of the Messiah. That is why Genesis contains a litany of genealogies: "these are the generations," "these are the generations," "these are the generations." The genealogies of Genesis are a seder of God's redemptive activity in the people of Israel.

It is not a coincidence that in the penultimate chapter of Genesis, Jacob blesses his twelve sons, showing that it is the tribe of Judah where God has placed the seed of the Messiah. (Genesis 49:8–12 is a wonderful example of grace, as Judah in no way deserved to receive by his behavior the promise that the Messiah would be born from his descendants.) The seder of God's promise to raise up a Redeemer from within Israel has now reached its goal, and the rest of the Old Testament is simply the record of salvation history as the promise of the Messiah is traced through the genealogies of Israel.

Seder takes on a new meaning after the Babylonian exile in 587 BC as the Jews were dispersed throughout the world. They were known as the "Diaspora." Because the Jewish people were not living in Israel, and therefore could not return to Jerusalem to engage in the sacrificial worship of Israel, seder came to mean "order of service." The Diasporan Jews were very strict and rigid in their Seders, their liturgies, because they were preserving for their people the faith of Israel in a time of persecution and separation from their homeland. Worship was the way of remembering who they were as God's chosen people and handing down the memories of their distinct identity from generation to generation. This is the time when the synagogue services developed as a way of hearing the Torah, praising God through psalms and hymns, and petitioning God for every need.

The Way of Prayer

Another fundamental structure in Jewish worship that has influenced Christian worship is the way of prayer. The Jews had a basic structure for all prayers called the *berakah*, which simply means "blessing." Although few Christian prayers bless God, the vast majority of Jewish prayers were blessings of God, who was a giver of gifts, especially the gifts of creation and redemption. Each blessing of God contained three parts: a greeting, a statement of motive (the reason for prayer), and a closing. Both the greeting and closing were brief and stylized, but the statement of motive had much room for expansion. The statement of motive was almost always about what God was doing for the people of Israel, especially as a God who gave gifts to His people. In most prayers, the people would petition God for what they needed on the basis of His goodness and loving-kindness. In every case, the petitions of the Jews covered all circumstances, and yet it was rare to find a petition that did not in some way relate to God's saving activity. An example of a Jewish *berakah* broken down into its three parts would look like this:

I. **Blessing**: a greeting to almighty God.
Blessed are You, Lord our God, King of the universe,

II. **Statement of Motive**: narration of God's goodness and grace.
for You nourish us and the whole world with goodness, grace, kindness, and mercy.

Petition: requests for God's actions based on His attributes.
Continue to give Your children what they need.

III. **Blessing**: close to the prayer.
Blessed are You, Lord, for You nourish the universe.

The prayer itself, then, would read as follows:

> Blessed are You, Lord our God, King of the universe, for You nourish us and the whole world with goodness, grace, kindness, and mercy. Continue to give Your children what they need. Blessed are You, Lord, for You nourish the universe.

Looking carefully at the statement of motive and petition, there is embedded in this form the essence of our biblical theology of worship. First, it is God who is recognized in prayer as the giver of gifts and the one who acts on behalf of His people, and then our response to God's gifts come in the petitions we bring before Him based on who He is and what He has done. This second part of the prayer is expandable, which means that it is possible to list a number of statements of motive and as many petitions as the assembly felt necessary to include. Although in formal liturgical worship most of these prayers would be carefully planned beforehand, the form of prayer allowed for flexibility and adaptability according to the situation.

Jewish prayers were ordinarily chanted because the natural response to the presence of God was to sing. When God was present with His gifts, it was always an occasion for celebration, and one normally sings at celebrations. The Jewish prayers were also chanted so the congregation could follow the movement of the prayer from greeting to statement of motive to petition to closing. The chant would change at each part of the prayer, signaling to the hearer what was being accented in the prayer. The chanting not only accented the meaning within the prayer but also signaled that prayer was always in the presence of God, who heard and answered prayer.

Early Christians adopted the *berakah* as their basic unit of prayer. It comes to us as the Collect. We pray the collects at the end of the entrance rite in the Divine Service, as well as in the Prayer of the Church. Collects are also prayed in Matins and Vespers. The Collect follows the basic structure of the *berakah*, beginning with a greeting and ending with a closing, and in between, containing both statements of motive and petition. Over the centuries, Christian collects have developed structures that do not always follow the form of the *berakah* to the letter, but it is surprising how many still do. A classic example of a collect that does follow the *berakah* form is the Collect of Grace from the service of Matins (see *LSB*, p. 228). Here it is with its structure marked out, and you can see that with the musical notations, significant shifts in the structure of the prayer are marked, indicated by those words in italics that suggest the raising or lowering of the voice.

I. **Greeting**

O Lord, our heavenly Father, almighty and everlast*ing* God,

II. **Statement of Motive**

You have safely brought us to the beginning of this day.

Petitions

Defend us in the same with Your mighty power and *grant* that this day we fall into no sin, neither run into any kind of danger, but that all our doings, being ordered by your governance, may be righteous in Your sight;

III. **Closing**

through Jesus Christ, Your Son, our Lord, who lives and reigns with You and the Holy Spirit, one God, now and forever. Amen.

The most common form of prayer for Christians is petitionary prayer. "Lord, teach us to pray, as John taught his disciples," requested one of Jesus' disciples (Luke 11:1). Jesus responded by teaching them the Lord's Prayer. Certainly, the disciples knew how to pray, for the center of the liturgical life of Israel was a continuous cycle of prayers based on a very simple prayer structure. When Jesus' disciples asked Jesus to teach them to pray, they used the word for *petition*, that is, teach us how to make requests of the Father as You petition the Father. The Lord's Prayer is the perfect prayer of petition, the perfect way to ask God the Father for all the needs that we could possibly have in our lives. Martin Luther said that "the Lord's Prayer is a prayer above all prayers, the greatest of all prayers, which has been taught by the greatest Master of all, in which all spiritual and bodily trouble is comprehended and which is the strongest consolation in all temptations, tribulations, and in the last hour."[1] This is why Christians now pray petitionary prayers more than any other form of prayer.

The Passover Seder

The Passover was the most important Seder in the life of Israel, the supreme celebration of the atonement in the life of the Jews. Lamb's blood was sprinkled over the doors of their homes so that the angel of death would pass over them. The Jews celebrated Passover every year as the most significant redemptive event in their lives. It focused on the coming Messiah and reminded them of all God's past blessings. It was a liturgical meal within an extended family with the head of the household (the paterfamilias) presiding over the Passover Seder.

The Passover is what anthropologists call a rite of passage that involves **separation** from the old life, **transition** to a new life by means of some ritualized act, then **incorporation** into a new life.[2] The Old Testament is replete with examples of such rites of passage: Noah and his family were *separated* from their heathen world by the flood, entered a period of *transition* in the ark, which represented the Church, and then were *incorporated* into a new world where they were the only eight people alive to repopulate the world. (The number eight represented eternity in the Old Testament, as may be seen in circumcision on the eighth day after birth, marking the entrance of a male child by the shedding of his blood into Israel, God's chosen nation.) The children of Israel were *separated* from their bondage in Egypt through a series of miracles that climaxed when the angel of death passed over their homes, sparing their firstborn. After fleeing Egypt, they passed through the Red Sea on dry ground as their *transition* and "baptism" (1 Corinthians 10:2) and were *incorporated* as the journeying people of God in the wilderness. After forty years of wandering, Israel was *separated* from the wilderness, made *transition* through the Jordan River (Joshua 3–5, another "baptism"), and was *incorporated* into the Promised Land flowing with milk and honey. The return from the exile was like a second exodus as God's people again traveled to the Promised Land and rebuilt the temple. While those events were unique in history, circumcision was to be performed on each male throughout Israel's generations. Circumcision represented the cutting off of the old sinful flesh, marking transition and incorporation as a member of God's people and a welcomed guest at the Passover feast.[3]

The Passover Seder was celebrated every year in the springtime to both commemorate the first Passover and to look forward to the coming of the very Lamb of God, the Messiah, whose blood would cleanse the whole creation. The Passover liturgy began with a series of blessings, one for the day and one over the first ritual cup of the Passover meal. Then the table was set with the food that was going to be eaten at the Passover. First, the paterfamilias, the male head of the household, would interpret the food, such as the bitter herbs that showed the bitterness of the journey out of Egypt into the wilderness, the unleavened bread that signified the haste in which they had to leave, and the lamb, which showed the blood that must be shed for Israel's deliverance from Egyptian bondage. After the interpretation of the food, the paterfamilias would tell the story of the exodus, narrating the story as his father and grandfather had before him (most families did not have a copy of the Bible). When the narration of the exodus was finished, the paterfamilias would take the second ritual cup, called the cup of redemption, and bless it as sign and recognition of God's redemption of Israel in the Passover in Egypt.

Now the meal would begin with the paterfamilias taking the bread, blessing it, breaking it, and giving it the family. The breaking of the bread signaled that it was time to eat the meal. After the supper had been eaten by all, the paterfamilias would take the third ritual cup, the cup of blessing, bless it as he then gave the grace after the meal, called the *Birkat ha-Mazon*, one of the most important prayers in Israel's liturgical life in both the Passover and Sabbath evening Seders. Through this prayer, God was blessed for creation, thanked for revealing Himself by giving the Promised Land to His people, and petitioned to redeem Israel in Jerusalem by the coming of the Messiah. (Christians would come to call this "eucharistic prayer," from the Greek word for thanksgiving.) Note the blessing that thanked God and the blessing that petitioned God were both centered in the land, first the Promised Land and then Jerusalem, the place of sacrifice and God's final salvation in the shedding of the blood of His Messiah. Liturgical scholars have traced the origins of early eucharistic prayers back to the *Birkat ha-Mazon,* showing the great continuity between Jewish and Christian worship. The *Birkat ha-Mazon*, then, would look something like this:

1. **Blessing:** Blessings for creation, for God's feeding His creation
2. **Thanksgiving:** Thanks for revelation, for His giving of the land
3. **Petitionary:** Petitions for future redemption in Jerusalem

Jewish scholar Louis Finkelstein sought to reconstruct what the earliest *Birkat ha-Mazon* might look like:

> Blessed are you, O Lord, our God, King of the universe, who feeds the whole world with goodness, with grace and with mercy. Blessed are you, O Lord, who feeds all.
>
> We thank you, O Lord, our God, that you have caused us to inherit a goodly land, the covenant, the Torah, life and food. For all these things we thank you and praise your name forever and ever. Blessed are you, O Lord, for the land and for the food.
>
> Have mercy, O Lord, our God, on your people Israel, and on your city Jerusalem, and on your Temple and your dwelling-place and on Zion your resting-place, and on the great and holy sanctuary over which your name was called and your kingdom of the dynasty of David may you restore to its place in our days, and build Jerusalem soon. Blessed are you, O Lord, who builds Jerusalem.[4]

There may have been a fourth cup following the cup of blessing, but there is much debate as to whether or not that cup was part of the Passover Seder at the time of Jesus. A rough outline of the Passover Seder would look like this:

Passover Seder

I. **The Preliminary Course**
  - **Blessing**—Cup I
  - **Blessing**—Feast of Unleavened Bread (Passover)
  - **Teaching at the Table**
  - Setting the Table
    - Interpretation of the Food
    - Narration of the Exodus
  - **Blessing**—Cup II, Cup of Redemption
  - **Blessing**—Bread
    - Breaking the Bread of Affliction

II. **The Meal**

III. **The Grace after the Meal** (*Birkat ha-Mazon*)
  - **Blessing**—Cup III, Cup of Blessing
  - 1. Blessing for creation: feeding
  - 2. Thanksgiving for revelation: land
  - 3. Petition for redemption: Jerusalem

The disciples had probably celebrated the Passover with Jesus before the night in which He was betrayed, not to mention the many Passovers they would have experienced within their own extended families. They came to this final Passover with Jesus in Jerusalem expecting that this would be like any other Passover, following the same order of service, with the same meaning given to each part of the Seder. However, in the last Passover Jesus celebrated with His disciples, He changed it from a "Jewish" Passover to the first Christian liturgy called the Last Supper. We might call this last Passover "Jesus' Passover" because He showed how it pointed to Him and came to fulfillment on this night in which He was betrayed.[5]

The Passover followed the clear outline given above, but there was flexibility within the ritual for the paterfamilias to tell the narrative of the exodus in his own way, and to use his own words to interpret the food that was set on the table. This flexibility allowed Jesus to interpret the various parts of the Passover Seder in a way they had never been interpreted before. He would have interpreted everything in terms of Himself, that is, He would have given the Passover meal a messianic interpretation because He was the Messiah who was about to fulfill God's plan of salvation on that very day. This meant the interpretation would have been Christological, for "Christ" is the Greek translation of "Messiah."

Therefore, when Jesus spoke of the food and the exodus, He would show His disciples that He was the new Israel, who would accomplish what Israel as a people could not. He would faithfully obey the Father's will and complete perfectly the exodus that Israel could not complete because of sin. The bitter herbs now spoke of the bitterness of His own suffering He was about to undergo on behalf of the world's sin, the unleavened bread of the haste is His body that must go to the cross to make that Passover from death to life. And He could now say that He was the Lamb of God whose blood would be shed on the cross to take away the sins of the world. This is, after all, "the day of Unleavened Bread, on which the Passover lamb had to be sacrificed" (Luke 22:7). As Jesus told the story of the exodus, He would show how His departure, His "exodus" (Luke 9:31), had brought Him from heaven into this world and would take Him to the cross, into the belly of the earth in a tomb,[6] and then raise Him up from the grave on the third day and take Him back to heaven on the fortieth. Needless to say, the disciples would have been shocked at His interpretation and struggled to understand the meaning of His words. They would have never before heard an interpretation of the Passover meal quite like this!

Nothing would be more shocking to them, however, than Jesus' interpretation of the bread and wine. When He took the bread to give thanks over it and break it, His interpretation of this bread must have been too much for them: "This is My body, which is given for you. Do this in remembrance of Me." And then when the supper was over, taking the third ritual cup, the cup of blessing, He gave thanks over it and gave it to them saying, "This cup that is poured out for you is the new covenant of My blood" (Luke 22:19–20). Bread, the food that only comes after the fall into sin because it is the food that comes from the sweat of the brow in planting, sowing, kneading, and baking, now becomes the means by which we receive Christ's body broken in death. Wine, the drink that rejoices the heart as a foretaste of our heavenly joy, now becomes the means for Christ's blood shed for our life. Body and blood in, with, and under bread and wine formed an interpretation of the Passover elements that, along with Jesus' other Christological interpretations, made this meal a meal to remember!

The Christian liturgy of the Sacrament is based on "Jesus' Passover" with His disciples in the upper room. It is from the Passover liturgy at the Last Supper that the early Christians received what was to become the liturgy of Holy Communion.

Luke is the only evangelist who preserves in his account a skeleton of the Jewish Passover that included two distinct cups of wine (22:17–18 and 22:20). These cups point toward the fuller structure of the Passover meal itself. The following diagram is an outline of a full Jewish Passover meal[7] in the left column and a summary of the Lukan account of the Last Supper in the right one.[8]

The Passover Meal	The Lukan Last Supper
A. Preliminary Course	
Word of sanctification (the *qiddush*, or blessing) spoken by the head of the family or host over the first cup (the *qiddush* cup).	**22:14**—The hour for the Passover observance begins with the disciples reclining at the table with Jesus.
Preliminary dish, including green herbs, bitter herbs, and a sauce made of fruit purée.	
The meal proper (see C) is served but not yet eaten; the second cup of wine is mixed and poured but not yet drunk.	**22:15**—Jesus announces His great desire to eat the Passover that is now set before them.
B. Passover Liturgy	
The Passover Haggadah (narrative teaching) spoken by the host.	**22:16**—In Jesus' explanation, He announces that He will not eat the Passover again until it is fulfilled in the kingdom of God.
First part of the Passover *Hallel* (praise psalms).	
Drinking of the second cup (cup of redemption).	**22:17–18**—The first cup mentioned by Luke is probably the second cup of the Passover, also called the "cup of redemption."
C. Main Meal	
Grace spoken by the host over the unleavened bread.	**22:19**—Jesus speaks the Words of Institution over the unleavened bread; the breaking of the bread begins the meal.
Meal, consisting of Passover lamb, unleavened bread, bitter herbs (Ex 12:8), with fruit purée and wine.	**22:20**—"... likewise, after the eating of the meal."
Grace (*Birkat ha-Mazon*) over the third cup (cup of blessing).	**22:20**—Jesus speaks the Words of Institu tion over the cup after the meal. (This is the second time a cup is mentioned by Luke.)
D. Conclusion	
Second part of the Passover *Hallel* (praise psalms).	
Praise over the fourth cup (*Hallel* cup).	

Jewish Christians who heard Luke's Gospel would be familiar with the Passover, but also might have been evangelizing those who were not aware of the Passover structure or realized that the institution of the Lord's Supper took place in the context of the Passover meal. The potential problem of Gentile ignorance is illustrated by the congregation at Corinth, where the celebration of the Lord's Supper apparently was held in conjunction with a congregational meal, and the congregation's celebration was plagued with problems and abuses (1 Corinthians 10–11). Today, we also are in need of learning the order of the Passover Seder to fully understand the significance of this meal that forms the foundation of our liturgy of Holy Communion.

Jewish Places of Worship

The most important place of worship was the temple in Jerusalem. The other two places were the synagogue, like our churches today, and the home, where special table prayers and readings attended the festive meals of the Jews such as the Passover and the Sabbath evening Seder.

Temple

As the place where God dwelt, the temple in Jerusalem was the supreme place of worship for the Jews. Here God was present for Israel for salvation, specifically in the Holy of Holies. The temple, therefore, was the place of holiness; the Jews understood holiness in terms of one's proximity to the temple. If you were outside Israel, on the eastern side of the Jordan River, you would be in a less holy space than if you were to cross the Jordan into Israel. Holiness radiated from the Holy of Holies outward into the world. (At one point, the temple was the home of the ark of the covenant, the jars of manna, and the Ten Commandments.)[9]

The bodily presence of Jesus Christ is the locale of God's holiness. That holy presence in Word and Sacrament unites us with Jesus and the first-century Church. The first-century world in which Jesus lived, taught, performed miracles, and accomplished the world's salvation was structured and ordered by people inhabiting that world. Each culture has its own core values. When people engage in the process of ordering their world, they are making a statement about who they are. They are defining their identity.[10] God's holiness in creation and the temple was one of the core values of first-century Judaism.

Jesus and His disciples shared the same culture as the people of His day, particularly the religious establishment. One reason Jesus was crucified was that He crossed some of the boundaries these religious leaders used to define themselves. He redrew the map of holiness and propriety. Many of these boundaries Jesus crossed directly affected the core value of purity and holiness: touching lepers, healing on the Sabbath, eating with tax collectors and sinners. But as Luke points out from the very beginning of his Gospel, Jesus crossed these boundaries because He was, as the Son of God, the embodiment of holiness and purity, and He was redrawing the boundaries of holiness not only for Israel, but for the entire cosmos. As the "Holy One of God" (Luke 4:34), whatever Jesus touched and proclaimed clean and holy—no matter how unclean and unholy it might be in the eyes of His first-century culture—then became holy because it had been transformed by the Creator who had broken into His creation to make all things new.

One of the great themes of Luke's infancy narrative is that the place of God's holiness is not only in Holy Scripture and the temple in Jerusalem, but now also in the flesh of Jesus Christ. It may have been quite shocking to first-century Jews to learn that Mary is described as the new Israel, the new temple, and even perhaps the ark of the covenant. God chose Mary's womb as the locale of His holiness, a temporary and portable vessel housing the imminent presence of the true God, thereby fulfilling the purpose originally given to Israel, the temple, and the ark. The body of Jesus is the new temple. In John's Gospel, when the Jews asked Jesus for a sign to verify His actions, He told them: "Destroy this temple, and in three days I will raise it up" (John 2:19). The Jews were incensed! It took forty-six years to build the temple in Jerusalem, and Jesus was claiming the power to rebuild it in three days? The evangelist John helps us understand the meaning of Jesus' words: "He was speaking about the temple of His body" (John 2:21). Jesus shows by these words He is not a revolutionary. As one author describes, "Jesus as the cornerstone of the true temple becomes the new center of the map and all holiness is measured by proximity to him."[11]

God chose Mary's womb as the locale of His holiness, a temporary and portable vessel housing the imminent presence of the true God, thereby fulfilling the purpose originally given to Israel, the temple, and the ark. The body of Jesus is the new temple.

This new map is now inclusive, for as Peter the Jew now tells Cornelius the Gentile, "God shows 'no partiality' " (Acts 10:34) because the map that Jesus has drawn breaks down the barriers that existed between people. But there are still boundaries, and Jesus, who draws the new map, also stands as guardian of the boundaries of that new map. The dividing line is Jesus Himself, as Simeon prophesied when Jesus was forty days old: "Behold, this child is destined for the fall and resurrection of many in Israel."[12] Jesus saw Himself as the ultimate arbiter of these boundaries.

The temple in Jerusalem was constructed into a series of courtyards that served as gathering places, but also as boundaries. Each person, according to status, rank, or sex, was only allowed so far. The Court of Gentiles was a far as a Gentile could go, the Court of the Women as far as a woman could go, and so on. Only Levitical priests could enter the Court of Priests and approach the altar of burnt offerings or enter the Holy Place, where the daily atonement sacrifices were made at the third hour (middle of the morning, around 9:00 a.m.) and the ninth hour (middle of the afternoon, at 3:00 p.m.). These atonement sacrifices took place while the people were praying in the Court of the Women, reminding them that God would send a Messiah to shed His blood for them to forgive them their sins. The people would stand outside the Holy Place and wait for the priest to come back.

Luke's Gospel begins and ends in the temple in Jerusalem, and glimpses of the temple appear throughout his record. At the beginning of Luke's Gospel, Zechariah enters the Holy Place, as is his duty as a Levitical priest. It is here that the angel appears to him and reveals that he and Elizabeth will bear a son, and that his name will be John. When Zechariah did not come out from the Holy Place, the people were perplexed because they did not know what was happening, and they were thinking that God was speaking to Zechariah (Luke 1:5–23). Another example of the temple in Luke is in the parable of the Pharisee and tax collector, who were both in the temple for prayer. This would have been during the morning or afternoon sacrifices. When Jews prayed publicly, they prayed aloud. The Pharisee placed himself front and center in the Court of the Women, probably in front of the Nicanor gate, for it was here that Jews gathered to pray during the atonement sacrifices. The Pharisee proclaimed in his prayer that he thanked God that he was not like other men, especially the tax collector. The tax collector, on the other hand, would have taken his place quietly in a obscure part of the courtyard. In a penitent manner, not lifting his eyes to heaven but beating his breast, his prayer during the atonement sacrifice is most appropriate for what he knows to be going on in the Holy Place. His prayer is literally: "Make an atonement for me, a sinner." He understood the true meaning of the temple rituals (Luke 18:9–14).

But there was a place more holy than the Holy Place, and that was the Holy of Holies. Only the high priest could enter the Holy of Holies once a year on the Day of Atonement. Leviticus 16 describes the sacrificial actions of Aaron, the high priest on this day. Blood was poured on the mercy seat for the sins of the people (Leviticus 16:15). Then Aaron laid his hands on the scapegoat, confessing over it all the sins of the people, as he sent it out into the wilderness bearing their iniquities (Leviticus 16:20–22). The shedding of blood for the sins of the people and the transference of sins from the people to the scapegoat were at the heart of the rituals on the Day of Atonement. That is why, when Jesus, our High Priest, shed His blood on the cross and died for the sins of the world, the temple curtain was torn asunder, for everyone now had access to the Holy of Holies through Jesus. There are no more physical boundaries to God's holiness. Hebrews 9 describes the significance of Christ's death in this way:

> But when Christ appeared as a high priest of the good things that have come, then through the greater and more perfect tent (not made with hands, that is, not of this creation) He entered once for all into the holy places, not by means of the blood of goats and calves but by means of His own blood, thus securing an eternal redemption. For if the blood of goats and bulls, and the sprinkling of defiled persons with the ashes of a heifer, sanctify for the purification of the flesh, how much more will the blood of Christ, who through the eternal Spirit offered Himself without blemish to God, purify our conscience from dead works to serve the living God. (Hebrews 9:11–14)

As a place of sacrifice, the temple in Jerusalem was very earthy and real. It was filled with the smells and sights that would accompany such sacrifices, resembling a slaughterhouse more than a Holy Place. Nevertheless, this reality signaled the presence of God in this space. There were perhaps 16,000 to 18,000 Passover lambs killed in the temple when our Lord was crucified. Estimates of pilgrims run around 125,000, adding in the inhabitants of Jerusalem for a total of about 175,000 people, and one lamb serving about ten people, this was a bloody affair. The blood was poured at the foot of the altar for the burnt offering. A bucket brigade of priests would transfer the blood for the place of sacrifice to the altar where it would be poured. The Mishnah, a document written by temple rabbis after the fall of Jerusalem (AD 70), describes the slaughter of the Passover lamb this way: "An Israelite slaughtered his [own] offering and the priest caught the blood. The priest passed the basin to his fellow, and he to his fellow, each receiving a full basin and giving back an empty one. The priest nearest to the Altar tossed the blood in one action against the base [of the Altar]."[13] The amount of blood from 18,000 was said to cover the ankles of the priests, and periodically they would have to wash the Court of the Women because of the volume of blood. The Kidron River that flowed between the temple and the Mount of Olives was said to run pink during the sacrifice of the Passover lambs. The burning of the entrails on the altar would accompany the pouring of the blood on the base of the altar, causing the temple to smell like a slaughter-house of burning flesh and bloody meat.

> When Jesus, our High Priest, shed His blood on the cross and died for the sins of the world, the temple curtain was torn asunder, for everyone now had access to the Holy of Holies through Jesus. There are no more physical boundaries to God's holiness.

The place where the blood of the Passover lamb was poured was Mount Moriah, the place David had chosen for the building of the temple (2 Chronicles 3). Mount Moriah was also the very rock where Abraham was asked by the Lord to sacrifice his son Isaac (Genesis 22:2). God provided a ram in place of Isaac so that Abraham would not have to give up his only-begotten son. This shows the wonderful continuity of God's saving action going back to Abraham, the father of the Jews, and then on to Moses where the blood of the lamb is placed on the doorposts, saving the firstborn of Israel from the angel of death on the first Passover. That action brought the children of Israel into the Promised Land that God had given them, and to Jerusalem, the place of the final sacrifice of the Passover lamb, Jesus Himself, on Good Friday when He was crucified for our sins. So when this Passover blood was poured on the rock of Abraham, the Jews understood this as the way God was going to save. There is no salvation, no forgiveness of sins outside of blood.

As a place of sacrifice, it is very difficult for us to identify with the worship in the temple in Jerusalem, which is one of the reasons early Christians borrowed almost nothing from the temple liturgy except the singing of psalms and the reading of Scriptures. With the all-sufficient sacrifice of Christ and the tearing of the Temple curtain, the liturgy of the Jerusalem temple became obsolete.

SYNAGOGUE

As discussed previously, synagogues developed during the Diaspora, the period when the Jews were scattered throughout the inhabited world and could not make a yearly pilgrimage to the temple in Jerusalem for Passover. The Sabbath liturgy of the synagogue is different from the temple liturgy because it contains no sacrifices. The synagogue liturgy centers rather around the reading of the Word, interpretation of that Word, the *Shema* or Old Testament "creed" from Deuteronomy 6:4–9 ("Hear, O Israel: The Lord our God, the Lord is One . . ."), prayer based on that Word, and the Psalms—the Old Testament hymns that accompanied the themes of the Word. The Sanctus from Isaiah 6 and Psalm 118 formed one of the earliest hymns. These services were very similar to our Matins, Vespers, Morning and Evening Prayer, and also helped shape the Word structure in the service of Holy Communion.

Synagogue worship looked somewhat like this:

Liturgy of the Synagogue

Invocation
  "Bless the Lord who is to be blessed."

The Sanctus
  (Isaiah 6 and Psalm 118—one of the earliest hymns)

The *Shema* or Old Testament Creed
  Deuteronomy 6:4–9: "Hear, O Israel: The Lord our God is one Lord. . . ."

The Eighteen Benedictions
  A series of blessings also known as the "Amidah" or the "Tefillah"

The Priestly Blessing or Aaronic Benediction
  Numbers 6:24–26

The reading of the Word
  Torah
    Psalm
  Prophets
    Psalm
  [Historical Writings]
    [Psalm]

Interpretation of the Word (Preaching/Teaching)
  Also known as Midrash

"Alenu leshabeah"
  "We must praise [the Ruler of all]"[14]

The reading of Scripture was central to the worship in the synagogue. As observed from the above outline, the manner in which the Jews read the Scriptures is very similar to the way we read the Scriptures. The major difference is that they began with the most important reading, the Torah—a selection from Genesis, Exodus, Leviticus, Numbers, or Deuteronomy. The Torah was the point of interpretation for the rest of the reading, that is, the prophetic reading interpreted the reading from the Torah, and so on with the historical reading. The rabbis used the important principle, that Scripture interprets Scripture, so that the prophets and other readings would serve as homilies on the Torah. Between each reading would be a time of meditation and reflection when they would chant Psalms chosen according to the theme of the reading. At the end of the Scripture reading, the rabbi or teacher would expound the Scriptures in his homily, called *midrash*, which means "interpretation." He would teach about what God had just said to the people through His Word.

The synagogue liturgy would take place in a simple space, men separated from women, with children around the central space ("bema") where the Word of God was read. Jews placed children close to the reading of the Word, for they believed that God was present in His Word, and they wanted their children to be as close to the presence of God as possible. Synagogue liturgies took place on the Sabbath, which for the Jews began at sundown on Friday and continued until sundown on Saturday. Most synagogue liturgies occurred on Saturday mornings after the celebration of the Sabbath evening Seder, which will be discussed in the next section.

Outside of Jerusalem, the synagogue was the most important place of worship for the Jews. In the temple, the chief priests from the Sadducean party were in charge of the temple sacrifices; in the synagogue, the pharisaical party of lawyers, teachers of the law, and scribes were leaders. They were considered the biblical scholars of their day, conservative in their interpretation of Scriptures. The Pharisees were in contact with Jesus during His extended Galilean ministry, and His manner of teaching and interpreting the Scriptures was closer to them than any other religious group in Israel. This is why He was regularly invited to teach in the synagogues and eat at their tables. However, as close as they were, there was one fundamental difference between Jesus and the Pharisees. His teaching centered in the Gospel, that salvation was by faith in the Messiah who would come to redeem Israel with the shedding of His blood; the teaching of the Pharisees was centered in the Law, that salvation was by works of the Law. This is why their preaching was moralistic while Jesus' preaching was Christ centered, an announcement that in Him the promises of the Old Testament were coming to fulfillment.

Thus, temple and synagogue were the two major public places of worship in Israel at the time of Jesus. There is, however, one more place where Jesus would have worshiped, and that is in the home in the context of the weekly family meal known as the Sabbath evening Seder.

House Worship

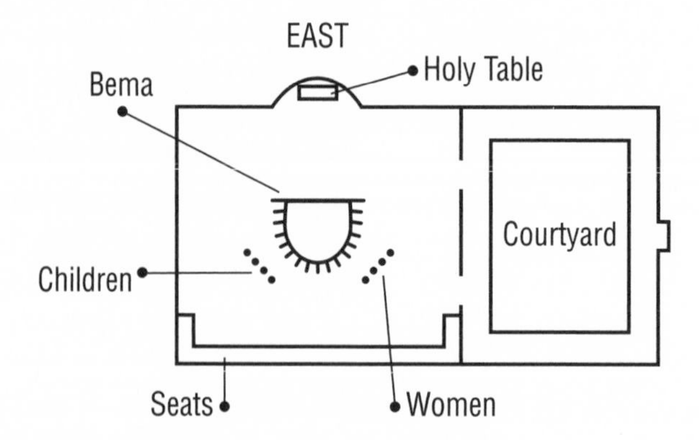

The house worship began on Friday night after sundown, the beginning of the Sabbath for the Jews. Every Friday night they would have a meal and a very brief but structured liturgy based on the Passover liturgy. It was called the Sabbath evening Seder (*seder* means "order," and here "order of service"). This meal reminded them every Friday night of the Passover, that is, the Lamb who would be slain. This Lamb was the promised Messiah, the Christ. This regular meal provided an occasion for the paterfamilias to keep the Passover alive in the lives of his family. On Saturday morning the family went to the synagogue for worship.

This house liturgy also had an influence on the development of the Christian Liturgy of the Word just as the Passover Seder provided the foundation for the Christian liturgy of the Sacrament. The following diagram shows the similarity between the Passover Seder and the Sabbath evening Seder:

Passover Seder	**The Sabbath Evening Seder**
I. The Preliminary Course	**I. The Preliminary Course**
Blesssing—Cup I	**Blesssing**—Cup I
Blessing—Feast of Unleavened Bread (Passover)	**Blessing**—Sabbath day
Teaching at the Table	
Setting the Table	
Interpretation of the Food	
Narration of the Exodus	
Blessing—Cup II, Cup of Redemption	
Blessing—Bread	**Blessing**—Bread
Breaking the Bread of Affliction	The Breaking the of Bread
II. The Meal	**II. The Meal**
III. The Grace after the Meal *(Birkat ha-Mazon)*	**III. The Grace after the Meal**
Blessing—Cup III, Cup of Blessing	**Blessing**—Cup II
1. Blessing for creation: feeding	
2. Thanksgiving for revelation: land	
3. Petition for redemption: Jerusalem	

Jesus participated at all three Jewish places of worship and in the liturgies they used. He cleansed the **temple** to make it a worthy place for His teaching (Luke 19:45–46), and prophesied that He would replace it with Himself (John 2:19–22). He often went into the **synagogues** to teach (Luke 4:16–30). Most of the occasions in the Gospel when He goes into people's **homes** are related to the Sabbath evening Seder (e.g., Levi the tax collector, Luke 5:27–32; Simon the Pharisee, Luke 7:36–50; Zacchaeus the chief tax collector, Luke 19:1–10).

Therefore, the temple liturgy had very little impact on Christian worship besides the affirmation of God's holy presence as central to Jewish and Christian worship. The synagogue service, however, gave birth to the Liturgy of the Word, and the Passover and house Seders were the foundation for the Liturgy of the Lord's Supper.

4

The Table Fellowship of Jesus

The most natural and intimate way of expressing common fellowship is at the table through a meal. In the ancient world, the meal itself was always prepared for with "table talk." For formal meals such as the Passover Seder or Greek banquets, this table talk would take the form of teaching at the table by an invited guest who would serve as "banquet speaker." Table talk, or teaching, and eating the meal formed the normal pattern of table fellowship in the ancient world.

Although we may not have as formal a structure, when we express fellowship together, we engage in table talk when we gather for ceremonial meals. For example, Thanksgiving, like the Jewish Passover, includes traditional foods such as turkey and dressing, potatoes, and pies. As important as the food is, what is at least as important is our "talk" when we come together as family and friends for table fellowship. This is one of the reasons many cultures have wine with meals. Wine enhances the food and aids in digestion, but it also facilitates the table talk and rejoices the heart as those who gather celebrate things they have in common.

The early Christian communities were liturgical and sacramental, that is, they belonged to the table fellowship of Jesus; they heard His teaching; they ate His food. All this sprouted from Jewish roots. So the language of the Jews at prayer was modified. Jewish prayers blessed God for His creation and thanked God that He promised to send a Messiah to redeem them. Christians thanked God for the redemption of all creation that was brought to completion in Jesus. The very Christian word *Eucharist* means "thanks."

As a worshiping Jew, Jesus would have prayed as a Jew. His teaching drew from Jewish forms and expressions, the same forms and expressions that would be shared by the earliest Jewish-Christian communities. These, then, would form the backbone of early Christian teaching to Gentiles.

Table Fellowship in the Old Testament

The Passover meal was central to Old Testament piety. So also was the weekly remembrance of the Passover in the Sabbath evening Seder. Table fellowship with God was a ready-made picture for Jewish Christians. They would use it to describe how God communicated His intentions for their salvation and established His presence with His people. The salvation history of the Jews is captured and expressed in the tradition and forms that are the structure of these meals. These ritual meals created a natural context for instruction in the Word of God, a Word that reconciles and unifies. The various peoples and cultures in the ancient Near East saw table fellowship as a high level of friendship and unity, and Israelites were no exception. To invite a guest to a meal was a universally understood act of hospitality. Therefore, in the New Testament, Jesus' meals sent a clear message to His contemporaries of His desire for God's reconciling action in Him to be extended to all people because Jesus ate with people of every class.

Ancient Israel bears witness to table fellowship as an occasion at which God often communicated His promised salvation. For example, God provided fruit trees in Eden, but Adam and Eve violated the fellowship boundaries set by God when they ate from the forbidden tree in the presence of the serpent, plunging the world into sin. In subsequent history, God begins to restore His fallen creation, and His redemption is often accompanied by or celebrated with a meal. We often see in these meals that God is establishing a covenant. One instance is in Genesis 18: God appears to Abraham via three men, one of whom turns out to be the Lord. Abraham and Sarah show hospitality to these guests by preparing a meal (cf. Hebrews 13:2), and the three eat real, human food. It is during that meal that God promises a son, whom God would use to continue the Seed of Eve until the coming of the promised Seed who would crush the serpent's head (Genesis 18:10–14; cf. Genesis 3:15).

The covenants Yahweh made with His people often were celebrated with a meal. When a covenant was established (or "cut," to use the more literal language), an animal would be cut in half, with the two parts laid side by side. The parties "cutting" the covenant would then walk between the two pieces of the sacrificed animal. This was a solemn agreement that if either party broke the covenant, the other could render the guilty party as that animal; the guilty party could be cut in two. When a covenant was cut, the animal used in the sacrifice was not left there to rot, but was eaten as a sign and symbol of the intimate fellowship that exists between the two parties.

While the patriarchs offered sacrifices at various times, a major fulfillment of the promise in Abraham's covenant began at the deliverance of the Israelites from their bondage in Egypt. At the Passover, the blood of the sacrificial lamb without blemish was applied to the lintel and doorposts. The Passover (Exodus 12; cf. Joshua 5:10–12; 2 Kings 23:21–23) celebrated the salvation that was the birth of the nation of Israel in which God gave them the gift of the Promised Land flowing with milk and honey. God instructed the Israelites to use the setting of the Passover meal to pass down the fundamental, gracious doctrines of God to future generations (Exodus 12:24–27). The exodus story would be told each year at the Passover meal. Teaching and eating at the Passover meal formed the Old Testament precedent for Jesus' table fellowship and Christian worship.

The Table Fellowship of Jesus

The Gospels record the table fellowship of Jesus, and that fellowship comes straight out of Old Testament patterns. For God to feed His people in the intimacy of the table would call to the Jewish mind the rich Old Testament precedent for this practice. *But for God to become flesh* and sit at table with them, giving them food from His own fleshly hands, was something new. Nevertheless, it was consistent with the character of God as portrayed in the Old Testament—the God who promised to dwell in the midst of His people and feed them (e.g., Deuteronomy 26:5–9; 1 Kings 8). God was present with His people at Old Testament meals such as the Passover and the shared temple sacrifices, but God was not yet incarnate. The Genesis 18 event with Abraham and the three men was but a hint, a cameo appearance of what was to come. In Jesus, God became present *in the flesh* to establish a table fellowship of eating and drinking with His people. And Jesus' practice, while new, was also scandalous. There were strict limits on those invited to many Old Testament meals (e.g., the Passover; the temple sacrifices), yet Jesus freely ate and drank with sinners.

The Passover Seder, the Sabbath evening Meal, and the early Christian Eucharist share table fellowship language that accurately describes the relationship between the three. For example, the evangelist Luke makes use of table fellowship metaphors and language as he systematically used Jesus' table fellowship to teach about the Eucharist, about Christian liturgy, and ultimately, about Jesus Christ and His kingdom. Luke shows Jesus eating with people frequently. He shows Jesus teaching during the meals frequently. The meals and the accompanying teaching become a dominant motif in the

Gospel that brings together many themes, making Luke's Gospel both catechetical and liturgical.

The act of table fellowship for Jesus, including both the meal itself and the participants of the meal, is also a form of teaching. Neither the teaching nor the eating is of greater importance; both must be considered together as the same activity. Table fellowship reveals something about the participants in that fellowship, particularly the host at the table. In Jesus' case, it shows who He is as the Christ, and what He must do. Jesus' lifestyle at the table is one of service, and He renders the ultimate service to humanity as God's innocent, suffering Messiah by giving up His life for the world on the cross and offering that same life at the table in His body and blood for the forgiveness of sins.

The table fellowship established in Jesus joins together those who participate in anticipation of the end time kingdom. Christianity embraces both the sinner and the righteous, and reveals the most intimate nature of the kingdom of God, namely that God and humans have fellowship with one another through teaching and eating together. Intimacy at the table is stuff that all people of all times understand. For Jews, this was the ultimate form of intimacy, which is why they maintained such strict requirements concerning who could eat together. To engage in table fellowship, one had to be clean, that is, to stand in God's presence and in the presence of His holy people forgiven and whole. This is why Jesus' table fellowship with sinners scandalized the Jews, and why His table fellowship always conveyed the forgiveness of sins.

Table Fellowship in Luke's Gospel

The table fellowship seen in Luke's Gospel provides the perfect vehicle for teaching about the nature of Christian eucharistic fellowship. Luke develops this theme by recording meals between Jesus and different categories of people: tax collectors, Pharisees, and disciples.[1] As one traces these meals throughout Luke, a pattern may be discerned: (1) teaching, (2) eating, (3) the presence of God.

Jesus' presence at the meal makes this table fellowship different from all other meals invoking the presence of God. In each of the meals featured in Luke's Gospel, Jesus is present to teach the participants about Himself, a teaching of the kingdom of God in which He, the King, is present to offer the forgiveness of sins. The occasion is always marked by the theme of conversion, a turning to God in repentance and faith. The true participants of the fellowship are repentant sinners, personified by Levi the tax collector, who initiates the table fellowship of Jesus with his invitation to feast at his house (Luke 5:29), and by Zacchaeus, the chief tax collector in whose house Jesus must stay and eat (Luke 19:5). In each meal, the teaching of Jesus is part of the table fellowship and essential to the meal. This teaching prepares for the meal and makes the meal a seal of the forgiveness taught by Jesus. In Jesus' table fellowship, three elements are apparent:

1. The meal is with sinners; it is an inclusive event.
2. Jesus teaches about the Kingdom.
3. The meal is an expression of the new era of salvation.

From its initiation at the feast with Levi (Luke 5) to its climax at the Emmaus meal (Luke 24), the basic pattern of table fellowship in Luke reveals that there is always teaching at the table, and eating as a seal of the fellowship, both of which take place *in the presence of God.* All of Jesus' meals are acts of table fellowship—teaching and eating in the presence of Jesus.

The table talk of Jesus' Galilean ministry focuses on the kingdom of God. For Jesus, that kingdom is about His own coronation on a cross where, through His death, Jesus reconciles all people to Himself through the forgiveness of sins. During the Galilean ministry, Jesus would travel from town to town each Sabbath, teaching in the synagogues and spending the Sabbath evening Seder with those who invited Him to preach. He would engage on a weekly basis in table fellowship, teaching at the table of the Sabbath evening Seder before the meal. (Note the table on page 71 for how the teaching at the table of the Passover Meal is paralleled in Jesus' teaching at the table in the Sabbath evening Seder.)

Jesus' meals are for repentant sinners who receive the forgiveness of their sins because of their fellowship with Jesus (for example, the meals of Luke 5 and 7). The call to repentance is made during Jesus' teaching at the table, as He does with Levi and Zacchaeus, as well as the sinful woman who comes repentant and whose penitence is affirmed by Jesus during His teaching. The climactic meal during His Galilean ministry is the feeding of the five thousand where Jesus first teaches about the kingdom of God and then feeds them with miraculous food (Luke 9:10–17). The language Jesus uses here at this meal links this feeding miracle with the Last Supper and the Emmaus meal, the other climactic moments in Jesus' table fellowship. "And **taking** the five loaves and the two fish, He looked up to heaven and **said a blessing** over them. Then He **broke** the loaves and **gave** them to the disciples to set before the crowd" (Luke 9:16, emphasis added). Here the King rules His kingdom by offering *now* the food that satisfies, and which is a foretaste of the banquet of heaven that is *not yet.*

As Jesus journeys to Jerusalem in Luke 13, 14, and 15, the emphasis shifts increasingly to the end times and the marriage feast of the lamb in heaven. The unmistakable elements of table fellowship are there. Jesus teaches how "people will come from east and west, and from north and south, and recline at table in the kingdom of God" (Luke 13:29). The banquet of the wedding feast in Luke 14 begins with the beatitude, "Blessed is everyone who will eat bread in the kingdom of God!" (Luke 14:15). This includes saints alive and saints asleep who will taste the banquet of the King. The parable of the prodigal son demonstrates that reconciliation and forgiveness take place when the entire community is invited to rejoice in the prodigal's restoration at the father's banquet of the fatted calf, for "it was fitting to celebrate and be glad, for this your brother was dead, and is alive; he was lost, and is found" (Luke 15:32). The meal with Zacchaeus demonstrates how Jesus' fellowship is about salvation for sinners. As the chief tax collector, Zacchaeus represents all sinners. Jesus' words to Him are representative of His ministry of salvation to the world as it is expressed in His table fellowship: "Today salvation has come to this house. . . . For the Son of Man came to seek and to save the lost" (19:9–10).

The Last Supper

The Last Supper is different from all previous Passover meals, for it is here that Jesus speaks for the first time of "the new covenant in My blood" (Luke 22:20). The Last Supper is the Meal of the new covenant, the new "exodus" (see Luke 9:28–31), the new Passover (see 22:17–19; cf. 1 Corinthians 5:7). As Jesus institutes the Sacrament of His body and blood, He directs the disciples, "Do this in remembrance of Me" (Luke 22:19), so that the Last Supper is Jesus' only table fellowship meal that is to be repeated, and it is to be repeated "until it is fulfilled in the kingdom of God" (22:16; cf. 1 Corinthians 11:26). It anticipates Christ's return and the consummation of the kingdom. Later Luke records that the disciples regularly celebrated "the breaking of bread" (Acts 2:42, 46). The Supper was held on the first day of the week—Sunday, the day of resurrection—in remembrance of the risen Lord. The chief reason for the Sunday gathering of Christians was "to break bread" (Acts 20:7). The Supper was not incidental or superfluous; its regular celebration lay at the heart and center of Early Church worship. St. Paul testifies to this in 1 Corinthians 11, and the evidence of the earliest liturgical documents show that the Lord's Supper was celebrated every Sunday until the time of the Reformation.

Promise of the Lord's Supper

At the Last Supper, Jesus issues sublime promises that pertain not just to that night, but to every occasion when the Church will gather around the Table of the Lord. Jesus promises to be with His disciples in a most intimate and miraculous way, with benefits that surpass those enjoyed by the people who reclined with Him in person during His earthly ministry up until the night on which He was betrayed. The guests at the Lord's Table—the Sacrament of the Altar—are actually in a more privileged position than were those who participated in the earthly meals of Jesus. The unique promise of the Last Supper, which holds true for every celebration of the Lord's Supper, is the bodily presence of Jesus' body and blood: "This is My body, which is given for you" (Luke 22:19); "This cup that is poured out for you is the new covenant in My blood" (22:20). According to these words, the body and blood of Jesus are truly present with the bread and wine. The body of Christ present with the bread is the body given into death for the salvation of the world; the blood of Christ in the cup is the blood shed "for the forgiveness of sins" (Matthew 26:28). At other meals with Jesus, the guests were able to see, touch (Luke 7:38–39), and hear Jesus, but only in the Sacrament of the Altar, the Supper He instituted, is Christ present in such a way that those who eat and drink receive His body and blood. The body and blood of Christ bring the forgiveness of sins and salvation He brought to the world through His ministry, His sacrificial death on behalf of all, and His resurrection.

Salvation and the forgiveness of sins through the body and blood of Jesus also bring the promise of eternal life. At the Last Supper, Jesus affirms that He will "not eat it [the Passover] until it is fulfilled in the kingdom of God," nor will He "drink of the fruit of the vine until the kingdom of God comes" (22:16, 18). Matthew includes a most significant additional phrase: Jesus tells the disciples, "I will not drink again of this fruit of the vine until that day when I drink it *new with you* in My Father's kingdom" (Matthew 26:29). The disciples who dine with Jesus will have a place at His table in the eternal kingdom feast. The Supper in which the disciples participate holds the promise of future eating and drinking when the kingdom of God fully arrives at the second coming. Like the penitent thief, they will join Jesus in paradise. (See Luke 23:39–43.)

These, then, are the unique benefits given by the Lord in His Supper according to His own words: His very body and blood, given and shed "for you" (Luke 22:19–20). With His body given into death and His shed blood come the communion of saints, the forgiveness of sins, the resurrection of the body, and the life everlasting. Disciples that faithfully continue in "the breaking of the bread" receive these blessings of the end times as they feast at His Table.

Baptism and the Lord's Supper

The Old Testament roots of both Baptism and the Lord's Supper are found in the Passover and ensuing exodus deliverance, as St. Paul indicates in his First Letter to the Corinthians:

> I want you to know, brothers, that our fathers were all under the cloud, and all passed through the sea, and all were baptized into Moses in the cloud and in the sea, and all ate the same spiritual food, and all drank the same spiritual drink. For they drank from the spiritual Rock that followed them, and the Rock was Christ. (1 Corinthians 10:1–4)

Paul sees a rite of passage in the events of the exodus through the Red Sea, crossing the Jordan River, and the accompanying cloud of God's presence. These incidents speak of Christian Baptism and of the Lord's Supper because the spiritual Rock that followed them was Christ (1 Corinthians 10:4). This shows us that Baptism and Lord's Supper are concrete events in our lives where Christ comes to us in His body to join us to Himself in the forgiveness of sins. The cloud and the rock were the presence of God in Christ; the water and the bread and wine are the presence of God in Christ. That is why Paul speaks of Israel's exodus in such a way that Christ is there as a Rock feeding His people food just as He is present among us giving us His body and blood for the forgiveness of our sins. Luke uses the same exodus imagery (Luke 9:31) to speak of Jesus' Passion, death, and resurrection. This exodus of Jesus, the crucifixion and resurrection, are the foundation for both Christian Baptism and the Lord's Supper.

Those who are baptized into Christ and who dine at His Supper are united with Christ in His death and resurrection. That means they, too, suffer because they are identified with Christ. It also means, however, that they receive the benefits of Christ's death and resurrection, namely, the forgiveness of sins and new life, so that after they die, they will rise by the power of

Christ's own resurrection. They will join Jesus in His eternal kingdom, where they will dine with Him anew according to His promise in His Supper.

Acts 2:38–39 says those who repent and are baptized in the name of Jesus Christ receive the forgiveness of sins and the Holy Spirit. In Matthew 26:28, Jesus, speaking of the cup in the Supper, refers to His blood shed "for the forgiveness of sins." Baptism into Christ entails dying with Christ and also rising with Christ to new life (Romans 6:1–11; Colossians 2:11–13). In the Last Supper Jesus promised His disciples that He would eat and drink with them anew in His Father's kingdom (Matthew 26:29), a promise that will be consummated in heaven (Revelation 19:6–9).

The Last Supper, then, is the highlight of Jesus' table fellowship. It is the meal Jesus earnestly longed to share with His disciples (Luke 22:15). It is the one meal Jesus has bequeathed to His Church as His testament. It is the ongoing feast that continues to be repeated in the Church in accord with Jesus' instructions, "Do this in remembrance of Me" (22:19).

The Church at the Table Rules and Judges

In Jesus' final teaching to His disciples at His Passover, in what amounts to His last will and testament to them, Jesus as the Lamb of God gives His body and blood and appoints a kingdom to these eleven disciples sitting at table with Him, just as His Father appointed to Him a kingdom. This kingdom brings with it the responsibility of serving as judges of the boundaries of this kingdom, in order "that you may eat and drink at My table in My kingdom and sit on thrones judging the twelve tribes of Israel" (Luke 22:30). Jesus' role as judge deciding who may enter His holy presence is handed down to the Church through the apostles and those who follow the apostolic pattern of teaching/preaching and administering the sacraments.

Sacraments are the new miracles of the post-Pentecost Church because they point to Jesus' presence in His creation bringing about the new creation. Just as the Old Testament judges were saviors and deliverers who led the people of God to repentance and faith (e.g., Judges 2:10–23; the LXX uses the verb "to judge," for their leadership [e.g., Judges 10:2–3]),[2] so the apostles and pastors in the apostolic ministry will "judge" in the following way: "The Gospel assigns those who preside over Churches the command to teach the Gospel [Matthew 28:19], to forgive sins [John 20:23], to administer the Sacraments, and also to *exercise jurisdiction* (i.e., the command to excommunicate those whose crimes are known and to absolve those who repent)."[3] Entrusted with the responsibility to oversee the mystery of Christ's holy presence, to apply Law and Gospel, to baptize, to absolve or retain sins, and to preside at the Supper, the apostles—and those who serve as their successors in Jesus' ministry—will lead the new Israel to gather around the Table of the Lord in His kingdom.

The Emmaus Meal

Throughout the Gospel of Luke, we read that all people around Jesus, even the apostles, never fully comprehend that Jesus as the Christ must suffer and die, even after He predicted His death and resurrection. As Jesus continues to predict His death and resurrection during His earthly ministry, the disciples are afraid to ask Jesus about them. However, the demons know who Jesus is and that His purpose is to destroy Satan's kingdom through His death and resurrection.[4]

Moving toward the final chapters of Luke's Gospel and the narrative of Jesus' Passion and resurrection, the reader sees how disciples such as Judas betray Jesus (22:1–6, 21–23, 47–53) and how Peter denies Him (22:31–35, 54–62). At the cross, very few of Jesus' followers are present: "And all His acquaintances and the women who had followed Him from Galilee stood at a distance watching these things" (23:49). When the women come to His tomb on that first Easter morning, they come to anoint a dead body (24:1). The disciples do not believe the women when they report that the tomb is empty (24:11).

The Last Supper was not Jesus' final meal with His disciples. After His resurrection, Jesus teaches two disciples on the road to Emmaus and breaks bread with them. There Jesus is present at the table for the first time after His crucifixion and resurrection. The reality of His bodily resurrection is confirmed later in Jerusalem when Jesus eats fish in the presence of His disciples (24:41–43). The Emmaus meal is distinct from the meals that precede and follow, for in the breaking of the bread (24:30, 35), the Emmaus disciples are the first people in Luke's Gospel to recognize that Jesus is the crucified and risen Lord. Only when Jesus opens up the Scriptures, and finally opens their eyes in the breaking of the bread, do these two men see before them Jesus the Christ, crucified and risen.

The evangelist's final word about Emmaus is a blueprint for Christian worship until the Last Day: "And they were expounding the things He taught on the road and how He was known to them in the breaking of the bread" (24:35, author's translation). The breaking of the bread recalls all of Jesus' table fellowship, particularly 22:19 and the words of institution, using the same pattern of words ("take, bless, broke, give"). Jesus' continuing practice of teaching and eating with His disciples at table has given the Church the norm for its liturgical worship. By His own unique example, the Lord Himself affirmed the pattern of liturgical worship, namely, teaching followed by eating in His table fellowship. He gave this norm in meals throughout Luke's Gospel (chs 5, 7, 9, 14, 19), at the Last Supper (22:14–38), and at Emmaus (24:35). In Acts, this same pattern of teaching and eating is present in the table fellowship of the Church (1:1–4). The meals in Acts confirm that from the beginning the Church followed the divine pattern through worship that included teaching and the celebration of the Lord's Supper. Worship in the New Testament Church is a continuing table fellowship with God that reaches back into the Old Testament and looks ahead to the wedding supper of heaven (Isaiah 25:6–9; Revelation 19:6–9), affording a foretaste of the feast to come. Jesus' table fellowship lies at the very heart of the kingdom of God as it is now present in the liturgical life of the Church. It is the classic liturgical formulation of Word and Sacrament that has continued in the church's celebrations of the Lord's Supper up to the present day.

Jesus' continuing practice of teaching and eating with His disciples at table has given the Church the norm for its liturgical worship.

The common bond between the meals of Jesus during His ministry, the Last Supper, after His resurrection, and the early Christian Eucharist is that they are first and foremost *acts of table fellowship* where Christ is *present* to *teach and eat* with His people. We might distinguish the mode of presence of Jesus in each of His meals, depending on where the meal falls in relation to the cross and the resurrection. Before the crucifixion, during His Galilean ministry and His Jerusalem journey, Jesus is present *locally*, that is, He is present as we are present to one another when we gather around the same table. At the Last Supper, Jesus is still present locally, however, in a miraculous and mysterious way He is also present *sacramentally* in, with, and under bread and wine. After His resurrection, at Emmaus, for example, Jesus is present in His resurrected body, as well as present sacramentally in the meal. Peter tells Cornelius of Jesus' appearances after His resurrection: "But God raised Him on the third day and made Him to appear, not to all the people but to us who had been chosen by God as witnesses, who ate and drank with

Him after He rose from the dead" (Acts 10:40–41, emphasis added). At Pentecost until now, Jesus continues to be present among us sacramentally in liturgies of Word and Sacrament.

At all these meals Jesus is present—present to teach about the kingdom of God by teaching about His death—present to break bread and reveal His intentions for our eternal salvation. In this way, we could say that table fellowship is revelatory. There is no difference between any of the meals of Jesus except their temporal relationship to the cross and the resurrection. Table fellowship of teaching and breaking bread becomes the occasion for the presence of the eternal kingdom because it is a celebration of the new covenant that is founded on Christ's death and resurrection. New Testament worship is a continuing table fellowship with God that reaches back into the Old Testament and looks ahead to the marriage feast of God at Jesus' second coming. Jesus' table fellowship goes to the very core of how the kingdom of God is now present in the liturgical life of the Church because Jesus the king is bodily present in His Church through Word and Sacrament.

Our liturgy of Word and Sacrament, then, is nothing more and nothing less than table fellowship with Jesus, firmly grounded in the Word of Jesus and the Meal of Jesus. As we observed, the basic structures of the liturgy have been in place from the New Testament, were given to the Church and instituted by Jesus Himself in the Last Supper, and then celebrated by the apostles in meals after Pentecost. If one approaches the liturgy from the perspective of Word and Sacrament, then one must approach it from the perspective of Jesus' ministry of table fellowship with His disciples before, during, and after His Passion. Christian worship is a continuation of the reconciled world's table fellowship with God in which He proclaims to us in His transforming Word salvation in Jesus Christ, and in His sacramental Meal He offers us the sacrificial death and resurrection of Christ's body and blood in, with, and under bread and wine. In both His Word and His Meal, salvation is present because Jesus Christ is present with His gifts of forgiveness, life, and salvation.

5
The Historic Liturgy and New Creation

As a faithful son of Israel, Jesus submitted Himself to the liturgical traditions of Israel in fulfillment of the Old Testament. He did not criticize the worship life of His time. Although He was harshly critical of many Israelite practices such as the purity laws and Sabbath laws, He simply did not comment on any of the liturgical rites in the temple or the synagogue. (His cleansing of the temple involved the marketplace within the temple walls, a place completely unrelated to the liturgical life in the temple proper.) We catch foretastes in the Gospels of the historic liturgy of Word and Sacrament, of the Divine Service as an act of table fellowship as we eavesdrop on Jesus, the faithful Israelite worshiper. These Gospel foretastes provide the basis for our current liturgical life as a participation in the forgiveness of sins and the life of the new creation Jesus reveals in His teachings.

Teaching and Proclamation

When Jesus arrived in Galilee to begin His ministry after His Baptism, He was greeted as a great prophet and teacher. John the Baptist was one of the best known prophets in Israel, and Jesus' Baptism by John now made Him famous, especially with the opening of the heavens, the Spirit's descent in bodily form upon Jesus, and the voice from heaven declaring, "You are My beloved Son; with You I am well pleased" (Luke 3:21–22). John proclaimed what everyone hoped, "Behold, the Lamb of God, who takes away the sin of the world!" (John 1:29). So when Luke writes that "Jesus returned in the power of the Spirit to Galilee, and a report about Him went out through all the surrounding country" (Luke 4:14), it was an acknowledgement that Jesus returned to His home country of Galilee with great expectations among the people. They looked to Him as the promised Savior, and they were stunned by His teaching, for He taught like no one else.

Instead of teaching how they were to behave, Jesus announced that a new era of salvation had arrived in Him, and that already signs of that salvation were present in His miracles. The primary place for Jesus' teaching was the synagogue, where, Luke tells us, Jesus was glorified by all because of His teaching. As Jesus went from synagogue to synagogue to teach on the Sabbath, the people were responding with great acclaim because He taught with such authority.

Although Jesus grew up in Nazareth, during His ministry in Galilee He lived in Capernaum because of its ideal location on the northwest shore of the Sea of Galilee. Capernaum was on what was called "the way of the sea" (Matthew 4:15), an international trade route running from Damascus to Egypt. Here Jesus would have contact with travelers from all over the Mideast. In the center of Capernaum was a synagogue, a place where Jesus communed with His Father through Word and prayer. There Jesus, the Word made flesh, read and interpreted Scriptures as to their fulfillment in Him, the Messiah who would come to teach about the kingdom of God and heal many who were broken by sin, sickness, and the devil. From the beginning, Jesus tied the presence of God in the Scriptures and His holiness as the Son of God to the cleansing of those who had become infected with effects of the fallen world. This cleansing is the necessary and blessed result of the Creator returning to His creation to make all things new.

Jesus' Sermon in the Synagogue of Nazareth (Luke 4:16–30)

Jesus did not confine Himself to Capernaum. He traveled all over the region of Galilee, including Nazareth, where he had been raised by Mary and Joseph. Luke's introduction to Jesus' preaching at the synagogue in Nazareth is filled with details about the rhythm of His ministry: "And He **came** to Nazareth, where He had been brought up. And **as was His custom**, He went to the **synagogue** on the **Sabbath day**, and He **stood up** to read" (Luke 4:16).

In His hometown of Nazareth, Jesus continued His custom of teaching in the synagogues on the Sabbath (4:15). The worshipers of Nazareth would expect Jesus, now a noted teacher (4:15, 23), to read Scripture and give an interpretation. However, Jesus came to the synagogue of Nazareth in order to read Isaiah 61 and to declare that the messianic era of salvation had now begun in Him. This is a climactic moment in salvation history. Here is Jesus, the Word made flesh, entering into a liturgical context in order to read the written word from Isaiah. Luke does not give us the full synagogue liturgy, but he does show that Jesus read and preached in the synagogue.

Here again is the format for the synagogue service (see p. 68), with those sections included in Luke in bold print:

Liturgy of the Synagogue

Invocation
"Bless the Lord who is to be blessed."

The Sanctus
(Isaiah 6 and Psalm 118—one of the earliest hymns)

The *Shema* or Old Testament Creed
Deuteronomy 6:4–9: "Hear, O Israel: The Lord our God is one Lord. . . ."

The Eighteen Benedictions
A series of blessings also known as the "Amidah" or the "Tefillah"

The Priestly Blessing or Aaronic Benediction
Numbers 6:24–26

The reading of the Word
Torah
Psalm
Prophets (Luke 4:18–19)
Psalm
[Historical Writings]
[Psalm]

Interpretation of the Word (Preaching/Teaching)
Also known as Midrash (see Luke 4:21, a very brief sermon indeed!)

"Alenu leshabeah"
"We must praise [the Ruler of all]"[1]

Jesus' sermon in Nazareth launches His ministry of "good news proclaimed to the poor, release proclaimed to the captives, recovery of sight to the blind, broken ones sent away in release, and the year of the jubilee proclaimed" (see Luke 4:18–19). This work of the Messiah is the work of the new creation, and to speak of the new creation is to speak of the kingdom of God. What Jesus read from Isaiah 61 He would preach throughout His ministry. And that ministry is continued in our worship today.

"The kingdom of God" occurs in Luke 4:43 for the first time in Luke's Gospel, and without explanation. It follows the sermon in Nazareth and the many miracles He performed in Capernaum. The kingdom of God is never defined in the Gospels, and one must deduce its meaning from the context. Its use here by Luke indicates what is yet to come. It is the Good News that God's plan of salvation is now being manifested in Jesus, who teaches and performs miracles. These miracles testify to the presence of God in Him. The connection between the kingdom of God and the teaching and miracles of Jesus is an intimate one. Thus, the kingdom of God and the ministry of the new creation are one and the same thing. Jesus, the preacher of the Gospel to the poor, is also the kingdom preacher who must preach the Father's redemptive plan, for this is His mission. This mission comes from God and through Jesus. It is messianic, in fulfillment of the Old Testament. It is a balance of teachings and miracles. It is the releasing power of the new era of salvation. It causes the demons to recognize the presence and dominion of God in the world.

Performative Speech

The proclamation of Jesus is performative speech, that is, Jesus' words create what they say. As a creative word (as in Genesis), when He speaks, things happen. Jesus' preaching declares that the new creation comes through His presence in the Creation. He comes as the Creator to make all things new, bringing relief and healing to the poor, the captives, the blind, and the broken ones. Jesus announces this by means of the Old Testament, which He now interprets in terms of Himself. Those words of promise in the Old Testament, when spoken by Jesus, become a present reality. Jesus' preaching proclaims reality and enacts it in the same moment. The people of Nazareth and people in synagogues throughout Galilee had never heard preaching like this before and must have been shocked by what they heard. Jesus' preaching was authoritative and declared that from now on everything would be different. With His presence in the creation as the Creator, His teaching and His miracles announced that *already* the new creation had dawned.

Jesus' preaching as performative speech continues in the Church today. When a pastor reads Scripture and preaches in the Divine Service, his word is also a performative word. It creates what it says not because of the pastor's compelling personality or character but by virtue of the office that he holds as a called and ordained servant of the Word. As one who speaks for Christ, the pastor brings Christ's gifts. When he preaches the Law, hearts are convicted and people turn in repentance and faith for the life-giving words of the Gospel where comfort and hope are given. When the pastor reads God's Word and preaches Law and Gospel, Christ is present bodily for His people to forgive them their sins and thereby give them life and salvation. The pastor's words actually forgive sins as if it were Christ Himself forgiving sins.

Martin Luther maintains that this is in fact the reality of the pastor's absolution: "Confession has two parts. First, that we confess our sins, and second, that we receive absolution, that is, forgiveness, from the pastor as from God Himself, not doubting, but firmly believing, that by it our sins are forgiven before God in heaven."[2] In our liturgy today during Confession and Absolution, the pastor announces this very same reality in forgiving the sins of the people in his congregation: "Upon this your confession, I, by virtue of my office, as a called and ordained servant of the Word, announce the grace of God unto all of you, and in the stead and by the command of my Lord Jesus Christ I forgive you all your sins in the name of the Father and of the Son and of the Holy Ghost" (*LSB*, p. 185).[3]

Miracles and Release from Bondage

The evidence that Jesus was the Creator present in His creation to make all things new was seen in the announcement of the forgiveness of sins and in His teaching and preaching of the dawning of a new creation. But nowhere was the reality of Jesus as the Creator, as God, seen more powerfully than in His miracles. In all cases—good news proclaimed to the poor, release to the captives, recovery of sight to the blind, freedom to those who are oppressed, and the Year of Jubilee—one thing is central: the release is from all misery that creation endures as a result of the fall into sin. What Jesus proclaims and the miracles He performs to demonstrate the reality of that proclamation actually release people from their bondage to demon possession, sickness, sin, and death. This release is always attached to His bodily presence, for He says, "Today this scripture has been fulfilled in your hearing" (Luke 4:21).

What does this release really mean to us and to this fallen world? The word for release is often translated as forgiveness—release from the bondage of sin—but for Jesus there is no distinction between spiritual and physical bondage, for both are demonstrations that we are captive to a world that needs restoration to wholeness. The captive and the oppressed include those who are physically in bondage to sickness or demon possession, spiritually in bondage to sin and death, and those who are in shame because of their sins or because they have been sinned against. Therefore, the more literal translation of "release" captures the meaning of liberation from the bondage of sin, sickness, death, and Satan. At times this will involve physical healing, exorcism, and rebuking destructive forces of nature, in addition to forgiving sins, because Jesus releases from physical bondage to show that He has the authority and power to release from spiritual bondage. Jesus in His ministry carries out this fulfillment of prophecy by releasing creation from its bondage to sin and restoring it to its proper state of harmony with the Creator. That is what forgiveness is—release from the burden of our sins that causes us guilt and shame. It is freedom like none other we might know, freedom to live in a broken world knowing that Jesus has taken upon Himself all our sins so that we might not have to bear the burden of those sins ourselves.

Bondage makes its destructive appearance in four ways: demon possession, sickness, sin, and death. These are demonstrations of the fallen creation in need of restoration to health and wellness. Although you will become sick and one day die, in Christ's death and resurrection, to which you have been joined through your Baptism, you now are completely whole and well, for your life is now His life. Although your body does not experience this freedom now during your Christian life in this world, because Christ dwells in you and you dwell in Him, you are free from the eternal consequences that follow bondage to the world, the flesh, and the devil.

The fiftieth Jubilee year liberated slaves, forgave debts, returned people to their homes, and stopped all sowing and reaping (Leviticus 25). It anticipated the Messiah's eternal salvation. Jesus announced in Galilee by citing Isaiah 61 that the Year of Jubilee is now present in Him and His ministry. This message of release, foreshadowed in Isaiah and the prophets and fulfilled in the ministry of Jesus, unites the Old and New Testaments.

Jesus' ministry was a continuous expression of release to the captives. In His teaching and healing, Jesus made no distinction between physical sickness and demon possession. Immediately following His sermon in

Nazareth, He rebuked the man possessed with demons (Luke 4:35), then rebuked the fever of Peter's mother-in-law (4:39). Jesus would rebuke both fevers and devils and say, "I must preach the good news of the kingdom of God to the other towns as well; for I was sent for this purpose" (4:43). "Which is easier," He asked the Pharisees, "to say 'Your sins are forgiven you' or to say, 'Rise and walk?' " (5:23). Jesus announced that the Son of Man has authority both to forgive sins and heal paralytics, for both are a demonstration that the Creator has come to His creation to release it from its fallenness. Jesus touched the sick and the dead, giving health and life while taking the sickness and death into His own body—the great exchange. This is what St. Paul meant when he wrote: "For our sake He made Him to be sin who knew no sin, so that in Him we might become the righteousness of God" (2 Corinthians 5:21).

The two acts of raising the dead in the Galilean ministry of Jesus—the widow's son at Nain (Luke 7:11–17) and Jairus's daughter (Luke 8:40–56)—are instructive of the great exchange. Jesus, the living one (Luke 24:5), gives life to those who are dead. The incident with the woman with the flow of blood is also instructive of the great exchange—power goes out from Jesus into her broken body and makes her whole as He, at the same time, is bearing her sickness. Matthew says it best: "This was to fulfill what was spoken by the prophet Isaiah [53:4]: 'He took our illnesses and bore our diseases' " (Matthew 8:17).

This incarnate Jesus creates the community into which these outcasts are now incorporated, the Body of Christ, whose Word has the power to free creation from the bondage into which it has fallen. For the later Church, this power will come through His resurrected body, for to be in Christ is to be joined by Baptism to His body, crucified on Calvary but raised again to show us what we are now and what we will one day be. "Today, this Scripture has been fulfilled in your hearing," says Jesus to His relatives and friends in Nazareth (Luke 4:21), and so it is. Even now, the Scripture is fulfilled in our ears, as His Word becomes alive in us. With the word today, Jesus announces the inauguration of the end times. That announcement reveals to the hearer how his Baptism initiates him into a life of continual release, sustained in the Lord's Supper.

Jesus and the New Creation

Jesus journeys to Jerusalem and to the cross, continuing to take into His body the world's sickness and sin, and releasing people from bondage through His Word and bodily presence. The great and final miracle of release is His Passion and death. Creation demonstrates that it is being re-created by the darkness that covers the whole earth from the sixth to the ninth hours (noon to 3:00 p.m.—Luke 23:44). This is an act of God in His creation because the creator of all things has died. It is an uncanny darkness, a cosmic sign that the creation is unraveling and a re-creation out of the darkness is about to occur. Matthew reports an earthquake and the resurrection of saints who, after Jesus' resurrection, walked around the holy city, as if the entire Church age had transpired in an instant and the second coming had come prematurely (Matthew 27:51–53). Here is a concrete example how with the death of Jesus "it is finished," the work of the new creation is done, and the Lord's second coming could happen at any moment following His resurrection from the dead.

For Luke, reporting the darkness is enough of a sign that evil is threatening to destroy God's creation and revert it to chaos. Creation's bondage to sin and the curse of death, which Jesus had been bearing since His conception, is now completely laid upon Him to do its destructive work for an unnatural darkness of three hours. The creation is being re-created and healed, and the process of re-creation causes it to plunge into darkness. The Creator who has come to His creation is at this moment of death bringing in a new creation. The darkness is a sign that *already* the end of all sickness and brokenness has come in the death of Jesus, even though it has *not yet* come in its fullness.

Yet the Creator, who took on flesh and was born into His creation, is at this moment of death, bringing in new and eternal life, a new creation. The darkness is a sign that already the end of the old world has come in a preliminary way in the death of Jesus (cf. Luke 21:25–26; Acts 2:20). A new and eternal day, a dawn from on high, is about to break forth and shine forever on those who dwell in "darkness and in the shadow of death" (Luke 1:78–79).

With Jesus' death, the old order finally gives in to the curse of death brought on by Adam's sin. At the same time, Jesus' work of atonement is completed, and He is about to enter into His own Sabbath rest (Luke 23:54, 56). God's provision for His new creation is completed; the new order is ready to shine forth, and it will do so with the first morning light of Easter. Together, darkness and light—the three hours of darkness while Jesus is on the cross and the brilliant light of Easter morning—inaugurate the new creation, the eternal Sabbath rest for the people of God (Hebrews 4:9–10). The new day of Sabbath rest has that beginning, but it will have no end; in the end times there will be no darkness, only light (Revelation 21:23–25); no crying or mourning from suffering and death, only joy (21:4).

When Jesus rises from the dead on the third day, after His Sabbath rest in the tomb, He brings all creation with Him. Jesus has shown His power over nature, demon possession, and sickness. These miracles lead up to the final miracle of the resurrection from the dead. This is the ultimate miracle, and it foreshadows Jesus' own resurrection where He frees once and for all the bondage of creation to sin seen in storms, demon possession, disease, and death.

All of us are broken people who experience the consequences of our sin through sickness, tragedy, and death. We yearn for that ultimate miracle where all of this suffering will be removed from our mortal bodies. Through Jesus' crucified and resurrected body, our restoration in the new creation to health and wellness is ongoing in the life of the Church. In that life of the Church His miracles continue in the Gospel and the Sacraments, testifying that Jesus is present to perform acts of release for His creation to re-create it and restore it to wholeness. In Baptism, our broken bodies are joined to His resurrected body and there in those purifying waters we are made whole. We are released from our brokenness, even though we do not "feel" that release outside of the gift of Baptism. But we not only learn to walk in this baptismal forgiveness as broken people, we also see in our brokenness His presence, as our sufferings join us to His sufferings. It is therefore through the means of grace, the Gospel and the Sacraments, that we find health and wellness.

Teaching and Miracles—Word and Sacraments

The ministry of Jesus was quite simple: He traveled from town to town in Galilee for two and half years teaching the people and performing miracles as signs that the new creation had dawned. Then He turned His face to go to Jerusalem for the final miracle, where through death He took on Himself all sickness and sin, and through His resurrection He demonstrated in His resurrected body what we shall one day become.

Teaching and miracles—that's what Jesus' ministry is all about. And those same two activities of Jesus continue in the Church today as the Lord continues to teach His people through the Word that is read and preached in our Divine Services. Through the miracle of Baptism we enter into the Body of Christ, His Church, so that we might partake of the Body of Christ in the miracle of the Lord's Supper. Sacraments are the new miracles of Jesus in the world today because they testify to the bodily presence of Christ in His creation bringing in the new creation. In Baptism, Christ is present in water through Word and Spirit where He turns sinners into saints, taking us across the boundary of death into a life that never ends, delivering us from darkness into His light. In the Lord's Supper, Christ is present in, with, and under bread and wine to give us the very same body and blood that was crucified on Calvary and raised again on the third day.

The teaching and miracles of Jesus, therefore, continue in the Church today through the liturgy of Word and Sacrament. We hear the voice of Jesus in His Word and we take Him into our bodies in body and blood for our health and salvation. How remarkable that these are the very same structures

> Our liturgy is nothing more and nothing less than table fellowship with Jesus.

of table fellowship—Word and Meal—in which we experience now a foretaste of the heavenly feast with angels, archangels, and with the whole company of heaven. Our liturgy is nothing more and nothing less than table fellowship with Jesus.

Jesus, the New Temple

Jesus is now the new temple (cf. John 1:14; 2:19–22), the holiest place that all may approach. Jewish Christians and God-fearers familiar with the Old Testament would be acquainted with the idea of the movement of God's presence, and that the Holy of Holies was moveable. God led Israel out of Egypt as a pillar of cloud by day and as a pillar of fire by night (Exodus 13:21–22). God's glory visibly came to dwell over the ark of the covenant and the tabernacle to guide Israel in her travels (Exodus 40:34–38; see also 25:22; 33:7–23). After the priests processed with the ark to the newly built Jerusalem temple, God took up residence there (1 Kings 8). Shortly before the first temple was destroyed, Ezekiel saw God's glory leave it (Ezekiel 10), and this same glory of God appeared to him in Babylon (Ezekiel 1). After the exile, the rebuilt second temple lacked the glory of the first temple (Ezra 6:13–18), but God promised one day to fill it with even greater glory (Haggai 2:1–9; Zechariah 8–9). That promise comes to fulfillment here, when the "King of glory" comes in (Psalm 24:7–10), and the Lord Himself comes to His temple (Malachi 3:1).

Mary and the Ark of the Covenant

Luke tells us much about the conception, birth, and infancy of Jesus, more than the other three Gospels. One of the great themes of Luke's infancy narrative is to announce in no uncertain terms that the place of God's holiness is not only in Holy Scripture and the Jerusalem temple, but is now also in the body of Jesus Christ. It may have been quite shocking to first-century Jews to learn that Mary is described as Israel, the temple, and even the ark of the covenant, not because of who she is, but because God chose her womb as the locale of God's holiness, thereby fulfilling the purpose originally given to Israel, the temple, and the ark.

The presence of Yahweh in a cloud overshadowed the tabernacle and the ark of the covenant, and the glory of Yahweh filled it (Exodus 40:35). As

John McHugh notes: "St Luke, when he wrote the word 'overshadow,' must have known what associations it would evoke in the Jewish mind. No Jew, reading the words 'A Power of the Most High will overshadow thee,' could fail to think of the Divine Presence or *Shekinah*."[4] When the Holy Spirit comes upon Mary, she conceives Jesus as holy, the Son of God.

As Luke moves the scene from Nazareth to a city in Judah for the visitation, we find an odd series of parallels between Mary's journey to the hill country of Judah and the movement of the ark of the covenant to the same locale on its way to Jerusalem, as has also been noted by McHugh:

> The two stories open with the statement that David and Mary "arose and made a journey" (2 Sam 6:2; Luke 1:39) up into the hill country, into the land of Judah. On arrival, both the Ark and Mary are greeted with "shouts" of joy (2 Sam 6:12, 15; Luke 1:42, 44). The Ark, on its way to Jerusalem, was taken into the house of Obededom, and became a source of blessing for his house (2 Sam 6:10–12); Mary's entry into the house of Elizabeth is also seen as a source of blessing for the house (Luke 1:41, 43–4). David, in terror at the untouchable holiness of the Ark, cried out: "How shall the Ark of the Lord come to me?" (2 Sam 6:9); Elizabeth, in awe before the mother of her Lord, says, "Why should this happen to me, that the mother of my Lord should come to me?" (Luke 1:43). Finally, we read that "the Ark of the Lord remained in the house of Obededom three months" (2 Sam 6:11), and that Mary stayed with Elizabeth "about three months" (Luke 1:56).[5]

As a temporary and portable vessel housing the local presence of the true God, Mary fulfills the purpose of the ark of the covenant. The presence of the Lord, who overshadowed Mary at Jesus' conception, now dwells in her. Luke has now shown that Mary is Israel reduced to one. The correspondence is now complete between the presence of God in the Jerusalem temple and in the temple of Mary's womb.

Destruction of the Jerusalem Temple

Jesus' final teaching before His Passion centers on the temple and Jerusalem (Luke 21:5–38). Jesus, teaching in the temple, is about to explain the temple's destruction in the near future. It is not simply the temple that is in view but the stones of the temple, along with two different perspectives on those stones.

One perspective is expressed by those who comment on the majesty of the magnificent setting provided by Herod the Great for the second temple (Luke 21:5). They see only the earthly grandeur and temporal significance of the temple, bound as they are by time and space. But Jesus begins His revelation of the end times by warning them that "days will come" (21:6) when these beautiful stones will be pulled down and not one will be left on top of another. Stones have already figured prominently in Jesus' previous sayings about Jerusalem: The stones would cry out in acclamation when Jesus enters Jerusalem if the people were prevented from responding (19:40). The enemies of Jerusalem "will not leave one stone upon another in [her], because [she] did not know the time of [her] visitation" (19:44). And Jesus is "the stone that the builders rejected . . . the cornerstone" (20:17). Jesus repeats here what He said before He entered the holy city: the "stones" that matter in the temple are not the ones that form the physical building, but the "Stone" whose presence has resided among those physical stones and who now prophesies the end of those stones.

The New Presence of God

Indirectly, Jesus announces a shift in the locale of God's presence—from the physical temple in Jerusalem to His own perfect body. The Jerusalem temple is rendered obsolete by Jesus' incarnation (cf. John 4:20–26). The destruction of the temple in AD 70 will prompt people to look for God's presence in the location where He has come to dwell forever—in Jesus, who, in turn, comes to dwell in His Church through the Gospel—His Word and Sacraments. God's grace will no longer come through animal sacrifices at the stone temple. Rather, His grace will come through what the Lord has instituted to be the worship life of the Church: Word, Baptism, Lord's Supper. This font of the Church's life prepares the people of God for the end times, which could come at any time. The Church must be prepared to see that the end times begin with the death and resurrection of Jesus.

Throughout His teaching Jesus warns His disciples that they will suffer betrayal just as He is about to be betrayed—through rejection by men even unto death—and that they must be prepared if they are to persevere to the end. Christians will experience persecution for no other reason than their connection with Jesus. The name of Jesus defines their identity, for Christians bear in their broken bodies Jesus, the new temple, God's holy presence. For that reason, Christians see their bodies as temples of the Holy Spirit, the Spirit of Christ. Opponents will hate them because the presence of God has shifted from the temple of Jerusalem to where Christ has promised to be present: in the Gospel, and in His Supper, and in those baptized in His name. How ironic that the temple of Jerusalem is destroyed by God through the Romans because the people refused to believe that a shift in divine presence had taken place. How ironic that Christians will be killed because they proclaim that this beloved presence now dwells in them and among them!

All of the Gospels emphasize this shift in the location of God's presence from the stone temple (Luke 21:5–6) to the new temple of flesh, Jesus Himself. (It is the point of Stephen's sermon in Acts 7.) As Jesus frequents the (stone) temple during Holy Week, the two temples are one—in the same place—reinforcing for the disciples that Jesus is the new temple. He is the source of divine teaching. He is the one who speaks the words of God. He is also the new place of atonement, the new Passover sacrifice. The forgiveness of sins comes through Him. The time will soon come when the stone temple in Jerusalem is destroyed (Luke 21:5–24) and the schism between Jews and Christians will be wide and deep. But for now during Holy Week the old and the new are together. The new temple teaches in the old temple, and the new people of God—His disciples—freely mingle with the people of the old covenant.

"But we have this treasure in jars of clay, to show that the surpassing power belongs to God and not to us."

(2 Corinthians 4:7)

Jesus' movement back and forth across the Kidron Valley links His temple teaching to the Mount of Olives, the place of Jesus' prayer, the location of His betrayal, the place of ascension (and the location where many believe the Lord will come again). During Holy Week, those in Jesus' company heard His teaching, shared meals with Him, and were with Him in His times of prayer (cf. 21:36; 22:39–45). In the Early Church, this pattern of Holy Week will be continued in the Divine Service. Jesus' disciples, rising early (cf. 21:38) on Sunday morning (Acts 20:7), the day of resurrection, will flock to the new temple, the church, in order to hear the teaching of Jesus—the words of God. There they will also break bread—celebrate the Lord's Supper from the night of His betrayal—and remain watchful in prayer (Luke 21:36). This is the picture of the Early Church in Acts 2:42, 46; 20:7. Hence Jesus' Holy Week pattern, continued in the Church's liturgy—the Service of the Word, the Service of the Sacrament, and the prayers—will preserve the Church in faith until the end, so that Jesus' followers will be prepared to stand before the Son of Man when He comes (Luke 21:36).

6
The Psalms in Worship

On the road to Emmaus, Jesus scolded two of His disciples for not believing what the prophets had spoken, namely that in fulfillment of the Old Testament the Christ should suffer and enter into His glory. Then "beginning with Moses and all the Prophets, [Jesus] interpreted to them in all the Scriptures the things concerning Himself" (Luke 24:25–27). Forty days later the risen Lord's final words to His disciples before His ascension instructed them that "everything written about Me in the Law of Moses and the Prophets and the Psalms must be fulfilled" (Luke 24:44).

Why that strange, last addition in Luke 24:44: "and the Psalms?" What could Jesus have meant by mentioning the Psalms alongside Moses and the Prophets, the only place in Luke's Gospel where the Psalms are referred to by name, even though there are more citations from the Psalms in the New Testament than from any other book of the Old Testament? To answer the question is to discover how the Psalms are Scripture's song in the worship of Israel and the Church, particularly the singing of psalms in the presence of God.

Blessing God in the Temple—Luke 24:53

The first clue as to the Psalms' importance in worship comes immediately following these final words of Jesus when He takes His disciples to Bethany, just outside Jerusalem, and raises His hands and blesses them as He is taken up into heaven. The spontaneous response of the disciples is to fall down and worship Jesus, then rise and rush to the temple to worship Him again, blessing God. Blessed by the ascending Lord, the disciples cannot do anything else but seek a place of His presence in order to bless Him.

To bless God is to praise Him, and we may be confident that they praised the Father for His Son, Jesus Christ, their crucified, risen, and now ascended Lord, as well as praising the Father for the communion they now had with Him through His Son. They blessed God even though their Messiah now appeared to be absent from them, removed from their sight by the clouds. They must have been confused, perhaps even fearful at that moment, for Christ had left them alone, so it seemed, and the Spirit had not yet come upon them at Pentecost. They needed to go to the only place they knew God was present—the temple and Torah—in order to have communion with God. We may also be confident as to the shape of the disciples' praise of God in the temple. They would have joined the singing of the psalms that was part of the ongoing life of temple and synagogue. The disciples were faithful followers of Jesus, and their instincts to worship God were noble and good even in this time between the ascension and Pentecost. After forty days of listening to the risen Lord's teaching, after forty days of eating and drinking with Him after He rose from the dead, even after watching Him ascend into heaven, all the disciples wanted to do was to sing the psalms in the presence of God!

How Jesus Knew the Psalms

How did Jesus come to know the psalms? The evangelist Luke reminds us that Jesus "grew and became strong, being filled with wisdom, and the grace of God was upon Him" (Luke 2:40). Luke is not only telling us about Jesus' physical growth, but how He also increased in wisdom. At age 12 (the age of maturity in religious matters), Jesus was in the Jerusalem temple in the middle of the teachers, listening to them and asking them questions. Although we have no way of knowing for sure, it is likely that Jesus traveled to Jerusalem every spring for the Passover, for that is what pious Jews did at the time of our Lord. Jesus was at home in the temple, for it was His Father's house, and He knew that God's presence filled the Holy of Holies. Like all other pious Jews, He came to the temple for sacrifice and prayer, to hear the Word of God, to listen to the teachers expound the Scriptures, and to sing the Psalms.

The teachers were astonished at the 12-year-old Jesus because He knew the Scriptures. Evidently, taught by faithful Joseph and Mary, and through the training in the faith He would have received through the synagogue in Nazareth, Jesus had come to know the Scriptures, especially the Psalms. He would return to Nazareth at age 30 to read the Scripture from Isaiah 61 and 58, and then interpret those words. On that occasion, Jesus made the bold claim that those Scriptures were now fulfilled in the ears of His hearers because He, the Word made flesh, had now come to His hometown synagogue in order to read the Word of God. Like all pious Jews, Jesus believed that God's presence was not only in the Holy of Holies in the temple in Jerusalem, but was also present in the reading of the Word of God. For Israel, God's Word was God's presence; in fact, God's Word was God's food, for to hear God's Word was to consume it as if it were food. Both the Old and New Testaments speak of God's Word in this way. The psalmist sees God's Word as something worth eating: "How sweet are Your words to my taste, sweeter than honey to my mouth!" (Psalm 119:103). Both the prophet Ezekiel and the evangelist St. John must eat the scroll of God's Word. It is to be digested in the stomach in order to bring either sweetness from its comforting grace or bitterness from its biting Law (Ezra 3:3; Revelation 10:9–10).

Psalms in the Temple

Jesus learned the Psalms from His worship of His Father in temple and synagogue. Although worship in the temple was centered in the sacrifices, especially the atonement sacrifices at the third and ninth hours (9:00 a.m. and 3:00 p.m.), there was a regular recitation of the Psalms in the temple:[1]

- Sunday: Psalm 24
- Monday: Psalm 48
- Tuesday: Psalm 82
- Wednesday: Psalm 94
- Thursday: Psalm 81
- Friday: Psalm 93
- Saturday: Psalm 92

This we learn from the Mishnah, a commentary on the worship of Israel from the end of the second century AD. Because of the destruction of the Jerusalem temple in AD 70, it is difficult to reconstruct the exact liturgy of the temple at the time of Jesus, although we know much about the temple liturgy from the Scriptures themselves. Psalms were sung by temple singers, often to the accompaniment of musical instruments. The Psalm of the Day, as listed above, came after the morning and afternoon atonement sacrifices. Feast days such as Passover, the Feast of Weeks, and the Feast of Tabernacles featured both the Hallel Psalms (113–118) and the Songs of Ascent (120–134); in other words, there was a full liturgical use of the Psalter throughout the temple that was carefully monitored by the Levitical priests and sung by Levitical choirs. For use in the temple, the Psalter was divided into five books: Book I: Psalms 1–41; Book II: Psalms 42–72; Book III:

Psalms 73–89; Book IV: Psalms 90–106; and Book V: Psalms 107–150.[2] "Psalter" refers to the Book of Psalms as they were used in Israel's worship.

> "Psalter" refers to the Book of Psalms as they were used in Israel's worship.

Psalms in the Synagogue

Scholars are not certain that the Psalms were used during synagogue services at the time of Jesus, even though the Psalter does play an active role in synagogue worship after the destruction of the temple. The hints of synagogue liturgies in the New Testament coincide with many of the elements that have been discovered in the documentary evidence of later synagogue liturgies. The chanting in the synagogue of the Hallel Psalms and the Songs of Ascent, and the singing of hymns and other songs of praise must have included other psalms as well. In fact, research into early Christian liturgies is bearing out a growing consensus that psalm verses were sung throughout the synagogue service in the first century, even though we are not sure where in the liturgy these verses would have been sung.

Psalms were used as interludes or moments of reflection between the readings in the synagogue services Jesus attended and preached in.[3] How else would Jesus, His disciples, the evangelists, and Paul have known the Psalms, since it was unlikely that any of them had their own copy of the Psalter? They had to hear it somewhere, and because attendance at the temple was at most a yearly pilgrimage for Passover, the only other place where Scripture was read, heard, and sung was the synagogue. The early Christian Church learned such a practice from Jewish synagogue services.

There are at least six ways the Psalms may have been used in Israel's worship in the first century:

The Use of the Psalms in Israel's Worship[4]

1. Daily use of complete psalms
2. Special psalms for feast days
3. Psalm verses used at various places in the liturgy, e.g. "O Lord, open my lips" (Ps 51:15) before the prayers in the synagogue
4. Triennial cycle of psalms in the synagogue based on the reading of the Psalter in the Temple
5. Responses of people to prayers, readings, and benedictions with Psalm verses
6. Psalter as a source of prayers and the language of prayers

Use of Psalms in Israel's Worship and Today

As Dietrich Bonhöffer notes in his marvelous little book *Psalms: The Prayer Book of the Bible*, the original impetus for most of the psalms may have come from David himself who sang songs with his harp before King Saul when the king was plagued by an evil spirit: "And whenever the evil spirit from God was upon Saul, David took the lyre and played it with his hand; so Saul was refreshed and was well, and the evil spirit departed from him" (1 Samuel 16:23).[5] The Chronicler makes it very evident that the entrance of the ark of the covenant into Jerusalem was accompanied by the singing of psalms:

> David also commanded the chiefs of the Levites to appoint their brothers as the singers who should play loudly on musical instruments, on harps and lyres and cymbals, to raise sounds of joy. . . . So David and the elders of Israel and the commanders of thousands went to bring up the ark of the covenant of the Lord from the house of Obed-edom with rejoicing. . . . David was clothed with a robe of fine linen, as also were all the Levites who were carrying the ark, and the singers and Chenaniah the leader of the music of the singers. . . . So all Israel brought up the ark of the covenant of the Lord with shouting, to the sound of the horn, trumpets, and cymbals, and made loud music on harps and lyres. (1 Chronicles 15:16, 25, 27–28)

David was not the only musician, nor was he the only composer of psalms. Peter Scaer notes that Asaph, "a companion of David, liturgist in the temple, a hymn-writer, and leader of the Asaphite guild of musicians,"[6] combined the two important characteristics of a psalmist—desiring God's presence in the temple and responding to that presence as a leader of the singing in the temple. Scaer writes:

> According to the Chronicler, David appointed Asaph chief of choral worship before the Ark of the Lord (1 Chron 16:37), where he served daily alongside fellow Levitical singers Heman and Jeduthun (to whom Psalm 77 is co-attributed). His musical duties included the "sounding of [cymbals]," and the singing of hymns (1 Chron 16:5). Not simply a musician, he "prophesied" according to King Solomon (1 Chron 25:1). This prophecy consisted of singing inspired songs, in which Asaph and his guild were trained.
>
> When Solomon brought the ark into the temple, Asaph and his guild were present, and offered songs of praise before the Ark

(2 Chron 5:12). As they sang, "the glory of the Lord filled the temple of God" (2 Chron 5:14). Evidently, close proximity to the Ark gave the Asaphites special access to the divine presence.[7]

The Psalms themselves indicate to us that they are to be sung. Originally the word *psalm* was synonymous with "hymn," and hymns were always meant to be sung. It is not an exaggeration to describe the Psalms as the "hymnbook" of the Bible, and certainly the "hymnbook" of the temple and the synagogue. In fact, most biblical scholars claim that the Psalms were written for liturgical use. As Sigmund Mowinckel notes in his monumental work *The Psalms in Israel's Worship,* "the title of the book of Psalms in Hebrew is *Tehillim,* which means 'cultic songs of praise.' "[8] Thus, Psalm 33:2–3: "Give thanks to the LORD with the lyre; make melody to Him with the harp of ten strings! Sing to Him a new song; play skillfully on the strings, with loud shouts."

Even the titles of the Psalms indicate that they were written to be sung, as in Psalm 4, where this psalm of David is addressed "To the Choirmaster: With Stringed Instruments," or Psalm 5, "To the Choirmaster: For the Flutes." Many of the strange Hebrew words scattered throughout the Psalter have led many to posit that words such as *Selah, Sheminith, Gittith,* and *Higgaion* may have been references for use by the musician, the Levitical singers in the temple, or the choirs and cantors in the synagogues. Even psalms considered to be prayers and laments were intended to be sung, because the Psalms as hymns, prayers, or laments were done in the presence of God.

That the Psalms were sung in the temple worship of Israel is without doubt, even though the debate goes on concerning their use in the synagogue. But a larger question looms: why were the Psalms *sung*? To say they were sung because this is what David did under inspiration begs the question. What is the theological rationale for singing the Psalms? Was there something about Israel's worship that demanded this? Was such a theological perspective operative for the Early Church, and is it valid for us today? Once we've answered these questions we can begin to understand why Jesus said that "everything written about Me in the Law of Moses and the Prophets and the Psalms must be fulfilled" (Luke 24:44).

There are many reasons to sing praises to God. Singing expresses joy. It also provides an appropriate vehicle for lamenting. Singing binds people together. It is a powerful teaching tool, aiding the memory. It seems that one must sing in the presence of God. Indeed, singing is a fitting activity for a wedding feast.[9]

John Kleinig aptly summarizes the significance of singing in the temple that applies also to the synagogue:

> Sacred song served to articulate the response of the people to the LORD's presence with them, for the singers acted on behalf of the king and his people before the LORD. By their performance of choral music, they expressed the people's gratitude for his benefits to them, articulated their jubilation at his goodness, enunciated their amazement with him, voiced their adoration of him, confessed their faith in him and interceded on their behalf before him.
>
> Thus the theological significance of sacred song was determined by its ritual function. It proclaimed the LORD's gracious presence to his people at the temple and articulated their response to his presence with them there.[10]

Christ the Suffering and Righteous Messiah in the Psalms

To understand the Psalms as Scripture's song sung in the presence of God is to understand that Jesus Christ is the center of the Old Testament, its purpose and its goal. Or, to return to Jesus' final words to His disciples in Luke 24, we might ask: what did Jesus tell the disciples as He began from Moses and the prophets, interpreting them in all the Scriptures the things concerning Himself? Did Jesus piece together isolated verses as proof texts, or did He appeal instead to the themes of longer passages or of whole biblical books? What passages might He have chosen from the Old Testament prophecies to show that the Christ would die and rise on the third day? We might find it difficult to discover any such passages from reading Luke's Gospel, for the evangelist does not cite specific Old Testament passages that refer to the death and resurrection of Christ, with the exception of Isaiah 53:12 at Luke 22:37, and this encourages the thought that Jesus was working more from grand Old Testament themes than from specific, brief proof texts.

Instead of citing prophetic proof texts from the Old Testament for Jesus' death and resurrection, Luke portrays Jesus as the consummation of the pattern set by Moses, the prophets, and the Psalms. Luke's use of the Old Testament to prove Jesus must suffer and die points to the recurring Old Testament pattern of suffering before glory, of violent opposition to the righteous, and to the hope of God's saints for rescue even beyond death. The evangelist weaves Old Testament allusions, ideas, and illustrations into the fabric of his narrative so that his Gospel sounds to the hearer as a continuation of the Old Testament narrative and therefore a continuation of salvation history. The Lord's larger pattern and plan determines the content of prophecy, where the overall thrust of God's redemptive activity in the Old Testament, in conformity with His righteous plan of salvation, demands that God's innocent and righteous Messiah suffer an agonizing death and be raised on the third day. Or to put it another way, John McHugh writes:

> *Suppose there were* a human being who was utterly without sin? What would have to happen "according to the Scriptures"? Clearly, whatever happened to such a person would have to vindicate, not to undermine, the Old Testament teaching that God is always and in every action utterly just and righteous. Now if there is one thing the disciples had observed *before* Jesus died, it is that he was in every single deed and word faultlessly obedient to God his Father. They knew him intimately for more than two years, and had every opportunity to observe him; and their judgement was that Jesus was completely without sin.
>
> That is why our Lord can chide them, on the day of his Resurrection, with not understanding the Scriptures, with not perceiving that it was inevitable that God would raise him from the grave. True, it had been necessary that he should first suffer and die and be buried, in order that his obedience to the Father should extend, and should be seen to extend, over the whole span of earthly human existence. But once that was done, and seen to be done, it would have been utterly unjust if his body had been left to decay and corruption. The Resurrection of Jesus *had* to happen, if the teaching of the Old Testament about God was true.[11]

The Passion and resurrection of Christ are the final consummation of all Scripture—the sign of fulfillment. Jesus follows the Old Testament pattern of suffering before glory in His life, and death and resurrection completes it. Conversely, from the New Testament perspective one could even say that Moses, the prophets, and the psalmists had to be conformed to the pattern that would be set by Christ Himself. Or to put it plainly, Christ's life, death, and resurrection dictated what the Psalms would say. But again, for our purposes, why does Jesus add to Moses and the prophets that His suffering and death are in fulfillment of the Psalms? Darrell Bock speaks to this question:

> Jesus, in the entrusting of his spirit to the Father, follows the pattern of an innocent righteous saint and fulfills specifically the plan of God for *the* innocent sufferer. Luke 24.46 points to the climax of the Passion narrative. It is intended to have the reader see that though Jesus suffered, surely he was righteous, a key Lukan theme in Acts.
>
> The allusions from the Psalms point to the context in which Jesus suffered by the plan of God. He suffered in the pattern of innocent, righteous saints in the hope that God would vindicate him and therefore validate his claims about himself. With the resurrection, Jesus' vindication occurred and all things were fulfilled so that now witnesses could be sent out with the message about Jesus as the suffering but raised Christ who can offer forgiveness of sins (Luke 24.44–47).[12]

An understanding of the Psalms as the Scripture's song becomes clearer with the advent of Christ and the interpretation of the Psalms through Christ by the New Testament authors. Or to put it even more radically, in paraphrasing Dietrich Bonhöffer, "Who in fact *sings* the Psalms?" Is it David, the believer today, or is it David and the believer who are both in Christ? Bonhöffer writes:

> According to the witness of the Bible, David is, as the anointed king of the chosen people of God, a prototype of Jesus Christ. What happens to him happens to him for the sake of the one who is in him and who is said to proceed from him, namely Jesus Christ. And he is not unaware of this, but "being therefore a prophet, and knowing that God had sworn with an oath to him that he would set one of his descendents upon his throne, he foresaw and spoke of the resurrection of the Christ" (Acts 2:30 f.). David was a witness to Christ in his office, in his life, and in his words. The New Testament says even more. In the Psalms of David the promised Christ himself already speaks (Hebrews 2:12; 10:5) or, as may also be indicated, the Holy Spirit (Hebrews 3:7). These same words which David spoke, therefore, the future Messiah spoke through him. The prayers of David were prayed also by Christ. Or better, Christ himself prayed them through his forerunner David.
>
> This short comment on the New Testament sheds significant light on the entire Psalter. It relates the Psalter to Christ. How that is to be understood in detail we still have to consider. But it is important to note that even David did not pray out of the per-

> sonal exuberance of his heart, *but out of the Christ who dwelled in him*. To be sure, the one who prays his Psalms remains himself. But in him and through him it is Christ who prays. . . .
>
> Who prays the Psalms? David (Solomon, Asaph, etc.) prays, Christ prays, we pray. We—that is, first of all the entire community in which alone the vast richness of the Psalter can be prayed, but also finally every individual insofar as he participates in Christ and his community and prays their prayer.[13]

It was Luther, of course, who first saw the Psalms as "a Christian book foreshadowing the life and death of the Redeemer."[14] Luther, an Augustinian monk who regularly prayed the Psalter according to the monastic cycle, discovered the Gospel through his lectures on the Psalms (August 1, 1513), along with his later lectures on Romans (fall 1515) and Galatians (1516–1517). These biblical texts were his "Damascus road."[15] The Psalms were his lifeblood, for in the suffering and *Anfechtungen* portrayed in these hymns Luther saw Christ in His suffering, and then Luther's own suffering and the suffering of all who had taken up Christ's cross to follow Him. "My God, my God, why have you forsaken me?" (Psalm 22) was for Luther not only the essence of the Christ's suffering—abandoned, deserted, and forsaken by His Father—but also the design behind his own suffering in Christ.[16]

Psalms in the Life of the Church

The New Testament theme of Christ in the Psalms is the foundation for the use of the Psalms in the life of the Church: "Every psalm is thus understood as an address between the Father and the Son, or between the church and its God or its Redeemer."[17] Sermons of Peter and Paul in the Acts of the Apostles rely on the Psalms to make the case that Jesus is the Christ. Those sermons are an indicator of how foundational the Christological reading of the Psalms was for the Early Church. Furthermore, for Christians, the use of the Psalms in the temple and synagogue paved the way for their use in the Church's liturgy as it developed in the first four centuries. That is to say, Psalms had both the status of biblical texts like any other readings from the Old Testament, but had a unique status as the hymns of the Church through which proclamation took place. Peter Brunner, the great Lutheran theologian of worship, notes the following about the Christian use of the Psalms:

> The Psalter of the Bible plus the Old and New Testament canticles are the church's prayer book and its hymnbook in one. When

> these Biblical psalms are prayed and sung in worship, *the words of Holy Scripture are directly proclaimed.* In verbal content, the singing of psalms is closely related to the reading of Scripture. The element of witnessing proclamation is not lacking either; this is already intimated in the manner of presentation. When the church takes the psalms on its lips, as for instance in the prayer psalms, it testifies that it has taken these words into its heart and now professes them as its own. Especially the antiphon and the Gradual psalmody present the Word of Scripture in such a manner that the hearers and certainly also the singers may, so to say, steep themselves in them. This type of presentation of the Word may effect a meditative appropriation, *a spiritual "eating" of the Word such as is achieved in hardly any other form of proclamation in worship.*[18]

The chanting of Psalms by the congregation in connection with choirs or cantors was a common occurrence early on in the Church's life. People would simply gather to sing Psalms. This practice became canonized in the vigils that occurred on the eve of a great festival. The ongoing singing of Psalms bound people together as they readied themselves for the great feast the next day. These acts of Psalm singing were as foundational for the piety of the people as the feast itself. Perhaps the most moving testimony to the meaning of such Psalm singing is given by St. John Chrysostom as he describes the significance of Psalms in the life of his community:

> If we keep vigil . . . in the Church, *David comes first, last, and midst.* If early in the morning we seek for the melody of hymns, *first, last, and midst is David again.* If we are occupied with the funeral solemnities of the departed, if virgins sit at home and spin, *David is first, last, and midst.* O marvellous wonder! Many who have made but little progress in literature, nay, who have scarcely mastered its first principles, have the Psalter by heart. Nor is it in cities and churches alone that, at all times, through every age, *David is illustrious*; in the midst of the forum, in the wilderness, and uninhabitable land, he excites the praises of God. In monasteries, amongst those holy choirs of angelic armies, *David is first, midst, and last.* In the convents of virgins, where are the bands of them that imitate Mary; in the deserts, where are men crucified to this world, and having their conversation with God, *first, midst, and last is he.* All other men are at night overpowered by natural sleep: *David alone is active*; and, congregating the servants of God into seraphic bands, turns earth into heaven, and converts men into angels.[19]

As we now look at some specific uses of the Psalms in the life of the Church, we will consider the use of the Psalms in the Divine Service and in the Daily Office.

Use of the Psalms in the Divine Service

From the very beginning, psalmody always accompanied movement in the Church's liturgy. Before Constantine, when there was very little movement in the liturgy, the use of Psalmody was in connection with the lessons of the day, or what came to be known as the Gradual. The earliest use of Scriptures in the Divine Service, both East and West, included the three lessons: Old Testament, Epistle, and Gospel. Early on, the psalm occurred between the Old Testament and Epistle lesson, with an Alleluia verse between the Epistle and the Gospel, a custom most likely borrowed from the synagogue. After a time, the Old Testament lesson dropped out of the service and the Psalm/Alleluia was conflated to form the Gradual, so named because it was sung on the step (*gradus*) leading to the pulpit. It was also very common for the lessons to be chanted along with the Psalms according to simple tones not unlike the tones used in the synagogues.[20] The use of the Psalms between lessons has continued down to our day, with the Gradual returning to its original location after the Old Testament lesson.

The manner in which the Psalms were sung has varied over the years. The reality is that much variety occurred in the singing of the Psalms. John

Entrance	**WORD**	**Preparation**	**SACRAMENT**	**Distribution**
Confession & Absolution INTROIT Kyrie Gloria Collect	Old Testament GRADUAL Epistle ALLELUIA Gospel Sermon Creed Prayers for the Faithful	Offering OFFERTORY PSALMS	Preface Proper Preface Sanctus Prayer Lord's Prayer Words of Institution Peace of the Lord	Agnus Dei COMMUNION PSALMS Canticle Collect Benediction

Lamb offers a concise summary of the various ways Psalms were sung in the history of the Early Church:

a. the psalms sung by the whole congregation;

b. the psalms sung by one person, all others listening;

c. the psalms sung alternately by the halves of the congregation, or by two choirs, verse about, or half-verse about, which is properly antiphonal;

d. one voice singing one verse or half-verse, and the congregation the next, which is properly responsorial;

e. a singer or body of singers singing a verse, and those assembled responding with Alleluia or Amen or with a phrase like "For his mercy endureth for ever," which also is responsorial.[21]

The final category was the most common because the availability of the Psalter for every member of the congregation was unlikely. Although some psalms were memorized by the congregation, they would not have the entire Psalter committed to memory. Since Vatican II, when liturgical communities began chanting the Psalms again, congregations have experimented with Psalm singing according to each of these categories. Among liturgical churches today, the final category has become the most popular, with choirs and cantors singing the verses of the Psalms and the congregation responding with an antiphon, though this form of Psalm singing is often combined with responsorial singing between congregation and choir/cantor in a manner similar to the way the Psalms have been arranged in many contemporary hymnals today.

The use of the Psalms at other parts of the Divine Service always covered the movement of clergy and their attendants during the procession to the altar at the beginning of the service, during the procession of the bread and wine during the Offertory, and during the distribution of the elements after the consecration. Evidence for the Introit, Offertory, and Communion psalms does not occur until the fourth or fifth centuries.

> On the one hand, we have the group Gradual-Alleluia-Tract, which form an integral part of the Mass. Their place is normally between the lections, which has been a place for psalmody as far back as records can take us. At this point nothing else is being done; the psalms are sung, not as an accompaniment to other rite or ceremony, but as themselves a vital part of the service. On the other hand we have items, such as the Introit, the Offertory and the Communion Psalm, none of which is an integral part of the Mass, but all are used as accompaniments to actions which them-

> selves are portions of the liturgy. Thus the Introit came into being as an accompaniment to the procession of the clergy from the vestry to the altar. We have therefore two groups whose origins were different and whose original purposes were different, though it is true that for a considerable portion of their history, there has been little noticeable distinction between them.[22]

The Introit form that we have today is a reduced portion of psalmody from the entrance rite that originally included many Psalms. Chanting whole Psalms was at the heart of the "vigil" kept by the congregation as they waited for the clergy to enter. Today, whole psalms may replace the Introit, a practice preferred by Luther, since it provides the same function today as would the Introit—the announcement of the theme of the day.[23] For both the Introit and the Psalm, the Gloria Patri was added early on to demonstrate the Christian use of the Psalter, as well as to make a bold trinitarian confession in orthodox communities to counter ancient heresies. It has been customary even among Lutherans to bow at the Gloria Patri because of the proclamation of the trinitarian name. In the Old Testament, the divine name was not even mentioned, for to speak God's name was to call forth His presence (the name the Lord, "Yahweh," was used instead of the divine name). God's holiness and God's name are inseparable. To bow one's head when the trinitarian name of God is proclaimed is a simple sign of reverence to the presence of the Creator and Redeemer of all.

The use of psalmody in the Offertory and Communion processions paralleled its use in the entrance rite of the liturgy. As the gifts of bread and wine were brought forward for Communion, along with other gifts like "fruit, wool, oil, milk, honey, olives, and cheese, and also silver and gold,"[24] psalms would be sung by the choir with the congregation singing an antiphon. No specific psalms are mentioned in the earliest references to the Offertory psalmody. This practice was clearly established at the time of Augustine. The singing of psalms during the Distribution, called the *communio,* was also the practice of the Early Church. Psalm 34 is mentioned in connection with the *communio* by *Apostolic Constitutions*, Augustine, and Jerome. With the introduction of the Agnus Dei, the singing of hymns with the Psalms became more common. Later on, portions of Psalms 1–26 were sung during Lent, whereas verses from Psalms 9–119 were used on the Sundays following Pentecost.[25]

Use of the Psalms in the Daily Office

An investigation of the Divine Offices of Matins and Vespers, Morning and Evening Prayer, illustrates how the Psalter was used outside of the Divine Service. The simple order of the earliest prayer office was Psalms, lessons, hymns/canticles, and prayers. In these offices of prayer in the ancient Church, the use of the Psalter was extensive, distributing all 150 Psalms across the daily rhythm of prayer so that the entire Psalter could be sung during the week throughout the course of the eight services of prayer (for these services, see below). When other portions of Scripture were read in the service of prayer, the Psalms always preceded the readings. It was not uncommon for prayers to be prayed after chanting the Psalms at this point in the service, later to be known as Psalm prayers.

As the monastic offices grew in the Middle Ages, the entire Psalter continued to be read throughout the week, though in many communities this became too rigorous an exercise. However, specific psalms became associated with a particular office, as the following breakdown of the Psalms in the monastic office indicates:[26]

***Nocturns* [middle of the night]**

Psalms 3 and 95 are sung as invitatories.
Twelve psalms follow, selected from Psalms 21–109

***Lauds (Matins)* [daybreak]**

Psalms 67 and 51 are sung daily, with Psalms 148–150 at the conclusion.

After Psalm 51, the following are appointed for each day:

Sunday: 118, 63
Monday: 5, 36
Tuesday: 43, 57
Wednesday: 64, 65
Thursday: 88, 90
Friday: 76, 92
Saturday: 143 and a canticle from Deuteronomy

***Prime* [shortly after daybreak]**

Four sections of Psalm 119 on Sunday
On other days, three psalms from Psalms 1, 2, 6–20

***Terce* [9:00 a.m.], *Sext* [noon], *None* [3:00 p.m.]**

Three sections of Psalm 119 for each service on Sunday
On other days, three psalms for each service from Psalms 120–128

***Vespers* [at the end of the working day]**

Four psalms each day from Psalms 110–118, 129–147

***Compline* [before bedtime]**

Psalms 4, 91, and 134 daily

Scattered throughout this daily rhythm of prayer were also psalm verses that gave direction and focus to the various offices. We are all familiar with the opening versicles of Matins and Vespers originally associated with *Nocturns*, the first service of the day. These versicles governed the entire day of prayer:[27]

V. O Lord, open my lips,
R. And my mouth will declare your praise. (Ps 51:15)

For all the other services of prayer, the following versicles were used:

V. Make haste, O God, to deliver me!
R. Make haste to help me, O Lord. (Ps 70:1)

There were many other versicles used throughout the Daily Offices that are familiar to us. Some other examples are as follows:

Attached to the canticle Te Deum:

V. O Lord, save your people and bless your heritage!
R. Be their shepherd and carry them forever. (Ps 28:9)

V. Every day I will bless you
R. and praise your name forever and ever. (Ps 145:2)

V. Lord, keep us this day without sin;
R. Have mercy upon us, O Lord, have mercy upon us. (Ps 123:3)

V. Let your steadfast love, O Lord, be upon us,
R. even as we hope in you. (Ps 33:22)

V. In you, O Lord, do I take refuge;
R. let me never be put to shame. (Ps 33:1)

Following the Kyrie Eleison and the Lord's Prayer:

V. As for me, I said, "O Lord, be gracious to me;
R. heal me, for I have sinned against you!" (Ps 41:4)

V. Return, O Lord! How long?
R. Have pity on your servants! (Ps 90:13)

V. Let your priests be clothed with righteousness,
R. and let your saints shout for joy. (Ps 132:9)

V. O Lord, save the king!
R. May he answer us when we call. (Ps 20:9)

V. Remember your congregation,
R. which you have purchased of old. (Ps 74:2)

V. Peace be within your walls
R. and security within your towers! (Ps 122:7)

During *Compline,* a responsory after the lesson and before the *Nunc Dimittis*:

V. Into your hand I commit my spirit;
R. Into your hand I commit my spirit;

V. You have redeemed me, O Lord, faithful God.
R. I commit my spirit. (Ps 31:5)

V. Glory be to the Father, and to the Son, and to the Holy Spirit.
R. Into your hand I commit my spirit.

V. Keep me as the apple of your eye;
R. hide me in the shadow of your wings. (Ps 17:8)

Other Psalm verses:

V. Our help is in the name of the Lord,
R. who made heaven and earth. (Ps 124:8)

V. Hear my prayer, O Lord;
R. let my cry come to you! (Ps 102:1)

Lutherans have followed the Church's tradition of using the Psalter as Introits or whole psalms in the Divine Service, as well as an extensive set of psalms in the Liturgy of the Hours. The Psalms are either chanted or spoken, and the variety of ways in which they have been used reflects the richness and variety of the great tradition. Whether Gregorian chant is used or Psalms are spoken, for the Lutheran Church they are first among the hymns and songs of the Church.

What better way to close this chapter than with a Psalm. Psalm 34:1–10 was sung during distribution of the Lord's Supper and also is appointed for All Saints' Day:

I will bless the LORD at all times;
His praise shall continually be in my mouth.
My soul makes its boast in the LORD;
let the humble hear and be glad.
Oh, magnify the LORD with me,
and let us exalt His name together!

I sought the LORD, and He answered me
and delivered me from all my fears.
Those who look to Him are radiant,
and their faces shall never be ashamed.
This poor man cried, and the LORD heard him
and saved him out of all his troubles.
The angel of the LORD encamps
around those who fear him, and delivers them.

Oh, taste and see that the LORD is good!
Blessed is the man who takes refuge in Him!
Oh, fear the LORD, you His saints,
for those who fear Him have no lack!
The young lions suffer want and hunger;
but those who seek the LORD lack no good thing.

7
The Christian Concept of Time

The Christian concept of time is filled with Jesus' presence as He enters our lives and into *our space and time* through the Church's liturgical marking of time. In Christian liturgical time, Jesus' death and resurrection is not simply a past, historical event, but He is present ***now*** in His Church through our observing of days and weeks and years. Christians affirm in their concept of time not only that Jesus died and rose again, but that Jesus died and rose again ***for us***, and the gifts of forgiveness, life, and salvation are present ***for us***, right here, right now, in Christian liturgical time.

Christians view time in three cycles: (1) the resurrection and the first day of the week celebrated each week, (2) the Church Year, and (3) the hours of the day. We will look at these three cycles in detail in this chapter.

Time is a part of our lives that we seldom think or talk about, except when we complain that we do not have enough of it. Few people think of time as holy or as a gift of God, but time is sacred, a trust from God to live in His creation with joy and contentment. Time is marked by Christians in a special way in their liturgical life because Christ entered time. By His presence in the creation to make all things new He changed our reckoning of time forever. From the beginning, early Christians lived with clarity about how, through Christ's resurrection, eternity now bore in upon our finite time. They lived in that tension between a life lived toward the end time within time itself, that tension between the now and the not yet. By their accounting of days and weeks and years, Christians gave meaning to time. Their timekeeping proceeded from Jewish timekeeping and also proclaimed that now all was fulfilled in Christ.

Liturgical time allows the Church to proclaim time's sacred character as Christ-centered. Through Sunday as the day of worship and rhythms of the Church Year, the Church teaches how our days and weeks and years are shaped and formed by the reality that Jesus entered our time and space. This rhythm shows us how we are to truly live in God's gift of time as temporal beings baptized into Christ's eternal life. The structure of time says as much about us as a people as anything else we do or say as Christians.

We have been uncovering the three major structures of our worship—the structure of the rite, the structure of space, and now the structure of time. By looking at some of the precedents for the development of the rite within the worship of Israel and the liturgical life of Jesus, we have focused on the pattern of worship as it developed among early Christians. Before proceeding to show how the liturgical rite of Word and Sacrament developed with the ordinaries into the Lutheran rite we have today, we need to reflect upon the Christian concept of time by focusing on Sunday (the Lord's Day, the Eighth Day), then proceed to the Church Year, and then conclude by observing how Christians marked their days by prayers at designated hours called the "Liturgy of the Hours."

How Christians View Time

Christians today are generally oblivious to the Church's unique way of looking at time. A clear sign of this loss of time as sacred is our thorough neglect of Sunday as the central day of worship.[1] For the first three hundred years of Christianity the Church organized time by the week, and Sunday was the day of celebration of God's restored creation because God's Son rose from the dead on that day. Early Christians regarded Sunday as "the Lord's day . . . an eighth day of creation, a day beyond the Sabbath rest, 'the beginning of another world' . . . the conclusion of the first creation and the new creation . . . 'the image of the age to come.' "[2] God's re-creation came to completion in the resurrection of Christ. Reverence for Sunday as the holy day was the way early Christians gave thanks to God for the redemption of all creation in the death and resurrection of Jesus Christ and *petitioned* Him to continue to act as Savior in their midst through the Gospel and the Sacraments. The Church saw Sunday as the day in which the future blessings of the kingdom were now present in the midst of the worshiping assembly. In a very real sense, the last days, the eschaton, had begun (see Hebrews 1:2). The Church's view was eschatological, that is, Christians saw that on Sunday through the presence of Jesus Christ in Word and Sacrament, the things of eternity were present. The celebration of the Lord's Supper on the Lord's Day demanded this view of Sunday and of Christian worship:

> In the eucharist the church met the sacramentally present Christ, risen and bringing the new creation, risen and revealed to his disciples in the breaking of bread. Eschatologically the meal was a participation in the end time—a foretaste of the kingdom rather than an expectation of its [future] coming. Historically, it was a meeting with the crucified and risen Christ now present with his church rather than a recollection of the events of his career. Until the sixteenth century, we have no evidence of a significant Christian community that did not celebrate the eucharist on the Lord's day. But in the first century and the second, we have no evidence that any commemoration of a particular event ever helped shape a Lord's day celebration of the new creation. General commemorations of specific points in sacred history were not present until well into the fourth century. Until then, and for a long time after, the Lord's day simply marked the presence with his church of the resurrected Christ.[3]

It was only after the Edict of Milan in AD 312 as the Church's liturgy grew that there was a shift from Sunday as the primary way of measuring time in the Church to both a weekly and yearly rhythm. This yearly rhythm we call the Church Year, the topic for a later section of this chapter.

The Bible and the Sabbath; The Bible and Sunday, the Eighth Day

Much has been said so far about Sunday as the Lord's Day and the day of worship, but where does this come from? Does not the Old Testament give a commandment that says we should worship on the Sabbath (Saturday), the seventh day of the week? If we look carefully at both the Old and New Testament understandings of the Sabbath we shall see that the Sabbath, like the temple, was provisional until the Messiah came to fulfill both temple and Sabbath by His presence in the creation, as well as through His suffering, death, and resurrection.

A careful reading of the words and deeds of Jesus in the Gospels shows why the Christian Church moved from worship on the Sabbath to worship on the first day of the week. That move from Saturday to Sunday doesn't come unannounced like a bolt out of the blue. Throughout His ministry, for instance, Jesus became involved in Sabbath controversies—invariably with miraculous healings—that pointed to Him as Lord of the Sabbath, King of the new era of salvation. That new era of salvation is fully revealed in Jesus' own resurrection on "the first day" or, alternatively, the "eighth day."

Every Lord's Day is a celebration of Jesus' resurrection, of "the Dawn from on high" (Luke 1:78, author's translation), the real presence of Christ. That presence was in His ministry of healing on the Sabbath and is now in His ministry of healing on the eighth day in His ministry of Word and Meal. There is a great deal of biblical precedent for understanding Sunday as the day of worship and as the eighth day in which God is continuing to make all things new.

Precedents from the Old Testament on the Eighth Day

The number eight first finds its significance in the rite of passage that rescues Noah and his family from the flood that destroyed the world. Noah and his family were *separated* from their heathen world by the flood, entered a period of *transition* in the ark, which represented the Church, and then were *incorporated* into a new world where they were the only eight people alive to repopulate the world. The Genesis account merely mentions Noah, his wife, his sons, and his sons' wives. It is the New Testament writer Peter who goes out of his way to do the math and notice that there are eight persons on that boat. The final judgment is certainly in view in the Genesis flood. Most perished, but eight were preserved, foreshadowing those who would be baptized into Christ (1 Peter 3:20–21). For this reason, the number "eight" points to the community of God's faithful people on earth and in heaven.

Circumcision was to be performed on each male throughout Israel's generations. Circumcision represented the cutting off of the old sinful flesh, marking transition and incorporation as a member of God's people and a welcomed guest at the Passover feast (cf. Luther on Genesis 17).[4] Thus circumcision, the Old Testament precedent for Holy Baptism (Colossians 2:11–13), was performed on the eighth day, the same day of the week as the birth, and so it suggested a new birth (cf. John 3:3–8).

In the Old Testament, circumcision on the eighth day not only indicated incorporation into Israel. It also included the eschatological hope of life in the age to come. In commenting on circumcision in Genesis 17:10–11, Martin Luther makes the following observation about circumcision on the eighth day:

> The mystic reason which the Master of the Sentences and other teachers adduce is passable. They maintain that circumcision was deferred to the eighth day because in the resurrection, which is signified by the eighth day, we shall be perfectly circumcised, in order that we may be free from every sin of the world.

> We not only do not reject this thought, but we confirm it as godly and learned. In an allegorical sense the eighth day signifies the future life; for Christ rested in the sepulcher on the Sabbath, that is, during the entire seventh day, but rose again on the day which follows the Sabbath, which is the eighth day and the beginning of a new week, and after it no other day is counted. For through His death Christ brought to a close the weeks of time and on the eighth day entered into a different kind of life, in which days are no longer counted but there is one eternal day without the alternations of night.
>
> This has been thought out wisely, learnedly, and piously, namely, that the eighth day is the eternal day. For the rising Christ is no longer subject to days, months, weeks, or any number of days; He is in a new and eternal life. The beginning of this life is perceived and reckoned, but there is no end. In that life the true circumcision will be carried out. At that time not only the foreskin of the heart will be circumcised—which happens in this life through faith—but the entire flesh and all its essence will be cleansed from all depravity, ignorance, lust, sin, and filth. Consequently, the flesh is then immortal.
>
> This allegory is a prophecy that when Christ rises again there will be a spiritual, true, and perfect circumcision outside time in eternal life.[5]

Jesus' circumcision most likely took place in Bethlehem as He began His mission of fulfillment on the eighth day—the first day of the new week of God's new creation, which will also be the day of His resurrection. His obedience to the Law involves the shedding of His blood for the first time, portending the greater outpouring of His blood in His flogging and crucifixion. His circumcision is a onetime event availing for all. The foreskin represents sin and rebellion against God (Colossians 2:13). While Jesus is without sin, He takes humanity's place under the Law as the sin-bearer, as also in His Baptism. The benefits of Jesus' circumcision are received in Holy Baptism (Colossians 2:10–13; see further on Luke 3:21–22). In Luther's exposition of Genesis 17:9–11, he includes among the benefits of circumcision for Old Testament believers the forgiveness of sins, justification, and incorporation into the people of God. These benefits accrued to those who received the sign of circumcision through their faith in God's promise, which is fulfilled in Christ.[6]

St. Paul speaks of Holy Baptism as a "circumcision made without hands" and as "the circumcision of Christ" (Colossians 2:11). Jesus' circumcision shows His fulfillment of the entire Old Testament on our behalf (Luke 2:21–24, 27, 39), for in the circumcision of the one who represents all humanity, all people are circumcised once and for all. How odd that the Sinless One should take into His life all the ritual marks of dealing with sin! This shows a strand of thought that runs from one end of the Bible to the other, that is, that God often does things in a way that is completely opposite to human expectations. We sometimes call this the Great Reversal. Evident too in the individual lament psalms is the Gospel theme of the Great Reversal. Psalms 22, 31, and 69 are all psalms of David, and the life of David offers many examples of reversal: the eighth and last son of Jesse became his foremost son; the shepherd boy was anointed by Samuel to shepherd Israel; the lightly armed youth slew the fearsome giant; the young man unjustly hunted by King Saul succeeded him as king; and while King David wanted to build a house for God, instead God established David's house (dynasty) to endure forever through the Son of David who would rule on the throne of David for eternity (Luke 1:32–33; 2 Samuel 7).

Jesus' Sabbath Theology (John 5, 20; Luke 6)

The movement in the Christian Church from worship on the Sabbath to worship on the first day of the week is one of the major results of Jesus' fulfillment of the Sabbath. Christ rose on the first day after the Sabbath (John 20:19), the first day of the new week of the new creation. The next Sunday, when the risen Christ appeared again, was called the eighth day (John 20:26: "eight days later"). When one counts inclusively, as in the Old Testament, the first day and the eighth day are the same day of the week.

Jesus' Sabbath controversies point to Jesus as Lord of the Sabbath, King of the new era of salvation. The Jewish-Christian community would have conceived it this way:

> First creation: Began on the *first* of six days; seventh day for rest and worship.
>
> Second creation: Began on the eighth day; the eighth day is devoted to rest and worship in anticipation of the eternal heavenly rest and worship in the "eschaton."

The word that instituted the Sabbath (Exodus 20:8; Deuteronomy 5:12) was to "remember/keep the Sabbath day to keep it holy." Observing its place within God's *created order* as a holy day of worship was the major reason for the Sabbath according to Exodus 20:8.

Although Genesis 2:3 reads, "So God blessed the seventh day and made it holy, because on it God rested from all His work that He had done in creation," God did not cease working in His creation. After the fall into sin, God worked mightily to restore His people. And the second time the Sabbath command is given (Deuteronomy 5:12), the reason is not *creation* (as it was in Exodus 20:9–11), but *redemption,* the exodus deliverance (Deuteronomy 5:15), which anticipates the final salvation accomplished by Christ at His "departure," His exodus (Luke 9:31).[7] Jesus affirms this redemptive purpose in John 5:17, where, in a controversy over His healing on the Sabbath, Jesus says: "My Father is working until now, and I am working." The work the Father and the Son are still doing is the *re-creation* of the world on the Sabbath that has no evening, that is, Sunday—the eighth day, the first day of the new creation.

The pattern of redemption builds on the pattern of creation but also supersedes it. The new creation supersedes the first creation. God created this world in six days and rested on the seventh, thereby establishing the pattern for the week. His command to "remember the Sabbath day, to keep it holy" (Exodus 20:8) instituted the corresponding practice of resting from the work of this world every seventh day. This brought the opportunity to hear of and meditate on the world to come, the world of God's promise. The six days of this creation and the six-day workweek for the life of this age, followed by a day set aside for God and for rest, are also a pattern for this world's history: a divinely ordained series of this-worldly kingdoms, followed by the kingdom of God and His holy ones, the kingdom of peace, of rest from toil (cf. Daniel 2:31–45; 7:1–28; 9:20–27). This is the "great Sabbath," the Sabbath rest for the people of God (Hebrews 4:9; cf. vv 1–10). It is eternal, even as the seventh day of Genesis has no evening. It is the kingdom of God, which Jesus, the dawn [sunrise] from on high (Luke 1:78), inaugurates in His appearing (Luke 1), in His ministry, and in His resurrection.

Thus the Third Commandment[8] points to the great Sabbath, the kingdom of God. When Jesus brought the kingdom, that to which the weekly Sabbath observation pointed, the kingdom had *arrived*, and so the Sabbath was *fulfilled.* After His resurrection from the dead, the weekly observation of the first creation (Genesis 1:1–2:3; Exodus 20:8) was made obsolete by celebration of the new creation.

Jesus in no way minimized the importance of the pious Jews' observance of the Sabbath during His earthly ministry, and His faithful followers also remained in rest on the Sabbath after His death (Luke 23:56). But His resurrection inaugurated a new aeon, the "great Sabbath age," in which all time and all space is hallowed for worship. Jesus frequently appeared to be breaking the Sabbath; His justification for those deeds was, ultimately, not that mere human regulations were involved but that He Himself was Messiah and Lord, the King of the Sabbath rest to which the (divinely instituted) Sabbath observation attested and for which it yearned—our redemption. This great Sabbath rest is sometimes called "inaugurated eschatology," and it shows that when Jesus stepped into our space and our time, and especially when He rose from the dead, all the blessings of that last day, that last aeon, the "eschaton," began to be revealed.

The Jews held that God continues two of His works also on the seventh day of each week: He makes alive, since children are born, and He judges, since people die on the Sabbath. Jesus picks up on that tenet and identifies Himself with His Father by saying that He—as God—does these same two works also on the Sabbath.[9]

Jesus sets the pattern for the Church's teaching, or expounding on the Word, in the Sunday liturgy. He does this by teaching and healing (the work of redemption) in the synagogue on the Sabbath, and in His teaching on the road to Emmaus on Sunday (the eschatological day). It is also on the first day of the week that the miraculous healing is instituted that comes through the forgiveness of sins in Holy Absolution and in the Supper of the Lord of the Sabbath.

And when He said this, He breathed on them and said to them, "Receive the Holy Spirit." (John 20:22)

Transfiguration (Luke 9:28–36)

The transfiguration event is a foretaste of the glory of Jesus both in His resurrection and His coming again in glory. Luke opens the scene of the transfiguration in 9:28 by saying: "Now about eight days after these sayings . . . " Why mention eight? Is it possible that Luke has the same interest in the significance of eight as Peter? The "eight days" are reminiscent of the eighth day as the day of the new creation, the first day of a new week, tying together the transfiguration and the resurrection.

Signs in Heaven and on the Earth and in the Temple (Luke 23:44–45)

The evangelists all report one extraordinary, cosmic sign at the death of Jesus that attests to a staggering and listing creation: darkness. The "power of darkness" (Luke 22:53) that God allowed to usurp authority over the world at Jesus' arrest wrought death and chaos. Just as Satan entered Judas (Luke 22:3), so now an unearthly darkness enters creation. Matthew reports an earthquake and the resurrection of saints who, after Jesus' resurrection, walked around the holy city, as if the entire church age had transpired in an instant and the eschaton had come prematurely (Matthew 27:51–53). But the darkness is enough, since it would signal to both Jew and Gentile that something was happening that threatened the very existence of creation. The darkness is a sign that evil is threatening to destroy God's creation and revert it to chaos.

In the first creation, before God set the primordial elements in order, "darkness was over the face of the deep" (Genesis 1:2). God then created light, which was "good," and separated the light from the darkness (Genesis 1:3–5). But as Satan, who had seized control of Judas, completes his scheme to kill Jesus, darkness reasserts itself over the light. Watching Judas leave the Last Supper, John comments portentously, "and it was night" (13:30). As Jesus, the source of life and light, dies, the sun, the source of natural light, fails to carry out its divine mandate to distinguish between night and day, darkness and light, and to rule over the day (Genesis 1:14–18). Instead, day and night are confused, confounded, and darkness usurps the rule of the sun as evil reigns over good—temporarily.[10] Creation's bondage to sin and the curse of death, which Jesus had been taking into His body since His conception and which He had borne on behalf of the people publicly since His Baptism, is now completely laid upon Him to do its destructive work. All demon possession, all sickness, all sin, all death are now placed upon Him.

Yet the Creator, who took on flesh and was born into His creation, is, at this moment of death, bringing in new and eternal life, a new creation. The darkness is an eschatological sign that already now the end of the old world has come in a preliminary way in the death of Jesus (cf. Luke 21:25–26; Acts 2:20). A new and eternal day, a dawn from on high, is about to break forth and shine forever on those who dwell in "darkness and in the shadow of death" (Luke 1:78–79).

As we already noted, in the record of the first creation, each of the first six days closed with the notice that "there was evening and there was morning" (Genesis 1:5, 8, 13, 19, 23, 31). The sequence of darkness and light signified the completion of each day. But on the seventh day, the day of Sabbath rest, there is no concluding notice of evening and morning (Genesis 2:1–3). That lack of closure leaves the first creation open-ended. God had finished His work, but God did not forever cease all activity. The rest of Genesis, and indeed the entire canon of Holy Scripture, witnesses to God's continuing involvement in earthly history and human affairs.

During Jesus' crucifixion, the darkness signals the imminent conclusion of God's work of redemption. In the cosmic history of the first creation, the three hours of darkness provide the closure to the Sabbath of Genesis 2:1–3. The history of the first creation draws to a close. With Jesus' death the old order succumbs to the curse of death brought on by Adam's sin. At the same time, Jesus' work of atonement is completed, and He is about to enter into His own Sabbath rest (Luke 23:54, 56). God's provision for His new creation is completed; the new order is ready to shine forth, and it will do so with the first morning light of Easter. Together, darkness and light—the three hours of darkness while Jesus is on the cross and the brilliant light of Easter morning—inaugurate the new creation, the eternal Sabbath rest for the people of God (Hebrews 4:9–10). The new day of Sabbath rest has that beginning, but it will have no end; in the eschaton there will be no darkness, only light (Revelation 21:23–25).[11]

The Resurrection (Luke 24:1–11)

All four canonical Gospels refer to Easter as "the first day of the week." Although they describe the *time* of day with various expressions, each writer views the time on the first day of the week from the perspective of darkness or light (Matthew 28:1; Mark 16:2; Luke 24:1; John 20:1). Since light was created and separated from darkness *on the first day* of creation (Genesis 1:1–5), viewing the resurrection from the perspective of darkness and light indicates that the evangelists understand "the first day of the week" as the eschatological, eighth day, which ushers in the new creation represented by the new week.[12] The shameful embarrassment of Jesus' crucifixion and the horror of His death are now surmounted as light banishes darkness at the dawn of this new day, the day of resurrection, the first day of the new era of salvation.

As soon as Easter Sunday, the first day of the new week, is introduced by Luke in 24:1, there is a shift in how this day is to be perceived thereafter. Easter is not just another day, but the climactic, third day in the sequence of

Jesus' Passion, the first day of the new creation, the day of the resurrection, the eighth, eschatological day. Here in the transition from the old Sabbath observances to Sunday, the eschatological day, there is a new reckoning of time because of the earth-shattering events of "these days" (Luke 24:18). The new era of salvation has dawned, the eschaton has arrived.[13]

Eschatological Time after the Resurrection (Luke 24:36–53)

Three interconnected scenes bring Luke's Gospel to a close and help illustrate that we are now living in the eighth, eschatological day: (1) Jesus' appearance to His disciples, when He greets them with peace and eats roasted fish in their presence (24:36–43); (2) His final teaching to them, in which He promises to send upon them the Holy Spirit from the Father (24:44–49); and (3) His ascension (24:50–53). A key issue for the interpretation of these final three scenes is their chronology. The opening words of 24:36, "as they were talking about these things," *give the appearance* that the three scenes in 24:36–53 all take place on Easter Sunday, the first day of the week, and are associated with the Emmaus account. But the first two chapters of Acts portray the ascension as occurring after forty days (Acts 1:3) and Pentecost after fifty (Acts 2:1), giving rise to what the Early Church called "the Great Fifty Days." Why does Luke give the impression in his Gospel that all three of these scenes belong with the Easter Sunday events?

The Emmaus story included five time notices (24:13, 18, 21, 29, 33), marking the day as Sunday, the first day of the week, the third day in the sequence of Jesus' Passion and resurrection. *Easter institutes a new reckoning of time:* the new era of salvation has dawned and the eschaton has been inaugurated. The revelation of this by Jesus Himself first takes place at the Emmaus meal.

After the last time reference in the Emmaus story (24:33), *no further time notices occur in the rest of Luke's Gospel.* Luke blends together the last three scenes of his Gospel in such a way that no delineation of time appears to separate them from Easter. *He wants the hearer of the Gospel to recognize that, once bread is broken and eyes are opened to the reality of Christ's presence, the community of the faithful live in the inaugurated eschaton*. In His Word and in His Supper, the crucified and resurrected Christ is truly present *now*, even though His disciples on earth do *not yet* enjoy full, complete communion in His presence. Time cannot separate disciples from their risen Lord or from Easter's promise of resurrection for them too. The Church now lives in the eternal Sabbath rest of Easter Sunday. This is why the early Christians had an eschatological perspective on liturgical time, with Sunday as the eighth, eschatological day. The Church's liturgical calendar, which grew around Easter, helps foster this Christological view of time. Instead of marking off passing years according to the secular world's clock, the Church's calibration of time ever revolves around Easter, returning to Easter each Sunday and moving from Easter toward the resurrection of all flesh. The past is never lost, since the entirety of salvation history is recapitulated every Lord's Day, and indeed every single day, for the baptized already have been buried and raised with Christ (Romans 6:3–4).[14]

The Eighth Day Today

The ramifications of this eschatology perspective are enormous. Early Christians marked the beginning of their life in Christ at baptismal fonts that were eight-sided to indicate that this is when they entered eternity by their union with Christ and His death and resurrection. Today, many baptismal fonts around the world are still eight-sided. We would do well to restore fonts that reflect this eternal dimension of our life in Christ. But even more, our pastors and people need to speak and act of Baptism as the constituting event initiating us into a life with Christ that never ends. Sunday was the primary day of worship for early Christians because this was the day when Christ rose. It is for this reason that His crucified and resurrected flesh was offered to the community in bread and wine at the Lord's Supper each Sunday. With Christ's bodily presence, the eschaton had arrived and Christians were now living in the Eighth Day of the new creation.

Today we like to say that Sunday is a little Easter. But for early Christians, Easter was a *big* Sunday, *the* day of worship. We must restore Sunday not only as the day of worship but also restore it as the day in which the Lord's Supper is celebrated as the moment when heaven and earth come together in Christ. The more we learn to live eschatologically, that is, to live knowing that Jesus Christ, the eternal one, lives among us and within us, the more local congregations will reflect in their worship the confidence and authenticity of Christ's redeeming action.

The Church Year

Time was a fundamental part of the creation; God created the world in six days, rested on the seventh, and declared the Sabbath a day of rest. After the fall, the Sabbath became a day to praise the Creator for His good creation, to thank Him for His ongoing presence in the creation with His mighty acts of salvation, and to petition Him to return as Messiah to restore the creation to what God had created it to be. As time went on, various feasts such as Passover, the Feast of Booths, and Pentecost became part of the rhythm of the Jewish year. By His resting in the tomb Christ fulfilled the ancient Sabbath day requirements. In His resurrection He restored creation. Sunday, the weekly celebration of the resurrection, was taken as the preferred day of worship by early Christians. As a Church steeped in the historical events of Christ's life, and the Jewish precedent of feast days during the year, Sunday was complemented by events from Christ's redemptive life, death, resurrection, and ascension. The Church Year developed to give the people of God access to the life of Christ through the unfolding of a proper understanding of the Christ of the Bible in light of His real presence. The Church Year tells the Church its story, which is Christ's story. It is the telling of that story that forms the Church into the Body of Christ.

The Church has seized this rhythm, taking up the incarnation and the crucifixion, the two scandals of Christianity, and establishing them to be the two great festivals of the Church Year, Christmas and Easter.

Time has always been a critical commodity, no less so in the Church. And the Church has no other choice but to be a good steward of time. Long, slow, annual rhythms in time serve theology. The Church has seized this rhythm, taking up the incarnation and the crucifixion, the two scandals of Christianity, and establishing them to be the two great festivals of the Church Year, Christmas and Easter. These are the pivots of the liturgical year. Within sacred time, the Church has harmonized the seasons of nature with the seasons of the Church Year. As nature experiences its yearly death in the fall and winter, the Church Year focuses on judgment, the ultimate death of the world as we know it. The transition to Advent is a natural one, for the Church now prepares for the birth of the Child who tolls the death of the old world and the resurrection of the new. When the sun reaches the point of death at the winter solstice and begins to rise again, the Church celebrates the birth of the new world when "the sun of righteousness shall rise with healing in its wings" (Malachi 4:2). Then Christian time goes on to coordinate the rebirth of nature in the spring and summer with images of new life through the resurrection of Jesus Christ. It is not a coincidence that Easter occurs in the spring. The themes of new birth and resurrection dominate, and Baptism becomes the reigning metaphor. The Pentecost season carries out the image of our full-grown, mature life in Christ as the summer fields become ripe with the fruits of God's creation. The Church has transformed the world by its liturgy and served the Gospel's goal. The Church has raised secular time to the level of the sacred. This sacred time becomes a revelation of grace because Christ now appears in it for the benefit of His people.

The specialization of our culture has often crept into the Church Year, revealing that liturgy and theology have been adapted to the culture. Most pastors can testify to the fact that they are bombarded by both Church and world with suggestions on how to use a particular Sunday to accent such things as specific charities, historical events, mission opportunities, and secular occasions. Such opportunities to recognize these special groups and events may be incorporated into the service in the prayers, the sermon, or even by a brief announcement. But it is unwise to allow these groups and events to trump liturgical time.

In contrast, observing the Church Year sometimes goes head-to-head with culture in order to form a body of believers around sacred rather than secular time. When the congregation does not observe the Church Year, it passes up a golden opportunity to elevate the Gospel of Him who died and rose for the life of the world. Isn't this the very center of our Christian faith? Why would we ignore Christ's death and resurrection in the way we mark time? **Reverence** of sacred time assists the congregation in worshiping a present person whose mighty deeds of salvation took place in time because that person enfleshed Himself in time and space. He still operates in time and space within the worshiping community. **Fidelity** to the historical acts of Jesus' life as marked in the Church Year gives the congregation a bridge across time so that it can see that these past acts of salvation are actually present realities. The future benefits of salvation are already now available to the congregation sacramentally. The Church Year exists for the sole reason of centering the Church's life in the life of Christ and proclaiming that the historical reality that "Jesus died" is now the sacramental reality that "Jesus died *for you.*" The Church Year brings the life, death, burial, and resurrection of Jesus into *your life*, into *your space and time*.

Christian time is God's time; the Church Year is God bringing home His Son to the congregation year after year. The daily, weekly, yearly rhythm of commemorating the saving deeds of Jesus Christ forms the congregation into a Christian community living in time sanctified by Jesus Christ. As restored creatures of a restored creation, we live our restored lives in restored time within the framework of the Church Year. Ordinary time has become sacred.

The Formation of the Church Year in Jerusalem

The development of the Church Year took place during the time of Cyril of Jerusalem (AD 315–386). A vital source for this development may be found in *Egeria's Travels*.[15] Egeria, a nun from Southern France, traveled to the Holy Land as one of the first Christian pilgrims. She reported back to the sisters in France by means of a detailed travelogue. Egeria wrote from a unique perspective; she did not miss much in the way of details and gave much information about Jerusalem at this time, particularly the liturgy and the Church Year. (She tended to report things different from life in Southern France.) The best dating of Egeria's travels is from AD 381–384.

An even better source for Cyril's church in Jerusalem are his lectures on the Christian Sacraments. The lectures are divided into two sections: one that is the "procatechesis" or the catechetical instruction before the rite of

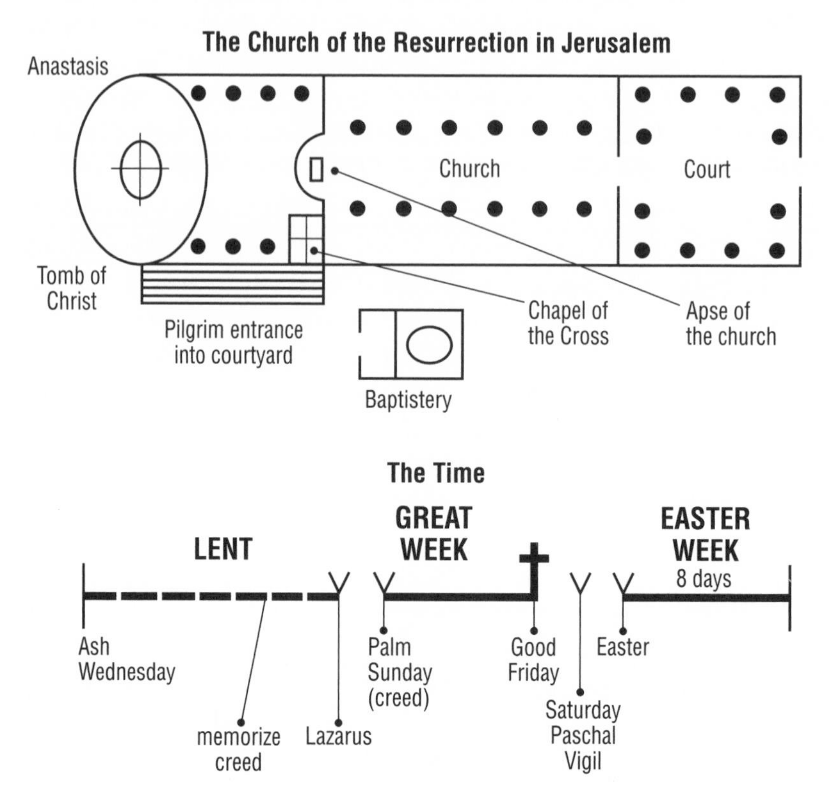

Baptism, and the other is the "mystagogical" catechesis that speaks of Baptism and Eucharist after the catechumen has experienced both of them during the Paschal vigil.[16]

A number of liturgical practices were instituted during this period of Cyril's bishopric that affect our Church today, especially the development of Lent and the Paschal season. Until the time of Cyril, the Church had measured time by the week, with the primary focus on Sunday, the eighth, eschatological day. Now the Church begins to bring history into the liturgy, measuring time by the year and creating a Christian calendar, the Church Year we are familiar with today. Now Christianity becomes located in space and time, and the following sacred places in Jerusalem now define the liturgical life of the Jerusalem church. If you followed Egeria during her pilgrimage to Jerusalem, you would find her visiting churches built in Bethlehem for Christmas, in Bethany for the celebration of Lazarus' resurrection on the eve of Palm Sunday and for the Ascension, the Mount of Olives for Palm Sunday, and the Church of the Resurrection at the place where Jesus was crucified, buried, and raised from the dead. What happens is that Jerusalem, the city, becomes the place of worship, and the town itself is a place of worship as huge numbers of people travel from place to place in liturgical formation, stopping here and there for Psalms, readings, and prayers. The rest of Christendom, fascinated by Jerusalem and the holy places, adopts this "urban liturgy" within their own city, and this "urban liturgy" becomes the standard for all liturgical worship in the west. Even after the barbarian invasions that began in AD 410, when the northern people of Europe swept down into the southern Roman Empire and sacked Rome and other cities, this liturgy becomes focused in a church building instead of a town. Instead of having a huge city in which to conduct the urban liturgy, the barbarians of the North built huge churches in their small villages so that the "urban liturgy" could be done in the basilica instead of the city.

The Church's departure today from the significance of Sunday, the eighth day, as the day of worship has affected its capacity to observe sacred time as centered in the extraordinary reality that on Sunday, through Christ's bodily presence in the Gospel and the Sacraments, heaven is on earth. The Church can never return to some golden age of the past (which, by the way, never existed) such as pre-Constantinian Christianity or even the flowering of liturgy during the fourth and fifth centuries. Nevertheless, early Christianity informs us once again that reverence and fidelity to sacred time are critical to liturgical renewal in our time. Reverence and fidelity to the Church

Year allows congregations to view all of reality, all of space and time through the life of Jesus.

SUNDAYS AND SEASONS

The Church Year may be divided into three parts: (1) the time of Christmas, which includes the seasons of Advent, Christmas, and Epiphany; (2) the time of Easter, which includes the seasons of Lent and Easter; and (3) the time of the Church, which is the Pentecost season. The times of Christmas and Easter follow the life of Christ from His birth until His death, resurrection, and ascension, whereas the Pentecost season reflects the life of the Church in its readings and accents. The story of how the Sundays and seasons developed is a complex one and, like much of the liturgy, we simply do not know the exact origins of many of our commemorations. But the theological accents of each time and season have come to us after many years of Christians celebrating these events through preaching and hymn singing. The following is a brief description of the theological overtones in each time in the Church.

THE TIME OF CHRISTMAS

The seasons of Advent, Christmas, and Epiphany focus on the incarnation of Jesus Christ. The tendency is to divide them into three different seasons, when in fact each in turn prepares for the incarnation, celebrates the incarnation, and manifests the incarnation. The feast of Christmas is the heart of the cycle, preceded by Advent as preparation and followed by Epiphany as the continued elaboration of the identity of the Christ Child born at Christmas.

Looking at these three seasons as part of one Christmas cycle, it makes sense that any plan for preaching and music during the first part of the Church Year would seek to discover the centrality of the incarnate One within the liturgical lessons for each Sunday. The seasonal Church Year then develops the full portrait of the Church's life centered in Christ, present among us and coming again in glory. The journey with Jesus from His birth all the way through His ascension gives a complete picture of the Christian's daily struggle of living in the flesh and yet by faith. At Christmas, we proclaim to one another that God in Christ came into this world to redeem us, and that now through Baptism He comes close to each of us—into our flesh! This Christ Child wants us to live, for His presence in our redeemed bodies makes us fully human. Later, during Lent and Holy Week we follow the

Christ Child to Jerusalem and to His death and resurrection where we see how in our Baptism we, too, take the same journey *in Him* as we suffer, die, are buried, and rise with Him to a life that never ends. We should not view or present the seasons of the Church Year in isolation from one another. Even in the Advent and Christmas seasons, the Church Year serves as a reminder and teacher that Jesus entered into the suffering and shame of our sinful flesh to deliver and sanctify us, and that it is His life that defines our life.

The seasons of Advent, Christmas, and Epiphany proclaim the tension of what God has already done in Jesus and what God will still do in Him. This is the dialectic of the now and not yet. Every Christian sees this tension expressed in his own life as saint/sinner or, as Martin Luther put it, *simul iustus et peccator*. This is the life we live under the cross in which we view ourselves as both condemned and redeemed. This tension is resolved in the incarnate Christ, crucified and now risen for the life of the world. Thus the Church offers liturgical lessons that allow the people of God to embrace that tension and proclaim this resolution in Jesus Christ whose presence is realized in the bread and wine.

Advent

The tension between the now and the not yet is one of the great themes of the Advent season. On one hand, we prepare for the Christ's coming in Bethlehem. On the other, we prepare for His second coming at the end of time. This tension between past and future is fully embraced by the congregation in the present as it prepares by meeting the coming Lord in the Lord's Supper, which proclaims His death and announces His coming in one sacramental act, as He commanded. Thus the tension of this season comes to life in the Sacrament, another expression of the constant tension of the Church's life under the cross and in light of the new creation.

The first Sunday of Advent follows immediately on the heels of four Sundays thick with end-times anticipation. They close off the season of Pentecost. With the first of these eschatological Sundays is the celebration of All Saints, the recognition of our oneness with all who have died and risen with Christ. The eschatology of these last Sundays is a natural one, for nature is dying all around us, the days are getting shorter and colder, and it appears as if the world is dying. What an appropriate time for us to consider the judgment and the end of all things.

Following the recognition of the saints and the final judgment, Advent is the dawn of the end-time, because Jesus, the end of all things, is born in

Bethlehem. But the eschatology here is different. Advent is a visual revelation of Jesus, the Holy One from heaven, invading our sin-laden cosmos and radically altering it by His presence for its good. Advent and Christmas are about how this apocalyptic invasion of the Christ in His incarnation and birth is *the eschatological event.* This is inaugurated eschatology, that is, that in the birth, death, and resurrection of Jesus the end times have already begun but have not yet reached their final consummation. When Jesus was made man, it was all over, so to speak, but not yet, in the context of human time.

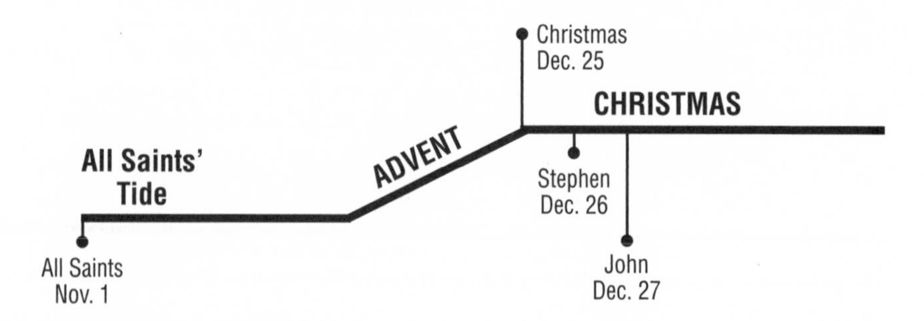

The Gospel for Advent I, the first Gospel of the Church Year, is Jesus' triumphal entrance into Jerusalem. There is such delicious irony in beginning our year this way, for the entrance of Jesus into Jerusalem is an end-time event. At the end of time, Jesus will come again, to enter and establish a new Jerusalem, where there will be "springs of living water, and God will wipe away every tear from [our] eyes" (Revelation 7:17). We begin our year of living out that reality *now* as we wait for that day, proclaiming the good news of Christ's new creation and traveling toward that day.

And so when Jesus enters Jerusalem for that first Holy Week, the end is near, the work of redemption is almost finished. What a way to begin a Church Year—in triumph—for Jesus enters Jerusalem as king, but also subdued, for He enters humbly, mounted on a donkey, and this King must die for the sins of the world. We begin the Church Year knowing from the start that Jesus was born to die. Already now on the first Sunday in Advent we have Palm Sunday, Good Friday, and Easter morning in our sights. The Church Year is fully immersed in historical time, chronological time, events that follow each other in sequence and as a consequence of one another. But historical time is merely a platform, a foundation from which eschatological time is erected. In eschatological time, the end has already come, and Jesus, the eschaton Himself, is present bodily in our first Sunday of Advent celebrations. The second and third Sundays of Advent continue with John the Baptist, who himself is an eschatological figure as he calls people to repentance and points them to God's final judgment when the winnowing fork of the Messiah clears the threshing floor to gather the wheat into His barns but to clear the chaff away to be burnt with unquenchable fire (Luke 3:17). The need for repentance because the end is near is a big theme in Advent. As John prepared for the coming of the Messiah by calling the people of Israel to repentance, so Advent prepares us through repentance for our celebration of the Child's birth in Bethlehem.

Advent is a penitential season, but not in the same way as Lent. Christmas is the first of two climaxes in the festival season; the greater climax at Easter is preceded by a greater time of penance. Advent and Christmas anticipate the birth of the Child, and His death and resurrection on Good Friday and Easter. This sense of hope in the midst of our penitential preparations is signaled by the fourth Sunday in Advent that already now looks to the Child about to be born. Either through the announcement of the birth of the child made to Joseph in Matthew or the one to Mary in Luke or Mary's great song after conceiving Jesus, we are on the threshold of one of the two great moments in our yearly celebrations—the birth of the Christ Child.

Christmas—Epiphany

There are two theories as to why Christmas occurs when it does, both of them probably correct, both of them pointing to the theological significance of Christmas and the incarnation. The first theory has to do with the winter solstice, which was celebrated on December 25 in the ancient world. For the Romans, a pagan feast to the "Unconquered Sun-God" (*Natale Solis Invicti*) acknowledged both the death of darkness as the sun reaches its lowest point and the birth of the light as each new day begins to get longer and longer. As with all pagan feasts, these were majestic in character and deeply attractive to the human spirit. They would often turn into raucous expressions of drunken and licentious behavior. Everyone was encouraged to participate in the feasting, so Christians were often tempted to join in the revelry.

The first recognized celebration of Christmas occurred in AD 336 in Rome, where Christians countered the pagan feasting with their own feast, for they had the true "light of the world," as John so clearly declares in his Gospel (8:12). The light born on December 25 is not only the light of the sun, but the birth of the "sun of righteousness," who "shall rise with healing in its wings," as Malachi so clearly proclaims (4:2). The great Christmas hymn by Charles Wesley "Hark! The Herald Angels Sing" captures this in the third verse:

> Hail, the heav'n-born Prince of Peace!
> Hail, the Sun of Righteousness!
> Light and life to all He brings,
> Ris'n with healing in His wings. (*LSB* 380:3)[17]

When Christ, the light of the world, is born in Bethlehem, so also is the eschaton born, that is, the end has come in the Christ Child who was born to die and bring with His death the completion of God's plan of salvation. This connection between the birth of the Child and His death brings us to the second theory as to the date of Christmas. In the ancient world, it was uncommon for people to know the date they were born. But the day of death was recorded, especially for people of renown. As early as the third century, many Christian communities thought March 25 was the day Christ was crucified, the day of the spring equinox. March 25 was also considered the first day of the new year, for many thought that on this day the creation of the world began. This united the creation and the redemption in their minds. The next logical step was to suggest that Christ died on the day He was conceived, as was the custom in this culture where birthdays were not known but the date of the death of a great person was always celebrated. It seemed natural that the day you left the world was the day you entered by conception. Good Friday, the Annunciation of the birth of Jesus to Mary, and Christmas all belonged together, or at least they did for the ancient world, for this combined Jesus' incarnation, birth, and atonement. Thus Christmas falls on December 25, nine months after His conception and His crucifixion.

Whether this date was true or not didn't really matter to the early Christians. What mattered was the larger theological truth behind the practice. The incarnation and the atonement belong together. Christmas and Easter are two sides of the same coin. Jesus was born to die. That's what the Church Year is all about, that is what Christmas, Easter, and the Annunciation are all about.

One pastor called me a few years ago and asked if it was okay to use white paraments with "Alleluia" on them for the celebration of the Annunciation, which always occurs during Lent. He was especially concerned about this after the careful removal of all "alleluias" during Lent. At least he didn't ask if we should sing Christmas carols. But maybe singing Christmas carols that announce that Christ is born is not such a bad idea? After all, the Annunciation is the day when Jesus breaks into our world. Didn't early Christians believe all this about the dates precisely because they held the annunciation of Christ's conception to Mary by the angel Gabriel in as high esteem as they did the birth of the Child and the death of the Child? For early Christians, there were four great days: (1) the day God created the world, (2) the day God came into this world, (3) the day God offered Himself up as a sacrifice for the sins of the world, and (4) the day that God showed He was the final conqueror over the enemies of the world—sin, death, and the devil—by rising from the tomb. The date of Christmas brings all this together in one theological tour de force.[18]

Epiphany and Christmas are intimately tied together by the theme of light. Light brings clarity in the darkness. The light of Christ born in Bethlehem now shines throughout the season of Epiphany as the Christ Child is made manifest to us as Messiah and Savior. In the time of Christmas, Advent prepares for the climax of Christmas, which continues in the season of Epiphany.

The day of Epiphany, January 6, is an older celebration than Christmas. It was originally celebrated as the birth of Jesus, since there was an alternate theory in the ancient Church that Jesus died on April 6, thus, nine months after His death and conception makes His birth on January 6. The parallels, then, between Christmas Day and Epiphany are very close.

The season of Epiphany shows clearly who the Child is. Epiphany begins with the Baptism of Jesus in the Jordan, where the Father proclaims: "This is My beloved Son, with whom I am well pleased" (Matthew 3:17). The season ends at the Transfiguration, where the Church looks over the valley of the shadow of Lent and sees a glimpse of the glory of the resurrection in the glory of Christ on top of the mountain. It also hears the Father reiterate what He said at Jesus' Baptism: "This is My beloved Son, with whom I am well pleased; listen to Him" (Matthew 17:5). The season of Epiphany is therefore framed with the voice of the Father proclaiming Jesus as the Son.

Throughout Epiphany we witness the teaching and miracles of Jesus. These show us that already now the Creator has come to His creation to bring in the new creation. This begins with His first miracle of turning water into wine at the wedding at Cana. It is a significant symbol of Epiphany as a manifestation of the glory of our Lord. The redemption of God's people was also portrayed as a marriage, the Lamb-Redeemer as the Bridegroom, the people of God as His Bride whom He loved so much as to give up His life for her. At the first official appearance of Jesus at the wedding feast of Cana, something is happening that has never happened before. Here is the Bridegroom coming to His bride, changing water into wine. This is the Messiah in the flesh, pitching His tent in the midst of a wedding feast, announcing that the feast that has no end was soon to begin.

The Time of Easter—The Seasons of Lent and Easter

A dramatic shift takes place as the Church Year moves toward the time of Lent and Easter. Although Lent is today celebrated as primarily a penitential season, it did not begin as such. Lent was a catechetical season that prepared those who were to be baptized (called catechumens) during the Easter Vigil for this momentous passage from darkness to light, from death to life. Ash Wednesday was first and foremost the enrollment of the catechumens for Baptism, and secondarily the pouring of ashes on those baptized members who had committed a public sin that offended both God and His community. That meant that Lent was focused on Baptism, both for those preparing for Baptism and those already baptized. It cannot be emphasized enough that the entire life of the Church was to bring people to the waters of Holy Baptism at the Easter Vigil. Cyril of Jerusalem tells us that the catechumens spent three hours every day hearing the Scriptures, first as to their literal/historical meaning and then as to their theological meaning. During the final week of Lent, our Holy Week (or Great Week as they called it), the catechumens would spend the entire day in preparation for Baptism through teaching, exorcisms, fasting, and prayer. The climax of the Church Year was when these catechumens entered the waters of Holy Baptism and the life of Christ in their initiation into the Christian Church.

It cannot be emphasized enough that the entire life of the Church was to bring people to the waters of Holy Baptism at the Easter Vigil.

The First Sunday in Lent defines the season in the same way the First Sunday in Advent defines Advent. The Gospel reading for Lent I has always been the temptation of Jesus in the wilderness (for both the one-year series and the three-year series), announcing the forty days of fasting in imitation of our Lord's fasting in the wilderness during His temptations by Satan. Jesus defeats Satan in the wilderness through His citation of the Word of God. Satan's temptations of Jesus are an attempt to have Jesus bypass the cross, but Jesus shows at the very beginning of His ministry that the cross is His destination. He must go the way of Jerusalem, and His journey to the cross is the foundation of one theme of Lent as we follow Him into the wilderness and beyond that to Jerusalem.

The temptation of Jesus by the devil foreshadows the conflict of the Passion and Jesus' victory on the cross. Already the triumph is anticipated, though it comes in a way that one might not expect. Jesus' battle and complete victory over the devil in the Passion and resurrection is one of the great themes of His life, giving rise to the expression of the Gospel that accents Christ's victory over Satan. But the devil is subtle, and he sees that his chance for victory lies in tempting Jesus to bypass the cross and reach for glory *now*. Each temptation attempts this: fill Your belly *now*, if You are the Son of God; worship me, and the kingdoms of the earth will be Yours *now*; throw Yourself down from the temple, and all will see *now* that You are the Son of God because God will rescue You. Had Jesus succumbed to any one of these temptations, He would have reversed the order of the kingdom, placing glory before suffering. The entire rhythm of His life was just the opposite, to show that suffering must precede glory. The rejected stone is the head of the corner. Jesus is both the new and greater Adam and the new and greater Israel, remaining the obedient man, Son of God, and Messiah.

And so He shows that this is the way it is with us. The world tells us to have prosperity *now*, demanding that the Lord show us His blessings *now*. The world would have us see suffering as a sign of God's rejection rather than fellowship with Christ where He draws us closer to Himself so that we might see His glory in our shame and suffering. Rather, the Church must preach "suffering before glory" right into the world's confusion to show that suffering is God's opportunity to demonstrate His mercy and forgiveness. Suffering forces us to recognize that we cannot depend on ourselves and must rely on God. Suffering is always God's opportunity to show us that He loves us.

The Psalm for Lent I is Psalm 91, the Soldier's Psalm for Israel, which enlists us in the battle. It is the song that accompanies us on our way to Jerusalem with Christ:

> When He calls to me, I will answer Him;
> I will be with Him in trouble;
> I will rescue Him and honor Him.
> With long life I will satisfy Him
> and show Him my salvation. (Psalm 91:15–16)

Here is another great Lenten theme, where we join in the battle with Christ as our captain in the well-fought fight against sin, death, and the devil. As the New Testament clearly portrays, Baptism enlists us in the apocalyptic battle as foot soldiers on the front lines. We do not fight by our own power, but we are clothed with Christ, who equips us for the fight and fights for us. St. Paul uses this imagery with the Ephesian congregation:

> Put on the whole armor of God, that you may be able to stand against the schemes of the devil. For we do not wrestle against flesh and blood, but against the rulers, against the authorities, against the cosmic powers over this present darkness, against the spiritual forces of evil in the heavenly places. Therefore take up the whole armor of God, that you may be able to withstand in the evil day, and having done all, to stand firm. Stand therefore, having fastened on the belt of truth, and having put on the breastplate of righteousness, and, as shoes for your feet, having put on the readiness given by the gospel of peace. In all circumstances take up the shield of faith, with which you can extinguish all the flaming darts of the evil one; and take the helmet of salvation, and the sword of the Spirit, which is the word of God, praying at all times in the Spirit, with all prayer and supplication. (Ephesians 6:11–18)

Luther uses this same symbolism in his great hymn of the Reformation, "A Mighty Fortress"—which is the Hymn of the Day for Lent I:

> A mighty fortress is our God, A trusty shield and weapon;
> He helps us free from ev'ry need That hath us now o'ertaken.
> The old evil foe Now means deadly woe;
> Deep guile and great might Are his dread arms in fight;
> On earth is not his equal.
>
> With might of ours can naught be done, Soon were our loss effected;
> But for us fights the valiant One, Whom God Himself elected.
> Ask ye, Who is this? Jesus Christ it is, Of Sabaoth Lord,
> And there's none other God; He holds the field forever.

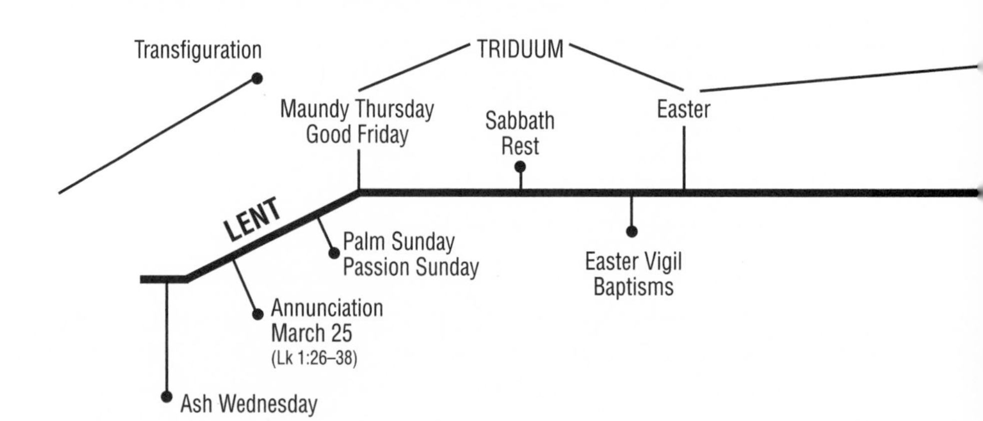

Though devils all the world should fill, All eager to devour us,
We tremble not, we fear no ill; They shall not overpow'r us.
This world's prince may still Scowl fierce as he will,
He can harm us none, He's judged; the deed is done;
One little word can fell him.

The Word they still shall let remain Nor any thanks have for it;
He's by our side upon the plain With His good gifts and Spirit.
And take they our life, Goods, fame, child, and wife,
Though these all be gone, Our vict'ry has been won;
The Kingdom ours remaineth. (*LSB* 656)

The climax of the Church Year comes with the three days or the Triduum: Good Friday, Saturday, and Easter Sunday (traditionally marked from sunset on Maundy Thursday until sunset on the evening of Easter). This marks the climax of Jesus' journey that began with Jesus' invasion into our world in the incarnation. From the moment of His breaking-in to our world, He has descended toward the belly of the earth. Now He brings that journey to completion as He suffers, dies, and is buried in the tomb. He will reverse this descent and begin His ascent on Easter morning when He rises from the dead. He completes His ascent on the fortieth day when He ascends into heaven. The diagram below illustrates this journey of Jesus.

This three-day journey through death into the belly of the earth and then back to life again is the journey of the newly baptized as they suffer, die, and rise with Christ in the waters of Holy Baptism (Romans 6). The restoration of the Easter Vigil as the climactic moment in the Church Year, as the first celebration of Easter and the time for Baptism in the Early Church, has been a healthy reminder in many parishes of the centrality of Baptism in our lives, as we die and rise daily in Baptism, and how our entire Church life is constituted

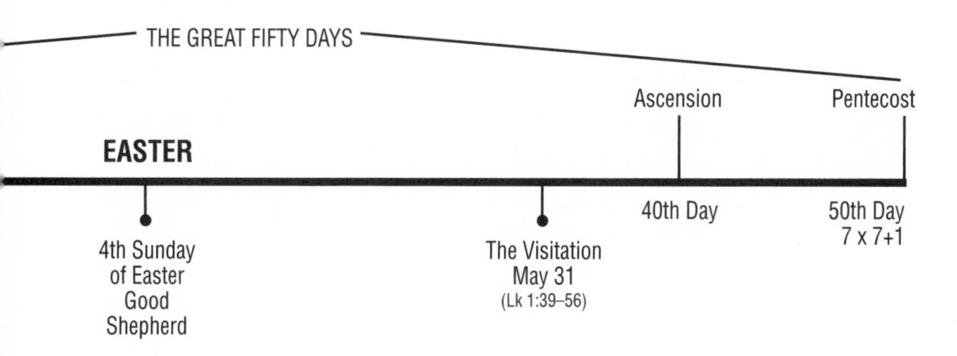

and organized around the process of catechizing, baptizing, and feeding the people of God with Christ in His Word and Sacraments.

The celebration of Easter in the spring, when new life is beginning to break forth in nature, corresponds to the new life celebrated in Christ's resurrection from the dead and our resurrection in Him in Baptism. This resurrection joy continues for the octave of Easter, when the song of Christ's resurrection continues for eight days. It was during this eight-day period that the catechumens in the ancient Church received their mystagogical catechesis on the mysteries of Baptism and the Lord's Supper. As Epiphany continues the climax of Christmas, the Easter season keeps the Easter celebration going, and for the Great Fifty Days from Easter to Pentecost—7 x 7 = 49 + 1 = 50—the Church lives out its eschatological destiny in its celebration of the resurrection of Jesus. Seven times seven is the number of perfection and the one additional day is the sign of eternity. This fifty-day Easter feast was interrupted by the celebration of Jesus' ascension into heaven, but this only enhanced the meaning of Christ's resurrection. His ascension is the final step in His ascent from the grave into heaven where He raises our human nature to His right hand and our humanity is enthroned with Him in heaven. The great ascension hymn of Christopher Wordsworth puts it best:

> He has raised our human nature On the clouds to God's right hand;
> There we sit in heav'nly places, There with Him in glory stand.
> Jesus reigns, adored by angels; Man with God is on the throne.
> By our mighty Lord's ascension We by faith behold our own.
> (*LSB* 494:5)

The Time of the Church—The Pentecost Season

Pentecost and the Church go together, as St. Luke tells us in Acts 2, where he describes the first Pentecost and the explosion of the Church from the Upper Room in Jerusalem, sending out shock waves that would eventually fill the whole earth. Pentecost is intimately tied to Easter as the fiftieth eschatological day, the week of weeks. If Easter was the celebration of the sacrifice of the Lamb, Pentecost is the offering of the firstfruits of that sacrifice in us, the baptized, through the ongoing presence of Christ in His Church by His Spirit. If the festival seasons of the Church Year are about Christ, the Pentecost season is about how Christ has now become a people. Pentecost is the season when the fields become ripe for the harvest as the baptized grow and proliferate and mature in Christ. Sometimes the Pentecost season seems endless, but that is precisely the point. As the Church moves toward the parousia with Christ present in His Church by His Spirit in Word and Sacrament, we already now have a foretaste of the end. Pentecost is the time when the end is celebrated among us every Sunday, and the harvest is ongoing each time baptisms are performed and suppers are celebrated. This is not the end focused on judgment but rather on the eternal feast.

There is, however, a distinct shift in the focus of the Pentecost season with All Saints' Day on November 1. All Saints' Day marks the transition in the Church Year to the last things, to the final consummation. From this point onward, the lessons for each Sunday begin to take on an eschatological quality. Since the Christian Church has always been conscious of time, it seemed most appropriate to the Church to choose apocalyptic texts for the fall of the year when all around it nature was experiencing its yearly death.

All Saints' Day was an appropriate day to mark this transition, for the Church could clearly see in its faithful departed the promise of Revelation that, clothed in white robes, the saints are the ones who have come out of the great tribulation, who have washed their robes and made them white in the blood of the Lamb, and who have entered into the kingdom of heaven. These saints are saints because they have been made objectively holy by Baptism; they have suffered and died with Christ; they have risen with Him and now appear before the throne of God, serving Him day and night in His temple. This festival boldly proclaims what we have been doing all season long: celebrating our union with Christ and all the saints at the foretaste of the heavenly feast. But now in these last weeks of the Church Year, our focus is on the end times and the marriage feast of the Lamb in His kingdom that knows no end.

The Liturgy of the Hours

Just as there is a yearly focus to our time, so also there is recognition of daily time. The disciples understood this when one of them asked Jesus: "Lord, teach us to pray, as John also taught his disciples" (Luke 11:1). Great teachers and religious leaders like John the Baptist had their own way of praying, and the disciples wanted Jesus to teach them how to pray to the Father, for they had come to see Him not only as a great teacher but also as the one whom the Father had sent as Messiah. Jesus responded by teaching them the Lord's Prayer, His way of petitioning the Father, a prayer that stands above all prayers because it is Jesus' unique way of praying to His Father in heaven and our Father as well. Certainly, the disciples knew how to pray, for the center of the liturgical life of Israel was a continuous cycle of prayers based on a very simple structure. What they wanted to learn was how to pray like Jesus prayed in the daily rhythm of their prayer life.

There were three essential prayers in the worship of Israel: (1) *blessing* God for His creation, (2) *thanking* God for His revelation of mercy, and (3) *petitioning* God to continue saving His people. When Jesus' disciples asked Jesus to teach them to pray, they used the word for *petition*. They wanted to know how to petition the Father as Jesus petitioned the Father. Daily prayer at fixed times of the day is petitionary prayer, that is, making our requests known to God at specific hours of the day. The Lord's Prayer is the perfect prayer of petition, the perfect way to ask God the Father for any need we could possibly have. Martin Luther said that "the Lord's Prayer is a prayer above all prayers, the greatest of all prayers, which has been taught by the greatest Master of all, in which all spiritual and bodily trouble is comprehended and which is the strongest consolation in all temptations, tribulations, and in the last hour."[19]

Do you find yourselves asking the same question the disciples asked of Jesus: "Teach us to pray"? Most people struggle with developing a regularized life of prayer, and that is true for pastors as well. Pastors have always been encouraged to take time out of their busy lives to read and meditate on Scripture, to pray for their people, their family, their friends, and for the world. A rich devotional life nourishes pastors in their pastoral work. And what is good for pastors is helpful for everyone. In our busy lives, however, it is difficult for all of us to find those quiet, reflective moments to address our Father in heaven with our petitions. So often it seems that we do not know quite how to say what we want to say to Him. We do well to consider how Christians have struggled through the centuries to "pray without ceasing" (1 Thessalonians 5:17). On Pentecost, after three thousand souls were added to the Church through Holy Baptism, it says that "they devoted themselves to the apostles' teaching and the fellowship, to the breaking of bread and the prayers" (Acts 2:42). Again, the word here for prayers is *petitionary* prayer, and certainly among their prayers that first Pentecost was the Lord's Prayer.

The Liturgy of the Hours is a daily remembrance of the world's story by embracing the same eschatological perspective found in both Sunday (weekly) and the Church Year (yearly). If Sunday and the Church Year provide the broad framework for our celebration of time, the Liturgy of the Hours (or the Divine Office) helps the Church mark its day by readings from

Scripture, singing of Psalms, and prayer. The Divine Service on Sunday with its special place in the Church Year gives meaning to the Liturgy of the Hours during the week. Although we may reorganize our offices of prayer in a way different from those who have gone before us, we still follow them using the same components as reading Scripture, singing psalms and hymns, and praying the prayers they have taught us while adding our own.

An investigation of the Divine Offices of Matins and Vespers, Morning and Evening Prayer illustrates how the Liturgy of the Hours might shape the devotional life of the Church. Christians have always set aside certain hours for prayer. For example, the *Didache* includes a church order used by missionaries from Antioch to plant churches. It was written between AD 40 and 60. In this order the faithful are instructed to pray the "Our Father"[20] three times a day. The main principle for a disciplined prayer life is simple: if one assigns hours for prayer, one will pray daily and regularly.

As early as third-century Rome, during the time of Hippolytus (around AD 215), these hours are associated with the Passion of Christ and the history of Israel. Perhaps the practice is even older, but Hippolytus is our earliest strong witness to a liturgy of the hours. His instructions in *Apostolic Tradition* are for all members of his congregation, and they mark the clear beginning of the Liturgy of the Hours, the Daily Office. Listen to these pastoral words from this third-century pastor to his people:

> And if you are at home, pray at the third hour and bless God [the third hour is 9 a.m.]. But if you are somewhere else at the moment, pray to God in your heart. For at that hour Christ was nailed to the tree. For this reason also in the Old (Testament) the Law prescribed that the shewbread should be offered continually as a type of the body and blood of Christ; and the slaughter of the lamb without reason is this type of the perfect lamb. For Christ is the shepherd, and also the bread which came down from heaven.
>
> Pray likewise at the time of the sixth hour [noon]. For when Christ was nailed to the wood of the cross, the day was divided, and darkness fell. And so at that hour let them pray a powerful prayer, imitating the voice of him who prayed and made all creation dark for the unbelieving Jews.
>
> And at the ninth hour [3 p.m.] let them pray also a great prayer and a great blessing, to know the way in which the soul of the righteous blesses God who does not lie, who remembered his saints and sent his word to give them light. For at that hour Christ was pierced in his side and poured out water and blood; giving

> light to the rest of the time of the day, he brought it to evening. Then, in beginning to sleep and making the beginning of another day, he fulfilled the type of the resurrection.
>
> Pray before your body rests on the bed. Rise about midnight, wash your hands with water, and pray. If your wife is present also, pray both together; if she is not yet among the faithful, go apart into another room and pray, and go back to bed again. Do not be lazy about praying. He who is bound in the marriage-bond is not defiled. . . .
>
> And likewise rise about cockcrow, and pray. For at that hour, as the cock crew, the children of Israel denied Christ, whom we know by faith, our eyes looking towards that day in the hope of eternal light at the resurrection of the dead.
>
> And if you act so, all you faithful, and remember these things, and teach them in your turn, and encourage the catechumens, you will not be able to be tempted or to perish, since you have Christ always in memory.[21]

Already in the third century, the hours of the day form the structure of prayer in the life of the believer. What is most remarkable about Hippolytus is that the rhythm of prayer is associated with Passion of Jesus (the third, sixth, and ninth hours), the death and resurrection of Christ (prayer at sunrise and sundown), and the last things (prayer before bedtime, which is eschatological). This is a well-ordered regimen of prayer urged on the faithful as part of their daily devotion to the Creator and Redeemer of all things. By the fourth century, Hippolytus' suggestions become what James White calls "the cathedral office . . . [the] daily services in the chief church of a city for the instruction in the Word, praise of God, and common prayer of all Christians."[22] In this cathedral office, we see the roots of our Matins and Vespers, our Morning and Evening Prayer, our Compline.

For 130 years, from AD 330 to 460, this cathedral office became the foundation for the devotional life of such major Church fathers as Augustine, Ambrose, Jerome, Basil, Gregory of Nyssa, Gregory of Nazianzus, John Chrysostom, Theodore of Mopsuestia, Cyril and Athanasius of Alexandria, and Cyril of Jerusalem, who were busy as bishops or theologians or both. St. Benedict in the sixth century formalized these offices into the monastic pattern of prayer that lasted until the 1960s and Vatican II, i.e. "Vespers (at the end of the working day), Compline (before bedtime), Nocturns or Vigil or Matins (middle of the night), Lauds (at daybreak), Prime (shortly thereafter),

Terce (middle of the morning), Sext (at noon), and None (middle of afternoon)."[23]

The Benedictine rhythm of prayer was rigorous, quickly becoming disassociated from the laity. That rhythm eventually comprised the exclusive prayers of the clergy. This unfortunate turn of events was reversed by Luther, who restored the Liturgy of the Hours to its proper place as the prayer services of the whole Church, laity and clergy alike. He returned the reading of Scripture to its original place as the major part of the liturgy from which flowed the psalms, hymns, and prayers of the Daily Office. The canticles of the Liturgy of the Hours were made simpler so people could sing them. Luther used the Daily Office as the foundation for his devotional life and his prayers.

We would be in good company if our prayer services found their place within the context of the Church's common prayer. To do this, we might return to using the Daily Office as the foundation for our daily, non-eucharistic services patterned after the daily prayers of early Christians. After all, James White's description of the cathedral office contains the essence of what we might consider the components of morning or evening prayer: "instruction in the Word, praise of God, and common prayer." The theological rationale of the Divine Office is worth considering.

The Liturgy of the Hours arose early in the Christian Church as a way for Christians to rehearse and retell the story of the world, to praise God for His mighty saving acts, and to petition the Father through the Son in its common prayer. Philip Pfatteicher in his *Commentary on the Lutheran Book of Worship* provides a summary statement of our peculiar Lutheran perspective on the Liturgy of the Hours, which was adopted by the North American Academy of Liturgy to describe the purpose and function of the Liturgy of the Hours. Pfatteicher writes:

> The mystery of God in Christ is the center of the liturgy of the church. By celebrating the Liturgy of the Hours at certain times of the day which recall creation and re-creation, the church, gathered together in the Holy Spirit, hears the life-giving Word of God and in response to it voices the praise of creation, joins the songs of heaven, shares in Christ's perpetual intercession for the world. This cycle of praise and prayer transforms our experience of time, deepening our understanding of how day and night can proclaim and celebrate the paschal mystery. Thus, the daily liturgy of the hours supplements and contrasts with the centrality of the Sunday Eucharist in the life of the church, edifying the one

holy people of God until all is fulfilled in the kingdom of heaven.[24]

There is something fundamentally sound about the theology of the Liturgy of the Hours that calls us back to it as the source of our services of prayer. As we pray Morning Prayer, we remember the resurrection of our Lord Jesus Christ and give thanks that He is the "rising Sun" of Malachi, the true "light of the world" of John's Gospel, and the "dawn from on high" of Zechariah's Benedictus.[25] Morning Prayer and Matins celebrate the newness of the morning that shows the triumph of light over darkness as Christ triumphed over the grave in rising from the dead. As we pray Evening Prayer, we remember that Christ has conquered death and darkness by going into the tomb for us. As the world lights its lamps and brings light into the darkness, we celebrate in the evening what we celebrated in the morning—that Christ is the light of the world. Evening Prayer recalls the ancient custom of Israel's life of prayer and devotion at the lighting of the lamps by families (described in Exodus 30) that became a Christian custom from the liturgy of Jerusalem.[26]

The natural rhythm of light and dark, of creation and re-creation in the Liturgy of the Hours continually reminds us of our re-creation in Christ in the waters of Holy Baptism. This pattern of nature provides the framework for our praise and prayer, for even our biological clocks are attuned to the rising and setting of the sun, and it seemed natural for many people in the history of the Church to pray on rising from their beds or in the evening when they retired for the night. And so the life of prayer of the people of God sanctifies the day in its movement from light to dark in the Liturgy of the Hours. In many ways, the Church's life of prayer is a continual renewal of time because time has been renewed in Christ.[27]

The challenge facing all of us in our busy, twenty-first-century world is how to make such a daily rhythm viable for us. Is the Liturgy of the Hours simply a quaint, historical remembrance for our Church that has little relevance to our lives? Recalling our previous discussion on the function of ritual in daily life, we know that without our daily rituals, we could not survive the many things that we attempt to accomplish in a day. Each one of us schedules things that are important to us, such as exercise or watching television or reading a book, and most important of all, time with our families and friends. These become routine, sometimes even mundane, like many household tasks such as cooking, cleaning, laundry, yard work, and car maintenance. But they are important to us—they are the very substance of our lives. Daily, weekly routines give our lives order in the midst of the chaotic busyness in which most of us live, and these routines allow us to survive and even thrive in this world of ours.

We all benefit from scheduling time for prayer and meditation, for listening to God's Word, and for silence. Even our secular world has awakened to this, which is why there is a movement within our culture for many different expressions of retreating from the busy schedules we keep to moments of contemplation and meditation, of deep breathing and silent retreat. The Christian Church has recognized this basic, human need from the beginning, and the Liturgy of the Hours is the Church's ancient response to help us make prayer a regular part of our lives where we join our Lord and His saints in Word and prayer.

This is not easy, however, and each person needs to decide for himself or herself how they might integrate daily, routine prayer into busy lives. Not many are able to do this as the ancient Church did, but stopping at 9 a.m. and noon and 3 p.m. to say the Lord's Prayer or some other brief prayer to recognize the Lord's hours on the cross takes little time and can offer a salutary reminder during the day that our lives are always lived under His cross. Scheduling prayer and reading of Scripture in the morning when one awakes or in the evening when one goes to bed is a simple way to observe the Liturgy of the Hours. Some congregations are even offering Morning or Evening Prayer on a regular basis so that people might pray in community.

Christians are the only ones in the world who know about the new creation in Christ, and what better way for them to tell the world the story of this new creation than to enter the rhythm of creation in their daily prayers and their Church Year observances? If the Church's prayer life is set by the daily cadence of Morning and Evening Prayer, and by the pulse of the Church Year, then we will rehearse for ourselves every day the marvelous Good News of the Father's love in sending His Son to redeem us from our sins. There will move within the community a story that takes on a fresh incarnation week in and week out.[28]

8

Baptism: Entrance into the Divine Service

Since the Early Church, full participation in the Divine Service in both Word and Sacrament was only for the baptized, even though those not baptized were welcome to hear the Word of God with the community. To take part fully in the Divine Service one needs to be baptized. Baptism is the "frontier" sacrament upon which all of Christian life is founded.[1] Thus it is important for us to describe the significance of Baptism in the life of the Church as entrance into full communion with Christ through the Divine Service.

The foundational picture of Baptism is both a journey with Christ to Jerusalem and our participation with Him in His suffering, death, and resurrection. However, Baptism is so rich that it may be explained from many viewpoints. This chapter will explore Baptism as a rite of passage—a rite of Christian initiation. Further, we will delve into the New Testament to see how St. Luke the evangelist shows Baptism to be a process, beginning with John's Baptism and culminating in Christian Baptism at Pentecost. From there we will move to the Early Church. Early Christians developed their baptismal practices from the Scriptures, and so it is important for us to see how they incorporated the New Testament into the world in which they lived, first within Jewish culture, then within Gentile culture. This will also include a description of the rite of Holy Baptism in the Early Church with all its rich biblical foundations. Baptism was a multifaceted, sensory experience, and this fit well the Mediterranean world of early Christianity. Next, we will describe Luther's baptismal rites. As we would expect, Luther's understanding of Baptism is intensely biblical, intensely Christ-centered, yet deeply imprinted by late medieval culture. Finally, with all that data in hand, we will consider a proposal for Baptism in our time and our unique cultural context.

Christ's Journey from Heaven and back to Heaven[2]

The Gospels record the narrative of Jesus' journey from heaven to earth and back to heaven. Jesus descended from heaven to become one of us. He was conceived by the Holy Spirit and born of the Virgin Mary, baptized by John in the Jordan River, to live among us as teacher and miracle worker and rejected prophet, to die our death on a cross, to be buried in the earth, to rise from the dead on the third day, and to ascend back to heaven on the fortieth day. This movement from heaven to earth to heaven is described in the transfiguration as Jesus' "exodus" He is about to fulfill in Jerusalem (Luke 9:31) as He dies on the cross, descends into the earth in the tomb, rises out of the earth and ascends back to heaven. This is the new exodus, where Jesus does what Israel did not and could not do throughout the Old Testament. Jesus' journey from heaven to earth to heaven may be pictured as a divine invasion from one world into another world that knew Him not and then back to the world from which He came.

The Path of Jesus in the Nicene Creed

The Nicene Creed captures this journey best as Jesus invades our cosmos:

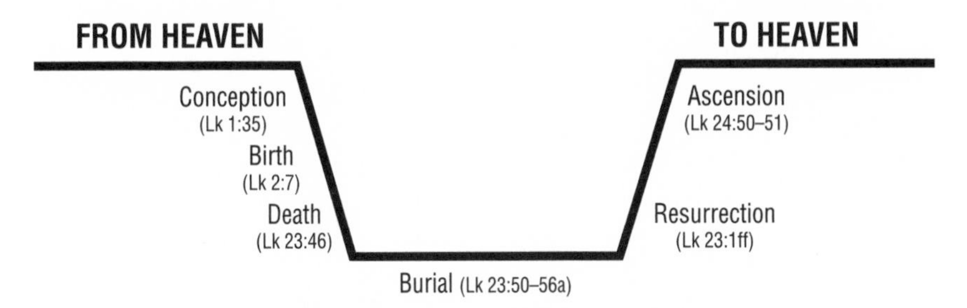

There are many journeys in the Old Testament, such as Abraham's pilgrimage from Ur of the Chaldees to the land promised him by God. These trips are not self-initiated but responses to God's call, travels under His guidance, aimed toward the destination He designates. God accompanies the pilgrims and promises to meet them in grace. The most important journey is the exodus, as the children of Israel travel from Egypt through the Red Sea, sojourn in the wilderness for forty years, and finally arrive in the Promised Land and ultimately in Jerusalem, where God's presence will reside in the tabernacle and then the temple. Israel's journey to the Promised Land was rehearsed every year at the Passover as Israelites from around the world journeyed to Jerusalem to eat a lamb that had been sacrificed in the temple and whose blood was poured out on the altar where God was present for salvation.

The psalms of ascent (Psalms 120–134) celebrate that annual journey to Jerusalem. Indeed, the entire Old Testament revolves around the journey of God's people to Jerusalem and God's promise to meet them there. Similarly, the entire Christian life may be viewed as a pilgrimage to the new Jerusalem, a journey to follow Christ into the heavenly sanctuary. The Old Testament sacrificial system awaited completion when God would fulfill His promise and return to Jerusalem in the flesh as the final *once-for-all-sacrifice* for the sins of the world. When Jesus speaks of His destiny as a journey to the Holy City of Jerusalem and turns His face to go there (Luke 9:51), those who know the Old Testament would see that the final "exodus" (Luke 9:31) was imminent. Jesus was the journeying prophet, ever in motion, ever homeless with no place to lay His head (Luke 9:58) except on a cross in Jerusalem.

Jerusalem, the City of Jesus' Destiny

The significance of Jerusalem as the goal of the journey of God's Old Testament people and their Messiah cannot be overemphasized. Each Gospel ends in Jerusalem with the death and resurrection of Jesus. Along the way, Jesus teaches His disciples about Himself and the kingdom of God. Jesus uses the journey as a time of teaching to help them understand the meaning of both past and future events, and to help them understand their Baptism, their mission, and His ongoing presence among them in the Lord's Supper. During this journey Jesus also reveals to us in words and deeds that He is the Messiah; that He must suffer, die, and rise from the dead; and that He will continue to be present with us through His Spirit.

Jesus' destiny is Jerusalem. Although for some in our culture the word *destiny* has taken on the meaning of "fate," it is a worthy expression of Jesus' destination in Jerusalem according to the predetermined plan of the Trinity for the redemption of the world. Jesus' destiny was ordained from the moment of His conception—and even before the foundation of the world (Ephesians 1:4–12)—for His destiny in Jerusalem is part of the Father's cosmic plan of re-creating the world. He will do this through the descent and ascent of His holy Son, Jesus, who was anointed with the Spirit at His Baptism to equip Him for His public ministry until His death. Throughout the Gospels this inexorable destiny waiting for Jesus in the Holy City is described. At 12 years old, Jesus knows His destiny is to be in His Father's house doing His Father's business. Satan tries to prevent Him from fulfilling His destiny of crucifixion by tempting Him in the wilderness (Luke 4:1–13) and again on the Mount of Olives (Luke 22:39–46), but Jesus conquered these temptations to bypass the cross, thereby anticipating His final victory. His destiny is clear: three times Jesus tells His disciples that He must suffer, die, and rise in Jerusalem.

In Baptism Christians Journey with Christ

Life is a journey from birth to death. For Christians, life is a pilgrimage from Baptism to death, which will be our entrance into full communion with Christ. St. Paul describes Baptism as a journey through death and burial with Christ to a resurrection into everlasting life (Romans 6). In the waters of Holy Baptism, the Christian gets death over with as he dies and is buried with Christ and is reborn to new life in Christ that never ends. Because Jesus has gone before us through the cross and tomb, we now rest assured that our journey in Baptism with Him will result in the destiny Jesus intends for us all: life in a resurrected body that knows no end.

Along the way to full communion with Christ in heaven, Christians live under the cross, where we are continually *in Christ*, hearing His Holy Word and feeding upon the holy food of His body and blood to sustain us on our journey. Our pilgrimage reaches completion just beyond our physical death, which is a portal through which we pass into *full communion with Christ* in His heavenly home. The goal of the journey is to live in Christ's presence forever and to feast at His table for eternity. The Christian pilgrimage is one that retraces the steps of Christ's journey, toward the inheritance and the heavenly communion and feast He has won for all. And it all begins with Baptism!

The life of Jesus is the prototype of the life Christians lead as catechumens—as students and disciples of Christ. Christian life, then, is also a journey from conversion and Baptism to the Lord's Supper. Baptized into Christ, we repeat this journey each week, recalling our Baptism as we prepare for the Supper. Hearing the words of Jesus in the Gospels is the perfect means for us to journey with Christ from His Baptism to the Last Supper and from His conception to His ascension to heaven. By journeying along the same "way" that Christ traveled, we receive fuller instruction about the mysteries of His Baptism and participation in the Lord's Supper. We journey from our second baptismal birth toward the heavenly wedding feast (Revelation 19:6–9).

Baptized into Christ, we also repeat this journey yearly. From Advent through Christmas we celebrate the dawn of His invasion into our world as He is born of the Virgin Mary. We continue to proclaim His revelation as the light of the world in Epiphany. Then we journey with Him into the desert to be tempted by Satan as our Lenten pilgrimage begins. It leads us to Jerusalem, where we suffer with Him on Good Friday, take a Sabbath rest during His rest in the tomb, and then rise with Him on Easter morning. For forty days we rejoice in our resurrected lives until we celebrate His journey back to heaven on Ascension, only to celebrate once more ten days later on Pentecost that He continues to be among us in His flesh by His Spirit.

Jesus is the itinerant, wandering missionary, ever *journeying* to the time and place of His "exodus" (Luke 9:31). And He is set before the eyes of the people who, likewise, are *in motion*—crowds, disciples, and apostles. They are people moving or being moved—from unbelief to faith, from an inquiring interest in Jesus to Baptism, to participation in the Lord's Supper, and to full communion with Christ in heaven at the end of their pilgrimage. It is to such hearers in Jesus' day and in ours that the evangelist might say: "Pilgrim, look at Jesus! See Him with eyes opened by baptismal waters; see Him with your ears as you hear the testimony of the Scriptures proclaimed, and as you eat and drink the Supper He has prepared for you." The Epistle to the Hebrews has a memorable exhortation to pilgrims trekking by faith through this world toward the world to come:

> Therefore, since we are surrounded by so great a cloud of witnesses, let us also lay aside every weight, and sin which clings so closely, and let us run with endurance the race that is set before us, looking to Jesus, the founder and perfecter of our faith, who for the joy that was set before Him endured the cross, despising the shame, and is seated at the right hand of the throne of God (Hebrews 12:1–2).

What Is Christian Initiation?

There are a number of ways to look at Baptism. It has been called the "frontier" sacrament because it begins life in Christ that is sustained during this lifelong pilgrimage to heaven through hearing the Word of God and receiving the Lord's Supper. The rite of Baptism is a simple act of applying water in the name of the Father, Son, and Holy Spirit through which the Spirit creates a life in Christ that knows no end. Baptism is nothing more and nothing less than this simple moment of water, Word, and Spirit. But surrounding this simple act of baptizing is a complex set of words and actions that highlight this entrance into a life by removing one from another life. That is why some call Baptism a rite of Christian initiation, because Baptism begins life in Christ as we are separated from the life we lived before Christ. In this way, Baptism is a "rite of passage." As discussed in chapter 3, rites of passage have three parts; *separation* from the old life, *transition* to a new life by means of some ritualized act, and *incorporation* into a new life.[3]

Baptism as Rite of Passage

Baptism is the supreme rite of passage because of what God does in Baptism as Paul describes in Romans 6, Ephesians 5, and Colossians 2. To be sure, separation, transition, and incorporation are ongoing aspects of the Christian life. Each continues throughout earthly life as the Christian daily repents, remembers his Baptism and Christ's promises, and leads the new life in the Spirit in communion with the whole Church. Separation, transition, and incorporation continue until death and Christ's return, when the body shall be raised incorruptible and the Christian shall enjoy full and direct communion in the unveiled presence of God.

Separation

With that in mind, we may still speak of major stages in the Christian life, stages that can be characterized as predominately separation, transition, or incorporation. *Separation* begins when one hears the Gospel and comes to believe through the power of the Holy Spirit that Jesus Christ is the way out of death to life. For baptized infants, separation and transition both occur in Baptism. But for adults, the Church, following New Testament practice, enjoins a period of instruction and catechesis prior to Baptism in order to teach all that faith in Jesus Christ entails.[4] It is a way of life calling for separation from the sinful practices of natural man. The new Christian life must be understood in light of God's unified revelation in the Old and New Testaments. In other words, catechesis involves instruction in how Jesus thinks (because this is how God thinks) and how Jesus lived, particularly the mercy and compassion He showed toward our dying world, which needs to be freed from its bondage. This catechesis is Christological in its instruction and in the lifestyle it inculcates. It is similar to Jesus' catechesis of the Twelve and the seventy(-two) with respect to their proclamation and behavior (Luke 9:1–6; 10:1–24).

Transition

Transition into fuller communion with Christ and His Church comes at the moment of Baptism—a water bath that brings a deep and complete cleansing within by Word and Spirit. Baptism moves a person across a boundary from one status to another, effecting a transformation from darkness to light, from being a child of Adam and of Satan into new birth as a child of God. Those baptized enter a heavenly community where they *now* receive the gifts of heaven and look forward to the consummation and full enjoyment of those gifts at death and the second coming of Christ. Baptism into Christ is *death* to the old world as Paul proclaims in Romans 6 and *resurrection* into the new one as Jesus describes in John 3.

In the earliest Christian communities, Baptism was rich in its theological and liturgical depth. It often began with an anointing with olive oil intended to represent the casting out of Satan and cleansing. After the actual Baptism in the font, it often ended with chrism: an anointing with perfumed oil. The similarity of the Greek words *chrism* (χρίσμα) and *Christ* (χριστός) accented the Christological character of Baptism, so the newly baptized are properly called "Christs," similar to Luther's intent when he said that through Holy Baptism we are "little Christs." The newly baptized have been anointed ("christed") so that they are ever after identified with Jesus, the Christ, which is why they are now called "Christians." Oil was applied in the Old Testament anointing that prefigured the Messiah—the Anointed One. In the Mediterranean world even today, oil is a staple in cooking, bathing, and healing. In the public baths in the ancient world, it was difficult to imagine bathing without both oil and water. Thus, it was not unusual for the baptismal bath to be accompanied by anointing with oil since both water and oil had biblical and cultural connotations.

Incorporation

Incorporation comes most visibly in the Lord's Supper. The baptized, who are in communion with Christ through Baptism, continue to be sustained and nourished by God in that communion in our very bodies through the holy eating of Jesus' body and blood. The baptized are preserved to life everlasting in their status as "Christs" through Holy Communion in Christ's body and blood. In the Lord's Supper, heaven and earth are joined together in the flesh of Jesus as angels, archangels, and all the saints worship the Lamb who was slain and raised again. Communion in Christ and participation in His flesh at the ongoing feast means communion with the end-time community of heaven, including those we have loved who have already gone to Christ, and all the saints here on earth in every place.

Christian Initiation

This passage that involves separation/catechesis, transition/Baptism, and incorporation/Supper may be called Christian initiation. The process of evangelization that sent the Church into the highways and byways to seek the lost (Luke 14) and proclaim the Gospel of release (Luke 4) had as its goal the enrollment into this process of initiation that begins with catechesis and comes to fruition with Baptism and Supper. The rhythm of the early Christian communities was the rhythm of evangelization, catechesis, Baptism, and Supper. This pattern was established by the earthly ministry of Christ Himself, in fulfillment of the pattern of the Old Testament. This pattern of Christian initiation continues in our churches today, which is why evangelical Lutheran churches see themselves as evangelical precisely because they are churches that center their life in Baptism, and all activity in reaching the lost and catechizing them culminates in the rite of Holy Baptism and the reception of the Lord's Supper. How different this is from much of American evangelicalism where Baptism is not perceived as central, even essential, to the mission of the Church.

Since the pattern of evangelization, catechesis, Baptism, and Lord's Supper comes from the New Testament itself, and in particular, from the ministry of Jesus and in fulfillment of Old Testament patterns, the Early Church continued it in the mission to both Jews and Gentiles alike. The Early Church saw no alternative, no other way to bring those from the highways and byways into the Church through Baptism than to continue the New Testament pattern.[5]

The Liturgy of Life

The question before Christians in all places and at all times is this: "What does it mean to live in Christ in the world around me, in the world as I know it?" It's a question of priesthood, and a priest stands between God and man. All Christians are priests who live, according to St. Paul, "to present your bodies as a living sacrifice, holy and acceptable to God, which is your spiritual worship" (Romans 12:1). To live in Christ is also to exercise one's priesthood in the world. It is to tell the world that Jesus Christ is present in our world in His gifts through us, through our lives of sacrifice and mercy as we love our neighbors as ourselves, interceding for them before

God with our prayers and our praise. These gifts we have through His flesh given to our flesh as the place and instrument of His presence. Eating and drinking the body and blood of Jesus is how we proclaim Christ's death until He makes Himself visible to the whole world. Jesus Christ is available to the world through the Church by the Holy Spirit through us. This Spirit is never detached from the person of Jesus Christ, and to know and believe in Jesus by the Spirit is a human, flesh-and-spirit knowing, and not some sort of "spirit knowing." Since our bodies are a "temple of the Holy Spirit" (1 Corinthians 6:19), Christ dwells in us and we dwell in Him by the Spirit, and as Christ's people we stand in the midst of a broken world as the presence of Christ to that world because, as the baptized, we bear witness in our words and lives to the Christ who dwells in us. Our lives testify that Christ's presence in the world transforms the culture and makes it new. Christ is present in the world through us, and He is present for the life of the world.

Baptism in Luke-Acts

Baptism into Christ is the sacrament through which we enter into the Christian Church. Baptized in Jesus' name, we experience what Jesus Himself experienced: we die with Him, are buried with Him, and are raised with Him (Romans 6:1–4; Colossians 2:11–13). Clothed with Christ (Galatians 3:27), His righteousness becomes ours (2 Corinthians 5:21). Therefore, to understand Christian Baptism, one first must understand Christ's own Baptism, His life, His death, and His resurrection. For this reason, it is necessary first to understand John's ministry of preparation.

John's Baptism

John's Baptism cleanses the people to make them ready to meet the Messiah when He comes. This cleansing comes through repentance and a Baptism into the forgiveness of sins. John's preaching is a call to repentance (Luke 3:7–9). John, like Jesus, is a lightning rod separating Israel into two groups: those faithfully waiting for the Messiah and those who have created for themselves something they believe is an alternative means of salvation, something which glorifies themselves and from which they are not willing to *turn* in repentance. In John's own words, he baptizes with water only (Luke 3:16), but Jesus will baptize with the Holy Spirit and fire (Luke 3:16).

Jesus' Baptism in the Jordan (Luke 3:21)

John prepares for Jesus and gives way to Him, since Jesus is the greater, yet John is a fundamental part of the process of salvation. It is Matthew who records that the fulfillment of righteousness comes *through both John and Jesus*: "It is fitting for us [John and Jesus] to fulfill all righteousness" (Matthew 3:15). John brings the Old Testament to completion; Jesus inaugurates the New Testament era. The opening of the heavens at Jesus' Baptism is the occasion for the Holy Spirit to come upon Him, His Baptism with the Spirit. Jesus has two baptisms, one by water, the other by fire. So also there are two openings of heaven at Jesus' baptisms. Since the temple curtain separated the Holy of Holies from the more earthly worship spaces, the opening of the heavens parallels the rending of the curtain at the death of Jesus (Luke 23:45), for His death is His Baptism of fire. The opening of heaven at Jesus' Baptism means that it will forever be opened to all humanity through the flesh of Christ by the Spirit of Christ.

The Holy Spirit Descends and the Father Speaks (Luke 3:22)

Jesus stands in the Jordan, ready to embark on His mission to redeem all creation. His way has been properly prepared by John. While He is praying after His Baptism, the Holy Spirit, in bodily form as a dove, descends upon Him and the voice of the heavenly Father proclaims Him the beloved Son. His mission is the will and the work of the triune God. As the Spirit is poured out on Jesus, so also He will pour out the Spirit on those He baptizes—those who are baptized in His name.

Along with the Spirit, the fire of God's wrath is also placed on Jesus at His Baptism, because Jesus is baptized with the Baptism intended for sinners who need repentance and cleansing. Jesus takes the place of sinners and begins His public ministry as the Lamb of God, the bearer of the world's sin. The fire of God's wrath placed upon Jesus will reach its full and complete fury at His crucifixion. Already in His Baptism, Jesus begins to journey to Jerusalem where His blood is poured out on behalf of all (Luke 22:20) and God's anger at sin—the fire of His wrath (Isaiah 66:15–16; Psalm 79:5–6; cf. Isaiah 29:6; Luke 3:17)—burns against Jesus, the bearer of the world's sins in His flesh. The Spirit who descends on Jesus is the same Spirit John referred to when he spoke of the Mightier One who is coming to baptize "with the Holy Spirit and with fire" (Luke 3:16) and the same Spirit who will be poured out on the Church at Pentecost. "Spirit" and "fire" are seen first in their coming upon Jesus.

The Fire of God's Wrath at the Crucifixion (Luke 12:49–50; 23:33–46)

As "the Anointed One," the "Messiah," the "Christ," Jesus stands in the waters of the Jordan both in solidarity with us and in substitution for us. From this moment on, Jesus is marked as the one to bear God's wrath that burns with "unquenchable fire" (Luke 3:17). Jesus' Baptism begins His public work as the Second Adam (Romans 5:12–21). The same Spirit that hovered over the waters at creation and gave life to the first Adam (Genesis 1:2; 2:7) now descends to participate in the work of re-creation through Jesus, the Father's "beloved Son" (Luke 3:22), the new Adam. Not without coincidence, Jesus' work of solidarity with Adam's fallen race begins with Jesus "full of the Holy Spirit . . . led by the Spirit in the wilderness" (Luke 4:1), being tempted in the wilderness (Luke 4:2). He will do what Adam and Eve and Israel could not do and we cannot do: be faithful to the Father in all things, even unto death, and therefore conquer the tempter. His Spirit-filled Baptism launches Him as the bearer of the Spirit in this work of obedience to the Father in all things.

Later in the Gospel, Jesus refers to His work as involving Baptism and fire: "I came to cast fire on the earth, and would that it were already kindled! I have a baptism to be baptized with, and how great is My distress until it is accomplished!" (Luke 12:49–50). Jesus' ministry begins and ends with Baptism (Luke 3:21–22; 12:49–50; 23:33–46). Jesus' water Baptism begins His ministry, and Jesus' "baptism" (Luke 12:49–50) on the cross at the end of His earthly public ministry is a bloody one. The fire of the full wrath of God against the entire sin of humankind rests on Him, and He bears it willingly, even to the point of shedding of His blood (Luke 12:49–50; 23:33–46).

In Scripture, fire can be portrayed as both destructive and purifying (e.g., Malachi 3:1–5). At Jesus' crucifixion, the fire of God's wrath is *destructive*. While Abraham's beloved son narrowly escaped being sacrificed as a whole burnt offering (Genesis 22), God's beloved Son will be consumed in the fire of God's wrath. Those who are joined to Him in a death and resurrection like His are free from that condemnation. Thus they are *purified* as they become children of Abraham through Baptism (Galatians 3:26–29). The "fire" of the Mightier One who comes baptizing "with the Holy Spirit and with fire" (Luke 3:16) includes both the judgment fire of hell for those who refuse to repent (Luke 16:19–31) and the purifying, sanctifying fire of the Spirit poured out on Pentecost as "tongues as of fire" (Acts 2:3).

Christian Baptism at Pentecost after the Resurrection and Ascension

When Jesus rises from the dead as the new Adam, He brings all creation with Him. At the ascension, Jesus makes no mention of the destructive fire when speaking of John's Baptism and Christian Baptism because the wrath of God has been quenched at the cross, and Christian Baptism will pour out the purifying fire of the Spirit. The Spirit brings those baptized into the Body of Christ, which is a necessary prerequisite for feasting on Christ's body and blood in the Supper. The Spirit also brings the Father's love and approval (Luke 3:22), because God's wrath was satiated when Jesus died on the cross and was raised again. Now for the baptized, the fire of God is not *destructive*, as it was at the cross, but *purifying*. In Christian Baptism, fire purifies the newly baptized of his or her impurities. Spirit and fire are inseparable after the ascension as Pentecost so graphically illustrates:

> And suddenly there came from heaven a sound like a mighty rushing wind, and it filled the entire house where they were sitting. And divided tongues as of fire appeared to them and rested on each one of them. And they were all filled with the Holy Spirit and began to speak in other tongues as the Spirit gave them utterance. (Acts 2:2–4)

Christian Baptism, then, will include water, Spirit, and fire.

Pentecost marks the starting point when the Spirit will now be poured out from the exalted Christ upon His Church, and when the Spirit will bring people into union with Christ through preaching and Baptism. There is a clean movement from John's baptism in the Jordan, to Jesus' Baptism, to the "baptism" of Jesus' Passion and death, to Jesus' resurrection and ascension, to Pentecost, and to Christian Baptism after Pentecost. In reality, these events must be understood together as embraced in the whole sweep of God's baptismal activity. John's Baptism prepared the Jews for their initiation into the Body of Christ. At Pentecost John's Baptism gives way to Christian Baptism, which embraces and draws on the fact that the Spirit came upon Jesus at His Baptism, the fire of God's wrath consumed Jesus at His crucifixion, and God's wrath was quenched by Jesus' bloody "baptism" (Luke 12:50) at the Place of the Skull. After Pentecost, the Spirit of Jesus now rests upon the apostolic Church and is poured forth from that Church as the apostles baptize "in the name of Jesus."

Christian Baptism encompasses John's Baptism, since Christian Baptism also is one of repentance for the forgiveness of sins (Acts 2:38; Luke

3:3). But Christian Baptism is much more because it is our entrance into the Body of Christ that bears the Spirit. In Christian Baptism, water, Spirit, and fire are combined in the believer's incorporation into the Body of Christ, the Church. Christ is now the baptizer in His Church's ministry as those baptized with water, Word, and the fire of the Spirit become members of His Body.[6]

The New Testament World of Christian Initiation

The rich contours of Baptism in the New Testament gave birth to the rites of Baptism in the early Christian Church. There were two dominant images of Baptism that began to emerge out of the New Testament documents. Baptism was perceived either as rebirth, echoing the words of Jesus to Nicodemus in John's Gospel that "Truly, truly, I say to you, unless one is born of water and the Spirit, he cannot enter the kingdom of God" (John 3:5), or as death and resurrection, as St. Paul writes: "Do you not know that all of us who have been baptized into Christ Jesus were baptized into His death? We were buried therefore with Him by baptism into His death, in order that, just as Christ was raised from the dead by the glory of the Father, we too might walk in newness of life" (Romans 6:3–4).

Rebirth and Dying and Rising with Christ

These images of Baptism as rebirth and death and resurrection dominated the thinking of early Christians who portrayed water and the Spirit in their depictions of early Christian Baptism. Baptism was indeed a rite of passage from death to life through a watery tomb, a rebirth that came about through water and the Spirit. Baptism, as the word itself means in its most basic sense, is a cleansing, a bath, where through God's Word the Holy Spirit is present to transform us from sinners into saints, to bring us out of darkness into light, to deliver us from eternal death into a life that has no end.

Bathing Practices in the Ancient World

Bathing practices in the ancient world give us a window into the Early Church's understanding of Baptism. Although many houses had indoor plumbing, most of them did not have the facilities for bathing. Roman citizens bathed in public baths provided throughout the cities and towns. Unlike the customs of many Americans today (but similar to the customs of some cultures outside the United States), people bathed once a week instead of once a day. To bathe in the ancient world meant to wash with water and anoint with oil. This may even be reflected in the customs of the Old Testament where, for example, Naomi sends Ruth to Boaz with the instructions to "wash therefore and anoint yourself" (Ruth 3:3). Oil was used as a substitute for soap, cleansing the body and sealing it from being easily soiled again. Oftentimes, among the more wealthy Romans, this oil was perfumed so that the effects of the bath would last longer. In some cultures today, scented oil in the form of colognes and perfumes are used because people do not bathe every day. Even in our culture, many of the cosmetic products are oil-based, providing the same protection from bodily odors that was provided the ancient world from their use of perfumed oils.

What is harder for us to relate to is the widespread use of oil in the Mediterranean cultures of the ancient world. Olive oil was a staple in the first century. People cooked in oil, spread it on their bodies for medicinal purposes, and bathed in it. Even today, while driving through Spain or Italy or Greece, one will frequently come upon miles and miles of olive groves. Therefore, when we look at the early Christian rites, we see the use of both water and oil in Baptism, since Baptism was a bath where sins were washed away as bodies were immersed in water and anointed with oil. Water and oil were inseparable for early Christians in Baptism because one could not imagine bathing without using water and oil; it was a self-evident part of washing.

Anointed in the Holy Spirit

There was another reason for using oil in Baptism that provided rich theological foundations for its use in early Christian baptismal rites. Oil was used in anointing kings and in other rituals where people and things were set apart for special purposes. The word *Messiah* in the Hebrew means "the anointed one," which when translated into Greek is the word *Christ*. Thus Christ is "the anointed one" because He is sent into the world to establish the kingdom of God. He is the King of the kingdom, reigning from a cross where He is coronated with a crown of thorns. Jesus is not anointed with perfumed olive oil, as the kings of Israel were before Him, but with the Holy Spirit, as Peter tells Cornelius: "God anointed Jesus of Nazareth with the Holy Spirit and with power" (Acts 10:38). This anointing occurred at Jesus' Baptism, where the Spirit came upon Jesus in bodily form as a dove, and the Father boomed in a loud voice, "You are My beloved Son; with You I am well pleased" (Luke 3:21–22).

To symbolize the anointing of the Holy Spirit in Christian Baptism, early Christians did what came naturally to them after bathing with water: they anointed with perfumed oil called "chrism." This oil acknowledged the reality that through water and the Word the Holy Spirit has come down upon the newly baptized and anointed him to be united with Christ in a death and resurrection like His. Christ now dwells in him and he dwells in Christ. Here again the Greek word for perfumed oil, *chrism*, sounds like the Greek word for Christ, showing the newly baptized is just like Christ, or as Luther said, he is a "little Christ."

Baptisteries and Fonts in the Ancient World

Not only did early Christians engage in symbolism in their use of oil with water in the rite of Holy Baptism, but they shaped their fonts to show what they believed about Baptism. As we have already described, for the first three hundred years of Christianity, Christians worshiped in their homes, small spaces that accommodated fifty to one hundred people. Following the practices of bathing in the ancient world, baptisms used as much water as possible, though the mode of application could be pouring, immersion, or even the use of water coming out of a wall or spigot as in a shower. The preferred method, however, was in a bath or tub, with liberal amounts of water. Baptism was generally done in the nude, and even though early Christians were accustomed to nakedness in the public baths, in their baptismal practices they were always discreet. Baptisms took place during the worship services but privately in another room that came to be known as the baptistery. The male priests and bishops would baptize men, but women deaconesses would actually assist in the baptisms of women while the priest or bishop stood behind a screen and pronounced the words as the water was applied. In the early Christian worship services in the house, these were small rooms attached to the larger room where the assembly gathered. These "bath rooms" were the place for washing and now became the place for Baptism.

As Christianity became a legal religion and Christian churches were built, baptisteries were constructed outside the church building as a separate place for Baptism. Many of these became filled with the images and symbolism of Baptism. They were considered "paradise" for the newly baptized. Here the baptized returned to the Garden of Eden through the waters of Baptism as they were united to Christ, the new Adam, whose incarnation, death, resurrection, and ascension showed them what true humanity looked like. This humanity was restored to them through the sacrament of Holy Baptism.

The baptistery in Ravenna, Italy, for example, is adorned with rich mosaics that portray the Garden of Eden, for this is the place of the creation restored and made new in Christ. Those who are by nature sinful and unclean by their birth into a fallen world are cleansed here and made new in this paradise restored.

Baptismal fonts provided another opportunity to portray the rich theological traditions of the New Testament. The very place where water was applied and the Spirit poured out with God's Word becomes filled with symbolic meaning. The most common shape for baptismal fonts were in the shape of a cross, showing the cruciform shape of Baptism as we die and rise with Christ. The font in Kelibia, Tunisia, a now found in the museum at Tunis, shows a four-sided shape that clearly represents the cross of Christ.

Baptismal font from Kelibia, Tunisia

The font is deep, with places for people to sit as they enter the waters. A Chi-Rho at the base of the font, the first two letters from the Greek word for Christ, shows that this is a Baptism into Christ. There is also an Alpha and an Omega, the first and last letters of the Greek alphabet, a symbol of eternity but also of Christ, who calls Himself the Alpha and Omega in the Book of Revelation (1:8). There are also images of fish and animals and plants throughout the font—images of paradise in a creation God had created good and re-created after the fall by His presence in the creation as the Creator. The cruciform font in Bulla Regia, also in Tunisia, clearly shows another picture of the font as a cross, as well as some of the fonts in Ephesus where Paul founded a church in the first century.

The author kneeling at the font in the baptistery of St. John's Church in Ephesus.

One of the baptisteries in Ephesus, as well as many others in the ancient world, was eight-sided. The number eight was the number that signified eternity in the ancient world, corresponding to the practice of circumcision that occurred on the eighth day after birth. Early Christians understood that in Baptism, they died with Christ and rose with Him to a life that never ends. This took place in an eight-sided eternal space to help proclaim the full meaning of their Baptism.

The world of the early Christian communities provided the backdrop for the theology of Baptism in the New Testament to come to life in a rich expression of rite and space. The rites themselves are a window into the full meaning of Christian Baptism.

The Rite of Holy Baptism in Early Christianity

The world of the New Testament and the early Christian Church was much different from the world in which we live. You can discover this for yourself by simply visiting Jerusalem or Rome or Athens and experiencing that even today the people in these cultures react to things differently than we do. We are truly children of the Enlightenment, that is, we process the things in our culture through our minds and emotions, and the signals that come to us through our senses are secondary. Unlike the culture of the first centuries of the Christian Church and those of the Mediterranean world today, we tend to trust only those things that come to us through our minds, not realizing that our senses together with our minds will provide the richest experience of reality for us. The early Christian rites will surprise you by their sensuousness, that is, that they communicated the simple act of washing with water, Word, and Spirit through a complex use of the senses. If you were to trace the baptismal practices of the Early Church through history, what would strike you more than anything else is that the earliest rites of water, Word, and Spirit involved both the body and the mind through the senses.

The early baptismal practices form the foundation of our baptismal life today, even though we no longer use many of these practices. By examining these rites, we are not in any way suggesting that we must return to performing Baptism as they did in the Early Church. The reason to examine them is to help uncover in our own practices the deep theological meaning of Baptism as it is portrayed in the earliest baptismal rites.

The Church of the Resurrection in Jerusalem

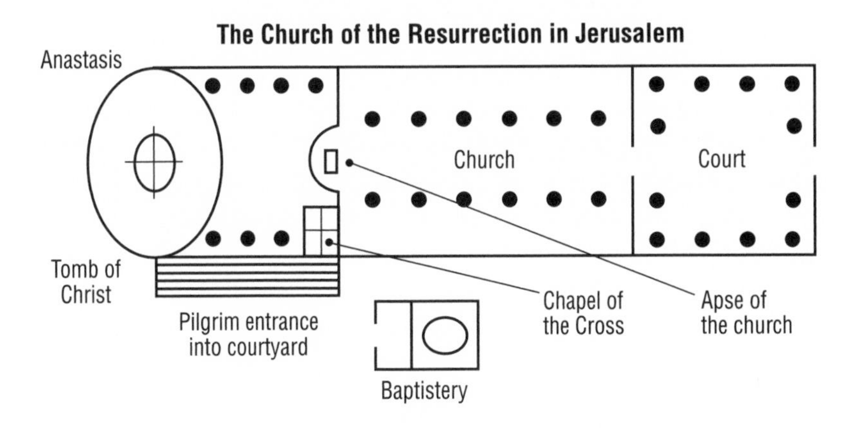

In describing the early rites, we will use the Church of the Resurrection in Jerusalem (AD 350–400) as an example. This was the church built by Emperor Constantine. Today the Church of the Holy Sepulchre stands on the foundations of Constantine's church. We have much data about the baptismal practices of Cyril of Jerusalem who recorded the baptismal rites of the Jerusalem church in the fourth century in his mystagogical catecheses (the word *mystagogical* refers to the mysteries of Baptism and the Lord's Supper). We also have the memoirs of a traveling nun, a pilgrim, from southern Spain called Egeria, who traveled to Jerusalem, witnessed the liturgy of the fourth century, and recorded in great detail what went on in the liturgical life in Jerusalem. The Church of the Resurrection is especially helpful since archaeologists believe that Constantine was able to build this church on both the place where Jesus died as well as the empty tomb from whence He rose from the dead. The rite we will describe will be a conflation of fourth-century rites, but it will serve as a summary of all that might have been possible at Baptism at this time in the Church's life. As a way of illustrating these rites, we will use the three phases of a rite of passage to describe the complex events that comprised the baptizing of adults and infants in the early Christian churches.

Separation—Catechesis

One of the vast differences between now and then is that those who came for Baptism were adults with their children. Adult Baptism was the norm, since most of the world was still composed of pagan unbelievers. The Church was just coming out of three hundred years of persecution in which it had to be very careful who was allowed to enter into the Church. What a disaster to bring someone quickly to the font for Baptism with that person not realizing that such an act would set one against the authorities and lead to persecution and even death! And what a tragedy for someone who came quickly to Baptism and then, when persecuted, betrayed the Christian community to the authorities, which could lead to widespread persecutions throughout the Church!

Like us, early Christians believed that conversion was instantaneous, that is, a person heard from another person that Jesus was the Christ, the Savior of the world who had died on Calvary, rose from the dead, and ascended into the heavens, and then on the basis of this witness the Holy Spirit worked faith in that person. All Early Church evangelization was one-on-one, Christians testifying to their unbelieving neighbors about the hope that was within them. But this instantaneous conversion took time to nurture. This nurture came through the Word of God that was read for an hour every Sunday in the liturgical assembly of believers, then explained through preaching for another hour by the pastor. The new believer would be invited to come and hear the Word of God in the midst of the believing community and be taught by the Lord Himself who speaks through that Word. This was called catechesis, that is, the teaching of the faith where the new believer echoes back what he or she hears in the Word of God. Catechesis taught the life of Christ through the Gospels, as well as the doctrines of the Church as they were expounded through other readings of Scripture as well as lengthy sermons that interpreted these words and demonstrated how the Word of God was to be lived out in everyday life.

Early Christians took this catechesis very seriously, so seriously that they would require an average of three years of teaching the faith before allowing most catechumens (those preparing for Baptism) to come to the font to be baptized. This seems like a long time to us, but remember their context of persecution. The Liturgy of the Word that preceded the Lord's Supper came to be known as the Liturgy of the Catechumens because catechumens were the focus of this service. They would be dismissed before the Liturgy of the Lord's Supper because they had not yet been baptized and were not ready to receive the Lord's body and blood. Each catechumen had a sponsor who observed his life to see if he was living out the teaching heard in the service. Catechumens not only had to give up their sinful lifestyles but also needed to perform acts of Christian mercy like visiting the sick and shut-in, and taking care of the widows and the poor in their midst.

Transition—The Rite of Baptism

The time of Baptism was normally the night before Easter, called the Easter Vigil, for Easter began at sundown on Saturday night in the ancient world. The Church would also baptize at times such as Pentecost, and infants would be baptized soon after they were born, but the majority of Baptisms occurred during the Easter Vigil. Lent was the time for the final preparations for Baptism, beginning on Ash Wednesday with the final enrollment of catechumens and penitents. Lent was first and foremost a catechetical time and only secondarily a time of penance. Remarkably, after three years of catechesis, the catechumens would meet for three hours every day during Lent. The bishop would take them through the Bible twice, first expounding the events of Scripture, and then interpreting those events through Christ.

On Saturday evening at the Easter Vigil, the faithful would gather in the main part of the church. In Jerusalem this was called the martyrium.[7] In darkness they would begin the vigil with the singing of psalms. Remember that in the Mideast in the spring it would be cold at night, and these stone churches would be very damp as well. Huddled together with a few candles providing some light, the rhythmic chant of psalms back and forth between a choir or cantor and the congregation itself would bind them together as a community.

After hours of chanting the psalms, the catechumens to be baptized would separate themselves from the community and move outside to the baptistery, men with their sons and women with their daughters. The baptisteries were buildings outside the church, normally with an outer and inner room. The outer room was smaller, and like the church they had just left, it was dark, damp, and cold. The first act of the catechumens was to turn to the west and renounce Satan and all his works and all his ways. They would face west for this was the place of darkness where Satan dwelled. This renunciation of Satan was part of the exorcism of Satan in which the bishop called for Satan to be cast out. After the renunciation, the catechumen would be sealed with exorcistic oil, the first of three anointings. Plain olive oil would be applied to the eyes, nose, lips, ears, and chest to seal out Satan. This oil was also considered part of the preparation the catechumen needed to fight Satan, as if he were a warrior readied for battle or an athlete trained to run a strenuous race.

Next the catechumens would strip off their clothes. In this dark, cold, and damp room, with oil on their eyes, nose, lips, and chest, these catechumens stood naked as Adam before the fall and also as Christ was upon the cross. Early Christians saw the catechumen in his nakedness as representing both Adam and Christ. Most people don't realize that Jesus was crucified naked upon the cross, emphasizing the shame of the crucifixion but also showing that in His humiliating and shameful nakedness, vulnerable to all, He had the power to defeat Satan. This is truly a profound proclamation of the theology of the cross.

While cold and naked and standing in the damp darkness, the doors to the baptistery would burst open and the catechumens would enter into a magnificent room that was warm and filled with light, beautifully arrayed with mosaics of paradise on the walls. "You have entered paradise," Cyril would say, for this was in fact the place where they would cross the boundary from death to life and enter into communion with Christ, a communion that never ends. The fonts from Kelibia and Ephesus show clearly how the newly baptized would step down into the font to be baptized with water. They would be immersed three times—once in the name of the Father, again in the name of the Son, and finally in the name of the Holy Spirit—also representing the three days that Jesus spent in the tomb. Here Cyril unites Baptism in the name of the triune God with Romans 6 and proclaims Baptism a tomb where we die and rise with Christ. Cyril writes that in the waters of Baptism we both died and were reborn, that the font was both our tomb and our womb.

Coming up the stairs on the other side of the font, dripping wet with water, the newly baptized would be anointed with chrism, that sweet-smelling oil representing the anointing of the Holy Spirit. The newly baptized now stand there as "Christs." A white robe would be placed upon them to soak up the water and oil, and also to represent the robe of righteousness they had now been clothed with through their Baptism into Christ. Washed, oiled, and robed, the newly baptized would now return to the assembly of believers waiting in the church. How incredible it must have been to smell the chrism covering these newly baptized Christians! The smell of Easter in the Early Church was not of Easter lilies, but it was the sweet aroma of those who had died and risen in Christ. And what a way to celebrate Easter, where the reality of Christ's death and resurrection was lived out by all in the Baptism of adults, children, and infants who now entered the paradise of God through the water, Word, and Spirit!

Re-incorporation—The Lord's Supper

To confirm what had taken place in the font, the newly baptized would be anointed a third time with the oil of confirmation in the presence of the baptized who were gathered in the main church. This post-baptismal anointing became the origin of our confirmation rites today.

Like newborn babes, the newly baptized would not wait thirteen years to be fed by their mother but immediately were fed the food of heaven, the Lord's Supper. This was part of their initiation into the Church where they were re-incorporated into the new world through the Lord's Supper. This would now be the meal that would sustain them on the long journey ahead. In the ancient Church, the newly baptized would receive three cups: (1) a cup of water to remind them of their Baptism, (2) a cup of milk and honey to signify that they had entered the Promised Land flowing with milk and honey, but also the pablum of the newly born, and (3) a cup of wine that was the very blood of Christ. Here now in the body of Christ, they would be supported through the Lord's Supper in their new life in Christ as they entered a world hostile to them. But because Christ dwelled in them and they dwelled in Christ, they could show forth who they now were in Christ by living the liturgy of life in their day-to-day lives. Through their acts of mercy, love, and compassion they would show forth in their lives the love, mercy, and compassion of Christ who suffered and died for the sins of the world.

These early rites inform our Lutheran baptismal practices and may suggest some changes in our practice and enrich the way we baptize both infants and adults.

Lutheran Baptismal Practices

Luther's Baptismal Rite

Martin Luther inherited a baptismal rite that reflected some of the practices of the early Christian Church but also contained elements of the practice of the Middle Ages. What stands out in Luther's rite are those early Christian practices that accompany the simple application of water with the Word. Luther understood that the rite of Baptism is nothing more and nothing less than baptizing with water in the name of the Father and of the Son and of the Holy Spirit. But he saw the value of surrounding this simple action with prayers and actions that communicated the fullness of what is happening in Holy Baptism.

Luther's rite begins with an exorcism: "Depart thou unclean spirit and make room for the Holy Spirit." Luther lived in an age when Satan was a discernible enemy, and until an adult or child was brought into the kingdom of God through the waters of Holy Baptism, Satan was his master. Luther follows the casting out of the unclean spirit with the sign of the cross on the forehead and the chest, a remnant of the exorcistic anointing of the senses. Having cast out the unclean spirit, the mark of Christ's cross sets apart the unbaptized for the great moment when he will pass from Satan's kingdom into Christ's, from death to life.

What follows the mark of the cross is perhaps Luther's greatest contribution to the baptismal theology of the Christian Church. His "flood prayer" shows how Baptism flows through both the Old and New Testaments:

> Almighty eternal God, who according to thy righteous judgment didst condemn the unbelieving world through the flood and in thy great mercy didst preserve believing Noah and his family, and who didst drown hardhearted Pharaoh with all his host in the Red Sea and didst lead thy people Israel through the same on dry ground, thereby prefiguring this bath of thy baptism, and who through the baptism of thy dear Child, our Lord Jesus Christ, hast consecrated and set apart the Jordan and all water as a salutary flood and a rich and full washing away of sins: We pray through the same thy groundless mercy that thou wilt graciously behold this child, and bless him with true faith in the spirit so that by means of this saving flood all that has been born in him from Adam and which he himself has added thereto may be drowned in him and engulfed, and that he may be sundered from the number of the unbelieving, preserved dry and secure in the holy ark of Christendom, serve thy name at all times fervent in spirit and joy-

> ful in hope, so that with all believers he may be made worthy to attain eternal life according to thy promise; through Jesus Christ our Lord. Amen.[8]

Luther then follows this prayer with a second exorcism, indicating how important this rite was for him: "I adjure thee, thou unclean spirit, by the name of the Father ✝ and of the Son ✝ and of the Holy Ghost ✝ that thou come out of and depart from this servant of God."[9] It is only after two exorcisms, the mark of the cross, and his flood prayer that Luther performs the central action of baptizing in the name of the Father and of the Son and of the Holy Spirit. Like the early liturgies, Luther calls for an anointing with oil upon the forehead following the application of water with these words: "The almighty God and Father of our Lord Jesus Christ who hath regenerated thee through water and the Holy Ghost and hath forgiven thee all thy sin, anoint thee with the oil of salvation in Jesus Christ our Lord to eternal life. Amen."[10] Here the newly baptized is marked once again, but this time with sweet-smelling chrism that visibly demonstrates that through water and the Word, this reborn child of God may now properly be called "Christ."

Luther then gives the child to the sponsors with a baptismal candle and these words: "Receive this burning torch and preserve thy baptism blameless, so that when the Lord cometh to the wedding thou mayest go to meet him to enter with the saints in to the heavenly mansion and receive eternal life. Amen."[11] The darkness has been cast out, and the light of Christ has now dawned in this newly born. Admission to the eternal wedding banquet of the Bridegroom is now the possession of this child who was washed clean with water and the Word, for Christ now dwells in him and he in Christ through the Spirit.

Throughout his life, Luther's theological accents on Baptism were the same, and Luther could be called a theologian of Baptism. More than anything, he stressed the water bath with the trinitarian name as central to the rite. Surprising to many, Luther preferred immersion to any other method of applying water at Baptism, to accent the person's death and resurrection in Christ, reflecting the practices of the early Christians with fonts in which one descended as one suffered, died, and was buried with Christ and rose to a newness of life. This may also be why Luther placed the baptismal garment on the newly baptized since they would be drenched in water after the immersion. Immersion was for both adults and infants.[12]

Luther has two rites, the first entitled "The Order of Baptism, 1523," which is a very mild revision of the medieval rite. He notes, however, at the end of this revision that "in baptism the external things are the least important."[13] This leads him to a second revision, "The Order of Baptism, 1526," a much more substantial one that eliminates many of the ceremonies such as the salt, the blowing under the child's eyes, the Ephphatha, the anointings, and the baptismal candle. Luther seems to be responding here to the pressures from those who were trying to separate themselves from medieval practices. He never returned to the rite to revise it again, but one wonders what he might have done had he revised the baptismal rite later in life. But after 1527, "baptism gains substantially greater prominence in the Reformer's mind," probably in light of his battles with Ulrich Zwingli and those who were trying to diminish the real presence of Christ in the sacraments. His Genesis lectures indicate that after 1527 there was "a sea change in Luther's attitude to the distinction between the subjective and the objective, between the inward and outward things . . . [with a] new stress upon the objectivity of the sacraments, upon the tight bond between water and word, and upon the validity of baptism in the absence of faith."[14] Luther's renewed sense of the value of "external things" has opened up the door for today's Lutherans to reconsider using ceremonial elements from the rich baptismal traditions of the Church catholic like exorcisms, anointings, the candle, but most especially, a rich and lavish use of water.

Our Baptismal Rites Today

Luther's rite has some significant differences from what we might be accustomed to today. Some may be familiar with the baptismal candle, but the exorcism and the anointing with oil may not only come as a surprise but may even offend our sense of what Baptism is and should be. Why add all of these other things when all that is necessary for Baptism is the simple application of water with the trinitarian words through which the Holy Spirit works the miracle of the new creation?

The answer to this question is quite simple. There is no requirement to add to the simple application of water with the Word. They may stand on their own without anything added or subtracted. All our Baptisms could be like an emergency Baptism where we simply apply water in the name of the triune God. But where possible, Christians throughout the history of the Church desired to adorn this life-giving Sacrament with surrounding practices that made this extraordinary event memorable in the life of the baptismal community. These other words and actions communicated through both mind and body the enormous significance of this movement from death to life. Even in our own baptismal rites we have added readings from Scripture, the renunciation of the devil, the confession of the Creed, as well as prayers for the sponsors and the newly baptized. Babies often wear white on this occasion. Parents are usually given a baptismal certificate. Families will often have some sort of feast following the service. Are these things necessary? Certainly not. But who could deny that all of these things help our communities remember the power of Baptism that begins our life in Christ?[15]

In *Lutheran Service Book* two rites are made available for congregations, both of them closer to Luther's rites than what many of us have experienced in the recent past. Both rites center on Baptism with water and the trinitarian formula. Both rites have similar structures, and both offer options for the inclusion of exorcisms, an anointing, the placement of the garment, and the baptismal candle. Most important is the centrality of Luther's flood prayer that "highlights baptismal imagery from the Old Testament (e.g. the flood and crossing of the Red Sea) which finds its fulfillment in the Baptism of our Lord and the Christian's own Baptism."[16] What may be seen in these two baptismal rites are possibilities to embrace the rich tradition of the Church in her baptismal practices that proclaim Baptism as death and resurrection in Christ and entrance into a life that never ends. Here is the basic structure of the two rites that illustrate how our churches are now able to reflect the baptismal theology of Luther and the early Christian Church:

Holy Baptism—Pew Edition	**Holy Baptism—Alternate Form** **Based on Luther's Baptism Rite**
Baptismal Address Naming of the Candidate Sign of the Holy Cross Flood Prayer Enrollment of Sponsors Holy Gospel from Mark 10:13–16 Lord's Prayer	Baptismal Address Exorcism Sign of the Holy Cross Flood Prayer Holy Gospel from Mark 10:13–16 Lord's Prayer
Renunciation of Devil with Sponsors	Renunciation of Devil with Sponsors
Confession of Creed with Sponsors	Confession of Creed with Sponsors
Baptism with Water with Trinitarian Formula	Baptism with Water with Trinitarian Formula
Anointing with Oil White Robe Candle Welcome and Prayers[17]	Prayers[18]

A New Proposal for Baptism in a New Millennium

As twenty-first-century Christians we have entered into a postmodern world much different than the world of our parents and grandparents. Today's world is more like the world early Christians confronted where people are asking questions about God and Church and life that are basic and foundational. There is no longer a collective, cultural biblical literacy. Christian presuppositions, which may have been badly skewed in previous generations, do not shape society in our time. Nor do the children of our postmodern culture process reality through a rationalistic structure, but instead perceive what is real through both their minds and their bodies, through visceral experience. Instruction in the faith in a classroom setting and format may not be the most appropriate way to form new converts into a life in Christ. People today learn differently. They yearn for a holistic approach that communicates the fullness of God's action in Christ through word and action, through what they hear with their ears, see with their eyes, smell with their noses, and taste with their mouths. Christians can rejoice over this context because it truly involves "heart, soul, mind, and strength," not just "mind." The ancient pattern of the initiation of Christians through evangelization, catechesis, Baptism, anointing, the Lord's Supper, and post-baptismal catechesis seems well-tooled to reach our increasingly unchurched world. This is especially true when those seeking God are allowed time in their process of formation to ask basic questions and be formed gradually by Scripture, liturgy, and catechism, the three sources of catechesis for life in Christ.

Catechesis, Catechumens, and the Catechumenate

To understand the new proposal for Baptism, one must first understand what the Early Church has to say about catechesis. "Catechesis" is what takes place along the journey from unbelief to Baptism into Christ. Catechesis is more than *instruction* in the faith—it is *formation* into the life of Christ. St. John Chrysostom points out in his baptismal homily that "catechumen" comes from "echo" because "instructions were to be so internalized that they 'echoed' not only in one's mind but in one's conduct."[19] In its use in the early baptismal and catechetical texts, "catechumens" are those who are preparing for Baptism, and a clear distinction is made between those who are "catechumens" and "the baptized." The catechumens would be dismissed after the Liturgy of the Word, while the baptized would remain for the Liturgy of the Lord's Supper. Only the baptized were admitted to the Holy Supper. The Liturgy of the Word came to be known as the "Liturgy of the Catechumens" or the "Mass of the Catechumens," because it was through the Liturgy of the Word that the catechumens were instructed in the Christian faith. Very early on, catechumens were known as "hearers of the word," for the Word of God heard in the worshiping congregation was the primary means of catechesis.

In the unique genre of the "mystagogical catecheses" of the fourth century, an explanation of the mysteries of Baptism and Eucharist was saved until *after* the catechumen was baptized during Easter week. For eight days, the pastor explained to the newly baptized what happened to them at the font and at the table. Although they had been catechized about the doctrine of Baptism and the Lord's Supper, they had not yet heard about the rites that accompanied these two great sacramental moments. Pedagogically, the Church believed that it was more important for the catechumens to first experience Baptism and the Lord's Supper and then have these rites explained to them.[20]

Catechesis is "a way" the catechumen follows Jesus and travels with Him along the catechetical road to Jerusalem. By journeying along the same way that Christ traveled, the catechumen is prepared to enter into the mysteries of Baptism and the Lord's Supper. Today the contemporary adult catechumen's journey to life in the Church follows the ancient pattern of making Christians: Catechesis—Baptism—Lord's Supper—Post-baptismal Catechesis.

The Adult Catechumenate

Throughout Christendom there has been a renewal of Baptism taking place. No longer may it be assumed that most adults have been baptized. Like the early centuries of the Church's life, unbaptized adults are coming to our churches asking primary questions that reflect no knowledge of what it means to be a Christian. They are not asking questions that reflect knowledge of Christian doctrine, such as what is the difference between Lutherans and other Christians on the Lord's Supper, but primary questions like who is Jesus, what is the Bible, what is the Trinity? Following the patterns of the early Christians, a rigorous and intense process of preparing adults for Baptism is taking place in Christian churches across denominations. The adult catechumenate practiced throughout the Christian church today[21] is divided into four time periods:

1. **Inquiry:** an open-ended period during which unbaptized persons make an initial inquiry into the Christian faith;

2. **Catechumenate:** an open-ended period during which catechumens explore more deeply the church's story of faith;
3. **Preparation for baptism:** a period of intense preparation prior to the celebration of Holy Baptism; and
4. **Baptismal living:** a life-long period during which the newly baptized grow more deeply into the practice of faith and Christian life.[22]

Between these times in the journey of the catechumen, various rites mark the transition from one period to another. A rite of welcome ushers the catechumen from "inquiry" to the "catechumenate," and a rite of enrollment from the "catechumenate" to "preparation for Baptism." Baptism, confirmation, and the Lord's Supper form the culmination of the entire process that moves the newly baptized into "baptismal living." That high point is followed by a rite of vocation after a short period of post-baptismal catechesis. Along the journey, the catechumen will be accompanied by a sponsor who will support him as he is instructed and formed in the Christian faith by pastors and teachers. Such instruction and formation comes through catechesis that involves:

- Studying **Scripture**, particularly by means of the lessons for each Sunday from the lectionary;
- Participating in the **liturgical life** of the parish and hearing the meaning and significance of the Divine Service and the other worship services of the church;
- Learning how to listen to the **proclamation** of Law and Gospel in the sermon;
- Teaching **Luther's Small Catechism** as a map for baptismal living;
- Modeling a **devotional life** of Scripture, prayer, and meditation;
- Practicing **ministry in daily life** by works of charity in the congregation and in the world.[23]

The journey of the catechumens to life in Christ through Baptism, the Lord's Supper, and an ongoing baptismal life also provides an opportunity for the entire congregation to be renewed in its own baptismal journey to the heavenly Jerusalem. The adult catechumenate offers the Church a process of evangelization and catechesis that is biblical, historical, and thoroughly Lutheran in its form and substance.

This chapter on Baptism as entrance to the Divine Service draws to an end. We have traveled from Jerusalem to Tunisia to Italy to Germany and back home again. Along the way we have discovered that Baptism brings us to our true home to be with God in the Father's house, a foretaste of our final homecoming at the Lamb's banquet in His kingdom that has no end. But our summons home in Christ has not ended, for by His Spirit His eternal presence goes with us, and we now go out from the font and the table as messengers of His peace, greeting pilgrims on the way as heralds of the kingdom.

9

The Historic Liturgy as Divine Service— The Liturgy of the Word

At last we come to a description of the Divine Service. In the Divine Service the world's story is told Sunday in and Sunday out, for this is where we hear and taste our Creator and Redeemer, Jesus Christ, as we are joined to Him in a union that knows no end. The story of creation and re-creation is told here, the story of the patriarchs, Abraham, Isaac, and Jacob, of David's kingdom and Isaiah's prophecies, of Mary and Joseph and Peter and Paul, the story of Jesus and the saints who have died and now live in Him. Here is our story—the story of our Baptism into Christ and into everything the Old and New Testaments embrace. The Divine Service is where the world is made new in Christ as He comes to His people with the gift of Himself through which we are forgiven, joined to His life, and saved from our enemies.

The following explanation of the components of the historic liturgy flows out of the biblical and Jewish precedents, as well as the historical developments of the Divine Service through various cultures and such influences as space and time. Much of what happens in the development of the historic liturgy comes to us anonymously, that is, we simply do not know who first introduced various elements into our worship life.

One of the principles of interpretation applied to "primary" liturgical texts (texts of our worship services) is that they tend to be more conservative than "secondary" theological reflections (the texts people write as they think about God). This comes from the belief that people at worship tend to change their way of thinking and speaking about God more slowly than theologians and scholars do. The assumption is that any changes over an extended period of time would be imperceptible to the congregation at worship and that over many generations people would worship in more or less the same way. For example, we would expect the liturgy of Justin Martyr in Rome in AD 150 to be very similar to the liturgy that might be celebrated there seventy years later.[1]

Our Lutheran liturgy traces its heritage back to the New Testament and the Early Church, which in turn comes from the Old Testament practices as were followed by Jesus Himself. Jesus' table fellowship with sinners sets the pattern of Christian worship as one of teaching and eating, and His ministry of teaching and miracles become manifest in the Church's historic liturgy of Word and Sacrament. Early sacramental rites and practices exhibited strong biblical foundations that confessed a Christ who was real and present and caused transformation. These rites were at the center of the formation of an identity in Christ. This is because sacramental rites were associated with the emotionally charged sacramental practice that brought early Christians into full fellowship with Christ and His Church. Sacramental rites integrated them into a community called the Body of Christ, a community created by the Spirit's working through Word and water and bread and wine.

Lutherans have been able to maintain a proper balance between Word and Sacrament, seeing the natural rhythm between the two. The Word prepares for the Meal by causing burning hearts, that eyes might be opened in the breaking of the bread, as happened in Emmaus (Luke 24). The Word cultivates the soil and plants the seed for the growth that continues with the eating and drinking of the body and blood of the crucified and risen Savior. As we shall see, the two climaxes in the Divine Service are the reading of the Holy Gospel and the Words of Institution, the two places where we hear the very words of Jesus Himself. One is not more important than the other. Both are necessary in the order given to us by Jesus and the apostles. However, because the Lord's Supper comes as the second high point in the Divine Service, it has a sense of bringing the liturgy to its complete and full end, and therefore sometimes feels more climactic.

The Church's rite of Word and Sacrament is the most central part of the liturgy, upon which both space and time depend. To begin, let us look at how the liturgy has developed into its fivefold shape.

The Fivefold Shape of the Lutheran Liturgy

The twentieth century experienced an explosion in liturgical research and literature. Scholars uncovered liturgical texts that were never known before. We know more than ever before about the Jewish precedents of Christian worship, the early liturgies of the Church, the development of those liturgies in the imperial period (AD 312–600), and the dissolution of those liturgies in the medieval period (AD 600–1500).

New sources have been discovered both hidden in libraries and from archaeological digs, increasing our historical knowledge that makes communication between current liturgical traditions not only possible but also commonplace. The influence of liturgical churches on non-liturgical churches and vice versa is unprecedented. Liturgy now crosses denominational bounds so that today there is among liturgical communities an "ecumenical basic form"[2] discovered through recent research in the area of liturgical structures. This "structural" approach to liturgy reflects the premise that form and theology belong together—in changing form one changes theology; in changing theology one changes form. The basic form of worship is comprised of two simple structures:

> Proclamation of the Word and the celebration of the Meal instituted in the night of betrayal, both of these executed with invocation and adoration of the Triune God—that comprises the entire worship of the church beyond the line of Baptism. Thus the part commanded by Christ's institution appears in the form of worship.[3]

The liturgical structures of Word and Sacrament are the stable cornerstones of the liturgy that have not changed since the time of the New Testament. These structures are foundational in every period, from the pre-Constantinian period (AD 30–312) through the imperial period (AD 312–600), the medieval period (AD 600–1500), the Reformation era (AD 1500–1650), the age of pietism and rationalism (AD 1650–1850), as well as during the origins of the Missouri Synod up until today (AD 1850–2007).[4] The only significant additions to these two structures are the great liturgical hymns of praise, the ordinaries, which have located themselves around the two structures of Christian liturgy. The ordinaries are those parts of the liturgy that do not change from Sunday to Sunday. The Kyrie (Luke 18)/Gloria in Excelsis (Luke 2) precede the Word, and the Creed/Hymn of the Day follows the Word; the Sanctus (derived from Isaiah 6 and Psalm 118) precedes the Words of Institution and the Agnus Dei (from John 1) follows them. This combination of Word and Sacrament and the ordinaries make up what is commonly called the historic liturgy of the Church. By the seventh century, a fivefold structure of the historic liturgy was fully in place, with the exception of the Creed, which came in the eleventh century.

The historic liturgy is derived both from the synagogue liturgy and from Jesus' last Passover with His disciples in which He instituted the Lord's Supper, and therefore is very Jewish. It developed in the Greco-Roman Empire and reached across the entire Roman world. One often hears the complaint that our Lutheran liturgy is somehow "German," but that is simply false. The liturgical music in many of our contemporary hymnals is shared by other traditions, and a surprising amount of it is composed by contemporary Americans.

Entrance	WORD	Preparation	SACRAMENT	Distribution
Confession & Absolution	Old Testament Gradual	Offering Offertory	Preface Proper Preface	AGNUS DEI (7th Century)
Introit	Epistle Alleluia		SANCTUS (3rd Century)	Canticle
KYRIE (5th Century)	GOSPEL Sermon		Prayer	Collect
HYMN OF PRAISE Gloria in Excelsis (6th Century) This Is the Feast (20th Century)	CREED (11th Century)		Lord's Prayer	Benediction
Collect	Prayers for the Faithful		WORDS OF INSTITUTION Peace of the Lord	

The Liturgy of the Word (known as the liturgy of the catechumens) contained readings from the Old Testament, the Epistles, and the Gospels, with psalms interspersed (the origin of our Introits and Graduals), and the homily (square number 1, an act of deliberation over the Word). The Liturgy of the Lord's Supper included the Preface (and with the formation of the Church Year in the fourth century, the development of the proper preface), the eucharistic prayer, and the Lord's Prayer (square number 2, an act of thanksgiving over the bread and wine).

It must be noted that both the structures of Word and Sacrament and the ordinaries are from the Scriptures. The historic liturgy is completely biblical and is meant to be transcendent and transcultural because of its biblical foundation. It is clean and elegant, exhibiting one of the central principles of liturgy: simplicity. The above image shows the shape of the historic liturgy and the dates of the ordinaries.

Preparation for the Divine Service

Invocation
Confession and Absolution

The core value of holiness in the first-century world of Jesus and the apostles is still our core value today as our people enter into the bodily presence of Christ in His Word and Meal. The temple had its boundaries that kept those who were not worthy or prepared from entering God's holiness; we today also enter God's holy presence confessing our sins in repentance and faith and hearing God's absolution. Public confession and absolution are not part of the Divine Service but preparation to enter Christ's bodily presence and receive the gifts from that presence.

The Invocation

Our services begin with the Invocation of the name of the triune God: "In the name of the Father and of the Son and of the Holy Spirit." Wherever the name of Jesus is, there is Jesus—present bodily with the gifts of salvation. The name of Jesus bears His presence. By beginning with the trinitarian name placed upon us in our Baptism, we are announcing that Christ is present among us in His Word, in His Sacrament, and in the baptized gathered as the Body of Christ, His Church. The trinitarian name may be spoken by the pastor facing the altar, where he stands with the baptized speaking back to God the name given us in Baptism. The pastor also may proclaim those words facing the congregation, where he announces the reality that Christ is present bodily among us. Facing the altar, the pastor signs himself with the cross as a mark of his Baptism; facing the congregation, he traces the cross over the congregation as he will during the Absolution and the Benediction. These are performative acts of proclamation that create what they say.

By beginning in the name of the Father and of the Son and of the Holy Spirit, the Church follows Jesus' liturgical practice at the beginning of His ministry in the synagogue in Nazareth. The first words of Jesus' public ministry are a citation from Scripture from Isaiah 61: "The Spirit of the Lord God is upon Me." Isaiah's words are clearly a reference to Jesus' Baptism, where the Holy Spirit descended upon Him and the Father's voice proclaimed Him the Christ, the One who would accomplish the trinitarian plan of salvation. But these words are also a reference to the Trinity: the "Spirit" is the Holy Spirit, the "Lord" is the Father, and "Jesus" is the one upon whom the Spirit is resting. Jesus begins His public ministry in a synagogue liturgy, "In the name of the Father and of the Son and of the Holy Spirit," setting the pattern for our own beginnings as we enter His presence with the proclamation of the trinitarian name and affirm together our baptismal identity.

The Confession of Sins and Absolution

In the Early Church, there was no practice of public confession and absolution. Confession and absolution were private, for individuals. Our Lutheran Confessions speak of this private, individual form of confession and absolution and not the corporate form that we are accustomed to as we prepare for the Divine Service.[5] What we practice today is a later development. But as an expected part of our liturgical heritage, it has become a salutary way for us to enter Christ's holy presence.

Reflected in our practice of public confession and absolution is the implementation of the Office of the Keys, which was instituted by the Lord after His resurrection from the dead. Luther summarizes perfectly the essence of confession and absolution: "Confession has two parts. First, that we confess our sins, and second, that we receive absolution, that is, forgiveness, from the pastor as from God Himself, not doubting, but firmly believing that by it our sins are forgiven before God in heaven."[6]

Luther's words remind us that confession should be a confession of sin, and absolution a pure word of release. There are many different forms of confession and absolution in our hymnals, and these should be followed, for they speak truth about our sins and about God's forgiveness and have had the benefit of long-term use, having been tested and tried and found to be true. Every congregation should hear at least monthly the absolution in the "indicative-operative" form that most clearly proclaims the reality that the pastor, in the stead and by the command of Christ, is forgiving the sins of those who will enter the presence of Christ to receive His gifts.[7] The indicative-operative form reinforces faith and assurance for those whose consciences are most troubled in ways that no other form does. Perhaps this is why our Lord instituted it in John 20. This absolution may be found in our services in the following form:

> Upon this your confession, I, by virtue of my office, as a called and ordained servant of the Word, announce the grace of God unto all of you, and in the stead and by the command of my Lord Jesus Christ I forgive you all your sins in the name of the Father and of the Son and of the Holy Spirit. Amen. (*LSB*, p. 185)

I. The Entrance Rite

Introit, Psalm, or Entrance Hymn
Kyrie
Hymn of Praise—Gloria in Excelsis or Worthy Is Christ
Collect

As the liturgy properly begins with the Entrance Rite, the destination of the first part of the Divine Service is the reading of the Holy Gospel. There is a symphony of movement to this climactic point in the service, and the entire liturgy from the opening moment points to the very words of Jesus in the Gospel.

Before the time of Constantine, the vast majority of Christians worshiped in houses. Due to the small space, there was no Entrance Rite. The area in the houses was so small it was impossible and unnecessary to stage any movement of people in the church. This changed, however, in the post-Constantinian era, when the churches grew both in space and in numbers. It was not unusual for some basilicas to accommodate thousands of people. Common practice was for people to gather for worship well before the actual service began. As they gathered, the cantor or the choir would begin to chant psalms and encourage the people to join in the antiphon with them or in certain responsories that could be memorized, since the people at worship did not have printed material until after the fifteenth century. As more and more people entered the church, they would join in the psalm-singing, and a rhythm would develop among the faithful. The way of chanting the psalms among these early Christians was similar to the way we do so in contemporary Lutheran service books, as well as in many other Christian liturgical traditions. This gathering of the faithful through psalm-singing could last a long time, and the process of rhythmic chanting formed them into a community.

When a critical mass of people had gathered, the clergy and their attendants would enter the church. The key issue was to find a reverent way to process into a church crowded with psalm-singing pilgrims. As in the secular world, when people needed to pierce through a crowd, the church had a procession. A cross on top of a pole to lead the procession into the church allowed the people to see the procession. For those who could not see the cross, there were servers with bowls of incense to swing behind the cross, to identify the procession by smell. At times of high solemnity and feasting, attendants would accompany the procession, forming a kind of flying wedge to make a path to the altar. The procession included many clergy, since thousands needed to be communed. As the clergy processed in, it became popular for the psalm-singing to shift to liturgical hymns like the Kyrie and Gloria in Excelsis that marked the final stages of the Entrance Rite. These were hymns that the entire congregation would know and could sing with gusto as they prepared for the reading of God's Holy Word.

In Kramer Chapel at Concordia Theological Seminary, Fort Wayne, Indiana, services are begun in the back of the chapel at the font with Invocation, Confession, and Absolution. By beginning at the entrance to the chapel at the font, we announce that we prepare to enter God's holiness by marking ourselves with the baptismal name, confessing our sins, and hearing God's absolution from the pastor. Some celebrants will dip their fingers into the font before making the sign of the cross over the congregation to connect Baptism to the absolution received at the beginning of the service. Then, accompanied by the Introit or the Kyrie, a cross leads the pastors and attendants into the chapel, capturing the sense of psalm, Kyrie, and Hymn of Praise as entrance rite. The responsive Kyrie is well-suited for this, for the assisting minister may chant the petitions as the congregation responds, "Lord, have mercy."

Introit, Psalm, or Entrance Hymn

It is important to note that our liturgy from Introit to Collect was simply the Entrance Rite to the Liturgy of the Word. It was a time of movement that accompanied the procession of the clergy by means of singing into the church. Today we have the option to use either the Introit, a part of a psalm, the full psalm of the day, or an entrance hymn. It is not uncommon for congregations to use both an entrance hymn and an Introit/psalm, which are used to introduce the people of God to some of the themes of the day.

The Ordinaries in the Entrance, Preparation, and Distribution Rites

The ordinaries in the Divine Service are liturgical texts and as such may be interpreted like any other text. They are the people's response to the gifts, and so our focus will be on the biblical content of the ordinaries, their place and function in the flow of the Divine Service, and their character as the proper response of praise, thanksgiving, and petition by the people of God.

The introduction to *Lutheran Worship* relates the significance of the ordinaries in the Church's life:

> Our Lord speaks and we listen. His Word bestows what it says. Faith that is born from what is heard acknowledges the gifts received with eager thankfulness and praise. Music is drawn into this thankfulness and praise, enlarging and elevating the adoration of our gracious giver God.
>
> Saying back to him what he has said to us, we repeat what is most true and sure. . . . The rhythm of our worship is from him to us, and then from us back to him. He gives his gifts, and together we receive and extol them. We build one another up as we speak to one another in psalms, hymns, and spiritual songs. . . . We are heirs of an astonishing rich tradition. Each generation receives from those who went before and, in making that tradition of the Divine Service its own, adds what best may service in its own day—the living heritage and something new.[8]

In all matters liturgical the principles of *reverence* and *fidelity* are watchwords for us. When it comes to the ordinaries, what could be more faithful and reverent in the acknowledgment of gifts received with thankfulness and praise than singing back to God what He has said to us with liturgical hymns that are grounded in Scripture, are true and sure, and have been sung by Christians in response to gifts received for thirteen hundred years? The ordinaries are a vital part of the rich tradition handed down to us, and which even now we continue to make our own in a new Lutheran hymnal for the Church.

The ordinaries form the core of our acknowledgment of gifts received with eager thankfulness and praise.

The ordinaries form the core of our acknowledgment of gifts received with eager thankfulness and praise. This means that Christ stands not only as the giver of gifts in Word and Sacrament but also as the one in whom we respond back to the Father with eager thankfulness and praise. The Church placed these ordinaries where they are to respond to the reality of Christ's presence in Word and Sacrament, that is, the ordinaries are where they are for both liturgical and theological reasons. To discover the theology of the ordinaries, we must look at the very words of these liturgical texts.

When looking at the specifics of the liturgical texts of the ordinaries there is a temptation to spend a great deal of time on the history of the development of these texts, not only as to when and where they came from but also as to the evolution of the text itself. Needless to say, the history here is complex and convoluted, sometimes obscure, as it often is when dealing with the origins of liturgical texts. Remarkably, there is not much written about the ordinaries in books or monographs, and any search for the origins of liturgical texts requires patience and diligence.

Kyrie

In the ancient world, the king would sometimes visit a village or city. Anticipating his coming, villagers would line the road waiting for him to appear, and as he entered the city they would cry, "Lord, have mercy!" Amid their shouts, one could also hear petitions from the crowd for gifts that reflected the king's mercy, such as food, protection, lower taxes, and always and most important, **peace**. Jesus' entrance into Jerusalem is an excellent example of this. In the Eastern Church, Christians adopted the practice of petitioning for gifts with cries of mercy as the clergy entered the church during the procession to the altar at the beginning of the service. This secular practice was adopted for their King—the King of the Universe—for He was coming to them in His Word to bring the gifts of His presence: "The *Kyrie* is not another confession of sins, but a prayer for grace and help in time of need—'the ardent cry of the Church for assistance.' "[9]

The cry for mercy is biblical, particularly for those seeking the release from bondage that only Jesus the King can give. It is the cry of the ten lepers, who, seeing Jesus and knowing He can heal, cry out, "Jesus, Master, have mercy on us" (Luke 17:13). It is the cry of a blind beggar at the gate of Jericho, who, on hearing that "Jesus of Nazareth is passing by," cries, "Jesus, Son of David, have mercy on me!" (Luke 18:37–38). This petition for mercy has been explained in this way:

> [It is] the most comprehensive and most expressive of all prayers. . . . To beg God's mercy is to ask for the coming of His kingdom, that kingdom which Christ promised to give to those who seek it, assuring them that all other things will be added (Matthew 6:33). Because of this, it is a perfect example of a universal petition.[10]

The Kyrie is the acknowledgment of gifts to be received with eager thankfulness and praise because the King is coming in His Word. The most ancient form of the Kyrie was the simple acclamation "Lord, have mercy," but early on it took the form of a litany similar to the one in many contemporary Lutheran service books.

In **peace** let us pray to the Lord.

Lord, have mercy.

For the **peace** from above and for our ***salvation*** let us pray to the Lord.

Lord, have mercy.

For the **peace** of the whole world, for the **well-being of the Church of God**, and for the ***unity*** of all let us pray to the Lord.

Lord, have mercy.

For this ***holy house*** and for ***all who offer here their worship and praise*** let us pray to the Lord.

Lord, have mercy.

Help, save, comfort, and defend us, gracious Lord.

Amen.

The cry for mercy in the Kyrie is a cry for **peace**. The entire Kyrie is prayed "in peace," and two of the first three petitions are for "peace from above" and for "the peace of the whole world." The petition for "peace from above" acknowledges that peace came from heaven to earth through the incarnation of Jesus Christ and petitions the Lord to continue to be present among us in our worship. The invasion of peace from above is why we petition for "the peace of the whole world"—a peace realized in salvation, the well-being of the Church of God, the unity of all, a peace for this holy house and for all who worship here. Peace is the condition of "wholeness and well-being"[11] that now exists on earth and in heaven because of the incarnation and atoning death of Jesus, a theme echoed in the opening verse of the Gloria in Excelsis from Luke's Gospel.

Peace is also the new greeting of the Church of the New Testament that provided the foundation for the post-Pentecost Church in mission. Jesus sent the seventy out to greet households in peace, and His first greeting to the eleven after the resurrection was the greeting of peace as He ate roasted fish before them (Luke 24:36). Peace and hospitality at the table go hand in hand in the mission of Jesus and His disciples. God's mercy is expressed at the table of His Son through forgiveness offered and received, the very mercy and forgiveness that Jesus showed to sinners as He went from house to house with the greeting of peace. The petitions conclude with a list describing the essence of our cry for God's mercy: "help, save, comfort, and defend us, gracious Lord." And so the Divine Service as table fellowship with Jesus begins in peace as the people cry for mercy in the Kyrie.

Hymn of Praise: Gloria in Excelsis

The movement from the peace of the Kyrie to the peace of the Gloria in Excelsis is seamless, as if the Gloria now interprets the peace of the Kyrie. Attached to the song of the angels from Luke's record of Jesus' birth in Bethlehem is a trinitarian hymn that reiterates the peace and mercy of the Kyrie as it centers itself in the Lamb of God who takes away the sin of the world. The Gloria in Excelsis first appeared in the liturgy in morning and evening prayer, though there is a liturgical "rumor" that it was first used in Rome by Pope Telesophorus at Christmas early in the second century (d. AD 136). Athanasius refers to the Gloria as a liturgical text in the fourth century. As with all the ordinaries, its origin is shrouded in anonymity, though it may be assumed with confidence that "the *Gloria* has been known throughout Christendom since the fourth century."[12]

From the beginning, the Gloria has been associated with the feast of Christmas and therefore with the incarnation itself. Although there is no conclusive evidence that the Gloria entered the Divine Service as a prelude to the Service of the Word to balance the Sanctus, the prelude to the Words of Institution, there may be some evidence for such a suggestion from none other than the evangelist St. Luke. This may be an excellent example of the biblical character of the liturgical development of the historic liturgy. In Luke's Gospel the Gloria in Excelsis is a foreshadowing of the Entrance Hymn of the people of Israel when Jesus finally arrives in Jerusalem for His death. The parallels between the song at Jesus' birth and the song of the people as He enters Jerusalem are striking, especially in view of Luke's version of the entrance hymn:[13]

Luke 2:14: "***Glory in the highest to God***, and **on earth** ***peace*** among men of His favor."

Luke 19:38: "Blessed the Coming One, the King, in the name of the Lord! **In heaven** ***peace***, and ***glory in the highest***!"

When Luke is compared to Matthew, Mark, and John, what he has in common with them is what liturgical scholars call the Benedictus from Psalm 118:26, that is, "Blessed is He who comes in the name of the Lord!" This may be seen in the following comparison of the texts:

Matthew 21:9	"**Hosanna** to the Son of David! ***Blessed the Coming One in the name of the Lord!*** **Hosanna** in the highest!"
Mark 11:9	"**Hosanna!** ***Blessed the Coming One in the name of the Lord!*** Blessed the coming kingdom of our father David! **Hosanna** in the highest!"
Luke 19:38	"***Blessed the Coming One***, the King, ***in the name of the Lord!*** *In heaven peace, and glory in the highest!"*
John 12:13	**Hosanna!** ***Blessed the Coming One in the name of the Lord,*** even the King of Israel![14]

What is unique in Luke compared to the other evangelists is the final two phrases—"In heaven peace, and glory in the highest!"—and it is here that Luke reports words that echo the angelic hymn of Luke 2:14, also unique to Luke, emphasizing his themes of peace and glory by placing them toward the center of the circular structure with "heaven" and "in the highest" as the frame. What is in the center is the Benedictus: "Blessed the Coming One, the King, in the name of the Lord." At the birth of Jesus, there is glory in the highest; this same highest glory is proclaimed as He enters Jerusalem for His death. The great mystery here concerns peace: at Jesus' birth, there is peace on earth; as He enters into Jerusalem for His Passion and resurrection, there is peace in heaven. Thus earth and heaven are joined together in peace through the incarnation and atonement of Christ.

This incarnational and biblical reality recorded by Luke is exactly the same reality that happens every time God's people gather for the Divine Service, where Christ's presence in Word and Sacrament joins heaven and earth together in peace. This is what we have earlier called "inaugurated eschatology." The Sanctus will state this plainly when Isaiah's vision is used to declare that "Heaven and earth are full of Your glory." What is most curious about this phrase in the Sanctus is that Isaiah does not include "heaven" in his record of the words of the seraphim, but has only "the whole earth is full of His glory" (Isaiah 6:3). It is the Church that added "heaven" to the Sanctus, and where do you think it came from?—from Luke's Gloria in Excelsis and the entrance hymn of the pilgrims into Jerusalem! The reality of Christ's presence in the Lord's Supper demanded that the Church acknowledge that heaven and earth are joined together in the breaking of the bread. When it came time to declare that this same reality exists in the hearing of Christ's Word, the source for the Sanctus' "heaven and earth" became the logical choice for the hymn that leads to the breaking open of God's Holy Word. Therefore, the Gloria prepares for Christ's incarnation in His Word, and the Sanctus prepares for His atoning presence in His Supper.

There is more to the Gloria in Excelsis than the opening verse from Luke's Gospel. The main body of the hymn is a liturgical text that is trinitarian.

Lord God, heavenly king, almighty God and Father:
We worship You,
we give You thanks,
we praise You for Your ***glory***.

Lord Jesus Christ, only Son of the Father,
Lord God, ***Lamb of God:***
You take away the sin of the world;
have mercy on us.
You are seated at the right hand of the Father;
receive our prayer.
For You alone are the ***Holy One***,
You alone are ***the Lord***,
You alone are ***the Most High***, Jesus Christ

With the Holy Spirit,
in the ***glory*** of God the Father.
Amen.

That this is a hymn of praise is clear from the opening acclamations. The reason for our worship, our thanksgiving, and our praise is that the glory of our Father, the heavenly King and almighty God, now dwells on earth in the flesh of Jesus Christ who is present among us in Word and Sacrament.[15] This glory is described in the center of the hymn, a proclamation of what Jesus Christ, the only Son of the Father, the Lamb of God, has done for the world through His death. On account of this we ask for His mercy, and because of His exaltation to the right hand of the Father, we ask Him to receive our prayer (an echo of the Kyrie). Here the Gloria announces what is at the center of the Divine Service: the heavenly conversation of the Lamb who was slain and raised again in the Word and the ongoing feast upon this very Lamb in the Lord's Supper.[16]

The congregation's proclamation of His atoning work and vindicating resurrection/ascension leads to our declaration of who He is: the Holy One, the Lord, the Most High Jesus Christ. The first and third title come from the annunciation in Luke 1:26–28. By calling Him "the Holy One," we join the angel Gabriel who announced to Mary at the moment of conception that what she bore in her womb was Holy, the Son of God (Luke 1:35b). Wherever God's holiness dwells, there is His temple, and just as Mary's womb became a temporary vessel for God's holiness, we declare in the Gloria in Excelsis that the humble space set apart for Divine Service is a temple of God's holiness.

By calling Jesus "Lord" we join Peter and the rest of the Twelve, along with the Jews converted at Pentecost when, at the climax of his sermon, Peter announces, "Let all the house of Israel therefore know for certain that God has made Him both Lord and Christ, this Jesus whom you crucified" (Acts 2:36). The acclamation, "Jesus is Lord," was the great confession of faith in the earliest Christian communities, and it is to this "Lord" that we have just petitioned for mercy and peace.

Finally, to declare Him "the Most High" returns us to the angel Gabriel who declared to Mary that the child she would bear in her womb would be called "Son of the Most High" (Luke 1:32). This designation acknowledges that precisely because He is the Lamb of God who takes away the sin of the world, He has ascended to the Father and received the honor of sitting at His right hand. This final designation leads us to the Holy Spirit through whom Jesus Christ is present in the glory of God the Father. Christ's presence through the Spirit concludes the hymn, so that the trinitarian portion of the Gloria begins and ends with the glory of God, whose presence we worship, give thanks, and praise.

Hymn of Praise: Worthy Is Christ

The magnificence of the Gloria in Excelsis has caused some to wonder why the Church ever agreed to add a new Hymn of Praise. It was only in the Roman rite (which is the foundation for the Lutheran rite) that there were no options for any other Hymn of Praise.[17] The introduction of "Worthy Is Christ" as another Hymn of Praise is perhaps the most significant innovation of contemporary Lutheran rites.[18] Its wide acceptance by the ecumenical church is a testimony to its appropriateness for the Divine Service as a worthy replacement of the Gloria in Excelsis during the season of Easter and other feast days. It also demonstrates how true liturgical change should take place, not by individual people or congregations, but by the Church through her worship commissions and the corporate use of the innovation over a period of many years. When a new worship resource comes into existence, commissions on worship could judge by acclamation of the Church at large whether this innovation should remain a part of the Divine Service. Such inclusion would then be a decision of the corporate church.

Most people are unaware that the text comes from the first two verses of the canticle *Dignus est Agnus*, a liturgical text from Revelation 5:12–13, 15:3–4, and 19:5–9. "Worthy Is Christ" joins to *Dignus est Agnus* texts from Revelation about "the Lamb who was slain" (Revelation 5:12). The Lamb of the Gloria is now the Lamb of the victory feast, showing the connection between these two hymns, as the antiphon-refrain of "Worthy Is Christ" suggests:

> The antiphon-refrain, "This is the feast of victory for our God," is, like many traditional antiphons in the church's liturgy, not an exact biblical quotation but rather a gathering and a restatement of the many biblical references and allusions to banquets and feasting as signs of the gladness and intimacy of God's kingdom. It draws upon the picture of the messianic banquet in Isaiah 25:6, which celebrates the destruction of death and which proclaims therefore God's victory and triumph (see also Rev. 5:5; 22:6, 17; Isa. 55:1). The New Testament image for the gladness of the kingdom is often the wedding feast (as in Matt. 22:1ff.; Rev. 19:9) but is sometimes simply a "feast" as in Matthew 8:11. Nonetheless, the image looks back to the Passover meal which celebrates Israel's deliverance from slavery, to the Easter victory both in its past and present (and future) dimensions, and to the messianic banquet of the future, when the kingdom comes in all its fullness.[19]

The text from *Divine Service, Setting One* is as follows:

> This is the ***feast of victory*** for our God. Alleluia, alleluia, alleluia.
>
> Worthy is ***Christ, the Lamb*** who was slain,
>
> ***whose blood set us free*** to be people of God.
>
> This is the ***feast of victory*** for our God. Alleluia, alleluia, alleluia.
>
> Power, riches, wisdom, and strength,
>
> and honor, blessing, and glory are His.
>
> This is the ***feast of victory*** for our God. Alleluia, alleluia, alleluia.
>
> Sing with all the people of God, and join in the hymn of all creation:
>
> Blessing, honor, glory, and might
>
> be to God and ***the Lamb*** forever. Amen.
>
> This is the ***feast of victory*** for our God. Alleluia, alleluia, alleluia.
>
> For ***the Lamb who was slain has begun His reign***. Alleluia.
>
> This is the ***feast of victory*** for our God. Alleluia, alleluia, alleluia.
> (*LSB*, p. 155)

"Worthy Is Christ" proclaims "the feast of victory for our God," and so a legitimate question is this: "What is this feast of victory?"[20] It is not, as some might think, simply a reference to the Lord's Supper but to all God's acts of table fellowship stretching back into the Old Testament where God's redemption is often accompanied by a meal. There is common ground between these Old Testament meals, especially the Passover, Jesus' meals during His earthly ministry, Jesus' Passover on the night in which He was betrayed, the breaking of the bread and opened eyes at Emmaus, and the celebration of the Lord's Supper in the Church since Pentecost. The feast of victory not only refers to the Liturgy of the Lord's Supper, but to both Word and Sacrament, because table fellowship with God in both Old and New Testaments and in our own churches today involves three essential elements: the presence of God in Jesus, in His teaching at the table, and in the breaking of the bread. The feast always includes breaking open His Word as well as the breaking of the bread. And because we share this fellowship at table with Him now, we have a "foretaste of the feast to come" where we shall "celebrate with all the faithful the marriage feast of the Lamb in his kingdom, which has no end."[21]

The content of this hymn comes from John's Revelation, and there is a progression of thought throughout the hymn as it proclaims the victory feast. In the first stanza from Revelation 5 John describes the heavenly liturgy, the new song of the four living creatures and the twenty-four elders who fall down before the Lamb with harps in hand and bowls full of incense that contain the prayers of the saints. Joining the new song of heaven we proclaim with them Christ's worthiness as the Lamb who was slain (Revelation 5:9–10). The atonement is the content of heaven's joyous song and the foundation for the rest of our hymn. Flowing from the Lamb's blood is the freedom we have now as His people in the new creation, realized in the forgiveness of sins as well as the healing of the entire creation through His blood. For this He is worthy.

The second stanza continues the new song of Revelation 5, but with the voices of myriads and myriads and thousands and thousands of angels joining our song, together with every creature in heaven and on earth and under earth and in the sea, that is, with all creation. What we announce with all creation is that the atonement of the Lamb—His scandalous suffering and humiliating death—is now the source of power, riches, wisdom, and strength, and honor, blessing, and glory. In Jesus' suffering and death, God is showing us His glory and power, and therefore, the essence of heaven itself.

The third stanza reiterates this heavenly song from Revelation 5 with the hymn of all creation that comes from Revelation 15 and 19. This hymn of all creation that we now sing as the people of God with the host of heaven is the song of the saints standing by the sea of glass with harps of God in their hands, singing the song of Moses and the song of the Lamb that signals victory in the battle with the beast (Revelation 15:2–5). It is also the song of the multitude at the marriage supper of the Lamb (Revelation 19:1–10). Notice how heaven and earth are joining together in the hymn of all creation, singing "blessing, honor, glory, and might be to God and the Lamb forever." And heaven and earth also sing together "Amen!" Here is another moment of "inaugurated eschatology," beautifully stated in the last stanza of the hymn: "For the Lamb who was slain has begun His reign. Alleluia." The beginning of the Lamb's reign is the ongoing victory feast of Word and Sacrament that Christians have been celebrating since that first Pentecost, and continue to celebrate even now.

The Gloria in Excelsis is appointed to be used as a hymn of praise during the Christmas and Epiphany seasons; minor festivals of the incarnation such as the Presentation, the Annunciation, and the Visitation; and throughout the Pentecost season. "Worthy Is Christ" is reserved for Easter Sunday through Pentecost Day, All Saints, and the Sunday of Fulfillment. There is wisdom in these rubrics, giving preference to the Gloria, the more ancient of these two hymns of praise, but recognizing the paschal character of "Worthy Is Christ."

The Collect of the Day

When the psalm, Kyrie, and Hymn of the Day had ceased, the presiding minister brought the Entrance Rite to a pious halt by chanting or speaking the Collect of the Day. These prayers form one of the most beautiful collections of prayers in the history of the great tradition, and most of them *collect* the thoughts of the people as they prepare to meet their Lord in His Word. The collect follows the pattern of the Jewish *berakah* that begins with a greeting of God, the statement of motive, petitions, and a conclusion. Even in our prayers, we follow the pattern of Jesus in the synagogue who prayed in a form similar to the collect's form.

The greeting of the pastor that announces the presence of the Lord to bless and give gifts precedes the collect: "The Lord be with you." This greeting occurs here, before the gifts are given in the Liturgy of the Word, and in the preface to the Liturgy of the Lord's Supper, where the gift given is the very body and blood of Christ. The greeting and response of the people announces the special relationship between the pastor and his flock, for as one who stands in the stead and by the command of Christ, he is the one through whom the gifts are given. The collect, following upon this pastoral greeting, is itself an intensely pastoral prayer and should be spoken by the pastor and not said in unison by the congregation. For the pastor, standing in the stead and by the command of Christ, prays in Christ on behalf of the people, presenting to the Father through the Son by the Spirit the deepest longings of God's holy people. Here is the pastor as intercessor, preparing the people of God to hear the Word of God through prayer.

II. The Liturgy of the Word

Old Testament
Gradual
Epistle
Alleluia
Gospel
Sermon
Creed
Prayer of the Church

The first major structure of the Divine Service that is part of the table fellowship pattern of Word and Meal is the Liturgy of the Word. Here Christ comes to us from the voice of the pastor to our ears through which He is present for us and for our salvation. We readily speak of the Eucharist as the real presence of Christ, but we should also speak of Christ's presence in His Word. We tend to say, properly so, that the Holy Spirit works through the Word in order to create faith. But we need to add that faith is created because of the real presence of Jesus Christ according to both His divine and human natures. In His Word, Christ is present in His body and soul, flesh and blood. He is present in the Word not to feed our bodies but our souls. The problem comes in describing this presence, and Lutheran dogmatic categories about the presence of Christ in the Word could well be more fully developed. This presence is, of course, a mystery, but one that we affirm as part of our understanding of Christ's real presence in the liturgy. The one present bodily in the Lord's Supper first invites us through the Gospel and preaching. Preaching cannot be divorced from the Sacrament, and all Christian preaching must in fact be Christological and sacramental. This affirms our confession that Christ promised to be present by His Spirit wherever His Word is read and preached in the Church's worship. This is, of course, a great mystery, but it nevertheless accents what we believe about Christ's ongoing presence among us through the Gospel and the Sacraments.

Viva vox Jesu

Viva vox Jesu—the living voice of Jesus—is what we hear when His Word is read and preached. The Word of Jesus is both a written and an oral word. This Word, though written in words inspired and canonically received, is also spoken and heard within a community called the Body of Christ. This voice is a living voice, for by it Jesus Christ is present for us bodily.

This Word comes from the Word made flesh, a Word that has creative power—power to cast out demons, heal the sick, raise the dead, and release us from our sins. With the Old Testament saints, we acknowledge that God's Word is God's food for hungry pilgrims who have journeyed in Christ through a baptism of His death and resurrection toward the final destination of full communion with Him in heaven.

This Word is interpreted within the community, broken open through preaching as hearts burn through proclamation of prophet and apostle. At the center of our task of interpretation is the understanding that exegesis is always undertaken with preaching as central to our explication of the Scriptures, for the Scriptures were meant to be preached. To interpret Scriptures rightly requires a proper method of interpretation that reflects a biblical theology of preaching. As a result, to confess our preaching as *Viva vox Jesu* is also to speak of the centrality of Christ in Holy Scripture. And those who proclaim Christ's living voice suffer for that proclamation.

Ulrich Asendorf, an enlightened Luther scholar, describes the *Viva vox Evangelii*. He provides a corrective to those who claim for Luther a narrow view of *sensus literalis*, which means "the literal sense." But he begins by stating how important it is to see the Word of God as a preached Word. Asendorf writes:

> [*Viva vox Evangelii* is] one of the key words and catch phrases in Protestant theology. Its common usage refers to the Word of God as kerygmatically understood. Accordingly, God's Word is first and foremost the preached Word. Certainly, thereby is meant one of the central concerns not only of the theology of Martin Luther but also that of the Reformation in general.[22]

Hughes Oliphant Old describes a very similar understanding of the Word of God among both the New Testament writers as well as the Early

Church fathers. He speaks of this as Christ's "kerygmatic presence" and cites numerous examples in the Gospels and Paul's Epistles where Scripture testifies that its very nature is kerygmatic, particularly Luke 10:16 and its parallel in Matthew 10:40. For Old, "kerygmatic presence" simply means "that when the word of Christ is truly preached, then Christ is present."[23] These observations are in connection with Paul's well-known words from Romans 10:14–17:

> How then will they call on Him in whom they have not believed? And how are they to believe in Him of whom they have never heard? And how are they to hear without someone preaching? And how are they to preach unless they are sent? As it is written, "How beautiful are the feet of those who preach the good news!" But they have not all obeyed the gospel. For Isaiah says, "Lord, who has believed what he has heard from us?" So faith comes from hearing, and hearing through the word of Christ.[24]

The Lectionaries

The dilemma of providing liturgical resources for the Church is to decide which lectionary to use. Does one include the lectionary of Luther, that is, the historic one-year series, or simply provide the Church with the three-year lectionary series that is used by the vast majority of the Church catholic? There are virtues to both lectionaries and persuasive arguments for keeping both.

One of the great virtues of the historic lectionary is its anonymity, that is, no one knows who chose these readings, how they came together, and what rationale was used. This shields the historic lectionary from the accusation of partisan meddling. Those who have lived through years of hearing this historic cycle justifiably treasure its catechetical value. There simply is great value in hearing the same lessons repeated year after year.

But there is also much romantic talk about the "ancient and venerable" historic lectionary. For all of its great catechetical value, there were no Old Testament readings until the nineteenth century, and the selection of readings was less than successful. The revision of the Old Testament readings is necessary so these readings could correspond more closely to the Gospel lessons in a hermeneutic of promise and fulfillment, as was the intent of the three-year lectionary. The stunning adoption of the new and innovative three-year lectionary by Western Christianity within a few decades of Vatican II is nothing short of miraculous. Clearly, the Church saw the need for more exposure to the Holy Scriptures within the Divine Service. The continuous reading of

Matthew, Mark, and Luke in series A, B, and C, along with readings from John during Epiphany and Easter, was embraced for a number of reasons. This new lectionary provided the Church with the more ancient practice of hearing the Gospel unfold as it was intended to be heard—as a complete narrative of the ministry, death, and resurrection of Jesus from the pen of a single evangelist. This refreshing approach to the weekly Sunday readings gave immediate context from one Sunday to another, providing continuity for the congregation as they heard the Gospel unfold from week to week. It also afforded preachers the possibility of deeper exegetical study as well as the prospect of unfolding the fruit of that study within the preaching.

Another reason for the quick adoption of the three-year lectionary was that congregations heard more of the Scriptures over a three-year period than when the same lessons were read year after year. With mounting biblical illiteracy among many in our culture today, the three-year lectionary shows that less Scripture, as with the historic lectionary, is not necessarily the best approach for those who know very little about the Scriptures. The enthusiastic reception of the three-year lectionary by our congregations was gratifying to those who feared the worst when this Roman Catholic innovation was introduced. To hear lessons read in the Church that had not been heard for generations had an immediate salutary effect.

Perhaps the most compelling reason to embrace the three-year lectionary was the restoration of the Old Testament to the readings of the Church with all its rich Christological implications. The hermeneutical intent of the Old Testament choices was to provide a promise/fulfillment rhythm between the Old and New, the very desire of Jesus and the inspired writers of the New Testament. Here was a lectionary that was shaped by some of the finest biblical and liturgical scholars in the world, receiving more careful attention and coordination between the Old Testament and Gospel lessons than any other lectionary in the history of Christendom.

Finally, there is an ecumenical benefit to the three-year lectionary within most of Western Christianity. This is especially true within church bodies where associations with other Christians are not as prevalent as in some denominations. To be reading the same texts on the same Sunday as other Christians throughout the world is a passive but significant expression of our common confession that Jesus is Lord and Savior of the whole world. This reality struck me during my three-month sabbatical in northern Spain taking care of the mission established there by missionaries from Argentina. In the small town of Pola de Siero in the local Roman Catholic church I heard the lessons read and proclaimed, and later that morning I read and preached from the same lessons in the fledgling Lutheran mission gathered in the home of Virginia Garcìa in El Berròn, Asturias. Those very same lessons were also being read and preached in my home congregation of St. Paul's in Fort Wayne, Indiana, where my wife, sons, colleagues, and fellow Lutherans would reflect on how Christ was present in these life-giving words. This reality was true throughout the United States, not only in Lutheran churches but also among millions of other Christians in other denominations.

As we have seen, there are strong values to each lectionary. Those congregations that want to accent continuity with the tradition and the catechetical possibilities of reading the same Scripture lessons every year will have the historic lectionary to choose from. Those who want to hear the voice of each evangelist in a continuous reading of the Gospel, hear more of the Scriptures each year, as well as join the vast majority of Christians in reading the same lessons every Sunday will want to choose the three-year lectionary.

The reading and preaching of Scripture in our churches today closely follows the pattern of the synagogue liturgy as celebrated by Jesus and the apostles, and the adaptation of that practice by the ancient Church. The historic liturgy that has been handed down to us in our worship books is very similar to what has been experienced by the Church for almost two thousand years, not to mention the practice of Jesus and His apostles. The reading and preaching of the Word of God is simple in its structure and direct in its focus. We begin by looking at the practice in the ancient Church and then upon the liturgy of the Word as it has come to us.

The Liturgy of the Word in the Ancient Church

In the ancient Church, everyone was invited to hear the Word of God. This included the baptized, those preparing for Baptism (the catechumens), visitors, the penitents (those who had committed a public sin and were being restored to the community), and those who were being restored from doctrinal error. The Word Service became known as the Liturgy of the Catechumens because it was available to everyone and was the means by which those preparing for Baptism were instructed in the Christian faith. As the Jews in the synagogue believed that God was present in the reading of the Word of God, so also Christians believed that this performative Word made Christ present for the people with the gifts of forgiveness, life, and salvation.

In the simple house setting described earlier, the liturgy would have little ceremony but rather be simple and pragmatic. There was no space in these house churches for any formal movement. As we have noted, there were no pews for sitting and hearing the readings in the church until the invention of printing in fifteenth century, so everyone would be standing for the entire Word service. With liturgies now in text form, to be followed by the eye, it was more convenient to sit than to stand in the liturgy, so pews were added to conform to the reading of the liturgy that was now taking its place alongside the hearing of the liturgy. It was also necessary to have a place to store the worship books.

The service would start with the reading of the Word, though there may have been the singing of a psalm beforehand. Normally, there would be three Old Testament readings, either from the Torah or Law (e.g., Genesis, Exodus, Leviticus, Numbers, Deuteronomy), or from the Prophets and Historical Books or Writings. Between the readings they would sing psalms reflecting upon those readings. This was a time to meditate on the message of the readings, its meaning and application. This part of the service would be very close to the synagogue liturgy discussed in the chapter on Jewish precedents.

Then would follow the Epistle reading, with psalms between each reading. The letters of Paul, Peter, and John would be read in their entirety if possible, so that this second lesson was a continuous reading of the letters of the New Testament.[25] Following the Epistle, there would be the reading of the Holy Gospel. These early communities would read an entire chapter of the Gospel or even a larger section. Since the people were already standing for the Gospel (they stood through the entire service), they honored the reading of the very words of Jesus by adding an Alleluia to the psalm that preceded the reading of the Gospel. This was how they set the Gospel apart. The flow of the Divine Service was always toward the Gospel, which is the climax because it is the very word of Jesus. All the lessons look toward the Gospel: the Old Testament prophets look forward to Christ; the Epistles are a commentary on the Gospels and the life of Jesus. The reading of Scripture in the Word service in the ancient Church could last as long as an hour. (Today, the average length of time for the reading of all three of the lessons is between six and eight minutes! We moderns are in such a hurry.) This is why the Liturgy of the Word was called "the liturgy of the catechumens." Hearing the word of God within the Body of Christ for one hour was a significant act of formation for the catechumens and the baptized.

After the Gospel reading came the sermon. The preaching could go on indefinitely, probably for a minimum of an hour. The sermon was a commentary on the Gospel first, and then a full biblical exposition on everything that was read. Thus the Word service could last two hours or longer. The congregation would participate and react more than we do, e.g., beating breasts when they heard the Law and crying out with joy when they heard the Gospel.

At the conclusion of the Word service there was the Prayer of Dismissal (in later centuries called the "Prayer of the Faithful"). The purpose of this prayer was to dismiss certain categories of people from the Word Service who were not worthy to enter the holy presence of Christ in the Lord's Supper. The word *mass* came from the word Dis-***miss***-al. This prayer form was a distinct part of the liturgy until medieval times. It would include prayer for the catechumens, the penitents, and for those who had confessed publicly a doctrine contrary to the teaching of the Church. After the dismissal of all but the baptized, the doors of the church would be closed. This is the origin of what we now call "closed communion." Even now in the Eastern Church at this point in the liturgy the deacon cries out "the doors, the doors," a remnant of this ancient practice preserved in the eastern liturgy. By this practice of dismissing those who are not worthy to receive the Lord's body and blood, one can see that the core value of holiness from the biblical culture of Jesus and the apostles is still in force among the early Christians. They took very seriously the bodily presence of Christ in the Lord's Supper, as well as following the Lord's instructions to the apostles in Luke 22.[26]

When all had been dismissed and only the faithful remained, they would exchange the kiss of peace. This would be a full kiss on the mouth—men to men and women to women—a sign of the reconciliation that existed among the members of the community before they came to the Eucharist. Only the baptized who were in complete fellowship with one another were capable of exchanging this kiss. This was not a cultural phenomenon, for even in this culture this would have seemed unusual, but the Gospel gave them the freedom to do this.

The Liturgy of the Word Today

Our reading and preaching of Scripture not only resembles the practice of the ancient Church but also carries the same sense of Christ's bodily presence. Through God's Word read and proclaimed, Christ chooses to make Himself present and the reality in which we dwell is heaven itself with all its gifts.

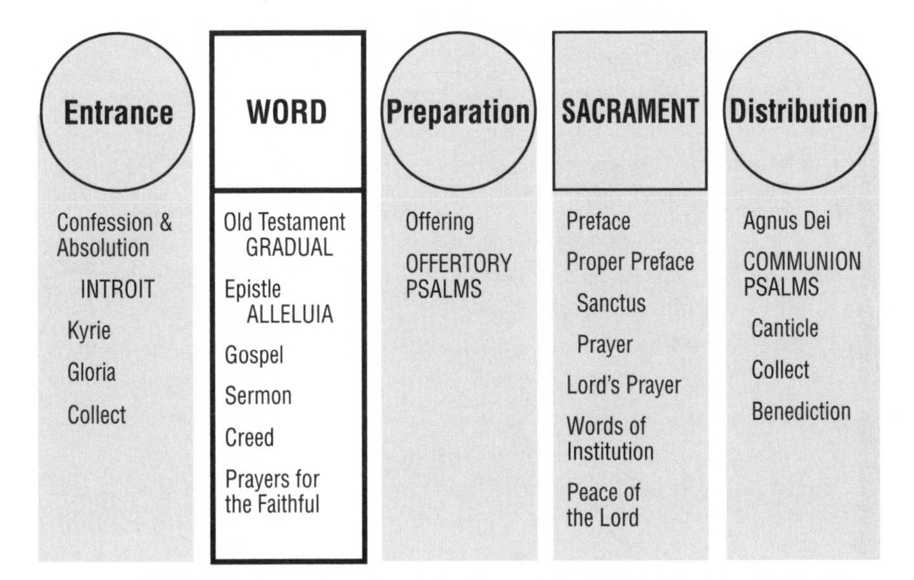

The pattern of reading is the same, with the movement of the entrance rite and the liturgy of the Word culminating in the reading of the Holy Gospel. The very words of Jesus provide the first of two climaxes in the liturgy, the other being the Words of Institution in the liturgy of Holy Communion which are also the very words of Jesus. The two climaxes in the liturgy are the very words of Jesus because they are the performative words of Jesus, the Word made flesh who created the world and recreated it through His death and resurrection. This means that the climax of the liturgy of the Word is the worship of Christ who is in our midst and taking action through His Word.

In our congregations, we acknowledge this climactic moment by singing the alleluia, or what Luther called "the perpetual voice of the church,"[27] and we rise to our feet. On festival days, the climactic character of the reading of the Holy Gospel may be honored by a Gospel procession where the book of the Gospel is brought down into the midst of the people, showing how Christ abides among them in both His divine and human natures. In our ears we hear His words of grace. We greet the Gospel reading with the acclamation, "Glory to You, O Lord," and acknowledge its conclusion with "Praise to You, O Christ," showing once again that it is the very words of Jesus that now bring us to the highest point of worship. We would do well in our congregations to teach our children and catechumens to recognize the climactic character of the Gospel, and carry out our liturgies in such a way that the Gospel is experienced by the congregation as climactic.

THE HYMN OF THE DAY, THE SERMON, THE CREED

Once the Gospel has been heard by the congregation, the Liturgy of the Word continues with the Hymn of the Day, the sermon, and the Creed. The Hymn of the Day and the sermon are interpretations of the Gospel, and the Creed is the baptismal faith confessed in light of the Gospel and its proclamation in song and word. The sermon and Hymn of the Day help the congregation see how Christ is proclaimed in the entire Liturgy of the Word that finds its fulfillment in Christ's very words, and the Creed as an ordinary is like the Kyrie and Gloria in Excelsis—an acknowledgment of gifts received with eager thankfulness and praise. The Creed did not enter the Divine Service as an ordinary until much later in the medieval period. The Creed first appeared in the West at the third Synod of Toledo in Spain, AD 589, but does not become part of the Roman Rite until AD 1014, so it is much later than the Agnus Dei (seventh century), which was the last of the ordinaries to be incorporated into the Divine Service. Until then, the Creed was associated with Baptism and not with the liturgy of Word and Sacrament.

That the Hymn of the Day and the sermon interpret the Gospel and proclaim Christ to the people of God suggests a number of things. It is fitting and respectful of the liturgy that the sermon be on the Gospel of the day, except for some exceptional circumstances, such as a series of sermons on the continuous reading of the Epistles. If the Gospel is central, then the Old Testament and Epistle help interpret the Gospel, as was the case in the Jewish synagogue and the Early Church. This is particularly true of the Old Testament lesson, which in both the historic lectionary and the three-year lectionary was chosen in connection with the Gospel.

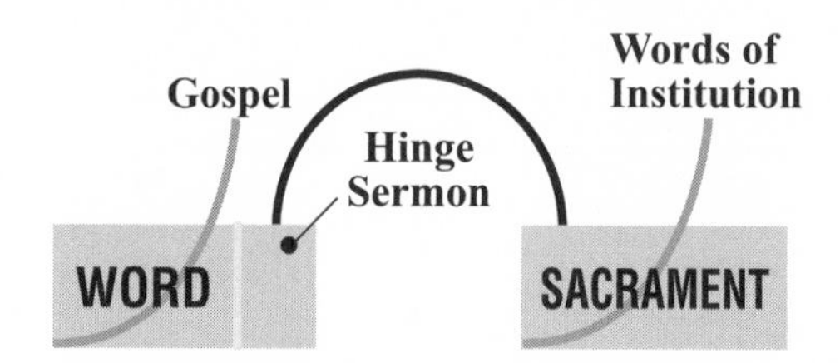

The sermon explicates the readings and proclaims the person and presence of Christ.

This means that the sermon explicates all of the readings, including the Hymn of the Day, as to how Christ is present and active as the agent of our salvation. Preaching proclaims both the person and work of Christ, focusing on the atonement and how that atonement is now present bodily for the people of God in the hearing of the Word and the eating and drinking of the Word made flesh.

The Prayer of the Church

The Prayer of the Church was formerly called the Prayer of Dismissal (see above) and provided the conclusion of the Liturgy of the Word. In this pastoral prayer, the needs of both church and world are brought before the people as they give thanks and petition the Father through the Son by the Holy Spirit. These prayers flow out of the readings and the sermon, using the themes of the day as a focus for the thanksgiving and the petitions. The prayers may take on various forms, normally responsive as the people respond with acclamations such as "Hear our prayer" or "Lord, have mercy." Another form that may be used is the bidding prayer where a member of the congregation on behalf of the people brings forward the bid, or petition, and the pastor prays concerning that request. Petitions should be brought to the pastor ahead of time, but there should be an opportunity during the service for the congregation to bring their concerns to the pastor through the elders or ushers.

In some settings of the Divine Service the Prayer of the Church comes after the offering and offertory and is attached to the Liturgy of the Lord's Supper. This is a more recent practice and does not reflect the practice of the Early Church where the prayers of dismissal marked the close of the Liturgy of the Word. Either place is acceptable, though the more ancient practice seems to make more sense both in terms of the rhythm of the Divine Service and the function of the prayers in the liturgy itself.

This brings our explication of the Liturgy of the Word in the Divine Service to a close. In the next chapter, we will explicate the Liturgy of the Lord's Supper.

10

The Historic Liturgy as Divine Service—The Liturgy of the Lord's Supper

The prayers bring to a conclusion the first two structures of the fivefold structure of the Divine Service, the Liturgy of the Word. The focus now shifts to the Liturgy of the Lord's Supper, framed by the preparation of the table and the distribution of the gifts. These final three structures complete the Divine Service, bringing it to a climax. The presence of Christ, having come first through hearing, now comes to us bodily in eating and drinking. From ear to mouth Christ feeds us holy food, and then out into the world we go, bearing witness to the Christ in us and bringing others into Christ's presence that they might receive the gifts.

III. Preparation of the Table

The Offering

The Offertory

A natural break in the service occurs at this point when the table is now set for the Lord's Supper. In the Early Church, when the Liturgy of the Catechumens ended, the bread and wine would be carried in from another room, probably the kitchen area. That would be the "pause" between the Word and Sacrament services. The elements would be very simple: a pitcher of wine, a cup, and some bread. There was no entrance rite or ceremony accompanying the placement of the elements on the altar; tight space simply would not allow it. The elements were carried in and placed on the table. The people would remain standing in their places because there was no place to go.

In the post-Constantinian Church, a more elaborate entrance rite for the bread and wine would take place that paralleled the entrance rite of the clergy at the beginning of the service. A procession of the bread and wine would proceed from a building outside the church where the wine was stored and the bread baked, equivalent to what we now call the sacristy. This procession would include a cross, incense, and whatever else was necessary to make a path through the congregation with the elements. In the Eastern Church this is called "the Great Entrance."

As in the entrance rite, psalms would accompany the procession, though no particular psalm or "ordinary" attached itself to the procession of the gifts of bread and wine. Any appropriate psalm could accompany the bearing of the gifts to the altar. One psalm most associated with the procession was Psalm 51, "Create in Me a Clean Heart, O God." Sometimes no psalm would accompany the procession, but a canticle would be used, such as those we now use in some of the settings of the Divine Service (e.g., "Let the Vineyards Be Fruitful," a biblical canticle,[1] as well as the canticle "What Shall I Render to the Lord," based on Psalm 116,[2] one of the Hallel Psalms that Jesus would have sung on His way to the Mount of Olives on that first Maundy Thursday after the Last Supper.)

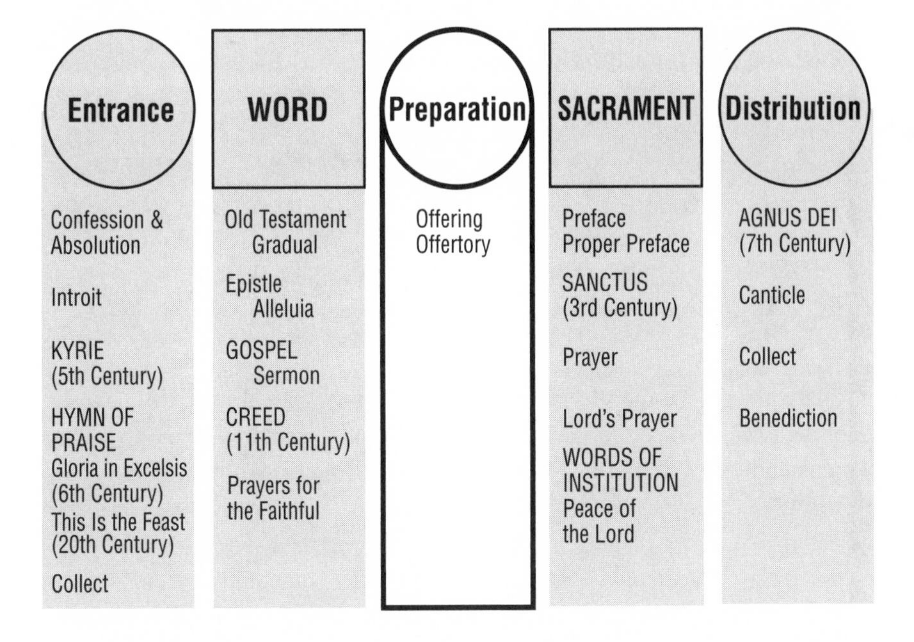

The bringing forward of the bread and wine is part of the sacrificial part of the liturgy where we offer our gifts to God, including our tithes and offerings. These gifts are given in response to the hearing of the very words of Jesus in the Gospel and are given in thanksgiving for the gift about to be received in the Lord's Supper, as we give back to the Lord what He has given us, acknowledging that we are unable to "outgive" the Lord. The people of God respond by bringing forward their gifts with the bread and wine as the table is set for the meal. The offering of our gifts for the extension of God's kingdom begins with the gifts of bread and wine that will be used as the means by which we will receive the very body and blood of Christ. We will need these gifts so that we can bear witness to Christ in the world. These gifts also are a means by which God provides for needs of the community. This is particularly poignant when the altar also functions as a table so that the preparation of the table suggests to the congregation that a meal is about to be eaten.

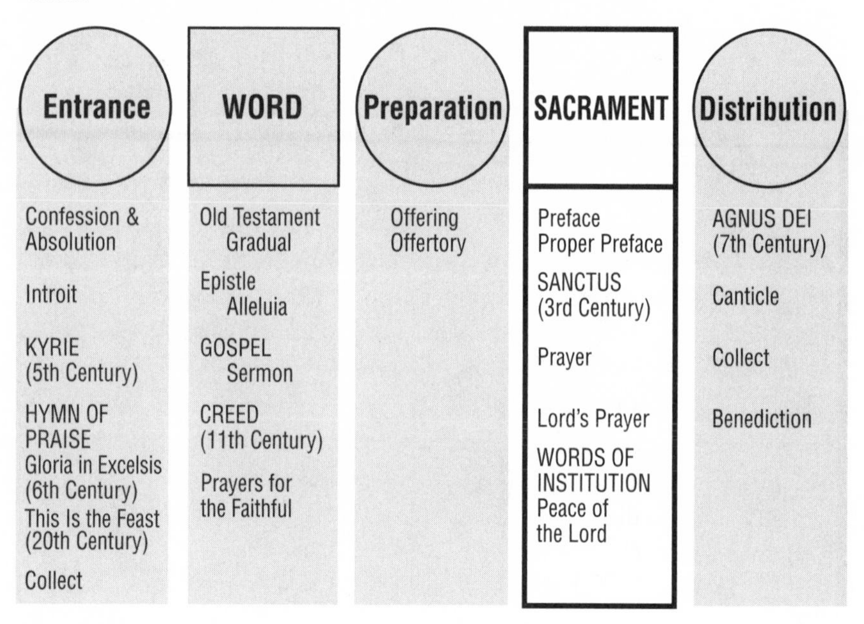

IV. The Liturgy of the Lord's Supper

Preface

Proper Preface

Sanctus

The Lord's Prayer

The Eucharistic Prayer

The Pax Domini

The second major structure of the Divine Service that is part of the table fellowship pattern of Word and Meal is the Liturgy of the Lord's Supper. Here

Jesus is present for us bodily, as He is in the Liturgy of the Word, but now He is present in, with, and under bread and wine. To come to the altar and receive these gifts is to enter the Holy of Holies. Here at the altar we come to the new Jerusalem, to the mountain of His holiness: "On this mountain the LORD of hosts will make for all peoples a feast of rich food, a feast of well-aged wine, of rich food full of marrow, of aged wine well refined" (Isaiah 25:6). Here we feast with Christ and all the saints at a banquet He has prepared for us.

The Liturgy of the Lord's Supper does not stand on its own but follows closely upon the Liturgy of the Word that has tilled the soil of the heart so that the good seed might be planted, grow, and bear fruit. As we saw on the way to Emmaus, where there is no hearing of the Word to cause hearts to burn, the meal cannot open eyes to the eternal realities of heaven on earth in Jesus Christ. This reality—that we join angels and archangels and all the company of heaven in feasting with Christ in His kingdom—is the reason why we give thanks. And so the Lord's Supper is also called the Eucharist, which means the giving of thanks to a God who graciously gives eternal gifts to temporal people. These gifts bring us into communion with Christ and all of heaven, which is why this is also called Holy Communion. It acknowledges that we have joined ourselves to the eternal One and His eternal kingdom. The destination of our journey from font to altar for these gifts is why we sometimes call this great feast the Sacrament of the Altar. But throughout this book we have normally referred to this as the Lord's Supper, for it is a meal of bread and wine, body and blood, and it is the Lord's Supper, not ours; He does the giving and the feeding, and we simply receive these gifts in faith and to His glory, recipients of heaven itself in our very bodies.

PREFACE

P: The Lord be with you
C: And also with you.
P: Lift up your hearts.
C: We lift them to the Lord.
P: Let us give thanks to the Lord our God.
C: It is right to give Him thanks and praise.

The Liturgy of the Lord's Supper begins with the Preface, which acknowledges this eschatological reality of heaven and earth joined together in Christ. The Preface is one of the oldest parts of the liturgy, and could have been used by the apostles.[3] We have already observed how the pastoral salutation, "The Lord be with you," preceded the Liturgy of the Word. Now the same greeting begins the Liturgy of the Lord's Supper. The pastor says, "Lift up your hearts," calling us to lift them up into heaven with Christ and all the company of heaven, which is exactly what we do when we enter into this holy meal. "We lift them to the Lord," we exclaim, for the Preface teaches us that the Lord's Supper is a joining together of heaven and earth in one great liturgy. "Let us give thanks to the Lord our God," proclaims the celebrant, for the Church throughout the ages gives thanks to God for the divine gifts of grace which flow to us from the sacrificial life and death of our Lord Jesus Christ. "It is right to give Him thanks and praise," we respond, and so our Lord's Supper begins with eucharistic joy, for all thanksgiving and praise come from the joy of our union with Christ.

The Proper Preface

In the Early Church before Constantine, before the Church Year was fully developed, the liturgy would move from the Preface to the Sanctus to the eucharistic prayer. But as the Church Year developed, the Preface expanded into what is now called the Proper Preface, a part of the Liturgy of the Lord's Supper that changes according to the season. The proper prefaces contain some of the most sublime theology in our liturgies, connecting us to both the life of Christ, the theological implications of His life, and the reality of that life present among us now in the gifts of bread and wine, body and blood.[4] Each proper preface begins with the words, "It is truly good, right, and salutary that we should at all times and in all places give thanks to You, holy Lord, almighty Father, everlasting God," and ends with "Therefore with angels and archangels and with all the company of heaven we laud and magnify Your glorious name, evermore praising You and saying . . ." These phrases have become connected to the eucharistic prayer that begins here and continues through the Words of Institution.

The final phrase concerning the angels, archangels, and all the company of heaven speaks with greater clarity than any other phrase in the liturgy to the reality of heaven on earth, a reality we have called "inaugurated eschatology." What we must always remember when we go to the Lord's Supper is that we commune with Christ and that wherever Christ is, there is heaven. And this communion includes all the saints who have died and risen in Christ: Abraham, Isaac, Jacob, David, Ruth, Peter, Paul, our grandparents and great-grandparents—perhaps even our spouses or our children—and all the saints now living all over the world, and those still to come. After someone dies, it is good to think of them at the Lord's Supper, knowing that as we commune here below at the table of the Lamb and sing His songs, we do join them since they are simultaneously communing at the marriage feast of the Lamb in His kingdom that knows no end, and singing the songs of the Lamb with angels and archangels. In Christ, in that great mystery of our union with Him, we are joined to all who are joined to Him.

In between these two formulaic phrases are the variable parts of the proper preface. For example, the Proper Preface for Holy Week contains language that speaks directly of the season and the atonement of Christ, the new Adam, as that which reverses the fall of the first Adam whose disobedience came from eating fruit from the forbidden tree:

> It is truly good, right, and salutary that we should at all times and in all places give thanks to You, holy Lord, almighty Father, everlasting God, through Jesus Christ, our Lord, who accomplished the salvation of mankind by the tree of the cross that, where death arose, there life also might rise again and that the serpent who overcame by the tree of the garden might likewise by the tree of the cross be overcome. Therefore with angels and archangels and with all the company of heaven we laud and magnify Your glorious name, evermore praising You and saying . . . (*LSB: Agenda*, p. 151)

Sanctus

After the Preface and Proper Preface comes the singing of the Sanctus. This hymn derives its name from the Latin word for "Holy" and prepares the people to hear the eucharistic prayer and receive the Sacrament. In it the congregation joins in the song of the angels, archangels, and all the company of heaven who are also singing songs to the Lamb in the heavenly places. It is a solemn act of adoration and thanksgiving in the spirit of holy awe. This is an appropriate way to begin the sacramental rite because this is now the Christian Holy of Holies.

Returning to the fivefold shape of the historic liturgy, the Kyrie and Hymn of Praise as the entrance to the Liturgy of the Word are balanced by the Sanctus that, with the Preface and Proper Preface, forms the entrance rite to the Liturgy of the Sacrament. Just as the Kyrie announced that the King was coming in His Word, so now the Sanctus announces that the King is coming in His Lord's Supper: "Blessed is He who comes in the name of the Lord." As we observed above, the Gloria's accent on heaven and earth being joined together in peace is echoed in the Sanctus so that both Kyrie and Gloria are embraced by the Sanctus. The following diagram illustrates the delicate, but significant balance between the ordinaries.

ENTRANCE	PREPARATION	DISTRIBUTION
Psalms/Introit (chanted)	**Psalms** (chanted)	**Psalms** (chanted)
Kyrie (Lk 16, 17, 18) *The Coming of the King* "In peace . . ." Lord have mercy	**Sanctus** (Is 6/Ps 118) *The Coming of the King* Blessed is He who comes	
Gloria (Lk 2:14) "Glory be to God on high		**Agnus Dei** (Jn 1:29)
"We praise you . . . **God the Father** Almighty **Lamb of God, Son of the Father** takes away the sin of the world with the **Holy Spirit** . . ."		**Lamb of God** takes away the sins
Collect of the Day		

The Sanctus is the most ancient of liturgical hymns, though it, too, has a textual history that is hidden in the mists of liturgical communities East and West, Jewish and Christian. Liturgical scholars affirm that the Sanctus was a hymn sung in both temple and synagogue during the time of Jesus. It is highly probable that Jesus sang the Sanctus at some point in His liturgical life. Appearing as early as the third century in Syrian and Palestinian churches, the Sanctus may be present even earlier in Christian worship. Clement of Rome may refer to the Sanctus as a liturgical text in his first letter, and Origen in a sermon on Isaiah. Clement was bishop from AD 92–101, meaning that the Sanctus may very well be present in the first century. Its first appearance as a liturgical text in a eucharistic liturgy is from a liturgy of Serapion, who died in AD 360,[5] and by the end of the fourth century it was present in every major eucharistic liturgy.[6] The general high estimation of the Sanctus by liturgical scholars is summed up by this statement: "[The Sanctus] has been called 'the most ancient, the most celebrated, and the most universal of Christian hymns.' "[7]

There are two parts to the Sanctus, and each comes from a different book of the Old Testament. The first part is from Isaiah 6:3:

> Holy, holy, holy Lord, God of pow'r and might:
> **Heaven and earth** are full of Your glory.

The biblical context of Isaiah's vision may be described as follows:

> The *Sanctus* . . . derives from Isaiah's breathtakingly majestic vision of the transcendent otherness of the All-Holy in confounding contrast to the mortality and impurity of humanity (Isa. 6:3; see Dan. 7:10; Rev. 4:8). The prophet sees the exalted and utterly unapproachable Thrice-Holy enthroned as sovereign, surrounded with seraph attendants who hide their faces from the divine glory. The swirling incense becomes the robes of the Holy One whose glory fills the earth, whose holiness radiates upon the world. Isaiah was terrified by what he saw. A sinful man had penetrated the heavenly court and gazed upon the face of God.[8]

We have no clear idea why the Sanctus was first placed as a preface to the eucharistic prayer and the Words of Institution; it is the presence of God that Isaiah's vision and the Lord's Supper have in common. Like Isaiah, we, too, are sinful human beings who are about to enter the heavenly court, preparing to approach the table where we will gaze upon Him in the Supper He has prepared for us. We are not to seek God in our own sinful flesh, even in the manner Isaiah encountered Him, or by rising up to God as if in spirit only, as many Christians in our culture would suggest. Even some Christians will ask, "Why may I not approach God?" What is lacking is an understanding of God's holiness and His humanity—that it is only "safe" and possible for us to see and approach God in His humanity, for His glory comes down to us as we gaze upon Him in Word and Meal; that is as much glory as we are able to bear.

As noted in the discussion of the Gloria in Excelsis, the Church added "heaven" to Isaiah's words for they believed, as we do, that in the Lord's Supper heaven meets earth in the flesh of Jesus. The liturgy of heaven and the liturgy of earth are joined together, and though we cannot see or hear the heavenly choirs, we are joined with them in singing songs to the Lamb who was slain and raised again. Perhaps the common hymn between the liturgies of heaven and earth is the Sanctus, for both in heaven and on earth saints stand on holy ground before God's holy presence with whom they have holy communion.

The second part of the hymn is from Psalm 118:25–26, one of the psalms used in the procession to temple and altar. Originally, processional psalms were sung as the ark proceeded down the *via sacra,* especially as David brought the ark to Jerusalem from Obed-Edom (2 Samuel 6). Later these "hallel psalms" were sung as the Israelites ascended to the temple for worship. Psalm 118 describes the "Gate of Righteousness" through which the faithful and righteous Israelites entered as worthy participants in the temple liturgy (Psalm 118:19–20: "Open to me the gates of righteousness, that I may enter through them and give thanks to the LORD. This is the gate of the LORD; the righteous shall enter through it"). The righteous enter with thanksgiving, for God has answered their prayers and has become their salvation in the very place they now stand (Ps 118:21: "I thank You that You have answered me and have become my salvation").

Psalm 118, then, continues with a verse cited in all three Synoptic Gospels in the parable of the workers in the vineyard as Jesus' final preview of what will take place in Jerusalem: "The stone that the builders rejected has become the cornerstone" (Matthew 21:42; Mark 12:10; Luke 20:17, all quoting Psalm 118:22; cf. Acts 4:11). Jesus uses Psalm 118 to describe His upcoming rejection by the Sanhedrin. What is so extraordinary about Jesus' imminent crucifixion is that His rejection is the means by which He will become the cornerstone and is therefore a reference to His glory. God's glory is manifested in the rejection of God's Son (v. 22). For the psalmist, this great reversal of rejection as a means for glory is the Lord's doing and therefore is marvelous in our eyes (vv. 23–24). For this day of rejection on Golgotha is the day the Lord has made, a day for rejoicing and celebration in the temple of the Lord, for Jesus begins His ascent to the heavenly sanctuary when He is lifted up on the cross. As Hebrews puts it:

> But when Christ appeared as a high priest of the good things that have come, then through the greater and more perfect tent (not made with hands, that is, not of creation), He entered once for all into the holy places, not by means of the blood of goats and calves, but by means of His own blood, thus securing an eternal redemption. (Hebrews 9:11–12)

This brings us to the words of the Sanctus in the second stanza of the hymn. As a Psalm of Ascent, these words begin with the people crying "Hosanna," that is, "Save us, we pray, O Lord! O Lord, we pray, give us success!" The priests, speaking for Yahweh, then pronounce a blessing on the righteous as they now enter the temple "in the name of the Lord." To enter in His name is to enter in His presence.[9]

Hosanna. Hosanna. Hosanna in the highest.

Blessed is He who comes in the name of the Lord.
Hosanna in the highest.

As we already observed, this is also the song of the people of Jerusalem when Jesus entered the Holy City on Palm Sunday. When Jesus the King entered Jerusalem, He entered to receive the kingdom promised Him by His Father (Luke 22:28–30). Before Jesus entered Jerusalem, He had prophesied that the people would acclaim Him, "Blessed the Coming One in the name of the Lord." As Jesus enters, all the evangelists announce that Jesus is the Messiah who will ascend the tree and then break the bonds of death from a tomb now empty. As Pius Parsh notes, the Church's placement of the Sanctus at this point in the service is to create in the worshiping assembly the image of "our Lord upon the cross, with all creation gathered about; the *Sanctus* proper brings in the angels, the Benedictus the disciples, and the entire composition assumes the character of a drama."[10]

So also today in our sanctuaries the righteous gathered in the presence of the Holy One of God are blessed as they prepare to ascend to the altar to receive the holy food of body broken, blood poured out. The Benedictus—"Blessed is He who comes in the name of the Lord"—announces the reality that the King now comes to us in His Supper to feed His people holy food to make us holy so that we might depart in **peace**. Here God gives holiness to the unholy that we might holy be (a paraphrase of "My Song Is Love Unknown" [*LSB* 430:1]). In some eucharistic liturgies, the Benedictus is the people's response "to the invitation to holy communion, 'Holy things for the holy people.' "[11]

Luther permitted the singing of the Sanctus during the consecration with the elevation occurring during the Benedictus.[12] Luther's concession shows that for him the Sanctus affirms his belief in the bodily presence of Jesus at the Lord's Supper, though the traditional placement of it as the conclusion to the Preface/Proper Preface is preferred. Along with the elevation during the Benedictus in Luther's rite there would be the ringing of the bells and genuflection.[13]

From the beginning, Lutherans have observed the practice of bowing during the Sanctus and making the sign of the cross at the Benedictus, though this custom has fallen out of use in most Lutheran churches today.

We bow at the holy, bodily presence of Christ crucified and risen, present for us, for the forgiveness of our sins, for our salvation. We make the sign of the cross to acknowledge that we are baptized, that this same crucified and risen Christ dwells in us bodily by Baptism and faith, and that only because He is holy and gives that holiness to us bodily are we now called holy. This was and is one of the most sacred and reverent moments in the liturgy, and Christians have always acknowledged, both with their minds and bodies, such moments of high sanctity. To bow and make the sign of the cross is to simply express with our whole beings both the reality of Christ's indwelling presence, and the single most important fact about us; we are baptized.

The association of the Sanctus with the real presence of Christ in the Lord's Supper caused some churches in the Protestant communion to drop it from the liturgy, including some Anglicans. This was especially true of the Benedictus. Lutherans, however, have remained steadfastly attached to the Sanctus as an affirmation of Christ's bodily presence in the Sacrament.

The Lord's Prayer

The Lord's Prayer has always been associated with the Liturgy of the Lord's Supper and precedes the eucharistic prayer. Since it only occurs here in the Divine Service, it was a prayer that only the baptized prayed, with catechumens first learning to pray it during their final preparations for Baptism. In the ancient Church, the Lord's Prayer followed the eucharistic prayer as a summary of that prayer in the words that Jesus taught His disciples to pray.

The context of the Lord's Prayer in the ministry of Jesus helps us to understand its significance in the Liturgy of the Lord's Supper. The prayer itself is evoked by a request (Luke 11:1). This is the only occasion on which any of the disciples ask Jesus to teach them something. What one of them asks Jesus is to teach them how to petition God. Each rabbi had a particular way of petitioning God, and the disciples are aware that John had taught his disciples how to petition. Jesus begins in typical Hebrew fashion by calling on God. By instructing His disciples to address God as "Father," Jesus places them into the same relationship with God that He has. Throughout the Gospel, the disciples will observe Jesus' relationship to God the Father and come to realize that through the Son of God they are sons of God.

The Petitions

Jesus first petitions the Father regarding who God is—His name—and what God does—His reigning as King. God's holy name and God's gracious rule in His (present) kingdom give the disciples confidence and freedom to approach the Father with their own petitions. When Jesus begins with God-centered petitions, He is instructing the disciples that the gifts they receive come from the one who is holy and whose kingdom is coming when they petition the Father. Jesus would have His disciples treat God's name as holy by calling on God as Father, trusting that He will respond graciously for the sake of His Son.

The Fourth Petition

The petition for daily bread in the Lord's Prayer is the first of the three petitions that focus on the needs of the petitioners. When Jesus mentions bread, He is pointing to table fellowship where those dining receive both the physical bread needed for life in this world *now* as well as the eschatological bread that provides the life of the age to come as spiritual sustenance *even now*. This follows the pattern of the Old Testament manna, which certainly was physical, earthly food, but which at the same time provided miraculously and in abundance for the people chosen to be a priestly nation, pointing to the fullness of God's gifts to come in Christ. Now in the Gospel, the heavenly and eternal kingdom of God *has broken into this age in Jesus*. He grants the forgiveness of sins, heals, and raises the dead. Already now He is furnishing, at least in part, the life—both physical and spiritual—of the age to come. Therefore, in the prayer Jesus taught His disciples,

> the bread for which we pray is *at the one and the same time* both earthly bread to meet the hunger and need of the present day, and also the future bread which will satisfy the elect in the eschatological kingdom and is already given to us in anticipation —miraculous feedings of the crowds were, in sign and reality, present experiences of the future messianic meal at which those who now hunger will be satisfied.[14]

Luther saw "daily bread" as encompassing all of God's gifts—spiritual and eschatological as well as physical and temporal. The petition for "daily bread," in Luther's view, subsumes the following petitions for forgiveness and protection from temptation, much as all of the Ten Commandments are summed up in the First Commandment. Those who know Luther's Small Catechism will recognize the close relationship between the Fourth Petition of the Lord's Prayer and the First Article of the Creed, for "daily bread" signifies "everything that belongs to our entire life in the world,"[15] such as "food and drink, clothing, house and home, and health of body . . . a godly wife, children, and servants . . . our work, trade, or whatever we are engaged in to prosper and succeed . . . faithful neighbors and good friends, and other such things," as well as beneficent government rulers and protection from enemies, tempest, war, famine, wicked people, and the devil.[16] In the new creation, the baptized are those who know how to use these earthy and physical gifts from the Fourth Petition, for we are fleshly people for whom our God provides the things of this world so that we might rejoice in the gifts of His good and gracious creation.

Yet particularly in earlier writings Luther gave special emphasis to God's spiritual, eschatological, and sacramental gifts. Luther's longest treatment of this petition is in *An Exposition of the Lord's Prayer for Simple Laymen* (1519), where he says, "The bread, the Word, and the food are none other than Jesus Christ our Lord himself. Thus he declares in John 6 [:51], 'I am the living bread which came down from heaven.' " God answers this petition for bread by sending faithful clergy, who supply "this Word daily and abundantly." Luther explains that "daily bread" is given "in two different ways: first, through words; second, through the Sacrament of the Altar. . . . In the sacrament Christ is received." Luther goes on to stress the importance of Gospel-centered preaching to accompany the Sacrament, and he says that "faith is nothing else than the eating of this bread."[17] In his *Personal Prayer Book* (1522) Luther has similar comments:

> This bread is our Lord Jesus Christ who feeds and comforts the soul. Therefore, O heavenly Father, grant grace that the life, words, deeds, and suffering of Christ be preached. . . . Help us through his death to overcome our own death with a firm faith and thus boldly follow our beloved Guide into the life beyond this one. . . .
>
> At our life's end do not let us be deprived of the holy and true body of Christ. Help all priests to administer and use the sacred sacrament worthily and blessedly. . . . Graciously help us and all other Christians to receive the holy sacrament at the proper time.
>
> And in brief, give us our daily bread so that Christ may remain in us eternally and we in him.[18]

Jesus' table fellowship, entailing the kingdom, bread, and forgiveness petitioned for in the Lord's Prayer, arrives at its fullness in the Last Supper. There Jesus will institute the Meal of the new covenant in His blood, shed for the forgiveness of sins (Luke 22:14–20). Jesus will take physical bread and state, "This is My body, which is given [compare Luke 11:3] for you" (Luke 22:19). During the meal twice He will say that He will not partake again until the full coming of "the kingdom of God" (Luke 22:16, 18). Thus in the Lord's Supper God gives bread that is truly physical and at the same time eschatological. This bread is a foretaste of the feast to come in the eschaton (Revelation 19:6–9). It is bread that brings the forgiveness of sins because it is the very body of Christ, "given for you" (Luke 22:19). Moreover, this gift of forgiveness leads the recipients to forgive others. Since God gives the forgiveness of sins with the bread and wine in the Lord's Supper, guests at the table likewise forgive the sins of those who owe them. We join our Lord when He forgives our neighbor's sins. The Lord's Prayer continues the pattern of Jesus' ministry throughout the Gospel: earthly and spiritual gifts are given together from the same hand of the Creator, who has united heaven and earth in the flesh of His Son, Jesus Christ. The incarnation of the holy Son of God by the Holy Spirit (Luke 1:35) is the prime manifestation of God's hallowing the creation; the heavenly, holy Child is born to inherit the throne of the earthly, Davidic kingdom (Luke 1:32–33). By instructing His disciples to address God as Father, as He has done, Jesus teaches them to confess that in His kingdom, His disciples on earth are united with the Father in heaven.

In worship, absolution and the table fellowship of the Lord's Supper give further expression to this joining of heaven and earth in Christ. In absolution, the human voice announcing forgiveness is at the same time a supernatural and eschatological announcement from Christ Himself. In the Sacrament, earthly bread is at the same time supernatural and eschatological bread, since according to Jesus' words, the bread is His body. When a catechumen prays for bread according to Jesus' instruction and remembers the recurring significance of bread in Jesus' ministry throughout the Gospel, the petitioner would likely include in mind the life-giving bread of the Supper—the God-given bread that is both earthly and heavenly.

The Fifth Petition

The forgiveness of sins, next in the Lord's Prayer, balances the petition for bread. Just as bread is the essential staple of physical life, and the Supper provides bread that is both earthly and heavenly, so forgiveness is the essential sustenance of spiritual life. Like the daily need for bread, the need for forgiveness is constant and ongoing, hence Jesus' provision of the Supper as the regular meal that provides forgiveness. It is only because forgiveness makes fallen humans holy that they may call on God as Father; His kingdom comes through the forgiveness of sins. There are dramatic examples of this in Jesus' ministry, for example, Luke 5:17–26; 7:36–50. In fact, Jesus lays out His mission in a sermon describing the purpose of His ministry, a ministry bringing "release" or "forgiveness" (see Luke 4:18–19). Just as "bread" involves both physical and spiritual nourishment, the forgiveness of sins brings release from the physical as well as spiritual consequences of sin. This Jesus demonstrated in His healing in Luke 5:17–26. In the Apostles' Creed, the progression is deliberate and explicit: "the forgiveness of sins" leads to "the resurrection of the body and the life everlasting." Disciples who pray the Lord's Prayer may have to wait until the resurrection to experience physical healing, but the promise of that release is as sure as the forgiveness of their sins in Christ.

The Sixth Petition

Both bread and the forgiveness of sins shed light on the final petition: "Lead us not into temptation" (Luke 11:4). The Father who gives all good gifts allowed even His Son to be tempted by Satan in the wilderness, and that temptation went so far as to include the suggestion to put (physical, earthly) bread ahead of the Word of God and to seek worldly glory instead of properly worshiping God alone (Luke 4:1–13). Jesus will also speak of Satan's desire to "to sift you [the disciples] as wheat" (Luke 22:31). Trials and sufferings come because of the preaching of the kingdom. The disciples will be rejected as Jesus was rejected. This opposition is a given with the coming of the kingdom. To pray not to be led into temptation is to pray for the resources necessary to avoid succumbing to that temptation. The disciples are to pray that though they are assailed by the devil, the world, and the sinful nature, God would preserve them from falling into apostasy. Taken together, the petitions for bread, for forgiveness, and for keeping them from succumbing to temptation are petitions to help the disciples be kept in the one true, saving faith, so that they "may finally overcome them and win the victory."[19]

Thus the Lord's Prayer petitions God to continue to give the eschatological gifts that already have a present reality for the disciples. So also for us today. This eschatological reality is about to be received by the communicants at the table set for them of the finest foods. They pray the Lord's Prayer knowing that the bread of life will be given into their mouths and they will partake of His life-giving death and resurrection. In the Liturgy of the Lord's Supper, the Lord's Prayer is a table prayer petitioning the Father that in this meal we may receive what we need to support us body and soul.[20]

THE EUCHARISTIC PRAYER

Following the Sanctus is the eucharistic prayer that balances the sermon as a recitation of God's mighty acts of salvation that culminated on the night in which He was betrayed. Like the sermon, the eucharistic prayer interprets for the baptized how God is a God who saves. Many of the ancient eucharistic prayers told the story of salvation, beginning with the Old Testament and stretching forward into the fulfillment of God's promise to save His world from sin and death in the incarnation of His Son, Jesus Christ. In the eucharistic prayers of the Church we see the story of the world told at a banquet where the host, Jesus Christ, is also the victim and the food. The Church's faith at the table is contained in the eucharistic prayers, just as the Church's faith at the font is told through her creeds.

From the very beginning, Christians have prayed at the Eucharist, giving thanks to God and including in that thanksgiving the Words of Institution, repeating the words Jesus spoke in the Upper Room to His disciples during the Last Supper. Within the eucharistic prayer, the Words of Institution are like the statement of motive in the Jewish *berakah*—they proclaim what it is that God has done for His people in this ultimate act of table fellowship, where Jesus gives His body and blood in, with, and under bread and wine. In both Jewish and Christian prayers, there are different accents, from greeting to statement of motive to petition to doxological ending. Not all prayer is petition, and the Jewish *berakah* and Christian collect are perfect examples of a biblical theology of worship where first God gives (statement of motive) and only on that basis do we respond (petition). Even within the Words of Institution themselves there are two different genres. The first part of each section of the *Verba* is the evangelist's narration, and only in the second part do we hear the very words of Jesus Himself,

> Take, eat; this is My body, which is given for you, This do in remembrance of Me. . . . Drink of it, all of you; this cup is the new testament in My blood, which is shed for you for the forgiveness of sins. This do, as often as you drink it, in remembrance of Me. (*LSB*, p. 162)

On the basis of this proclamation of Jesus' very words the people of God are able to petition the Father in prayer, asking that He continue to save them by His bodily presence in this heavenly meal. The Words of Institution are a statement of God's final saving action of the atonement of His Son for the sins of the world and the very body and blood of that atonement given to us in bread and wine.

The Breaking of the Bread

At the Last Supper, Jesus "took bread, and when He had given thanks, He broke it and gave it to them" (Luke 22:19). The act of breaking bread calls to mind, both for the disciples at the Last Supper and for the Christians of the Early Church, all the meals that the disciples had with Jesus.

Yet the Last Supper stands as the most significant meal of Jesus and the most important occasion of His breaking of bread. This is because it is the only meal in which Jesus identifies the bread as His very body and the (contents of the) cup as His very blood. It is also the only meal that Jesus directs His disciples to repeat. When the Christian Church later breaks bread in celebrations of the Lord's Supper, this is in response to Jesus' Words of Institution at the Last Supper.[21]

Bread itself can represent physical and/or spiritual sustenance (cf. Luke 4:4; 14:15). It may be understood as standing for all food, and even for all necessities of physical and spiritual life, as in the Lord's Prayer. Like manna from heaven, Jesus Himself is the "bread of heaven": "For the bread of God is He who comes down from heaven and gives life to the world" (John 6:33). Some Old Testament passages use bread and wine as metaphors for God's salvation (e.g., Isaiah 55:1–5; Proverbs 9:1–6). Daily bread, by contrast, is the food that comes by the sweat of people's brow after the fall into sin (Genesis 3:19). The broken bread in the Lord's Supper bears Christ's broken body, "broken" in the sense of "pierced" and "crushed," with His bones "separated" but not "broken" in death (Isaiah 53:5, 10; Zechariah 12:10; Psalm 22:14–17 [Matthew 22:15–18]; John 19:36). Jesus took the curse of the Law to Himself by becoming this bread of sorrow and misery. He also sweat drops of blood to signify the "brokenness" of His condition as He suffered the torments of hell in the Garden of Gethsemane (Luke 22:44).

On the other hand, wine is the eschatological drink of heaven that gladdens the heart (Psalm 104:15) and declares the presence of the Bridegroom at the feast (Luke 5:33–39; cf. John 2:1–11). The shed blood of Jesus drunk from the cup proclaims that the community is now restored and united from its brokenness through Christ's blood.[22]

The bread and wine in the Passover meal and the Last Supper are real, not just metaphorical, and these sacred meals provide spiritual benefits as well as physical nourishment. The Old Testament sacrificial blood was real, even though it was only from animals. How much more the fulfillment of this sacrifice of animals in the blood of the Lamb of God who takes away the sin of the world! How much more that we drink the blood of this Lamb who takes away sin in the Lord's Supper where His blood cleanses us and makes us holy!

The bread Jesus used at the Last Supper was unleavened. God had stipulated the use of *matzah* for Passover to recall the history of His greatest redemptive act for Israel. The unleavened bread was the bread of the exodus: "You shall eat no leavened bread with it [the Passover meal]. Seven days you shall eat unleavened bread, the bread of affliction—for you came out of the land of Egypt in haste—that all the days of your life you may remember the day when you came out of the land of Egypt" (Deuteronomy 16:3). The New Testament comments on the unleavened bread of the Passover in passages such as 1 Corinthians 5:7–8, applying it to the Christian Church in a way similar to Jesus' application in Luke 12:1. Both those passages warn against hypocrisy and impurity as a kind of leaven that should not be found in the Body of Christ because they are not found in Christ Himself. St. Paul's interpretation is first of all *Christological*, that is, Christ is our Passover sacrifice, our Passover redemption (1 Corinthians 5:7). Christology then leads to our understanding of the Church: the unleavened loaves required for the Old Testament Passover foreshadow the purity of the Christian Church, which must be purged of scandalous immorality (1 Corinthians 5:1–8).

> So already in the first century AD we can trace the eschatological interpretation of the unleavened bread: on it God had miraculously fed Israel during their journey through the desert, and had thus given a type of the abundance of bread in the Messianic time. It is no accident that in the New Testament the unleavened loaves are also eschatologically interpreted: I Cor. 5.7b-8. . . . The unleavened loaves are interpreted eschatologically in two ways: as pure dough they represent the purity and truth which characterizes the new world (I Cor. 5.8), and as new dough they symbolize the redeemed community (I Cor. 5.7a).[23]

God's provision of unleavened bread in the Passover meal and manna and water in the wilderness coincided with His provision of salvation and life. The exodus event encompassed salvation in both physical and spiritual terms: the people God redeems, He also feeds. God's ability both to save and to feed are represented by the unleavened bread of the Passover and by the manna of the wilderness.[24] In 1 Corinthians 10:1–4 St. Paul interprets the exodus and the manna and water provided in the desert *Christologically* and *sacramentally*: Christ is the rock who provided "spiritual food" and "spiritual drink" for those who were "baptized into Moses."

Jesus' Words Over the Bread and Wine

The breaking of the unleavened bread is invested with new meaning by the words of Jesus: "This is My body, which is given for you" (Luke 22:19). Jesus thereby summarizes His prophetic task: He has come to give His body in vicarious atonement on behalf of all. His words at the table also foreshadow His completion of His prophetic task on the cross. At the table He teaches about the kingdom and performs the miracle of the new era of salvation by offering His body, crucified on behalf of the world, in bread.

According to Jesus' words, *the bread is His body.* This is not a parabolic or metaphorical use of language. "Is" means "is." The giving of His body with the bread is just as real as the giving of His body into death on the cross. The body of Jesus given in the Supper is the same body of Jesus given into death on the cross, buried, and raised on the third day (Luke 23:52, 55; 24:3, 23). How can this be? It can only be a miracle (a mystery—μυστήριον), greater than the exodus miracles of manna and quail in the old covenant. Jesus is the new prophet in fulfillment of Moses, but greater, as Moses himself promised (Deuteronomy 18:15, quoted by Stephen in Acts 7:37). This is the new covenant that embraces and overtakes the old one. Jesus' prophetic actions are in keeping with the prophetic Christology of the New Testament: Jesus is the teacher and miracle worker who gives His body in the Supper as food for His disciples. He is also the rejected one who gives His body into death on the cross for the life of the world. At the Last Supper, Jesus, by His words and actions, fulfills His prophetic task as He foretells the *continuing presence of His body* for salvation, accomplished through offering His body in substitutionary death for the life of all, in the Lord's Supper.

Thus, Jesus' words with the bread and the wine make the Last Supper—and every Lord's Supper—miraculously different from all other meals. Those words declare the bread and wine truly to be His body and blood, given and shed for the forgiveness of sins (cf. Matthew 26:28).

Also unique to the Last Supper is Jesus' teaching about Himself as the sacrificial Passover Lamb in fulfillment of the Old Testament—the final fulfillment of the exodus deliverance (cf. "exodus" in Luke 9:31[25]). Jesus' impending death signals the beginning of the new, eschatological era of salvation. By stating that the bread is His body "which is given for you" (Luke 22:19) and the cup is the new testament in His blood, Jesus is interpreting the Passover meal *as a prophecy of what He will do—in a greater way—on the cross, and then in the Church's celebration of His Supper.* Those Israelites who ate the first Passover, with the blood of the lamb smeared on their doorways, were in fact spared from God's judgment; they then participated in the exodus deliverance from bondage. Those who now feast at the table of the Lord receive the benefits earned by His crucified body and shed blood: with His body and blood they also receive deliverance from divine wrath, freedom from bondage to evil, and safe passage to the new promised land (cf. Hebrews 4).

In Remembrance of Me

When the Lord instructs His disciples, "Do this in remembrance of Me," these words establish every Lord's Supper as a "remembrance" (*anamnesis*) of Jesus' atoning death and His promise to return again (1 Corinthians 11:26). The vital question as to the meaning of "anamnesis" is whether it is God who remembers us for Christ's sake or it is we who remember God because of His grace in Christ.[26] Certainly both are true, but God is the one who first remembers His promises in Christ and who prompts our response of remembering in faith. God's grace in Christ precedes and is the cause of the Church's remembrance. Every time God showers us with His gifts, it is because He remembers His promises in Christ to save us. That is especially true of the Supper, where the divine gifts are Jesus' own body and blood for the forgiveness of sins. The communicant receives the benefits of Christ's perfect life, atoning death, and new resurrection life. God "remembers" us for Christ's sake as He bestows these gifts.

Yet it is also true that the disciples are called by Jesus to celebrate the Supper in remembrance of Him. The call to remembrance at the Last Supper recalls God's covenant promises at creation and at the Passover. God called Israel to "*remember* the Sabbath" because of His rest on the seventh day of creation (Exodus 20:8–11) and because He redeemed Israel in the exodus (Deuteronomy 5:12–15). Within the liturgical worship of Israel were celebrations that were a remembrance of the great deeds of Yahweh throughout the history of His redemption of His chosen people. This was particularly true at the Passover celebration.

In worship, as God reminds the Church and the Church remembers, eternity unfolds in earthly time. For the Christian congregation, remembering is not so much fondly recalling something that happened in the past as it is having that distilled event from the past inserted into our present. As an act of remembering, the Lord's Supper is an eschatological event in which eternity is present because the eternal God is present with His grace, which will usher us into the eternal state. The communicant receives a foretaste of the eternal feast and is joined in "the communion of saints" (Apostles' Creed) with all the faithful—past, present, and future, on earth and in heaven.

When Jesus says, "*This* do . . . ," the remembrance of the Church entails important features of the meal. There were many other elements of the Passover meal besides the bread and wine, but Jesus intends His disciples to remember Him specifically by faithfully recounting and receiving His Words of Institution over the bread and wine, as well as by eating the bread of heaven and drinking from the cup of salvation. Thus, the Church's celebration of the Lord's Supper retains and highlights those distinctive features of the Last Supper.

In addition to being a faithful remembrance of and participation in the Last Supper, the Lord's Supper is a reminder of the entire table fellowship that Jesus engaged in from His incarnation to His ascension. It recalls and fulfills all the covenantal meals God celebrated with His people in the Old Testament, particularly the Passover meal, in celebration of the first exodus deliverance. As an act of divine remembrance, the Lord's Supper is a continuation of the table fellowship of Jesus with sinners. God remembers His new covenant promises and bestows His gifts. And as an act of remembrance by the Church, the Supper ties together both memory of Jesus' words and action according to those words: "Do this in remembrance of Me" (Luke 22:19).

The Cup of the New Testament in Jesus' Blood

The Words of Institution over the bread are separated from those over the wine by the Passover meal. Jesus calls the cup "My blood of the new testament," recalling Exodus 24, the ratification of the old/first covenant. In an unusual rite, Moses sprinkled half the blood of the sacrificed offerings on the people. The application of blood formally brought them into the covenant and made them beneficiaries of God's covenant promises. The covenant was then sealed when Moses and the elders ascended Sinai and "ate and drank" a sacred meal in the presence of God (Exodus 24:11). The parallels to the Last Supper are clear. The blood of the new covenant is applied to those who drink it in the cup. They are brought into the covenant and receive all its benefits made possible by the sacrifice of Jesus. The new sacred meal, too, is in the presence of God, since God incarnate is the host and He gives His body and blood with the bread and wine.

The Words of Institution stress the "new" testament. "New" alludes to the promise of a new covenant in passages such as Isaiah 42:9; 43:18–21; 55:3; 61:8–11; and Jeremiah 31:31–34, which Jesus fulfills by the shedding of His blood so that sins may be remembered no more. The theme of forgiveness, which recurs throughout these prophetic passages (notably Jeremiah 31:34), is made explicit in Matthew 26:28, where Jesus says His blood in the cup is shed "for the forgiveness of sins." "This is the *cup*" accents the *blood* of Jesus shed to create the covenant: "this is *My blood* of the covenant/testament" (Matthew 26:28; Mark 14:24). There is also a stress here on the unity of those who partake of the (one) cup, as St. Paul emphasizes in 1 Corinthians 10:16–17 with regard to the *one loaf.* Jesus' words over the cup include the same prepositional phrase He used over the bread as He repeats the substitutionary language of vicarious atonement: "for you" (Luke 22:19–20).[27] "Being poured out" suggests both the pouring from a cup and the blood that pours from the body of Jesus on the cross (cf. Psalm 22:14–15 [Matthew 22:15–16]).

The whole meal is concluded with these words: "This cup is the new testament in My blood, which is shed for you." God's plan demanded that God's righteous Messiah shed His innocent blood, as Jesus Himself explained to the Emmaus disciples by His teaching on the basis of the Old Testament (Luke 24:25–27). Jesus fulfills all the many bloody sacrifices of the Old Testament, including "the blood of the [first] covenant," which was poured out or sprinkled on the people (Exodus 24:6–8).[28] Jesus is the completion of a long line of suffering prophets who shed their blood in Jerusalem. He is also the nexus between those Old Testament prophets and the martyred New Testament apostles. Jesus says that His disciples are participants in and beneficiaries of the new testament in His blood as they partake of the cup and thereby drink His blood. The drinking of blood was an extreme offense to the Jews, but through it Christ's death becomes the disciple's life. To accept the cup and drink it is to accept Jesus' suffering and death as the atoning sacrifice for one's sins. To refuse to recognize Christ's body and blood in the Supper is to court condemnation (1 Corinthians 11:27–30).[29] Sharing in Christ's suffering and death is the only means to glory—in accord with the interpretation that Jesus gives of His death and resurrection in Luke 24:26: "Was it not necessary that the Christ should suffer these things and enter into His glory?" The Church, sharing in that suffering and death of Christ in the Sacrament of His body and blood, is bound together as the new creation, the Body of Christ. The words over the cup bring the action at the meal to a close by focusing on the death of Jesus.

Jesus' great desire to celebrate "*this* Passover" (Luke 22:15) with His disciples is to join Himself to God's people as He provides a greater salvation through a new "exodus" (Luke 9:31). He reinterprets the Passover events in terms of Himself, making Himself the fulfillment of Israel's redemption, for He is the Passover Lamb whose sacrificial death now does away with all other sacrifices. His flesh and blood replace the roasted lamb in the meal. His new covenant is one of forgiveness and eschatological hope. By His death and resurrection, Jesus leads God's people in victory procession from the old era of salvation into the new, transforming the old creation into the new one. This transformation is eschatological, embracing the past Passover meal, the Last Supper of Jesus, and the institution of the Lord's Supper—the new meal of the Church by which He will feed His disciples, strengthening and preserving them to life everlasting. All three meals anticipate, and are tied into, the final eternal feast (Revelation 19:6–9; Isaiah 25:6–8).

Jesus' Last Supper with His disciples is the new meal of the new era of salvation. The Last Supper of Jesus—and subsequent celebrations of the Lord's Supper—is different from all other meals, for Jesus gives His body with the bread and His blood with the wine. The miraculous and mysterious provision of these gifts in the Supper bestows forgiveness of sins and new life with God, based on Christ's death. This communal meal is Jesus' new Passover by which He establishes a new community that will celebrate this meal in remembrance of His death and resurrection and in anticipation of His return. The Last Supper is the climax of Jesus' table fellowship with His disciples. Indeed, it is the most important meal of all God's table fellowship from Eden to His visible return. Its greatest significance lies in what it bestows: the real presence of Christ, His very body and blood, offered up in death on a cross and now given with the bread and wine for the forgiveness of sins and life eternal.

The Words of Institution are the climax of the Liturgy of the Lord's Supper. The Lord's Supper is the ultimate expression of the forgiveness of sins through Christ's body and blood. This forgiveness flows from the cross through the blood of Christ directly to the faithful. In the minds of the early Christians, it is as though they were standing there at the foot of the cross on Calvary eating the body of Christ, broken for them in death and offered now in bread, and drinking the blood of Christ, poured out for them and given in wine. So also for us today. When we celebrate this Holy Supper, we remember, in the Jewish sense of "participate in," what Jesus did for us on the cross and in the resurrection, and God remembers us. As Paul said, "For as often as you eat this bread and drink the cup, you proclaim the Lord's death until

He comes" (1 Corinthians 11:26). Early Christians had a marvelous understanding of the Real Presence that continues among us today!

The following diagram shows that the movement of the Sacramental Service is toward the same climax as in the Word Service, i.e., the very words of our Lord. In the Word Service the climax was the Gospel Reading and continued through the sermon, which was the hinge between Word and Sacrament; in the Eucharistic Service, the climax was Christ's Words of Institution, anticipated by the recital of salvation history in the eucharistic prayer and continued through the Distribution. Therefore, the Gospel and the Words of Institution are different, but mirror images of one another.[30]

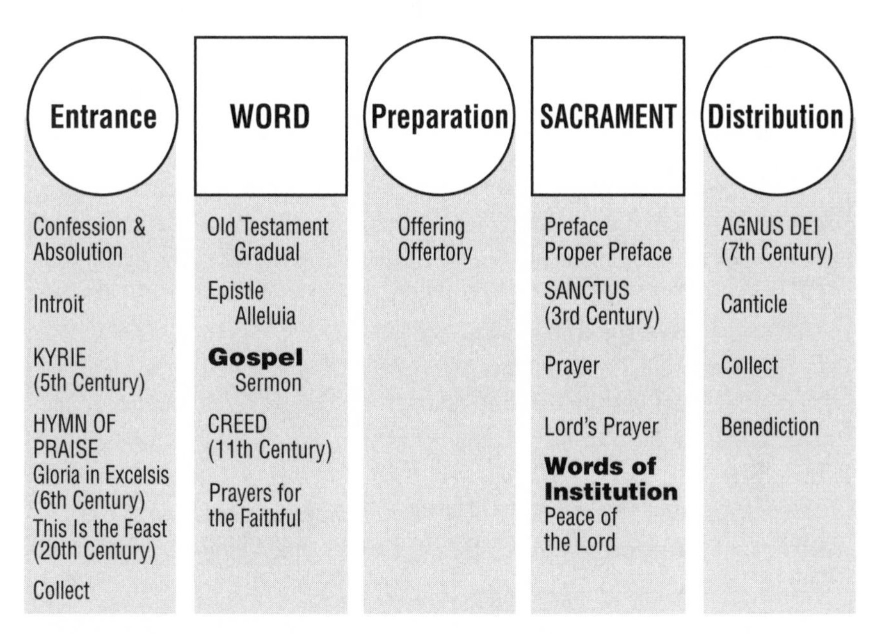

The Pax Domini—The Peace of the Lord

When the instituting Words of Jesus have ended, the pastor takes the bread and holds it over the cup and proclaims "the peace of the Lord be with you always." This is the peace first announced in our petitions in the Kyrie, the peace the angels declared at the birth of Christ in the Gloria in Excelsis, the new greeting of the people of God, because in Christ there is now peace on earth and peace in heaven. The peace announced now at the end of the Liturgy of the Lord's Supper is focused in the bread and cup where, in eating the body of Christ and drinking His blood, His peace rests in us because He now dwells within us. Luther thought so highly of this peace that he described it as a form of absolution:

> But immediately after the Lord's Prayer shall be said, "The peace of the Lord," etc., which is, so to speak, a public absolution of the sins of the communicants, the true voice of the gospel announcing the remission of sins, and therefore the one and most worthy preparation for the Lord's Table, if faith holds to these words as coming from the mouth of Christ Himself.[31]

The Distribution and Departure

The distribution of the Lord's Supper begins with the Agnus Dei. Like the Entrance Rite and the preparation of the table, the distribution is a time of movement, so it, too, is accompanied by other hymns and psalms. In the ancient Church, the distribution was done by stations to expedite the communion of thousands of communicants. Today, it is best done either by tables, where the communicants come forward in groups, or in a continuous manner. Regardless of the method, the distribution of these precious gifts should be done reverently. Kneeling at the table to receive the Sacrament is a more recent custom since the time of pietism, emphasizing the individual reception of the Sacrament and not the Sacrament as an act of the fellowship of the community (*koinonia*). The continuous distribution of the Sacrament suggests that we are communing at one table in one fluid act of reception. The host is placed either in the right hand as it is supported by the left one (the more ancient custom) or in the mouth, depending on the preference of the communicant.[32] The pastor announces the simple reality: "the body of Christ, given for you." The common cup is to be preferred. (For the sake of avoiding spillage it is probably best for the communicant to assist in the reception of the blood of Christ.) Here the words "the blood of Christ, shed for you" state with clarity and directness exactly what is received.[33] When the distribution is over, the pastor dismisses the congregation by announcing the reality of what they have received: "The body and blood of our Lord Jesus Christ strengthen and preserve you in body and soul to life everlasting. Depart in peace." The peace announced after the eucharistic prayer is reiterated here, framing the distribution of the gifts where the peace of Christ's body and blood is given and received.

Agnus Dei

The final ordinary, and the last one to become a permanent part of the Divine Service, is the Agnus Dei. It is the only medieval addition besides the Creed and has been dated anywhere from the sixth to the eighth century. Philip Pfatteicher notes that it was "introduced as an independent song, according to the *Liber pontificalis*, by Pope Sergius I around A.D. 700."[34] Liturgical scholars offer little comment on it, though most agree that it is the first hymn accompanying the movement during the distribution and was sung during the breaking of the bread and repeated as long as there was bread to break. Perhaps it was introduced into the liturgy because there were questions about Christ's real presence, for the Agnus Dei states in unequivocal terms that what is present on the altar is none other than the Lamb of God who takes away the sin of the world.

> ***Lamb of God***, You take away the sin of the world;
> *Have mercy on us.*
> Lamb of God, You take away the sin of the world;
> *Have mercy on us.*
> Lamb of God, You take away the sin of the world;
> Grant us **peace.**

Christ as the Lamb of God is a prominent description of Him in the New Testament, beginning with John the Baptist's declaration: "Behold, the Lamb of God, who takes away the sin of the world" (John 1:29). Thirty times Jesus is called the Lamb in John's Revelation, the fulfillment of the messianic prophecy of Isaiah 53:7: "Like a lamb that is led to the slaughter, and like a sheep that before its shearers is silent, so He opened not His mouth."

Within the Divine Service, the Agnus Dei sums up the themes woven throughout the ordinaries. The atonement of the Lamb is the most obvious, hearkening back to both the Gloria in Excelsis and "Worthy Is Christ." Likewise, the petition for mercy begun in the Kyrie now takes concrete shape as the communicants ascend to the altar to receive Christ's mercy in the Supper singing "**Lamb of God**, You take away the sin of the world." Most remarkable, however, is that the Agnus Dei ends as the Kyrie began, with the petition for **peace**. Peace describes the condition of the faithful in the Divine Service from beginning to end, and the Lord who joins earth and heaven together in peace now gives the Prince of Peace into the mouths of the communicants.[35]

The Post-Communion Canticle

As the distribution of the Lord's Supper began with the Agnus Dei, and was accompanied by hymns as the body and blood were given to the communicants, so it ends with another hymn, the Post-Communion Canticle. In Lutheran liturgies, the Nunc Dimittis, normally associated with Compline or

Vespers, became the most commonly used canticle to conclude the distribution. This is an inspired way to bring the communion to a close. We join Simeon in recognizing God's peace in the Christ Child who has opened our eyes to His salvation in the breaking of the bread. "My own eyes have seen" Christ in the flesh on the altar, as Simeon did in the baby Jesus, who is "the salvation . . . prepared in the sight of ev'ry people" (*LSB*, p. 165). Not only is the tone of peace sounded—a theme that we have observed throughout the liturgy from Kyrie to Gloria in Excelsis to Pax Domini—but the inclusivity of the Gospel as incorporating both Jew and Gentile is also proclaimed. The table is a table of unity for all who confess the true faith and repent and who believe that Jesus is present bodily to offer the gift of Himself in bread and wine. Eyes have beheld His salvation from invocation to communion, as He re-creates us through His Word and Sacrament.

The Nunc Dimittis, however, is not the only option here. A new possibility reflects a different reality than the Nunc Dimittis, namely, that having received this extraordinary gift of His Supper, we "Thank the Lord and sing His praise," a song in which we give thanks for the incarnation of Jesus and our reception of Him in His body and blood at the Lord's Supper. This joyful hymn comes from the opening verse of Psalm 105: "Oh give thanks to the Lord; call upon His name; make known His deeds among the peoples!" The deeds that have been made known in the liturgy are the incarnation, atonement, and sacramental presence of Jesus for the forgiveness of our sins. Psalm 34 was also used as a Post-Communion Canticle in the Early Church during the Communion.

The Post-Communion Collect

Three collects have been prayed at the end of the distribution. The first one is Martin Luther's post-communion collect. Here giving thanks is the natural response of prayer to the gift of the Lord's Supper, and the petition is that this salutary gift may indeed bear fruit in our lives. This prayer reflects the Two Tables of the Law—love for God and for one's neighbor—in the beautiful words "in faith toward You and in fervent love toward one another" (*LSB*, p. 166).

The second collect has a statement of motive concerning the Father that sums up the entire service by connecting the incarnation to the Lord's Supper: "the fountain and source of all goodness, who in loving-kindness sent Your only-begotten Son into the flesh." On the basis of the incarnation we give thanks for the "pardon and peace" we receive in the Sacrament

(*LSB*, p. 166). Here is the objective reality of Christ's incarnation, His bodily presence, and the gift of forgiveness. The petition is that He not forsake us but enable us to serve Him as the proper response to the gift.

The third option echoes the former canticle at the offertory that acknowledges that our eating and drinking the very body and blood of Jesus has "given us a foretaste of the feast to come." As pilgrims journeying to the heavenly Jerusalem, the collect looks forward to that day when "we may, together with all Your saints, celebrate the marriage feast of the Lamb in His kingdom which has no end" (*LSB*, p. 166). What a way to conclude our eucharistic repast, by thanking our gracious God that in this holy supper heaven has come to earth as our feasting here joins the banquet of the saints in heaven.

Another option is a collect from Maundy Thursday by Thomas Aquinas. Here the atonement (Passion) is connected to the Lord's Supper, as Luke does in his Gospel (Luke 22:14). The petition is for its proper use in our lives. We pray that His redeeming work—both on the cross and in the Sacrament—may be manifest in us.[36] This collect affirms what is said about the Lord's Supper in the service of corporate confession and absolution: "Therefore, whoever eats of this bread and drinks of this cup, confidently believing the words of Christ, dwells in Christ, and Christ in him, and has eternal life" (*LSB: Altar Book*, p. 423). We bear witness to Christ in our very bodies, and His suffering is manifest in our suffering as we "bear one another's burdens, and so fulfill the law of Christ" (Galatians 6:2).

The Benediction

In the ancient Church, the distribution was so long and involved that people would leave the church after receiving the Sacrament, leaving only the final communicants present for the dismissal. In most cases, the service simply sputtered out, with the presiding minister announcing: "The Mass has ended. Go in peace." And the remaining congregation would reply: "Thanks be to God." The newer setting for the Lord's Supper in our hymnals reflects the shorter, more truncated ending of the ancient eucharistic liturgies.

It was not until much later in the Church's life (tenth and eleventh centuries) that a more formal ending to the service was instituted with a blessing or prayer over all the people. Framing the invocation at the beginning of the service where the name of the triune God was placed upon us, so here, too, at its conclusion His name is placed upon us as blessing. He sends us with His blessing and His presence. In the Benediction the Church imitates her Lord who, as He ascended into heaven, lifted up His hands and blessed the disciples (Luke 24:50–51).

The unique Lutheran contribution is the Aaronic Benediction: "The Lord bless you and keep you. The Lord make His face to shine on you and be gracious to you. The Lord look upon you with favor and give you peace." The people respond: "Amen." The final word of the liturgy is "peace"—the peace that comes from Jesus who joins heaven and earth together in peace—one of the great themes of the Divine Service.

Filled with Christ, the faithful depart in peace to engage in the liturgy of life as they bear His presence wherever they go through their deeds of mercy and love.

11
The Historic Liturgy among Lutherans

This last stage of our journey focuses on what is distinctly Lutheran about the historic liturgy. In the now familiar words of Norman Nagel, Lutherans are "heirs of an astonishingly rich tradition." Yet, as is the case throughout the history of the Church, each generation of Lutherans "receives from those who went before and, in making that tradition of the Divine Service its own, adds what best may serve in its own day—the living heritage and something new."[1]

"The living heritage and something new" is what defines the spirit of Martin Luther and the Lutheran reformers in their evangelical reform of the medieval liturgy. To tell their story, however, we must enter their world and gain a sense of what they inherited that needed reform. What we find is that Luther, through his application of the theological principle of justification by grace through faith, restored the historic liturgy to the simplicity and beauty it had before the decay it suffered during the medieval period. Thus to know Luther's reforms we must see how the liturgy came to need reformation. This means we must go back into the fourth and fifth centuries and observe the changes that led to the dissolution of the liturgy. This brief historical interlude provides a glimpse into the world of Luther and his reforms painted with broad brushstrokes.

Liturgical history may be divided into a number of different periods. Throughout this book, we have referred to the earlier periods in church history, but the following brief descriptions are meant as summaries of each period. Included are key dates in church history to locate each period in relation to major events in the life of the Church.

THE DOMESTIC PERIOD (PRE-CONSTANTINE, AD 30–312)

49	Jerusalem Council
70	Destruction of the temple in Jerusalem
100	Death of John the Evangelist
100–150	Justin Martyr
189–190	Controversy over the date of Easter
249–250	Edict of persecution
311	Edict of tolerance (Christianity now a legal religion)
312	Constantine emperor

The story of the development of the liturgy in the Early Church is the story of persecution and zeal for mission. The blood of the martyrs was indeed the seedbed of the Church's growth. The Church grew as Christians gathered in simple spaces with a simple rite. This is called the domestic period because most worship took place in the homes of Christians, and this limiting space kept the liturgy simple. The two structures of Word and Sacrament were all that was necessary in this small space. The Church's life was centered in the liturgy to which the baptized brought others so that they might be catechized through hearing God's Word, then baptized and welcomed to the reception of the Lord's Supper. Since Christ was present bodily in Word and Meal to offer the gifts of forgiveness, life, and salvation, early Christians brought their neighbors and friends into this presence so that they might receive His gifts. Living under persecution, early Christians valued their liturgical life and guarded it carefully. They handed down to their children and grandchildren a way of worship that embodied what they believed and confessed—a confession that could lead to martyrdom. During this period of persecution, the liturgy changed very little and may best be portrayed by the following diagram of the two structures that are the stable cornerstones of the historic liturgy.

ROMAN SYNAXIS AD 220

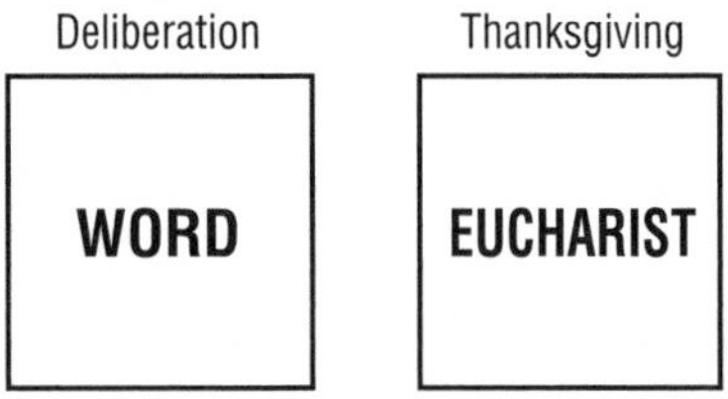

Deliberation	Thanksgiving
WORD	**EUCHARIST**

The Imperial Period (AD 312–600)

325	Council at Nicaea (Nicene Creed)
354–430	Augustine of Hippo
375	Cyril of Jerusalem
410	First barbarian invasion
440	Leo the Great, bishop of Rome
451	Council at Chalcedon
476	Fall of the Roman Empire
590–604	Pope Gregory the Great (Gregorian chant)

Constantine took control of the Roman Empire in AD 312, and as the official religion of the empire, Christianity took on an imperial character. In previous chapters we observed that as space expands, so does rite, and this affects the way Christians conceive of time as well. At this point, Christianity was no longer a Jewish sect; rather, it was very Gentile in nature, and the Church had assimilated itself into the Gentile communities. Christianity took a great risk in attempting to evangelize the whole imperial world. What a bold step for this humble group of Christians gathered primarily in house churches to challenge a non-Judaic and pagan worldview!

Roman culture was deeply entrenched, so much so that Constantine as emperor was unable to build a major Christian basilica in the center of pagan Rome. Healthy and vibrant, paganism was the culture of the empire, and it was there to stay. From the Roman perspective, Christianity appeared to be a meaningless sect that lacked influence or power. What authority could Christianity wield in the Roman culture and in her public life, since what the Christian Church called for was a simple but radical transformation in Jesus Christ? What resulted, however, was the conversion of the empire to the Christian faith, and this extraordinary evangelistic effort took place primarily through the historic liturgy.[2]

The imperial period was a period of growth and expansion in the liturgy. This occurred because of the expansion in space that was brought about by the construction of large basilicas in the fourth century in response to the Edict of Milan, which had made Christianity the religion of the empire. As we have described, three elements surround the structures of Word and Sacrament, accompanying movement in the liturgy with psalms and singing: the entrance rite, the preparation of the table, and the distribution of the Sacrament. The following diagram shows the growth of the liturgy into its fivefold shape, which is now known as the historic liturgy.The

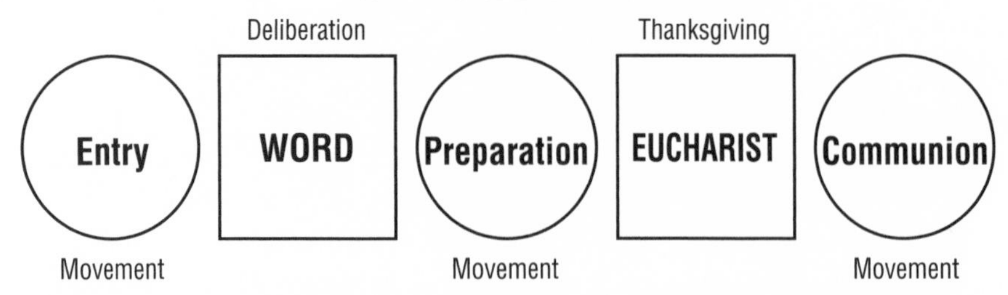

Edict of Milan was good, as far as it went. But how would the Church actually evangelize the Roman Empire? One attempt during this time was the introduction of the "urban liturgy."[3] The numerous house churches in Rome and other urban areas and the place where the bishop celebrated the Lord's Supper were quite separate so that a sense of unity in the Church was missing because the small churches were scattered throughout the city. A pastoral decision was made to bring the entire group of believers of a city together at one table on a number of occasions during the year. The bishops of these urban communities took the liturgy into the streets so that more people might be exposed to it and see the Church embody her faith in action.[4] To take the liturgy out on the road offered an opportunity for the pagan world to see the bishop and to hear the Gospel. Such a venture necessitated parades and advertisement, and these parades were very complex.

The urban liturgy used the entire day of Sunday as well as the whole city as the time and space for worship. Not everyone attended the entire day's liturgical events, for people would come and go. The reason for such a liturgy may sound strange to our twenty-first-century Church. These people saw this public, urban liturgy as God's *leitourgia*, His service to a lost world that needed to know that in Jesus Christ it had been re-created and restored. The urban liturgy was simply the Church manifesting its nature as the presence of Christ in the world. Here was the Creator doing His work of re-creation through Word and Sacrament.

This worship was constructed in seven related but distinct services.

The first service occurred around daybreak with psalms of praise. This was patterned after the synagogue and began when the pagan world began its business day.

The second service was a gradual gathering of clergy and laypeople either early in the day or at midmorning at a designated place called a station—typically in some city neighborhood or open space that could hold a large number of people. After prayer and Scripture, the procession began to the church building designated for the celebration of the Lord's Supper. The procession was accompanied with psalms. When the crowd arrived at the church, the entire procession entered the building, clergy and laity together singing psalms of entry.

The third service occurred in late morning or at midday at the stational church. This was the Liturgy of the Word, which included readings interspersed with psalms of meditation. This service concluded with the reading of the Gospel and a homily by the presiding minister (normally the bishop).

The fourth service was that of petitionary prayers, followed by the dismissal of the unbaptized, penitents, and certain others, in short, all those not worthy to attend the Lord's Supper. This became a very important pastoral function. Petitions were made for all those dismissed plus prayers for the faithful, the world, the Church, the city, and so on. After the prayers, which were considered part of the reconciliation process, a sign of that reconciliation was made with the kiss of peace.

The fifth service was the preparation for the Lord's Supper. By this time it was afternoon, and bread and wine were brought to the altar table in a procession accompanied by psalmody and with increasing ceremony. In the Eastern Church this became known as the Great Entrance. Like the entrance rite, this took a great deal of organizing and would be very complex.

The sixth service was the Lord's Supper itself. Once the gifts were arranged on the table, the bishop prayed over them, and then distributed Communion until all had participated in the bread and the cup. With thousands to commune, this became a lengthy process. It was mid-afternoon or later when the distribution was over.

The seventh and final service concluded before sundown when all business had ceased. This service, called *lucernarium* or lamplighting, was similar to our Vespers or Evening Prayer.

Within the urban setting, this liturgy on the town demonstrated that the Lord's Supper was the sacrament of unity and that the bishop makes this unity happen. The Christians of this time believed very strongly in one faith, one community, one Communion, one bishop, one grand liturgy on the town, thus affirming St. Paul's words to the Ephesians: "There is one body and one Spirit—just as you were called to the one hope that belongs to your call—one Lord, one faith, one baptism, one God and Father of all, who is over all and through all and in all" (Ephesians 4:4–6). When such a great urban Communion was celebrated, the elements of bread and wine were sent to some of the smaller churches from the consecration at the stational church so that as much of the city as possible could commune together from one table.

This was a very strong missionary church. It understood from a pastoral perspective that the liturgy creates confidence; it is what drives the Church forward and is celebrated for the life of the world. The festival described above was one grand attempt to keep a sense of community in a very complex, urban setting. And the Church of this period had the courage to face and solve its problem. It is an example of a Church that took risks, made some mistakes, but for better or for worse attempted to proclaim the Gospel of Jesus Christ to the Roman world.[5] The urban church was an attempt to proclaim the Gospel in a pagan world, and while we may not have the public gathering spaces of that time, we, too, live in an increasingly paganized world.[6]

The Medieval Period (AD 600–1517)

The history of the Church and her liturgy experienced a dramatic shift with the first barbarian invasion in AD 410. The invasions that followed caused great upheavals in both Church and world. The influx of cultures from the north forever changed both the Roman Empire and the Church. Roman culture was leveled, and in places such as North Africa, where luminaries such as Cyprian and Augustine had been leaders in their churches, Christianity ceased to exist. In comparison to the barbarian peoples, Roman culture appeared moral, sophisticated, and simple. We may not think of the Rome of gladiators and slave traders as a moral society, but when placed alongside barbarian morality, the Roman Empire appeared downright puritan. Barbarian mentality was completely different from that of the Roman mind, which was reflected in the liturgical changes that occurred under the influence of barbarian cultures.

Adapting Liturgy to Culture or Culture to Liturgy?[7]

We often speak today about the challenges of proclaiming the Gospel in a multicultural world, but our struggle to reach other cultures with the Gospel pales in comparison with the challenges facing pastors who confronted a culture that had no law or morality to guide it. Bishops such as Leo the Great (AD 440) and Gregory the Great (AD 590–604) found that they had to create a Christian culture from the ground up, since these new peoples could not understand their sermons and resisted any efforts at full conversion. Catechesis of the barbarians focused on the basics, especially the Ten

Commandments, to help people learn that indiscriminate killing and rampant unfaithfulness cannot go hand in hand with a Gospel of mercy and grace. The challenge of catechizing a people who had an axe against the evangelists' throats and who resisted most efforts to engender an ethical life in Christ was difficult if not impossible. Compromises were made, many of which we might consider outrageous and unacceptable. Some of these compromises opened the door for the abuses that led to the demise of faith and doctrine through regrettable liturgical innovations.

It is easy for us to be critical of the pastoral decisions that led to the dissolution of both doctrine and practice, but these pastors were responding to an enormously difficult situation. Not only were their lives at stake, but the lives of the faithful under their care also were in jeopardy.[8] In their efforts to convert these alien peoples to the truth, these pastors attempted to accommodate the Gospel to barbarian culture, not vice versa. As a result, culture shaped the liturgy; liturgy did not shape the culture. It is one thing, however, to adapt liturgy to culture when our lives are at stake and quite another to adapt the liturgy simply to conform to a prevailing culture that finds success in compromising the theology of the cross and the truth of Scripture.

It is one thing, however, to adapt liturgy to culture when our lives are at stake and quite another simply to conform to a prevailing culture that finds success in compromising the theology of the cross and the truth of Scripture.

The pastoral adaptations of the liturgy to the barbarian culture were efforts to convert the barbarians to a new and living hope. The barbarians had vivid imaginations and were fascinated by the high ceremony of the liturgy, thus they demanded more ceremony and were delighted by additions that added color and style to the staid Roman rite that was quite simple and flat-footed. The move to add ceremony to the liturgy went contrary to the liturgical instincts of centuries of Christians. But to appeal to the barbarian propensity for complexity and ornamentation, the liturgy began to grow in places where it was unnecessary to expand the rite. Examples of this abound. Normally, two candles appeared on the altar, but soon candelabras appeared and the table became cluttered with unnecessary vessels. Processions grew and expanded, and instead of being utilitarian, they became events unto themselves. In the end, the clutter obscured the simple fivefold structure of the historic liturgy of Word and Sacrament, accompanied by the ordinaries.

The Urban Liturgy in the Medieval Church

What really fascinated the barbarians, however, was the urban liturgy. Here was the kind of ceremony that took into account the entire city and the entire day. They were so taken with this liturgy on the town that they attempted to move it north into their smaller villages. By this time in the Christian Church, a cruciform structure was common for church buildings (see figure at right), with expansion on both sides of the building near the altar to accommodate increasing numbers of worshipers. Again, this was purely a utilitarian move. As the barbarians returned to their hometowns, they built huge basilicas in a cruciform shape in their villages, and they shifted the urban liturgy from the city to the building. The church building itself became a substitute for the city, and the procession took place within its walls. Stations were set up inside the church for the first service at daybreak, and the liturgy proceeded throughout the seven-service sequence, with Word and Sacrament being celebrated at pulpit and altar.

A number of other factors went hand in hand with this processional liturgy inside the church building. As mentioned before, the barbarians were not given to a high moral standard and the Ten Commandments cramped their style, so they would appoint members of their community who were more inclined to a pious life to represent them and lead the Christian life on their behalf. It was during this time that the monasteries and convents grew in number, and a bifurcation now took place between the clergy and the laity. The clergy were considered "professional" Christians. They would not only live the Christian life on behalf of the people, but they would also worship and receive the Sacrament on their behalf. The clergy, particularly the monastic choirs, now did the liturgy as they took over singing the ordinaries, hearing the Word of God, and receiving the Sacrament.

Within the church building itself, a space was created around the altar, choir, and lectern where the clergy would participate in the liturgy as the people observed from outside this space. Walls were built, and these internal structures became almost fortresslike in keeping the people out and the clergy in. If one visits Europe today, many of the great cathedrals exhibit this "church within a church" in which the two main structures of Word and Sacrament take place. The rest of the church building outside this space seems almost superfluous, since the main action takes place within the confines of the altar and choir. This "church within a church" became a place for great art, and the reredos on some of these altars and the wood carvings in the choir provide examples of the greatest artwork of the Middle Ages. This pattern is most striking in Cordoba, Spain, where Charles V built such a structure, not in the center of a large basilica but within a huge mosque that had existed for centuries. From the outside one may see this church, but upon entering the mosque, one would never know that a significant Christian church is located in its center.

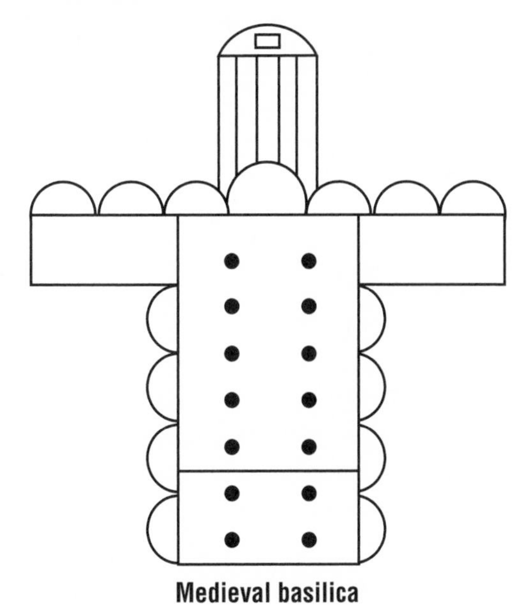

Medieval basilica

As the laity became increasingly disenfranchised from the liturgy, they were given things to entertain them while the liturgy was taking place. The rosary was introduced as a means for private piety while the people milled around the church during the service. Since barbarians, as animists, worshiped inanimate objects such as trees and stones and lightning, pastoral decisions were made to shift their worship from these natural things to more pious objects such as the bones of the apostles or the wood of the cross or other religious objects.[9] Chapels were needed to store these objects of veneration, so they sprang up along the outer walls of the church building. These chapels became excellent places for the laity to visit for veneration of the relics and prayer with their rosaries while the clergy were within the walls of their inner church doing the liturgy on their behalf. The chapels also became an ideal place for the beginning of a procession or its conclusion. Stained-glass windows and statues became fixtures in the church to add to the entertainment of the laity and to teach them the stories of the Bible and the basic tenets of the Christian faith. The Church Year, which had been devoted to the life of Christ, was now obscured by the proliferation of commemoration days for saints, particularly local saints. It became increasingly difficult to maintain any Christological focus in the daily, weekly, and yearly observances.

Changes in the Historic Liturgy

Barbarian innovations had a profound effect on the Roman rite, which had been simple and elegant. The new rite became complicated and overlaid with accretions that obscured its clean fivefold shape. The people no longer heard the Word of God read or preached unless they placed themselves close to the choir and listened intently. The Scripture readings themselves were shortened, and the Old Testament lesson fell out of use, replaced instead by legends of the saints. The life-giving, performative Word read and preached to nourish the people of God was now unavailable to most laity and reserved for the clergy alone. The great liturgical hymns that are the core of our acknowledgment of "gifts received with eager thankfulness and praise"[10] were now sung only by the monastic choirs as the chants became increasingly complex and were given only to the clergy to perform.

Perhaps the greatest changes took place in the Liturgy of the Lord's Supper. The Eucharistic Prayer became a vehicle to promote the doctrine of meritorious works, and instead of being a recital of the mighty deeds of God in saving His people, it turned the Mass into an unbloody sacrifice to God in which the priests offered the Father this Sacrament as their good work to earn His grace and favor. Not only that, but the Eucharistic Prayer was spoken so softly that only the clergy standing at the altar could hear what was being said. Even the monks in the choir could not hear the Liturgy of the Lord's Supper. This is why, at the Words of Institution, the bells were rung so that everyone in the church could rush to a place where they could see the elevation of the host and the cup. The host and cup were elevated both as offerings to God as part of this unbloody sacrifice but also so the people could commune with their eyes. Communion by mouth was infrequent (about four times a year), so this communion with the eyes became the more common way to receive the Lord's Supper.

Because of the doctrine of transubstantiation—which states that the bread and wine become the body and blood and cease to be bread and wine—great care and reverence were taken to be sure that no bread fell to the ground or wine was spilled. This doctrine was an attempt to preserve the real presence, but it became a means for withdrawing the cup from the laity. Because of this fear of falling bread and spilled wine, Communion was only in one kind—the bread—and it was placed directly in the mouth. The ancient practice of receiving it in the hand was discontinued because people would keep the host, take it home, place it on their mantel, and worship it because they believed it was the very body of Christ and that alone.[11]

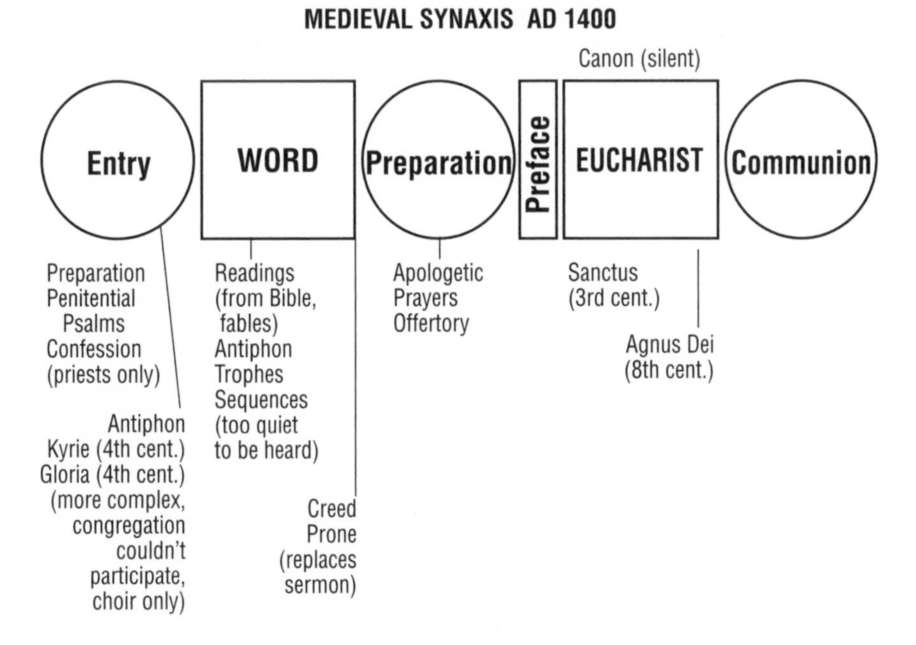

The Allegorization of the Liturgy

Since the liturgy had become almost unrecognizable, there was a pastoral desire to explain the liturgy to the people. The allegorization of the liturgy now began to take place. Two excellent representatives of this are Germanus (eighth century) and Amalarius of Metz (ninth century). Some of their explanations are biblical (Germanus), while others ignore the Bible and use the natural world to explain what is happening in the liturgy (Amalarius). For example, in fourth-century Rome, when it became warm, men would wave large fans in the chancel to cool the priest and to keep away insects. As Christianity moved north into colder climates, the barbarians kept the fans, but because they no longer filled a utilitarian purpose, they were allegorized to represent the beating of angels' wings in heaven at the moment of consecration. The bishop climbing to his chair was like the ascension of Christ into heaven. As a sacrifice, the Mass now became a reenactment of the Passion of our Lord: the bread and wine brought to the table were like Jesus' body brought to the tomb; the priests washing their hands were like Pontius Pilate washing his before Jesus' crucifixion. The more fanciful allegories adopted nature as their source: antiphons in the Introit represented two turtledoves calling back and forth in the forest.

The liturgy was allegorized because the lean fivefold structure of the historic liturgy had become obese and obscured with elaborate additions and changes. Remarkably, underneath it all the fivefold structure remained, though hardly discernable and the natural rhythm that moved toward the climaxes of the Gospel in the Liturgy of the Word and the Words of Institution in the Liturgy of the Lord's Supper was obscured beyond recognition.

Before moving on to the Reformation, it must be noted that the medieval period lasted for more than a thousand years. We date its beginning with the bishopric of Gregory in AD 590–604, but in reality its source and beginning was in AD 410 with the first barbarian invasion. This was a long period of time, and not everyone in every place succumbed to the abuses enumerated here. But this was clearly a period of dissolution in the liturgy: the loss of the real presence of Christ, the structures obscured, and the participation of the people reduced to a bare minimum. Private devotion supplanted participation in the public liturgy of the Church. The historic liturgy was no longer centered in Christ but in the works of the people. The professional clergy and the unprofessional laity both came to believe that they were saved by works—the clergy by doing the Divine Service, the laity by their devotion to the cult of the saints.[12]

The Reformation Era (1517–1580)

1517 Ninety-five Theses nailed to the door of the Wittenberg Church
1580 Book of Concord

Luther knew no other way to worship than this medieval liturgy. As an Augustinian monk, he was one of the professional clergy who believed that he was saved by his meritorious actions, particularly the performing of the liturgy. Luther was a medieval man who submitted himself to the liturgical life of the Roman Catholic Church. In his first Mass, his need to perform it perfectly as an acceptable sacrifice to the Father caused him to break down and become almost paralyzed during the Canon of the Mass (the Eucharistic Prayer). But there certainly were some benefits to this liturgical life. As a monk, Luther prayed the entire Psalter every week, so the Psalms became his lifeblood and were foundational in his proclamation of the Gospel and his interpretation of the Scriptures.

Luther's Principle of Reforming the Liturgy: Justification by Grace through Faith

Reforms of the medieval liturgy were evident already in the fifteenth century, so that when the Reformation began under Luther, there was already a sense that reform was necessary. Luther was not a liturgical scholar but a biblical one, and most of his liturgical reforms reflected utilitarian changes that he was compelled to make on biblical and pastoral grounds. Luther was conservative in his reforms. As a pastor, he valued freedom and love for one's neighbor in matters liturgical, but as a theologian, he applied theological principles to his reforms of the liturgy. His operating principle was simple. As he looked at the medieval Mass, he removed everything that did not preach Christ. His interpretive key was the doctrine of justification by grace through faith.

> Indeed, Christian freedom and love of neighbour spring from justification, and while Luther takes these latter things into account, worship and liturgical forms are governed not primarily by these, but by the gospel, and therefore by the doctrine of justification.[13]

Luther could see that the Gospel had been obscured and that much of the liturgy was meaningless to people because it had become hidden under layers of medieval compromise. Luther did not eschew the liturgy, for he knew that through this means Christ was present in Word and Sacrament as He had been since its institution on the night in which He was betrayed. Luther submitted himself to its forms and desired to blow away the mists that had obscured the historic liturgy so that people could see the beauty of its clean structure and its salutary character as a means of preaching Christ. Luther restored the liturgy to the people so that they could worship as the Church once had: hearing the Word of God, singing the ordinaries, and receiving the body and blood of Christ.

For Luther, the liturgy was the means by which God's Word came to God's people, thus the people needed to hear this life-giving Word read and preached.

These reforms worked themselves out in a number of ways. Luther made the liturgy simpler and more accessible by allowing Christ to speak clearly and plainly through His Word. For Luther, the liturgy was the means by which God's Word came to God's people, thus the people needed to hear this life-giving Word read and preached. Throughout the Divine Service, the Word of God dominates the liturgy from Kyrie to Gloria in Excelsis to the Scripture readings to Sanctus to Agnus Dei. As you read Luther's description of the rite, you see his evangelical impulse bringing forth the Gospel throughout the flow of the service. For example, the Alleluia that precedes the Gospel is "the perpetual voice of the church"[14] responding to the gifts given in the very words of Jesus. In the same way, the Pax Domini after the Words of Institution is considered by Luther to be a form of absolution. Luther's perception of the Word of God was not wooden, that is, for him it was not simply the text of the Scriptures. Rather, it is Jesus, the Word made flesh, who comes to us through preaching. "For Luther, the word of God is not primarily a text; it is first and foremost an oral event—the act of preaching."[15] This is why Luther's greatest contribution to liturgical reform was the revival of preaching. Luther preached constantly, and some estimate that he preached more than 2,300 sermons in his lifetime.[16] As a biblical scholar, his sermons were expositions of the text, and it was in his interpretation of the Scriptures that Luther proclaimed the Gospel of Jesus Christ.

> Luther was articulating a new understanding of the word. The word is as much a means of grace as the sacraments, but grace no longer understood in terms of substance but in terms of communication: address and response. In the Lutheran liturgy the hymn that came to surround the sermon or the pulpit office both furthered the proclamation of the word and provided a devotional response to it. However, the response sought by the preachers was the Spirit-gifted response of faith. As God's self-communication, the word of God is an encounter with the Person of God himself. One cannot encounter God without responding in faith and hope, in fear and love. *The preaching of the word is sacramental, because it conveys Christ himself.* . . . God's word

> always attaches itself to something created, even to something physical. As a form of self-communication from person to person, it is never disembodied. The word may be in the book or text of the Bible, the mouth of the preacher, or the earthly elements in the sacraments. The Word that was incarnated in Jesus the Christ, the divine Logos, is always taking on flesh not only in the way in which it is conveyed, but also in the life of the believer who receives it. The word of God is communication between persons, an "I" addressing a "you." But such communication is never only verbal. It is just as "real," just as "living," when it is conveyed through those sacramental signs that are also forms of the word of God, the divine self-communication. It was this incarnational understanding of the word of God for which Luther contended in his controversy over the real presence with Zwingli and the Swiss Reformers.[17]

Perhaps as important as the restoration of preaching to the historic liturgy was Luther's emphasis on hymns that could be sung by the people of God. Luther prized music almost as much as he did God's Word, and his musical talents, as a composer of texts and tunes, led to an outpouring of evangelical hymns from his own pen as well as from many others whom he encouraged to write hymns for congregational singing. Luther's hymns became a means for handing down faith, since they were filled with the content of the biblical faith.

> While the original purpose of these songs was to make congregational participation practical in evangelical liturgies, they became such a formidable means of disseminating doctrine that the Jesuits later said of Luther's songs that they "destroyed more souls than his writings and speeches."[18]

For Luther, singing was an act of proclamation as well as praise, and he established within Lutheranism this great tradition of music and singing. Even today, Lutherans are known for their music and hymns, and they still are a primary means of teaching the people about the truths of Christ and the Scriptures.[19]

Luther's reforms, however, did not lead to an immediate translation of the liturgy from Latin to German. In fact, Luther insisted that in the cities the liturgy remain in Latin, for everyone knew this language, whether they were Italian, German, French, or Spanish. The Latin liturgy was part of caring for the mission, for people from other countries would know Latin. The only place

Luther called for the use of German in the liturgy was in the rural areas where there were very few people who knew Latin or were from other cultures.

Luther called the Canon of the Mass a "cesspool" because of its meritorious works and its focus on the sacrifice of the Mass. Many would say that it was Johann Tetzel and his indulgences that most influenced Luther in reforming the Church, but it could also be argued that what Luther found to be the most objectionable abuse was the sacrifice of the Mass. Luther found it abhorrent that the liturgy, the primary way in which the faith was handed down to God's people, smacked of works-righteousness, and the sacrifice of the Mass was the greatest abomination of all. The Canon of the Mass was beyond rescue, so Luther cut out everything but the Words of Institution. This is why Lutherans have never had a Eucharistic Prayer, because Luther reduced the prayer to Jesus' own words. This does not mean he was against the Eucharistic Prayer. Rather, the Roman Canon of the Mass was so corrupt that there was nothing worth preserving except the very words of Jesus Himself.

As important as this was for Luther's reforms, it was Christ's real, true, and bodily presence in the Lord's Supper that was central to Luther's theology of worship, and much has been written about this.[20] Luther became so consumed in defending Christ's real, true, and bodily presence in the Lord's Supper that his earlier accent on our communion with Christ and His saints was lost in the polemical battles with Ulrich Zwingli and others. Luther's theology of worship as it is expressed through his understanding of the Lord's Supper is the "source of the church's life as a merciful body." Matthew Harrison notes that "Luther's indictment of his age strikes us in our time"[21]:

> Christians [in the early church] cared for one another, supported one another, sympathized with one another, bore one another's burdens and affliction. This has all disappeared, and now there remain only the many masses and the many who receive this sacrament without in the least understanding or practicing what it signifies.[22]

What Luther suggests to us is that our liturgical theology is incomplete unless we complement it with a corresponding theology of *diakonia*, that is, service, especially to one another within the Church. Our life of *leitourgia* in the Lutheran Church attempts to embody the treasures handed down to us in our Lutheran liturgical tradition. However, our *leitourgia* needs to be balanced by a healthy understanding of *diakonia*.

> The church's activities fall into three categories. *Leitourgia*, or Divine service, is the foundational activity of the church where

> God is serving us with His gifts of forgiveness, life, and salvation through the bodily presence of Christ in Word and Sacrament. *Marturia*, or public witness, is our response to the gifts as we confess to God and to the world that which He works in us, namely, our faith. *Diakonia*, or service, is Christ in us in the midst of the world as we act out the love, mercy, grace, and charity God gives to us in Christ amongst one another as He satisfies the needs of our neighbor through us . . . *Leitourgia* takes place regularly in the public worship service at font, pulpit, and altar, as Christ comes to us and as we come into communion with Him. In the Divine Service we do not serve ourselves inwardly by turning in upon ourselves, but rather Christ serves us through the office of the public ministry as the pastor stands in the stead and by the command of Christ. Through the pastor Christ speaks His Word and serves His Bride, the church, at His table. *Marturia* occurs both as an act of worship, in the Creed of the church, in hymns and prayers, as well as proceeding from the church into the highways and byways as we bear witness to the hope that is in us. *Diakonia* flows from the altar where we are served, and takes place outside the doors of the worship service, finding expression wherever suffering and sin afflict and infect our lives.[23]

Throughout Lutheranism today, the traditional threefold office of bishop, pastor, and deacon/deaconess is being promoted as reflecting the ecclesial structure of the Early Church.[24] The bishop most represents the activity of *marturia* as he embodies in his office the witness of Christ as the gracious Gift-giver. The pastor represents *leitourgia* because through him God serves the people with gifts. The deaconess/deacon represents *diakonia* in which Christ's love and mercy is embodied in compassionate acts. The bishop as the overseer of pastors represents *marturia* and *leitourgia*; bishops, pastors, and deacons/deaconesses all represent *diakonia*; but only bishops and pastors represent *leitourgia*. Luther's theology of worship as *Gottesdienst* embraces both *leitourgia*—what happens in the church on Sunday morning where faith receives the gifts from Christ's bodily presence and responds in love to God as the gracious Gift-giver—and *diakonia*, which is what happens outside the *leitourgia* through works of mercy and compassion to our neighbor. Through their *diakonia*, deacons/deaconesses point those who are broken and in need to the pastor and to *leitourgia*.

> Standing alongside the Pastor who dispenses Christ's gifts as a steward of the mysteries, deaconesses bind up the brokenhearted

> and the distressed. They go out from the door of the church, and bring in Christ's lost and broken lambs into His sheepfold where the Pastor feeds these lambs by bringing them into communion with Christ as He comes to them in Word and Sacrament.[25]

The presence of the worship wars throughout Christendom is both puzzling and troubling, and especially in the Lutheran Church because our understanding of the Lord's Supper was formed by our confession of the bodily presence of Jesus Christ. If people realized that the Creator of the universe, the very Lamb of God who hung on the cross and rose triumphantly from the grave, is bodily present among us, *along with the entire company of heaven, saints, angels, and archangels*, then reverence for that presence would shape our liturgical worship. Thus much of what is called "contemporary" worship in our circles would no longer be an option. If our congregations worshiped believing that heaven is on earth in Christ, the worship wars would soon come to an end.

If our congregations worshiped believing that heaven is on earth in Christ, the worship wars would soon come an end.

How ironic, then, that the same consuming influences Luther faced concerning the Lord's Supper continue in our broad evangelical, religious culture, our "Protestant" culture. Even as Luther did in his day, Lutherans today struggle to maintain the catholic confession that Christ is present bodily through Word and Sacrament. Why? Because Luther's Small Catechism shows us that the heart of the Supper is the gift of forgiveness of sins. As Luther so clearly states on the basis of Jesus' instituting words on the night in which He was betrayed, the forgiveness of our sins through the eating and drinking of the body and blood is why we come to the Lord's table. And as Luther so clearly and emphatically states, forgiveness is the primary gift, for "where there is forgiveness of sins, there is also life and salvation."[26] From forgiveness flows life—Christ's life—and His salvation, which is rescue from all our enemies, especially the devil, the world, and our flesh. Forgiveness of our sins joins us to Christ and His eternal life and gives us eternal rescue from all our foes.

In this individualistic society in which we live, the problem comes when forgiveness of sins becomes for us so personalized that all we see is my forgiveness and not the sufferings of the saints who are with us at the table. Unfortunately, for many Lutherans today, their understanding of the Lord's Supper is shaped only by Luther's Small Catechism and not by Luther's other writings, such as "The Blessed Sacrament of the Holy and True Body of Christ."[27] In preserving what is central to the Supper, we may have lost other, eternal realities that are swirling around us as we receive the gift of forgiveness by means of the body and blood in the Supper.

For example, many Lutherans do not fully grasp what we say in our liturgy when the pastor chants the final phrase of the Proper Preface concerning "the angels, archangels, and all the company of heaven." More than in any other place, here our liturgy speaks with great clarity about the reality of heaven on earth. What we must always remember when we go to the Lord's Supper is that we commune with Christ, and wherever Christ is, there is heaven. This communion includes all the saints who have died and risen in Christ—Abraham, Isaac, Jacob, David, Ruth, Peter, Paul, our grandparents and great-grandparents, perhaps even our spouses or our children—and all the saints now living throughout the world and those still to come. After someone dies, it is good to think of them at the Lord's Supper, knowing that, as we commune here below at the table of the Lamb and sing the Lamb's songs, we join the saints in heaven at the marriage feast of the Lamb in His kingdom that knows no end. In Christ, in that great mystery of our union with Him, we are joined to angels, archangels, and the whole company of heaven.

Luther's liturgical theology certainly embraced this reality, but as a pastor he took it one step further. He connected this extraordinary gift of communion with Christ and His saints in our *leitourgia* to the response of love that gives birth to *diakonia* as we share our sufferings with one another.

> This fellowship [at the Lord's Supper] consists in this, that all the spiritual possessions of Christ and his saints are shared with and become the common property of him who receives this sacrament. Again all sufferings and sins also become common property; and thus love engenders love in return and [mutual love] unites.[28]

By joining Himself to us in this sacred meal of holy food, we are now joined to all the saints who have died and risen in Christ. This communion of saints is where heaven and earth are joined together in Him. We are members of this eternal community, a community that even now participates in heavenly things as through Word and Sacrament we have a foretaste of the feast to come.

This means that we are not alone when we commune at the Lord's table; rather, we are joined in Christ with all the saints *and their sufferings*, and they bear our burdens and we bear theirs. As St. Paul tells the Galatians: "Bear one another's burdens, and so fulfill the law of Christ" (6:2). The Law may now be called "the law of Christ" because Christ fulfilled the Law in one word: "You shall love your neighbor as yourself" (Galatians 5:14). Christ fulfilled that Law by loving His neighbor all the way to the cross, where He bore the burdens of all humanity as the very Son of God. The law of Christ is fulfilled in us when we love our neighbors as ourselves, bearing their burdens and sufferings "as if they were our own." The following excerpts from Luther indicate that there is no better way to love one's neighbor as oneself than to go to the Lord's Supper and share with our neighbor Christ's suffering and the sufferings of the whole company of saints.

> Whoever is in despair, distressed by a sin-stricken conscience or terrified by death or carrying some other burden upon his heart, if he would be rid of them all, let him go joyfully to the sacrament of the altar and lay down his woe in the midst of the community [of saints] and seek help from the entire company of the spiritual body . . . . The immeasurable grace and mercy of God are given us in this sacrament to the end that we might put from us all misery and tribulation [*anfechtung*] and lay it upon the community [of saints], and especially on Christ. Then we may with joy find strength and comfort, and say, "Though I am a sinner and have fallen, though this or that misfortune has befallen me, nevertheless I will go to the sacrament to receive a sign from God that I have on my side Christ's righteousness, life, and sufferings, with all holy angels and the blessed in heaven and all pious men on earth. If I die, I am not alone in death; if I suffer, they suffer with me. [I know that] all my misfortune is shared with Christ and the saints, because I have a sure sign of their love toward me." . . . Be certain that Christ and all his saints are coming to you with all their virtues, sufferings, and mercies, to live, work, suffer, and die with you, and that they desire to be wholly yours, having all things in common with you. . . . You must take to heart the infirmities and needs of others, as if they were your own. Then offer to others your strength, as if it were their own, just as Christ does for you in the sacrament. This is what it means to be changed into one another through love, out of many particles to become one bread and drink, to lose one's own form and take on that which is common to all.[29]

Luther set the ordinaries, which had been the private domain of the monastic choirs, to tunes that everyone could sing and made the texts simpler and more straightforward. Many of the ordinaries were wed to existing hymn tunes or folklike tunes, as well as to liturgical music. These biblical canticles are the primary response of the people of God to the words of Jesus and His life-giving meal, so it was imperative that the people be able to sing these hymns with understanding. Luther's gift of music greatly added to his ability to restore the Church's song to the people.

The Church Year, which had become weighed down with commemorations of obscure saints, now focused on Christ's life. Commemorations of nonbiblical saints or those who lacked gravity in the great tradition were removed, though Luther still commemorated the great Church Fathers. Luther even had an understanding of Sunday as the eighth day on which God was re-creating the world through the bodily presence of Christ and His gifts. Luther restored Sunday to its character as *the* feast day, and only major feasts were allowed to overshadow Sunday as the eternal day of Christ's ongoing resurrection. The Church Year in use today is the result of Luther's Christological focus on proclaiming Christ and His Gospel every Sunday. This focus caused Luther to throw out anything that did not clearly proclaim that we are saved by grace and not by works of the Law. Because Luther applied justification by grace through faith to the medieval liturgy and simplified the liturgy, he uncovered the clean, crisp fivefold structure of the historic liturgy. For all intents and purposes, he returned the Church to the fourth and fifth centuries, when the historic liturgy was being developed and the structures were coming together in the beautiful symphony of sound and action that we know today. Luther made it possible for the people of his day to worship in continuity with the faithful of generations and generations of Christians that had gone before them. He returned the Church to its New Testament roots and to the historic liturgy known to the Church before its medieval demise.

A COMPARISON BETWEEN LUTHER AND LUTHERAN WORSHIP TODAY

Entrance	WORD	Preparation	SACRAMENT	Distribution
Confession & Absolution	Old Testament Gradual	Offering Offertory	Preface Proper Preface	AGNUS DEI (7th Century)
Introit	Epistle Alleluia		SANCTUS (3rd Century)	Canticle
KYRIE (5th Century)	Gospel Sermon		Prayer	Collect
HYMN OF PRAISE Gloria in Excelsis (6th Century) This Is the Feast (20th Century)	CREED (11th Century) Prayers for the Faithful		Lord's Prayer Words of Institution Peace of the Lord	Benediction
Collect				

If one would compare Luther's order of service (1523) to the contemporary Lutheran Divine Service as seen above, it is clear how our liturgies today closely follow the shape of the historic liturgy of the sixth and seventh centuries.

Luther's Order of Service

Entrance Rite

Introit—retained old Introits and preserved the Psalms

Kyrie

Gloria in Excelsis

Collect—traditional and evangelical

Liturgy of the Word

Epistle—emphasis on lessons in which faith is taught, not morality

Gradual—two verses only with Alleluia, "for the Alleluia is the perpetual voice of the church, just as the memorial of his passion and victory is perpetual"[30]

Gospel—candles and incense are neither forbidden nor prescribed

Nicene Creed—sung or spoken

Sermon—before Introit or after Creed. "Since the Gospel is the voice crying in the wilderness and calling unbelievers to faith, it seems particularly fitting to preach before the mass. For properly speaking, the mass consists in using the Gospel and communing at the table of the Lord."[31]

Liturgy of the Lord's Supper

I. Preparation of Bread and Wine—wine mixed with water (Offertory/Offering)

II Preface and Proper Preface

III. The Words of Institution—chanted

IV Sanctus—during Benedictus ("Blessed is He who comes in the name of the Lord") bread and cup are elevated for the weak in faith—this concession becomes "orthodox" when "through sermons in the vernacular they have been taught what the elevation means."[32]

V. Lord's Prayer—chanted or read

The Peace of the Lord ("a public absolution of the sins of the communicants, the true voice of the gospel announcing remission of sins, and therefore the one and most worthy preparation for the Lord's Table, if faith holds to these words as coming from the mouth of Christ himself"[33]) is pronounced facing the people. Luther claims it is the only custom of the ancient bishops left.

VI. Agnus Dei—pastor may commune himself at this time

VII. Post-Communion Canticle

Post-Communion Collect

Benedicamus Domino—Benedictus from Vespers possible

VIII. Benediction

Roman—"May Almighty God bless you: the Father, and the Son, and the Holy Ghost."

Aaronic—Numbers 6:24–27

Psalm 67:6–7—"God, our God, shall bless us; God shall bless us; let all the ends of the earth fear Him!"

Blessing similar to the one used by Christ at ascension (Luke 24:50–51)[34]

Abolitionists, Traditionalists, and Luther

Luther was very pastoral in his reforms, choosing not to change some ceremonies because he did not want to upset the people, though he left in place the fivefold shape of the liturgy that went back to the sixth century. Lutherans today, if they were to worship with Luther and his liturgy, would find it to be very similar in style to liturgical churches today. The liturgy of Luther was reverent to the presence of Christ, who was offering His gifts in Word and Sacrament. Of course, Luther never considered himself anything but a member of the one catholic Church, intending to reform it from within and not from without. As a liturgical reformer, Luther would not have been considered a restorationist or an innovator;[35] rather, he would have been an evangelical reformer who simply wanted to give people access to Christ and His gifts.

> Whatever its defects may have been, and they were . . . medieval defects pushed to their extreme, this Lutheran mass preserved for the faithful all that they had found best about the mass of the Middle Ages. . . . Along with the ceremonial, liturgical chant, sacred vestments, the crucifix and statues, incense and candles, the mass of devout Lutherans still found in their worship the whole atmosphere of adoration which the best Christians of the Middle Ages found in the holy presence and the evocation of the saving cross.[36]

During the Reformation, there were other liturgical movements that conflicted with Luther's reforms. In fact, the other two groups that formed as alternatives to Luther's liturgical reforms represent the extremes that have existed in the Church since the time of the Reformation. Both groups operate with the same principle—liturgy is adiaphora.[37] The "abolitionists," led by Andreas Carlstadt, claimed that since the liturgy is adiaphora, then everything needs to be changed. Here one is able to see the disastrous consequences of the radical Reformation. The movement of this group was toward a more "Protestant" liturgy similar to the liturgy of the followers of Zwingli, who denied the real presence. Carlstadt's group literally took the axe to altars, organs, and statuary; burned music libraries; and reduced the liturgy to nothing more than a service of Word and preaching. The Lord's Supper was relegated to a secondary position, for the only thing that mattered was the sermon, which, in following the Pharisees in Jesus' day, was more of a moralistic diatribe than a proclamation of Christ that created the reality of His bodily presence. These sermons were folksy and popular, appealing to the people in common speech with their own idioms.

Luther came out of hiding in the Wartburg to respond to this great threat against the Church and her Gospel. His Wittenberg sermons reflect his thinking at this time. Luther responded to Carlstadt and his dismantling of the historic liturgy by creating the German Mass, a Divine Service in the vernacular with the ordinaries as hymns accompanied by familiar melodies. Luther was reluctant to do this, and this was not his preferred liturgical setting. However, Carlstadt's abolitionist reforms had captured the imagination of the people, and Luther wanted to respond quickly with an alternative that would keep people from succumbing to the attractive but misleading positions of the radical Reformation.

The other group at the time of the Reformation could be called the "traditionalists," and they were led by Philip Melanchthon, who began with the same premise as the "abolitionists," that is, that liturgy is adiaphora. However, the traditionalists believed that the traditions would continue, and therefore nothing should be changed. This group appropriated the medieval liturgy without changes since liturgy did not matter. Like the abolitionists, the most important part of the liturgy was the sermon, which was academic in tone and style, a moral lecture. These sermons reflected a different homiletic style than the sermons of abolitionists, yet they still included many of the same theological accents. It must be said that Luther was much more at home with the traditionalists than the abolitionists and did not consider the traditionalists as great a danger to the Gospel. His reforms indicate that he did recognize the need to change the liturgy, though his changes were conservative and pastorally sensitive.

Luther's reforms take the mediating position between the two extremes, though in his respect for the liturgy he leaned more toward the traditionalists than the abolitionists. Luther was a liturgical man whose lively sense of the bodily presence of Christ and his reverence and fidelity to that presence necessitated that he keep the liturgy handed down to him with some evangelical changes. Luther's mediating position should be a guiding light for all Lutherans today as we attempt to "receive from those who went before and, in making that tradition of the Divine Service [our] own, add what best may serve in its own day—the living heritage and something new."[38] This mediating position is normally represented in the official hymnals of the Church. These worship books carefully consider the great tradition to provide continuity with those who have used the historic liturgy for more than fifteen hundred years, attempting to reflect the principle of "the living heritage and something new," following in the tradition of Luther and many of the other reformers.

From the Reformation to the Age of Pietism and Rationalism (1580–1850)

The history of Lutheranism from the time of the Reformation through the age of Pietism and Rationalism (1580–1850) is the battle between the two extremes proposed by Carlstadt and Melanchthon. The impulse is to follow either Carlstadt and the radical Reformation (which led to Pietism) or Melanchthon and the traditionalists (which led to Rationalism). Curiously, these two extremes are more alike theologically than they are different, and though they eschew the liturgy as adiaphora, they use the liturgy as a means to promote a different Gospel.

For the abolitionists, that Gospel is tinged with a strong sense of works-righteousness, and it infects much of Protestantism today, particularly with the individual focus on "me and Jesus" and the decision theology that runs rampant through its songs and sermons. Among the Rationalists, there are restorationist tendencies in which the liturgy becomes an object of devotion, turning this rite that bears the salutary means of grace into an idol to be worshiped. The liturgy becomes a good work, the platform for presenting the propositional truths of the faith. This ultimately undermines the incarnation and destroys the Church's sacramental life. Throughout the last five hundred years, the Lutheran Church has vacillated between these two extremes, moving toward one and then the other. Luther's mediating position keeps the Church in balance as it negotiates these two opposing alternatives to the truth of the Gospel expressed in the historic liturgy.[39]

Liturgy and Adiaphora

Today many appeal to Article X ("Church Practices: Called *Adiaphora*, or Indifferent Things") of the Formula of Concord, Solid Declaration, to claim that the historic liturgy of the Church is adiaphora.[40] Clearly, there are certain customs and ceremonies within the liturgical life of the Church in which Christians are free. However, in no way do the Confessions suggest that we ought to depart from the historic liturgy with its structure of Word and Sacrament accompanied by the ordinaries. In fact, it could be argued that the section on adiaphora in the Formula of Concord suggests the opposite. Article X must be read in the context of what the entire Lutheran Confessions say about liturgy, which, as we have seen, maintains Luther's strong emphasis on the Divine Service. What is often overlooked in Article X is the important caveat offered in the Formula that "at a time of confession" one must not depart from the historic liturgy of the Church.

> We also believe, teach, and confess that *at a time of confession*, when the enemies of God's Word want to suppress the pure doctrine of the Holy Gospel, God's entire church, indeed, every single Christian, but especially the ministers of the Word, as the directors of the community of God ‹God's church›, is bound by God's Word to confess the doctrine freely and openly. They are bound to confess every aspect of ‹pure› religion, not only in words, but also in works and actions. In this case, even in adiaphora, they must not yield to the adversaries or permit these adiaphora to be forced on them by their enemies, whether by violence or cunning, to the detriment of the true worship of God and the introduction and sanction of idolatry.[41]

Even Walther used the above section of Article X not to argue against the historic liturgy but to argue for the freedom within the Church to use the historic liturgy to form a Lutheran identity and as a statement of confession against the prevailing Protestant religious culture: "For 'at a time of confession' the Formula of Concord says quite correctly, 'one dare not yield.' Now, however, that 'time' is for us 'always,' because we are everywhere surrounded by Reformed and other sects."[42] The question facing today's Lutheran Church is whether we are "in a state of confession" when, like Walther, we are surrounded not only by the Reformed and other sects but also by the theology of our country's Protestant religious culture that has made its way into our church body through the new liturgies we borrow from other denominations.

Lutheran Liturgy in the Twenty-first Century

This brings us to the modern era and, in particular, to a number of practical ramifications for the Lutheran Church today. The remainder of this chapter will consider the cultural context in which we live and offer some suggestions about modern liturgical renewal.[43] Lutheran churches today are experiencing the results of the blossoming of contemporary liturgical scholarship and how liturgical renewal might take on a concrete shape. Our cultural context and its impact on our liturgy make liturgical renewal an issue these days. We are tempted to think we are in uncharted waters, but liturgical renewal has always been with the Lutheran Church since the Reformation.

Discussing liturgical renewal tempts one to rear back and give people what they think they want—a panacea, a recipe, a perfect liturgy, ten easy steps to a relevant, Lutheran, liturgical service. Such an approach centers on *tactics* of renewal, another how-to manual to achieve relevant liturgy that next year will be irrelevant. The Roman Catholic Church, with its rich and ancient liturgical heritage, is the seedbed for our Lutheran liturgy, yet it has succumbed to liturgical trends. This is borne out by a cursory reading of the literature on the liturgical movement since Vatican II. The search continues for the perfect liturgy, for the secret to liturgical renewal, yet no one appears to have *the* answer. The tactical approach to liturgical renewal never satisfies. It ignores the complexity of the context in which liturgy is acted out, confusing a church with liturgies with a liturgical church. This approach assumes that the liturgical structures need to be renewed.

But perhaps this is assuming too much. Perhaps what is wrong is not the liturgy but those who do the liturgy, their understanding, their commitment to it, and their execution of it. The targets of liturgical renewal are the clergy and the congregation. The problems are less liturgical and more theological, centering more in our anthropology and ecclesiology than our liturgiology. What is wrong is not the liturgy but the culture; thus instead of constantly asking what's wrong with the liturgy, we should be asking what's wrong with the culture. We should concentrate our attention on the renewal of the culture through liturgy, not vice versa. The goal of good liturgy is always the transforming of culture by the Gospel of Jesus Christ. This is not accomplished if the liturgy is subject to the whims of culture. Untransformed by liturgy, culture effectively destroys that liturgy. The Church becomes indistinguishable from the culture, and the Gospel is lost. This is the real secularization and destruction of the Gospel.

The goal of good liturgy is always the transforming of culture by the Gospel of Jesus Christ.

This does not mean that we ignore the cultural context of the liturgy. Instead, the dominating principle in renewal is to conform the world to the Gospel, not the Gospel to the world. This seems to be what Jesus meant in His constant polemic against the religious establishment of His day. He certainly showed how not to conform to culture by suffering the humiliating death of crucifixion. Even His disciples were so fearful of the consequences of His cultural scandal that they deserted Jesus until after the resurrection.

This also seems to be the intent of the apostle Paul in places such as Corinth, where he was insistent on adapting the culture under the criteria of the Gospel, willing to be a fool for Christ. In evaluating our liturgies, we must not see them as efforts to help us conform to the world's values. The essence of our Lutheran belief in the theology of the cross warns us against such liturgies. Rather, the liturgy helps us show the world how to live under the cross.

Thus our approach should be *strategic* rather than tactical. Renewal should be the result of viewing the whole life of the Church through the liturgy, a holistic view that calls for strategy, not tactics. A tactical approach trivializes our life in Christ, focusing that life in today's relevancies and today's style. A strategic approach focuses more on *reverence*, not just relevance; more on *renewal of substance*, not just reinforcement and strengthening of form; more on *theology*, not just practice. If we are reverent in worship, we will be relevant; if our life in Christ is substantial, we will develop forms to support that life; if our vision is biblically theological, we will be confessionally practical.

Such an approach may disappoint those who advocate change. A cut-and-paste approach is presumptuous and flies in the face of the tradition. In our changing culture, today's congregations are often too likely to subject the liturgy to the same criteria by which they judge everything else in society. If it doesn't work, fix it, change it, tinker with it until it is right. After all, this is what we do with our cars, our marriages, our lifestyles, and, sadly, our theology. Liturgy and theology should not conform to this world; they should transform the world.

On the other hand, one of the worst results of the liturgical movement in the 1960s and 1970s was the notion that there must be change for the sake of change. This period of the liturgical movement gave many of us the opportunity to work some things out of our systems. This period serves as a warning against shallowness and exposes the danger of excessiveness. Liturgical surprises were so frequent as to be unsurprising. The faithful, who knew the liturgy from their youth, were stumbling through pages and inserts so that worship measured the dexterity of their fingers and the quickness of their mind. No one would argue against change if something needs changing. But it is a cultural assumption that it is the liturgy that needs to be changed, when, as we have already suggested, it is we who need to be changed through the liturgy, for here Jesus Christ comes to us most completely Sunday in and Sunday out.

Although there are many laypeople who are dissatisfied with the liturgy, there are many more who are very satisfied. Perhaps it is the liturgical experts who are bored and demand the changes. One concern identified by laypeople is that committees of experts do not always understand a specific congregation and its cultural context. This is one of the dangers of liturgy from above. Liturgical conferences become promotional venues for the latest fads.

Instead, the liturgical movement must give priority to restoring the liturgy to the faithful, to recognizing that the liturgy does not belong exclusively to any one congregation, to the clergy, or to the commissions on worship of any church body. It belongs to the whole Church as it is expressed in a congregation. Since liturgy is the expression of God's people as they respond to His Word, lasting liturgical change must come from below, from the congregation, not from above, from the commissions on worship or self-styled liturgical experts.

There is great historical precedent to suggest that for fifteen hundred years liturgy came from the community at worship and not from committees of worship. Liturgy was not a text until the invention of the printing press, and what a congregation did on a Sunday morning evolved imperceptibly over a long period of time from within the congregation. As soon as the liturgy became a text, it could be edited or rewritten or even frozen in time. No one expects us to go back to textless liturgies, but it is important to see how liturgy develops and evolves in today's Church.

But this view must be tempered before we find ourselves returning to those makeshift liturgies of our very recent past. We need to take a hard look at who we are as the Lutheran Church. We do have a tradition with a cultural and historical context, and that tradition is both evangelical and catholic, a tradition our forefathers attempted to shape into a distinct Lutheran identity that mediated between our catholic and Reformation roots. Luther was both catholic and evangelical. To resolve this tension, his followers decided to call themselves "Lutheran." In many ways we are as much at a watershed in our history as our forefathers were in the sixteenth century. A battle is taking place for the heart and soul of our church body. This battle is being waged between those who want to move the Lutheran Church toward an American form of Protestantism with its Calvinistic roots and those who want to regain historical Lutheranism. At stake in liturgical renewal is nothing more and nothing less than the very ethos of our church body.

One of the goals of Lutheran liturgical renewal is the development of a distinct *Lutheran* ethos. The problem today is that our congregations are generally ignorant not only of biblical theology and Lutheran liturgical traditions, but, what is worse, they also do not know the Lutheran tradition as a positive evolution of the New Testament and early postapostolic Church, which in turn comes from the Old Testament as was practiced by Jesus Himself. They do not know what it means to be Lutheran. But people want to be Lutheran, and they accomplish this because they sing hymns that are foreign to them and listen to sermons that are without meaning for them. In the end, they mime those meaningless rituals we call liturgy. But true to the character of ritual, those hymns and sermons and liturgies bind them together as Lutherans. And true to the nature of liturgy, its conservative character caters to the confessional character of our church body that helps preserve its Lutheran identity. If people lose their Lutheran identity, it will result in the irrecoverable loss of the liturgy, a loss that in both cases would be an unimaginable tragedy.

One of the great contributions to liturgical studies in this century has come from the anthropologists and their work with rituals in primitive societies. Anthropologists have recognized the importance of rhythm and ritual in binding people together into a community. In our individualistic society, where we all want to do things our own way, one of the worst things we can do in our liturgies is cater to all these individual tastes. Variety does not solve problems; it creates them. The reason people are bored with the liturgy is not because there is no variety but because what takes place in the liturgy is perceived to be insignificant. Such a view suggests that God is not really present, a view encouraged by vapid liturgies that seek to adapt the liturgy to the culture. Anthropologists have discovered that ritual encourages the perception that the deity is present, a spiritual presence that binds the worshiping community together. In our liturgies, a fuller expression of our Lutheran liturgical traditions would nurture a fuller recognition that a major part of the Lutheran ethos revolves around an encounter with God in worship.

Concerned liturgical scholars are well aware of the consequences of lost liturgy, and they are equally aware of the sad condition of the biblical knowledge and the traditional awareness of many in our congregations. Scholars recognize that it is disastrous to leave the liturgy in the hands of those who know little of liturgy, theology, or Scripture. Thus liturgy cannot be an exclusive enterprise from below, from congregations who are not in touch with their historical roots. We still need liturgical scholars to give us liturgy from above. The challenge facing current liturgical renewal is mediating between the two. How do we resolve the tension between the scholars and the people who actually carry out the liturgy? How can we incorporate the findings of liturgical studies into our tradition and make them our own? How we resolve this tension will determine whether our church body remains Lutheran with both its Reformation and catholic foundations.

These questions give rise to a methodology of liturgical renewal that may satisfy both the strategists and the tacticians. For as the faithful see changes sweeping over them from the liturgical and cultural scholars, they must be provided with some criteria to judge these changes. This method of diagnosis will assist them in deciding, as congregations and parish pastors, whether these changes are good. The first question is: What things need to be renewed in our congregation? Such a question requires them to become liturgical critics who are capable of analyzing liturgical structures and diagnosing liturgical diseases. This approach to liturgical renewal will have important side effects for theology, pastoral care, evangelism, catechesis, preaching, architecture, and language. But the real benefit of this approach is that congregations will do what they should be doing—shaping a liturgy through strict parameters, a liturgy that is relevant and meaningful within their own context even as they take advantage of the expertise of liturgiologists who know the tradition and who are trying to be faithful to it.

As an example of this, consider a more practical analysis of the congregation's structuring of space and rite. These two areas of renewal are intimately related because they both deal with the two basic structures of Christian worship: the proclamation of the Word and the administration of Holy Communion. The way we structure our liturgical space and rites depends on our desire to make the Word of God accessible to the people in the Liturgy of the Word and the Supper of the Lord accessible to the people in the Liturgy of the Lord's Supper. Here are the questions the Church must face: Are our liturgical spaces reverent to the presence of Jesus Christ in Word and Sacrament? Are our liturgical rites faithful to Scripture and the tradition that has handed down to us Word and Sacrament as the two basic structures of Christian worship that form Christians together as the Body of Christ? These questions make us diagnosticians of space and rite under the criteria of Word and Sacrament, criteria basic to a Lutheran and apostolic construction of theology and worship.

As diagnosticians of liturgical space, there is no single way to structure the worship space, but there are guidelines to follow. First, the tension between the horizontal axis (human to human) and vertical axis (God to human) must be balanced. The foci for the Liturgy of the Word and the Liturgy of the Lord's Supper must be organized so that both human and divine communication can occur.

Second, the architectural placement of pulpit, altar, and font needs to be firmly fixed. Focus on the Bible-pulpit, on the food-altar-table, on the washing-font sends certain theological signals—all of which relate to the congregation's belief or lack of belief that Jesus Christ is present sacramentally and in His Word to bind them together as the Body of Christ. The Gospel is to be heard by all people when it is read and preached; the Sacrament is to be central to the liturgical space; Baptism, as initiatory in the life of the Church, is to be perceived as the way in which the congregation enters worship and is constituted in worship.

Third, the congregation is composed of people who are the Body of Christ. The space is both God's space and their space as God's people. Therefore liturgical space is utilitarian, providing shelter and ease of movement as people shift focus from pulpit to altar to font. It is simple, allowing the Gospel to be heard, the meal to be eaten, the bodies to be washed without distraction or disruption. It is flexible, giving the community freedom to express the Gospel freely from the pulpit, around the table, and at the font. It is intimate, revealing to the congregation a presence that is incarnate to absolve, to forgive, to reconcile, to save.[44] Finally, the worship space must fulfill Augustine's maxim that "beauty is the splendor of truth."

As diagnosticians of liturgical rites, our task is really very simple since the Church has handed down to us two basic structures: Word and Sacrament. When all the accretions are cut away, all that remains is the Liturgy of the Word and the Liturgy of the Lord's Supper. Our analysis of our rites begins with an awareness of these two structures and a commitment to maintain their integrity. These structures are as ancient as Scripture and will not change. They reflect the basic need of human beings to meet together to talk and eat. When the early Christians were gathered together in one small room in a domestic house church, they simply read His Word and ate His meal. Their songs and prayers were offered in light of His Word and in thanksgiving for His meal. They did not need any elaborate liturgies because they did not have the space in which to act them out. Our rites must fit our spaces, for a "high church" service in a small country parish is not just bad liturgy, it is bad taste.

Therefore a congregational analysis of rite must see to it that the rites of Word and Sacrament remain central to congregational worship within the setting of that worship. The decisions of a congregation about the shape of these two structures will determine the liturgical style of that congregation, and, in turn, this style is directly related to the pattern of liturgical participation. Each congregation must carefully decide these things for itself, with reverence to Christ's presence in His Word and in His Sacrament and with fidelity to the Scriptures and the traditions of the Church. Whatever the congregation decides, those decisions will determine the identity of that congregation as Lutheran and will define the nature of that community as a people who embody a Lutheran ethos. The point here is not that "everyone pick your own liturgy," but that everyone ought to be taught and should learn the beauty and richness of our liturgy. This should not be imposed from above, but the people of God should treasure the liturgy and benefit from its richness, seeing how it continually refreshes and renews.

As promised, no recipes or panaceas for liturgical renewal have been offered. Instead, these thoughts about liturgy principles about renewal have been suggested to guide congregations as they contemplate liturgical renewal. The hoped for outcome is that people think seriously about what it is we are about as we worship. The process of liturgical renewal is the responsibility of everyone in the Church. We can all participate. And if that participation is reverent to God's presence and faithful to His Word, then it will result in right worship.

Conclusion Lutheran Liturgy in the Postmodern World

At the end of the twentieth century, many of us were caught up in the excitement of a new hymnal. Two new Lutheran hymnals (*Lutheran Book of Worship* and *Lutheran Worship*) emerged during this time when many were ready for a change in worship, and many others were convinced that a new hymnal was the work of the devil. So much has happened in the liturgical life of the Lutheran Church during these twenty years that none of us could have ever guessed that we would be where we are today. As a result of the liturgical upheaval in the sixties, seventies, and eighties, we know more today about the history and development of Lutheran worship, as well as that of all major liturgical traditions, than at any other time in history. But this was not always the case. During this time of liturgical change a great gift has been given the Church with the emergence of scholars, pastors, musicians, and laypeople who are interested and informed about what it means to worship God rightly. Talk of the Divine Service and a proper understanding of worship is a regular part of the conversation of the Church. Worship is a hot topic not only in our circles but also throughout the Christian Church.

Many look back at the end of the twentieth century as the era of the "worship wars," choosing this kind of language to characterize what was happening in the Christian Church during this time of liturgical renewal and liturgical change. Certainly it felt like a war at times. A number of years ago, in the very midst of the conflict, something happened to me that changed the way I spoke about the challenges facing the Church in her worship life. Like Augustine, my conversion came through the innocence of a child, my son to be exact, who was no more than 5 years old at the time. He probably has no recollection of the questions he asked me as he watched the suitcase get packed and the briefcase prepared for another trip away from home. "Where are you going, Papa?" he asked. "I'm going to a conference of pastors," I replied. “Why?” he wondered. “To talk about the liturgy of the church.” Again he asked, “Why?” “Well,” I said, “the liturgy is under attack, and I am going to defend it.”

I immediately realized what I was saying as I tried to explain to my 5-year-old that the liturgy was some sort of thing that needed to be defended from an attack and that I was being sent to the front lines of this worship war to muster a defense. That’s the way it felt back then, and still does to some people today—hand-to-hand combat, us against them, an all-out war with one side pitted against the other. But that little conversation with my son changed the way I approached my presentations on liturgy and worship. It was time for a different approach. It was time to go on the offensive, not in a polemical or contentious way, but in a positive and winsome manner. It was time to highlight for people the gifts that are contained in our liturgical tradition.

Such an approach involved two issues for me, the very two things that go into the title of this book. *Heaven on Earth: The Gifts of Christ in the Divine Service* suggests two elements about the liturgical heritage of the Lutheran Church that this book has attempted to accent: that our worship is biblical and that our worship is apocalyptic.

The Divine Service Is Biblical

Our conversation on worship must accent the biblical content and biblical ethos of the historic liturgy. Many have recommended that for the Church to grow it needs to depart from traditional Lutheran worship because it is too “German.” One seldom hears such a comment anymore (except maybe from first-year seminarians in “Lutheran Worship” class), but I bring it up because of what it says about the way people perceive the liturgy. It is seen as very narrow, bound by a particular “culture” and therefore inaccessible to people who were not of that culture. Certainly, there are hymns written by Germans and hymns that use German tunes, but the shape of our liturgy and its content are not German but biblical, reflecting the teaching of Jesus in the Gospels, the shape of worship in Acts and the Epistles, the biblical culture of Palestine and the early Christian ethos of the North Africa of Augustine and Cyprian and Tertullian.

What we have come to discover in the past twenty years is that Lutheran worship invites us into a different world than the one we inhabit. This world gives a different perspective because it is its own unique culture: a mixture of first-century Judaism and fourth-century North Africa, of sixteenth-century Germany, nineteenth-century America, and twentieth-century Lutheranism in such places as the United States, Africa, Russia, South America, and in other places around the world. It transcends all cultures and represents no single culture because *it is its own culture.*

T. S. Eliot once defined culture as "a whole way of life." The Divine Service teaches "a whole way of life" as it tells the world its story. The Divine Service gives what I will call later "a map of the world in which we actually live."[1] From the very beginning, especially among the earliest Christians, Christian worship invited people into its own culture as it conveyed "a whole way of life," and that life was the life of Christ. Frank Senn describes the culture created in worship by the first Christians in this way:

> Their regular gatherings around the words of Scripture and the "visible words" of the sacraments, for the life of prayer and fellowship, had the effect of generating a *Christian culture*—a value system and a way of life that stems from nothing less than a worldview, a perspective on reality.[2]

It is into this *Christian culture* we enter when we take our seat in the pew at the beginning of the Divine Service to confess our sins, sing hymns, hear the words of Jesus, and eat His holy meal. We are entering a different world—stepping on holy ground—for this world is where Christ's presence permeates everything, a world that has its own language and rhythm, its own music and sounds, its own smells and tastes, a world that is separate and distinct from the world of your home or work, separate from the evening news or your favorite mall. This is the world as God intended it to be, a world transformed by the presence of Jesus Christ, the Creator of the cosmos, who invaded our world to make right what had gone wrong and who continues to make right what is wrong even now, here among us as He speaks to us in His Word, gives us to eat and drink of His body and blood, and thereby offers us forgiveness of all our sins, offers us His life, and salvation from our enemies. The *Christian culture* of worship is that of Christ, a first-century Palestinian Jew who is at the same time the eternal Son of God. And what makes our worship distinct from all other "cultures" is that it is governed by Christ's Word from beginning to end. In this Christian culture we are told the story of the world that has been created and re-created in Jesus Christ. Our liturgy splices us into this story that relates the entire witness of God's mighty acts of salvation in the cosmos since the fall of Genesis. The liturgy calls us to embrace the biblical story as our story, and the people that inhabit this story to be our ancestors.

Back in the heat of the worship wars when people commented that our worship was "German," I used this as an opportunity to say something about the biblical and transcultural character of the liturgy. The comment about the German character of our worship was a sincere attempt to open up our worship and the Gospel to other "cultures." To accent how biblical the liturgy is, I would ask them to name something German in the liturgy, noting again that some hymns were Teutonic in origin. Of course, they were always stumped by this request, and I would begin to list elements of the liturgy to illustrate that they were not bound by any culture: the Word of God, the Kyrie, Gloria in Excelsis, Creed, Sanctus, Words of Institution, Agnus Dei. What I was listing were the main components of the liturgy that were directly from Scripture, and with the exception of hymns, the core of what is commonly called the historic liturgy of the Church. The ordinaries of the Liturgy—the Kyrie, Gloria in Excelsis, Hymn of the Day, Creed, Sanctus, and Agnus Dei—are biblical and reflect a community shaped and formed by Christ through Scripture.

The Divine Service Is Apocalyptic

To speak about worship is to speak of a larger, cosmic reality that engages us not in a worship war but an apocalyptic one. Let me explain what I mean.

When we gather around Christ as He comes to us in Word and Sacrament, a divine invasion is taking place.[3] An alien is invading our space. Heaven is breaking into the earth. This apocalyptic invasion, through Christ, comes to be present among us here and now in our worship. This is possible because of Christ's first invasion, His journey from heaven into our world in the incarnation to make right what had gone wrong. Jesus, the eternal Word of God by which the Father created the heavens and earth and called them good, returned to His creation as a creature with flesh and bones. He had to become one of us because what had been created so good and so right had become so terribly wrong by the disobedience and rebellion of our first parents. Their sin transformed God's presence into something to be feared. They needed to cover themselves from the shame of their nakedness. Their newfound hunger and thirst caused them pain and suffering, yet they hungered for more than food and they thirsted for more than water—they hungered and thirsted for God, for righteousness—for God to make right what they had made so terribly wrong.

Only God the Creator of all things could do this. And He made right what was now so wrong by making all things new. And so as St. Paul says,

"But when the fullness of time had come, God sent forth His Son, born of woman, born under the law, to redeem those who were under the law, so that we might receive adoption as sons" (Galatians 4:4–5). Jesus invades our world to journey from heaven to earth and back to heaven again. He descends from heaven to become one of us, live among us as teacher and miracle worker and rejected prophet, die our death on a cross, be buried in the earth, rise from the dead on the third day, and ascend back to heaven on the fortieth. Jesus invades our world in order to journey all the way to Jerusalem and to a tree—a tree of life planted not in a Garden but on a rock pile outside the holy city. A tree on which God's Son was nailed. This Son of God shared our humanity, our hunger and thirst, so that He might make right what was wrong by being lifted up on that tree. The world God created good went so wrong that the Son of God Himself must be nailed to this tree and suffer the agonies of hell and be led to cry out, "I thirst." And just before He died, He said, "It is finished," for the work of making all things right and all things new was done. The earth shook and darkness covered the earth because our justification was finally accomplished—and such an act of atonement was physical and cosmic, and therefore it was apocalyptic.

How clearly the Church grasped this biblical and apocalyptic reality in the way in which the historic liturgy developed, from its extraordinary confession of Christ's bodily presence in Word and Sacrament to its final placement of the Gloria in Excelsis and Sanctus in the Divine Service. God is revealing Himself to His people through the means of grace, which is an apocalypse because that's what apocalyptic means: God's revelation of Himself for our salvation. This is not just the reality of what takes place in our worship, this is exactly the way the Scripture describes what happened to our cosmos with the incarnation and atonement of Jesus Christ and with His invasion in us in Holy Baptism. What God made right on the cross He continues to make right by His presence among us in our worship. Biblical worship is the means by which Jesus Christ becomes apocalyptically present to us, for us, and in us.

That means that biblical worship is also cosmic and it is physical, and that is because the Gospel is cosmic and physical. The world was transformed physically by Christ's incarnation and atonement, and we, too, are changed in our bodies when Christ invades us by His Spirit. No one understood this better than St. Paul, who suffered as a pastor with the saints scattered across Asia Minor, Macedonia, and Greece. He helped them understand the radical change that had taken place in them since the apocalyptic invasion of Christ in His incarnation and the corresponding invasion of the Spirit into their hearts at Baptism when they cried, "Abba, Father." That the Gospel Paul preaches is an apocalyptic one, he asserts at the theological center of his passionate Epistle to the Galatians. Not only does Paul say that in the fullness of time God sent His Son into our cosmos to redeem those who are under the Law, but that God also "*sent* the Spirit of His Son into our hearts, crying, 'Abba! Father!' " (Galatians 4:6). The one who cries to the heavenly Father is the Spirit of Christ in us.

To be born under the power of the Law is to be born in the present evil age. It describes those things of the old aeon under whose power we are enslaved and from whom Christ has set us free in the new creation, that is, free from sin, death, and the devil. To redeem us who live under the power of the Law is to liberate us from one of the enslaving powers in which we live and from which we are set free.

Just as the Father sent His Son into the cosmos to redeem it, so now the Father and the Son sends the Spirit into our hearts and we give the baptismal cry: "Abba, Father." Our birth and identity come through the Spirit. Paul ties the apocalyptic event of Christ's incarnation with the apocalyptic entrance of Christ in us by water and Word—where our identity is formed by the gracious work of the Holy Spirit. Paul states unequivocally that our identity is "in Christ" because we have been baptized into Him. We are now a part of the family of God as God's sons, for the Spirit of God has invaded our hearts (baptismal language for Paul) and that Spirit of God "is now that of the crucified and resurrected Christ."[4]

This apocalyptic invasion means one thing for us—instead of fighting a worship war, we are enlisted by Baptism into an apocalyptic battle. By our Baptism we are God's foot soldiers in the cosmic battle against the principalities and powers of the universe. This is the war we should be worried about, and this book is intended to equip you with the armor that you need to fight in the front lines of this war. No one needs to tell you that the apocalyptic war out there is fierce and that you need all the help you can get to survive the onslaughts. You know that there is only one weapon against sin, death, and the devil that can prevail, and that weapon is Jesus Christ—His bodily presence—the treasure that gives us access to heaven even now.[5]

The Treasure of the Bodily Presence of Jesus Christ

The time has come for Lutherans to stop apologizing for their liturgical heritage. Instead, we need to proclaim the gifts we inherit in our worship life as

Lutheran Christians who continue the catholic tradition. And these gifts are innumerable. Any liturgical scholar could list them for you: the historic fivefold shape of our Divine Service, the two pinnacles of the Divine Service—Jesus' words in the Gospel and Jesus' word in the Sacrament—the biblical ordinaries that surround Jesus' words as the major hymns of the liturgy, the centrality of preaching centered in Christ and liturgical in character, our hymnody in both its content and its music, as well as our musical tradition with its deep resources to support the flow of the liturgy from beginning to end. The list could go on. And this is not to mention the most important treasure of all: that within this fivefold shape we believe, teach, and confess that Jesus Christ is present offering the gifts of life, salvation, and the forgiveness of sins as we hear His Word and receive His holy meal. In the Divine Service we are confident that we have entered heaven itself because Jesus Christ inhabits our worship with His bodily presence. This confident liturgy is embodied in a life of worship that "receives from those who went before and, in making that tradition of *the Divine Service* its own, adds what best may serve in its own day—the living heritage and something new."[6]

Jesus Christ is the treasure of our liturgical heritage through which we receive the gifts of forgiveness, life, and salvation. To speak of Christ as the treasure of our worship is to simply follow Jesus in the way He spoke about Himself. Jesus tells the parable of the rich fool to show that if you lay up treasures for yourself in this life, then you will not be rich toward God (Luke 12:13–21). To be rich toward God is to be a recipient of Christ and His gifts, a member of His kingdom through catechesis, Baptism, Word, and Supper. And this can only happen in our worship, for only there is the treasure of Christ Himself whose bodily presence feeds us holy food. Jesus is quite clear on this: there are two alternatives, either fleeting treasure on earth (Luke 12:21) or eternal treasure in heaven (Luke 12:33–34). He promises that on our journey from earth to heaven, the "little flock" gathered for worship (Luke 12:32) will be graced with eternal heavenly gifts through Christ, the Shepherd who washes His flock in Baptism, feeds His sheep with the new Passover Lamb—His body and blood in the Supper—and tends them with the guidance of His Word.

The ramifications of the presence of this treasure (Christ) in our worship are mind-boggling. The problem is that with the modern mind-set of the past fifty years, Lutherans have not recognized the very treasure of Christ's bodily presence as they gathered to hear His Word and receive His Supper.

As modernists, we were caught up in the culture's inability to grasp the mystery of the Creator of the cosmos deigning to humble Himself under the means of simple words, simple water, simple bread and wine. With our scientific worldview we ceased to believe in such miracles as that which the liturgy proclaims—that with "angels and archangels and all the company of heaven" we here on earth join the worship of heaven in the person of Jesus. This was just too incredible for modern men and women to believe. We wanted more, and catechized by a secular culture bent on entertaining itself to death and a religious culture that exalted experience and feelings, we succumbed. Forking over the greatest possible treasure for the sake of fleeting treasures on earth we settled for trinkets from the world's marketplace, when in the Divine Service we were being offered heaven itself.

To survive the apocalyptic war we need to commune with Christ bodily in Word and Sacrament. This is all that we mean by "heaven on earth," namely, that God sent His Son in the flesh to make all things right in the world and that God sent the Spirit of His Son into our hearts to make all things right in us. The person of Jesus Christ, according to both His divine and human natures, is present in His creation, and wherever Christ is, there is heaven. Our communion with the flesh of Christ *now* through the means of grace prepares us for our full communion with Him in the heavenly liturgy that has *not yet* reached its consummation.

The apocalyptic reality of our worship makes for us all the difference in the world. Our liturgy, hymns, and spiritual songs proclaim that our worship is biblical. That our worship is both biblical and apocalyptic makes it fully Lutheran. Jesus Christ is central to our liturgy and hymns—the Jesus whose real absence is accessible only by experience and feeling, or the Jesus whose bodily presence feeds us the bread of life in His Word and His very body and blood in His holy Supper. Or to put in another way, is heaven truly on earth in the person of Jesus Christ as we gather as Christians to worship, or are we just on a holding pattern since the ascension until Christ comes again in glory?

Our worship is about the Father sending the Son to His creation to bring in a new creation. Christ comes not as leader but as the servant at a table He prepares in the midst of His enemies. Nothing new is made when Jesus visits His creation, but all things are made new. He takes what is broken and makes it whole; He frees the captives, gives recovery of sight to the blind, releases those who are oppressed, and forgives the sins of all. The Son frees the world from the bondage of its fallenness—to absorb into His own flesh our sin, our sickness, and our death, so that when He climbs up on that tree, the new creation He brings means the end of slavery to sin and death and the beginning of a new, liberated cosmos that waits for full release at the parousia.

Summoned Home to God in Christ

And so in worship Christ is summoning us home to be with Him when He invites us to sit and listen to His Word with our ears or our eyes and then come forward and receive His flesh with our mouths. Our eyes are opened to His bodily presence where He offers us the best seat at the table and the finest food. We have come home to be with God in the Father's house, a foretaste of our final homecoming at the Lamb's banquet in His kingdom that has no end. Worship is our home, our *own unique culture*, inhabited by Christ Himself, where we know by heart its language and its rhythms for we have immersed ourselves in its life because it is His life.

When the Benediction is spoken, the liturgy does not end, our summons home in Christ has only begun. As we depart from the Divine Service, the gifts Christ has given us become the gifts He gives our neighbors through us, gifts of mercy, love, compassion, and forgiveness. This is *the liturgy of life*, nothing more and nothing less than a recapitulation of His life in our lives *because we bear His presence in our bodies.*

What is given us in our worship is a map of the world in which we live. With this map in hand we navigate this fallen world with an apocalyptic worldview, one in which we see Him revealed daily in humble acts of Christian charity and mercy and forgiveness. This is so because we are the baptized, invaded by Christ's Spirit, released from the bondage of our sins by forgiveness, joined to Christ's life and given His character. The world we live in is both this present evil age and the world made new by Christ's real presence. But time is different for us now. We are already now in the end times, living as if tomorrow Christ would come again in glory even as He comes daily to us by His grace. The Christ we commune with in the liturgy of Word and Sacrament sends us forth to preside over the liturgy of life as we follow the map of the world in which we now live, Christ's world and ours, a world where heaven has come to earth to dwell among us, full of grace and truth.

Appendix
Seasonal Proper Prefaces

From *Lutheran Service Book: Altar Book*, pp. 145–64

Advent

It is truly good, right, and salutary that we should at all times and in all places give thanks to You, holy Lord, almighty Father, everlasting God, through Jesus Christ, our Lord, whose way John the Baptist prepared, proclaiming Him the promised Messiah, the very Lamb of God who takes away the sin of the world, and calling sinners to repentance that they might escape from the wrath to be revealed when He comes again in glory. Therefore with angels and archangels and with all the company of heaven we laud and magnify Your glorious name, evermore praising You and saying:

Christmas

It is truly good, right, and salutary that we should at all times and in all places give thanks to You, holy Lord, almighty Father, everlasting God, through Jesus Christ, our Lord; for in the mystery of the Word made flesh You have given us a new revelation of Your glory that, seeing You in the person of Your Son, we may know and love those things which are not seen. Therefore with angels and archangels and with all the company of heaven we laud and magnify Your glorious name, evermore praising You and saying:

Epiphany

It is truly good, right, and salutary that we should at all times and in all places give thanks to You, holy Lord, almighty Father, everlasting God, through Jesus Christ, our Lord; for what had been hidden from before the foundation of the world You have made known to the nations in Your Son. In Him, being found in the substance of our mortal nature, You have manifested the fullness of Your glory. Therefore with angels and archangels and with all the company of heaven we laud and magnify Your glorious name, evermore praising You and saying:

The Baptism of Our Lord

It is truly good, right, and salutary that we should at all times and in all places give thanks to You, holy Lord, almighty Father, everlasting God, through Jesus Christ, our Lord; for at His Baptism Your voice from heaven revealed Him as Your beloved Son, and the Holy Spirit descended on Him, confirming Him to be the Christ. Therefore with angels and archangels and with all the company of heaven we laud and magnify Your glorious name, evermore praising You and saying:

The Transfiguration of Our Lord

It is truly good, right, and salutary that we should at all times and in all places give thanks to You, holy Lord, almighty Father, everlasting God, through Jesus Christ, our Lord, who at His transfiguration revealed His glory to His disciples that they might be strengthened to proclaim His cross and resurrection and with all the faithful look forward to the glory of life everlasting. Therefore with angels and archangels and with all the company of heaven we laud and magnify Your glorious name, evermore praising You and saying:

Lent

It is truly good, right, and salutary that we should at all times and in all places give thanks to You, holy Lord, almighty Father, everlasting God, through Jesus Christ, our Lord, who overcame the assaults of the devil and gave His life as a ransom for many that with cleansed hearts we might be prepared joyfully to celebrate the paschal feast in sincerity and truth. Therefore with angels and archangels and with all the company of heaven we laud and magnify Your glorious name, evermore praising You and saying:

Holy Week

It is truly good, right, and salutary that we should at all times and in all places give thanks to You, holy Lord, almighty Father, everlasting God, through Jesus Christ, our Lord, who accomplished the salvation of mankind by the tree of the cross that, where death arose, there life also might rise again and that the serpent who overcame by the tree of the garden might likewise by the tree of the cross be overcome. Therefore with angels and archangels and with all the company of heaven we laud and magnify Your glorious name, evermore praising You and saying:

Easter

It is truly good, right, and salutary that we should at all times and in all places give thanks to You, holy Lord, almighty Father, everlasting God. And most especially are we bound to praise You on this day for the glorious resurrection of Your Son, Jesus Christ, the very Paschal Lamb, who was sacrificed for us and bore the sins of the world. By His dying He has destroyed death, and by His rising again He has restored to us everlasting life. Therefore with Mary Magdalene, Peter and John, and with all the witnesses of the resurrection, with angels and archangels, and with all the company of heaven we laud and magnify Your glorious name, evermore praising You and saying:

Ascension

It is truly good, right, and salutary that we should at all times and in all places give thanks to You, holy Lord, almighty Father, everlasting God, through Jesus Christ, our Lord, who after His resurrection appeared openly to all His disciples and in their sight was taken up into heaven that He might make us partakers of His divine life. Therefore with angels and archangels and with all the company of heaven we laud and magnify Your glorious name, evermore praising You and saying:

Pentecost

It is truly good, right, and salutary that we should at all times and in all places give thanks to You, holy Lord, almighty Father, everlasting God, through Jesus Christ, our Lord, who ascended above the heavens and, sitting at Your right hand, poured out on this day the promised Holy Spirit on His chosen disciples. For all this the whole earth rejoices with exceeding joy. Therefore with angels and archangels and with all the company of heaven we laud and magnify Your glorious name, evermore praising You and saying:

Holy Trinity

It is truly good, right, and salutary that we should at all times and in all places give thanks to You, holy Lord, almighty Father, everlasting God, who with Your only-begotten Son and the Holy Spirit are one God, one Lord. In the confession of the only true God, we worship the Trinity in person and the

Unity in substance, of majesty coequal. Therefore with angels and archangels and with all the company of heaven we laud and magnify Your glorious name, evermore praising You and saying:

Apostles and Evangelists

It is truly good, right, and salutary that we should at all times and in all places give thanks to You, holy Lord, almighty Father, everlasting God; for You have mightily governed and protected Your holy Church, in which the blessed apostles and evangelists proclaimed Your divine and saving Gospel. Therefore with patriarchs and prophets, apostles and evangelists, [with Your servant *name of saint being commemorated* ,] and with all the company of heaven we laud and magnify Your glorious name, evermore praising You and saying:

The Presentation of Our Lord

It is truly good, right, and salutary that we should at all times and in all places give thanks to You, holy Lord, almighty Father, everlasting God, through Jesus Christ, our Lord, who, sharing Your eternal splendor, was presented on this day in Your temple in the substance of our human flesh and revealed by the Spirit as the glory of Israel and the light of all peoples. Therefore with angels and archangels and with all the company of heaven we laud and magnify Your glorious name, evermore praising You and saying:

The Annunciation of Our Lord; The Visitation; St. Mary, Mother of Our Lord

It is truly good, right, and salutary that we should at all times and in all places give thanks to You, holy Lord, almighty Father, everlasting God, through Jesus Christ, our Lord; for by the Holy Spirit Your only-begotten Son was conceived in the womb of the blessed virgin Mary and brought forth in the substance of our human flesh that we might partake of His divine life. Therefore with angels and archangels and with all the company of heaven we laud and magnify Your glorious name, evermore praising You and saying:

St. Michael and All Angels

It is truly good, right, and salutary that we should at all times and in all places give thanks to You, holy Lord, almighty Father, everlasting God, through Jesus Christ, our Lord. Through Him Your majesty is praised by all the holy angels and celebrated with one accord by the heavens and all the powers therein. The cherubim and seraphim sing Your praise, and with them we laud and magnify Your glorious name, evermore praising You and saying:

All Saints' Day

It is truly good, right, and salutary that we should at all times and in all places give thanks to You, holy Lord, almighty Father, everlasting God. In the communion of all Your saints gathered into the one body of Your Son, You have surrounded us with so great a cloud of witnesses that we, encouraged by their faith and strengthened by their fellowship, may run with perseverance the race that is set before us and, together with them, receive the crown of glory that does not fade away. Therefore with angels and archangels and with all the company of heaven we laud and magnify Your glorious name, evermore praising You and saying:

Common I

It is truly good, right, and salutary that we should at all times and in all places give thanks to You, holy Lord, almighty Father, everlasting God, through Jesus Christ, our Lord, who on this day overcame death and the grave and by His glorious resurrection opened to us the way of everlasting life. Therefore with angels and archangels and with all the company of heaven we laud and magnify Your glorious name, evermore praising You and saying:

Common II

It is truly good, right, and salutary that we should at all times and in all places give thanks to You, holy Lord, almighty Father, everlasting God, through Jesus Christ, our Lord, who, having created all things, took on human flesh and was born of the virgin Mary. For our sake He died on the cross and rose from the dead to put an end to death, thus fulfilling Your will and gaining for You a holy people. Therefore with angels and archangels and with all the company of heaven we laud and magnify Your glorious name, evermore praising You and saying:

Common III

It is truly good, right, and salutary that we should at all times and in all places give thanks to You, holy Lord, almighty Father, everlasting God, through Jesus Christ, our Lord, who, out of love for His fallen creation, humbled Himself by taking on the form of a servant, becoming obedient unto death, even death upon a cross. Risen from the dead, He has freed us from eternal death and given us life everlasting. Therefore with angels and archangels and with all the company of heaven we laud and magnify Your glorious name, evermore praising You and saying:

WEEKDAYS

It is truly good, right, and salutary that we should at all times and in all places give thanks to You, holy Lord, almighty Father, everlasting God, through Jesus Christ, our Lord. Therefore with angels and archangels and with all the company of heaven we laud and magnify Your glorious name, evermore praising You and saying:

Notes

Introduction

1. See Robert W. Jenson, "How the World Lost Its Story," First Things 36 (October 1993): 19–24.
2. Norman Nagel, "Introduction," *Lutheran Worship* (Concordia: St. Louis, 1982), 6.

Chapter 1

1. See the introduction to John Kleinig's commentary on Leviticus where he describes this reality of God's presence in exquisite detail (Leviticus, Concordia Commentary [St. Louis: Concordia, 2003]).
2. The LCMS Commission on Theology and Church Relations articulates the New Testament understanding of inaugurated eschatology that underlies the very nature of Christian worship:

   > The term *inaugurated eschatology* embraces everything that the Old and New Testament Scriptures teach concerning the believer's *present* possession and enjoyment of blessings which will be fully experienced whenever Christ comes again. . . . Therefore, the Christian lives in the proverbial tension between the *now* and the *not yet.* This tension underlies everything that Scriptures teach about eschatology. On the one hand, the end has arrived in Christ. The believer now receives the promised eschatological blessings through the Gospel and sacraments. On the other hand, the consummation is still a future reality. The Christian has *not yet* entered into the glories of heaven. (Commission on Theology and Church Relations, *The End Times* [St. Louis, 1989], 17, 19.)

   See also James Voelz, *What Does This Mean? Principles of Biblical Interpretation in the Post-Modern World* (St. Louis: Concordia, 1995), particularly pp. 244–62, "Addendum 11-B: The Christocentricity of the Scriptures: The Kingdom of God and Biblical Eschatology as Key."
3. Philip Melanchthon captures the definition of *leitourgia* and shows that liturgy is the public service of God for the world through Word and Sacrament:

   > *Leitourgia*, they say, means a sacrifice, and the Greeks call the Mass *liturgy*. (Why do they leave out here the old name *synaxis*, which shows that the Mass used to be the communion of many?) Let us discuss the word *liturgy*. This word does not properly mean a sacrifice, but rather the public ministry. Liturgy agrees well with our belief that one minister who consecrates gives the Lord's body and blood to the rest of the people, just as one minister who preaches offers the Gospel to the people. As Paul says, "This is how one should regard us, as servants of Christ and stewards of the mysteries of God" (1 Corinthians 4:1), that is, of the Gospel and the Sacraments. And, "We are ambassadors for Christ, God making His appeal through us. We implore you on behalf of Christ, be reconciled to God" (2 Corinthians 5:20). So the term *leitourgia* agrees well with the ministry. For it is an old word, ordinarily used in public civil administrations. (Ap XXIV 79–81).
4. See Bryan Spinks, *Luther's Liturgical Criteria and His Reform of the Canon of the Mass* (Bramcote, Notts: Grove Books, 1982).

5. Luther's theology of worship as it is expressed through his understanding of the Lord's Supper "as source of the church's life as a merciful body" is evident in his treatise "The Blessed Sacrament of the Holy and True Body of Christ, and the Brotherhoods." See AE 35:45–73.
6. J. Pelikan, "Worship between Yesterday and Tomorrow," in *Worship: Good News in Action*, ed. Mandus A. Egge (Minneapolis: Augsburg, 1973), 59.
7. See Mark Searle, "Reflections on Liturgical Reform," *Worship* 56 (1982): 430. Pelikan insists that the watchword for the Church is "not innovation, but fidelity." Fidelity to the Fathers "does not mean living in the past, but living from the past and being faithful to it in facing the present and the future" (Pelikan, "Worship," 58–59).

Chapter 2

1. The dates for the ordinaries come from Frank Senn, *Christian Liturgy: Catholic and Evangelical* (Minneapolis: Augsburg, 1997), 85–86, 138. There is much debate about the dates of the liturgy. For earlier dating, see Luther Reed, *The Lutheran Liturgy* (Philadelphia: Muhlenberg Press, 1947); for the Kyrie, 255ff; the Gloria, 258ff; the Creed, 284ff; on the Sanctus, 313ff; the Agnus Dei, 344ff.
2. When Constantine declared Christianity the religion of the empire in AD 313, he opened up the treasuries of Rome and encouraged Christians to build large churches. As many Roman citizens became Christians, new problems of space for the church were created that needed to be solved in a short period of time.
3. This definition comes from Aidan Kavanagh's seminar, "An Anthropology of Ritual Behavior" (class notes, Yale Divinity School, September 27, 1983).
4. This section comes from Aidan Kavanagh's seminar, "An Anthropology of Ritual Behavior" (class notes, Yale Divinity School, October 4, 1983).
5. This ambiguity is captured in the words of Luke in describing the reaction of the disciples when Jesus appeared to them in the Upper Room: "they still disbelieved for joy" (Luke 24:41). It is too good to be true—Christ comes to us with the gift of Himself in the flesh.
6. Acts 1:12–13; 2:1–2, 44–47; 4:23–31; 5:42; 8:3; 9:11, 17; 12:12–16; 16:31–34; 17:5; 18:1–8; 19:8–10; 20:7–20; 21:16.
7. For example, Romans 16:5; 1 Corinthians 16:19; Colossians 4:15; Philemon 1–2; see also 2 John 7–10; 3 John 9–10.
8. *Seder* means "order" and eventually came to mean "order of service," so the Sabbath evening Seder is the structure of worship for this Friday evening meal.
9. That is, with Levi (Luke 5:27–39); the Pharisees (7:36–50, 14:1–24); Zacchaeus (19:1–10).
10. Paul indicates in his correspondence, particularly with the Church at Corinth, that his communities were quite diverse (see 1 Corinthians 12–14). Hippolytus gives us a hint of what his community was like in his description of the catechumenate. Some of the categories are slaves, panderers, sculptors of idols, charioteers, gladiators, and concubines. See Part II, XVI of his Apostolic Tradition "Of the Laity" (Geoffrey J. Cuming, *Hippolytus: A Text for Students* [Bramcote, Nottingham: Grove Books, 1976], 23–28).
11. This section was adapted from Arthur A. Just Jr., *Luke 1:1–9:50*, Concordia Commentary (St. Louis: Concordia, 1996), 16–18.

12. Louis Bouyer, *Liturgy and Architecture* (University of Notre Dame Press, 1967), 14–15.
13. Pulpits are an absolute necessity; lecterns are not. If a church does not have a lectern, Scripture may be read from the pulpit or, preferably, from the horns of the altar.
14. Scripture may also be read from the horns of the altar, the Old Testament and Epistle read from the southern corner and the Gospel read from the northern one. This northern proclamation symbolized in the ancient Church the proclamation of the Gospel to the unchurched pagans who lived "north" of Christian Rome. Today, this tradition is kept in some churches, though the significance of reading the Gospel from the northern horn has mostly lost its meaning.
15. "On this mountain the LORD of hosts will make for all peoples a feast of fat things, a feast of wine on the lees, of fat things full of marrow, of wine on the lees well refined" (Isaiah 25:6, RSV).

CHAPTER 3

1. Martin Luther, "Table Talk," *D. Martin Luthers Werke. Kritische Gesamtausgabe. Tischreden* (Weimar: Hermann Böhlau, 1912–21) vol. 5, no. 6288.
2. The concept of "rite of passage" comes from Arnold Van Gennep, *The Rites of Passage* (University of Chicago Press, 1960), who applies this concept in his own work in cultural anthropology. Although it is possible to push these three stages too far in applying them to the Christian faith, they can provide an order that helps explain the highly ritualized moment of Baptism, where one crosses a boundary from death to life, from time to eternity.
3. Cf. Luther on Genesis 17, AE 3:101–12. This paragraph is adapted from Arthur A. Just Jr., *Luke 1:1–9:50*, Concordia Commentary (St. Louis: Concordia, 1996), 7–8.
4. Louis Finkelstein, "The Birkat ha-Mazon," *Jewish Theological Quarterly* 19 (1928–29): 211–26, quoted in Frank Senn, *Christian Liturgy: Catholic and Evangelical* (Minneapolis: Fortress, 1997), 57.
5. This phrase comes from Xavier Léon-Dufour, *Sharing the Eucharistic Bread* (New York: Paulist Press, 1982), 192–93.
6. Jesus calls this the "sign of Jonah" in Luke 11:29–32.
7. The modern Jewish Passover meal is a historical reconstruction. Its exact form at the time of Jesus is unknown. The earliest primary sources are compiled in the Mishnah, which was committed to writing some two hundred years after the Last Supper, but the traditions reach back centuries earlier. Chapter 10 of the tractate *Pesachim* in the Talmud concerns the Passover meal (folios 99b–121b of the Soncino edition), but the discussion assumes that the reader is already familiar with the liturgical order, and so it does not provide a complete outline. It also bears witness to variations in some of the practices. Luke's account, with some background provided by the Mishnah, does indicate the general shape of the Passover Seder that Jesus celebrated.

   The most thorough study is that of Joachim Jeremias, *The Eucharistic Words of Jesus* (London: SCM, 1966), and the Passover outline is adapted from pages 85–86 of that book. For a modern Passover Seder with the Hebrew and an English translation, see, for example, N. Glatzer, ed., *The Passover Haggadah* (New York: Schocken, 1989).

8. This diagram is from Arthur A. Just Jr., *Luke 9:51–24:53*, Concordia Commentary (St. Louis: Concordia, 1997), 825.
9. The priestly party within the Sanhedrin, led by the Sadducees, would have been in charge of the temple cult. They had very little influence on Jesus until the end of His ministry when He entered their precincts during Holy Week for His final teachings on the Temple Mount. The Sadducean party, and therefore the majority of priests, focused on the first five books of Genesis as their canon, as that was where one found instructions concerning the sacrifices and ceremonies associated with the tabernacle.
10. Jerome Neyrey, *The Social World of Luke-Acts* (Peabody, MA: Hendrickson Publishers, 1991).
11. Neyrey, *Social World*, 293.
12. Luke 2:34, author's translation.
13. Herbert Danby, *The Mishnah* (Oxford University Press, 1992), 142.
14. See Senn, *Christian Liturgy*, 68–70, 85.

Chapter 4

1. The essential Lukan meals are the following: the feast with Levi the tax collector (5:27–38); the Bridegroom and the ascetic (7:18–35); anointing the feet of Jesus and the forgiveness of a sinful woman (7:36–50); feeding of the crowd (9:10–17); Sabbath healing, meal etiquette, and the banquet (14:1–24); meals with sinners and the prodigal son (15:1–2, 11–32); the meal with Zacchaeus (19:1–10); the Last Supper (22:14–38); the Emmaus meal (24:13–35); the eating of fish (24:36–43).
2. Paul uses the language of judgment when he warns the Corinthians that "anyone who eats and drinks without discerning the body eats and drinks judgment on himself" (1 Corinthians 11:29).
3. *Treatise on the Power and Primacy of the Pope* 60, emphasis added.
4. See the following: "Have You come to destroy us? I know who You are—the Holy One of God" (Luke 4:34). "And demons also came out of many, crying, 'You are the Son of God!' But He rebuked them and would not allow them to speak, because they knew that He was the Christ" (Luke 4:41). "I saw Satan fall like lightning from heaven" (Luke 10:18).

Chapter 5

1. See Frank Senn, *Christian Liturgy: Catholic and Evangelical* (Minneapolis: Fortress, 1997), 68–70, 85.
2. SC, "Confession," p. 26.
3. "The Power of the Keys administers and presents the Gospel through Absolution, which is the true voice of the Gospel. We also include Absolution when we speak of faith, because 'faith comes from hearing,' as Paul says in Romans 10:17. When the Gospel is heard and the Absolution is heard, the conscience is encouraged and receives comfort. Because God truly brings a person to life through the Word, the Keys truly forgive sins before God. According to Luke 10:16, 'The one who hears You hears Me.' Therefore, the voice of one absolving must be believed no differently than we would believe a voice from heaven" (Ap XII 39–40).
4. John McHugh, "A Sermon for Easter Sunday," *Clergy Review* 71 (March 1986): 58.

5. McHugh, "Sermon," 62.

CHAPTER 6

1. William Lee Holladay, *The Psalms through Three Thousand Years: Prayerbook of a Cloud of Witnesses* (Minneapolis: Fortress, 1993), 139ff.
2. These divisions come from Massey H. Shepherd, *The Psalms in Christian Worship: A Practical Guide* (Minneapolis: Augsburg, 1976), 21.
3. While there is no agreement that the use of the Psalms between the readings extends back to the first century, liturgical scholars such as Frank Senn suggest that such use of the Psalms between the reading of Torah and the Prophets is probable. See Frank Senn, *Christian Liturgy: Catholic and Evangelical* (Minneapolis: Fortress, 1997), 70.
4. These six points come from John Alexander Lamb, *The Psalms in Christian Worship* (London: Faith Press, 1962), 12–17.
5. Dietrich Bonhöffer, *Psalms: The Prayer Book of the Bible* (Minneapolis: Augsburg, 1970), 17–18. There are some exceptions, of course; for example, Psalm 90 is the prayer of Moses.
6. Peter Scaer, "Asaph and Jerusalem," in *All Theology Is Christology: Essays in Honor of David P. Scaer*, ed. Dean O. Wenthe, William C. Weinrich, Arthur A. Just Jr., Daniel Gard, and Thomas L. Olson (Fort Wayne, IN: Concordia Theological Seminary Press, 2000), 35–36.
7. Scaer, "Asaph and Jerusalem," 35–36.
8. Sigmund Mowinckel, *The Psalms in Israel's Worship* (New York: Abingdon Press, 1962), 1:2.
9. For more discussion on this see: Paul Westermeyer, *Te Deum: The Church and Music* (Minneapolis: Fortress, 1998), 27–29; Mowinckel, *Psalms in Israel's Worship*, 1:2; Aidan Kavanagh, *Elements of Rite* (New York: Pueblo Publishing Company, 1982), 31.
10. John Kleinig, *The Lord's Song: The Basis, Function and Significance of Choral Music in Chronicles* (Sheffield, England: Journal for the Study of the Old Testament Press, 1993), 181. "Ritual function" simply describes the purpose of Psalm singing in the context of the rite.
11. John McHugh, "A Sermon for Easter Sunday," *Clergy Review* 71 (March 1986): 92.
12. Darrell Bock, *Proclamation from Prophecy and Pattern: Lucan Old Testament Christology,* Journal for the Study of the New Testament, Supplement Series 12 (Sheffield, England: Journal for the Study of the Old Testament Press, 1987), 148.
13. Bonhöffer, *Psalms*, 18–19, 21 (emphasis added).
14. Roland Bainton, *Here I Stand* (New York: Abingdon-Cokesbury Press, 1950), 62.
15. Bainton, *Here I Stand*, 60.
16. Bainton, *Here I Stand*, 62.
17. Shepherd, *Psalms in Christian Worship*, 35.
18. Peter Brunner, *Worship in the Name of Jesus* (St. Louis: Concordia, 1968), 137 (emphasis added).
19. Cited from J. M. Neale, *A Commentary on the Psalms* (London: Joseph Master and Son, 1869), 1:1 (emphasis added).
20. Although this information is found in many places, this brief summary is indebted to

Shepherd, *Psalms in Christian Worship*, 36–38. "Tones" refers to the simple melodies used for chanting the Psalms in the liturgical worship of both Judaism and Christianity.

21. Lamb, *Psalms in Christian Worship*, 38.
22. Lamb, *Psalms in Christian Worship*, 82.
23. "We approve and retain the introits for the Lord's days and the festivals of Christ, such as Easter, Pentecost, and the Nativity, although we prefer the Psalms from which they were taken as of old" (AE 53:22).
24. Luther Reed, *The Lutheran Liturgy* (Philadelphia: Muhlenberg Press, 1947), 292.
25. Lamb, *Psalms in Christian Worship*, 97.
26. See Shepherd, *Psalms in Christian Worship*, 58–59.
27. This data comes from Shepherd, *Psalms in Christian Worship*, 61–65.

Chapter 7

1. This does not mean that we cannot worship on other days of the week such as Saturday or Monday evening services, for in our world today, such services are necessary to accommodate the diverse schedules of the people in our congregations. Although every day is a good day for worship, the community knows and affirms that Sunday is the central day of worship, the day of resurrection, the eighth day.
2. See P. V. Marshall, "The Little Easter and the Great Sunday," *Liturgy* 1, no. 2 (1980): 28, who quotes the *Epistle of Barnabas* 15:8b–9, Ignatius' *Ad Magnesios* 9:1, and Basil's *De Spiritu Sancto* 27 in support of his view. Used by permission of Taylor & Francis; see www.informaworld.com.
3. Marshall, "The Little Easter," 29.
4. See AE 3:101–12.
5. AE 3:140–41.
6. AE 3:125–42.
7. This "exodus" is the topic of conversation between Moses and Elijah on the Mount of Transfiguration that simply continues the conversation of heaven. While much of the Old Testament looks back to the exodus from Egypt as the great salvation event for Israel, many other passages look forward to a new and greater exodus that God promised to bring to pass (e.g., Isaiah 11:11–16; 43:16–20; 51:9–11). Just as the first exodus was laden with baptismal overtones, as St. Paul expounds in 1 Corinthians 10:1–5, so also is the new exodus. In the first exodus the water was the means of death; in it the Egyptian foes drowned. The new exodus also involves death—the death of Christ—and those baptized into Christ die to sin as they die with Christ (Romans 6:1–5; Colossians 2:11–13). But in the new exodus God will pour out water to sustain His people in the arid desert of this world (Isaiah 43:16–20), and this outpouring of water is accompanied by His outpouring of His Spirit on His people (Isaiah 44:3; cf. Pentecost). The Father's words at Jesus' Baptism (Luke 3:22) are now echoed at His transfiguration (9:35). By means of the new exodus God will vanquish the primordial serpent, Satan, and redeem His people (Isaiah 51:9–11). The fulfillment of all these themes can be seen in the depiction of Jesus' "exodus" in Luke-Acts.
8. Lutherans follow the historical western numbering of the Commandments. The eastern church numbers them differently, and since the Reformation, other Protestants have found it convenient to their theology to embrace that eastern numbering.

9. See Arthur A. Just Jr., *Luke 1:1–9:50*, Concordia Commentary (St. Louis: Concordia, 1996), 254–55.
10. The significance of darkness as a portent of curse, death, and chaos is also seen, for example, in Job 3. In despair Job wishes that he had never been born, that darkness would have blotted out the light on his birthday, and that the stars would not have shined on that night. He also wishes for that day to be cursed and invokes Leviathan, the primordial enemy of God (cf. Isaiah 27:1).
11. See Arthur A. Just Jr., *Luke 9:51–24:53*, Concordia Commentary (St. Louis: Concordia, 1997), 941–42.
12. Such an eschatological view of the Sabbath forms the conclusion of Augustine's *Confessions*, book 13, chapters 35–37 (trans. R. S. Pine-Coffin [New York: Penguin, 1961]), 346:

    > [35]O Lord God, grant us peace, for all that we have is your gift. Grant us the peace of repose, the peace of the Sabbath, the peace which has no evening. For this worldly order in all its beauty will pass away. All these things that are very good will come to an end when the limit of their existence is reached. They have been allotted their morning and their evening.
    >
    > [36]But the seventh day is without evening and the sun shall not set upon it, for you have sanctified it and willed that it shall last for ever. Although your eternal repose was unbroken by the act of creation, nevertheless, after all your works were done and you had seen that they were very good, you rested on the seventh day. And in your Book we read this as a presage that when our work in this life is done, we too shall rest in you in the Sabbath of eternal life, though our works are very good only because you have given us the grace to perform them.
    >
    > [37]In that eternal Sabbath you will rest in us, just as now you work in us. The rest that we shall enjoy will be yours, just as the work that we now do is your work done through us. But you, O Lord, are eternally at work and eternally at rest. It is not in time that you see or in time that you move or in time that you rest: yet you make what we see in time; you make time itself and the repose which comes when time ceases.

13. Just, *Luke 9:51–24:53*, 959–60.
14. Just, *Luke 9:51–24:53*, 1041–42.
15. For an excellent critical edition of both Egeria's travels and the liturgy of Cyril of Jerusalem see John Wilkinson, trans., *Egeria's Travels to the Holy Land* (Ariel Publishing: Jerusalem and Aris and Phillips, Warminster, England, 1981).
16. For an excellent source of Cyril's catechesis see F. L. Cross, ed., *St. Cyril of Jerusalem's Lectures on the Christian Sacraments* (London: S.P.C.K., 1966). (Now published by St. Vladimir's Seminary Press: Crestwood, New York, 1986.)
17. See A. Adam, *The Liturgical Year: Its History and Its Meaning after the Reform of the Liturgy* (New York: Pueblo, 1981), 121–22.
18. See T. Talley, *The Origins of the Liturgical Year* (New York: Pueblo, 1986), who is the most thorough and passionate proponent of this theory. See also Frank Senn, *Christian Liturgy: Catholic and Evangelical* (Minneapolis: Fortress, 1997), 160, for a brief summary of the origins of this view of the date of Christmas.
19. Luther, "Table Talk," *D. Martin Luthers Werke. Kritische Gesamtausgabe. Tischreden.* (Weimar: Hermann Böhlau, 1912–21), vol. 5.
20. In English, we tend to call this prayer "the Lord's Prayer," but other languages such

as German (*Vater unser*) or Latin (*Pater noster*) simply named the prayer by the first words. It is in that sense that the *Didache* speaks.

21. Geoffrey J. Cuming, *Hippolytus: A Text for Students* (Bramcote, Nottingham: Grove Books, 1976), 29–31.
22. James White, *Introduction to Christian Worship* (Nashville: Abingdon, 1980), 116.
23. White, *Introduction to Christian Worship*, 119.
24. Philip Pfatteicher, *Commentary on the Lutheran Book of Worship* (Minneapolis: Augsburg Fortress, 1990), 340–41.
25. Pfatteicher, *Commentary on the Lutheran Book of Worship*, 373.
26. Pfatteicher, *Commentary on the Lutheran Book of Worship*, 352.
27. But a similar rhythm of nature is captured in the Church Year that sanctifies the year by retelling the world's story through the story of Jesus Christ and the Church.
28. The resources here are vast. For the Daily Office, one begins with *Lutheran Service Book*, *Lutheran Worship*, *The Lutheran Hymnal*, or *The Service Book and Hymnal*. The hymns of the Church in our hymnals are always a wonderful source of devotion. The APLB has published four devotional books called *For All the Saints: A Prayer Book For and By the Church*. Concordia Publishing House will be issuing *Treasury of Daily Prayer* in 2008, a comprehensive prayer book for the laity using the schedules and orders as they are arranged in *Lutheran Service Book*. Besides these, there are numerous other devotional materials that are liturgical and filled with the wisdom of the ancients such as the aforementioned *The Private Devotions of Lancelot Andrewes*. See an article by J. Robert Wright, "The Genesis of a Book: Readings for the Daily Office from the Early Church," *Worship* 67, no. 2 (March 1993): 144–55, that describes the process of choosing readings from the Early Church for the Daily Office in the American Edition of *The Book of Common Prayer*.

CHAPTER 8

1. See David P. Scaer, "Baptism as the Foundational Sacrament," in *Baptism*, vol. 11, *Confessional Lutheran Dogmatics*, ed. John Stephenson (St. Louis: The Luther Academy, 1999), 1–4. Scaer argues that "Baptism was for Luther the foundational sacrament out of which all the other sacraments took their meaning."
2. See Arthur A. Just Jr., *Luke 1:1–9:50*, Concordia Commentary (St. Louis: Concordia, 1996), 21–25.
3. A man *leaves* his father and mother, *cleaves* to his wife, and they *become one flesh*. A wedding ceremony is possibly the most paradigmatic of all rites of passage.
4. For adults and infants, it is God who separates by the power of the Holy Spirit working through God's Word. For adults, however, it is by the Holy Spirit that their cognizance and will are transformed so that they no longer work against the teaching they now receive from the Lord as gift.
5. Excerpts of this section are from Just, *Luke 1:1–9:50*, 7–10.
6. Adapted from Just, *Luke 1:1–9:50*, 135–43.
7. From the Greek word μαρτυρέω, "to give witness," because here the Church proclaimed Christ's death and resurrection, thus "giving witness" to the transforming reality of Christ's redeeming presence.
8. AE 53:97.

9. AE 53:98.
10. AE 53:100.
11. AE 53:101.
12. For example, see "The Babylonian Captivity of the Church" where Luther says: "It is therefore indeed correct to say that baptism is a washing away of sins, but the expression is too mild and weak to bring out the full significance of baptism, which is rather a symbol of death and resurrection. For this reason I would have those who are to be baptized completely immersed in the water, as the word says and as the mystery indicates. . . . The sinner does not so much need to be washed as he needs to die, in order to be wholly renewed and made another creature, and to be conformed to the death and resurrection of Christ, with whom he dies and rises again through baptism" (AE 36:68).
13. AE 53:102.
14. Jonathan D. Trigg, *Baptism in the Theology of Martin Luther* (Boston, Leiden: Brill Academic Publishers, Inc., 2001), 147–48. Trigg's entire book forces us to reconsider Luther's revisions in "The Order of Baptism, Newly Revised, 1526," and whether, later in life, he might have gone back to some of the ceremonial elements in "The Order of Baptism, 1523."
15. In recent revisions of Lutheran baptismal rites, much of Luther's baptismal service is now included, especially the exorcisms, the flood prayer, and the anointing.
16. *LSB: Agenda*, 2.
17. *LSB: Agenda*, 5–11.
18. *LSB: Agenda*, 12–16.
19. T. M. Finn, *Early Christian Baptism and the Catechumenate: West and East Syria* (Collegeville, MN: Michael Glazier, 1992), 4. Cf. also E. Yarnold, *The Awe-Inspiring Rites of Initiation: The Origins of the R.C.I.A.* (Collegeville, MN: The Liturgical Press, 1994), 7, who also notes that "the instruction the catechumens received was not only for their ears, but should resonate in their minds and find expression in their lives."
20. Compare this to the rites of the Enlightenment and modernism of our own recent past where we talk things to death first, then experience them. This is especially true of many liturgies today where so much is explained *during the rite* that the liturgy becomes even more incomprehensible. See chapter 3.
21. The liturgical studies in the early twentieth century led to the institution of the adult catechumenate in the Roman Catholic Church after Vatican II called the "Rite of Christian Initiation of Adults" (RCIA). Many Protestants adapted the RCIA for their own context, including the Episcopalians, Methodists, and even the Mennonites. Lutherans approached the RCIA very cautiously, since they perceived rightly that these rites were semi-Pelagian. The discussion among North American Lutherans in the 1990s that led to a form of the catechumenate in many Lutheran churches studiously avoided a simple adaptation of the RCIA, and the results demonstrate that they have not only captured the spirit of the early Christian rites but also reflect a deep Lutheran ethos. As an example, the period of mystagogy now focuses for Lutherans on vocation, reflecting Luther's theology of vocation. See below *Welcome to Christ: A Lutheran Introduction to the Catechumenate.*
22. P. Nelson, "Introduction," *Welcome to Christ: A Lutheran Introduction to the Catechumenate* (Minneapolis: Fortress, 1997), 8.

23. Adapted from *Welcome to Christ*, particularly p. 8 and pp. 13–15, "How does the catechumenal process work?" by R. Hofstad on the "apprenticeship in faith."

Chapter 9

1. This principle was borne out when our church body maintained the same hymnal through the turmoil of the sixties and seventies. It was not until the theological controversies had subsided that a new hymnal was offered. Some might argue that this was purely coincidence, but one should never underestimate the subtle power of the liturgy as it forms people and church bodies. If one really wants to know what a church body believes, just open up their worship book and read their hymns and their liturgies. This will tell you more about their theology than any of their theological documents.
2. This expression comes from the great Lutheran liturgical scholar Peter Brunner, *Worship in the Name of Jesus*, trans. M. H. Bertram (St. Louis: Concordia, 1968), 231, who writes: "the form of worship, by reason of its concrete historicalness, strives toward an ecumenical basic form."
3. Brunner, *Worship*, 225.
4. In fact, there have been only two significant *structural* changes in the history of the liturgy. The first occurred during the Reformation when an entire structure dropped out of the liturgy (the Sacrament of the Altar). The second is happening now in some churches where the Liturgy of the Sacrament *precedes* the Liturgy of the Word.
5. See Fred Precht, "Confession and Absolution," in *Lutheran Worship: History and Practice* (St. Louis: Concordia, 1993), 338. For his full discussion of the history of corporate confession and absolution, see pp. 358–69.
6. SC, "Confession," 26.
7. See Precht, "Confession and Absolution," 333. He calls this the "so-called sacramental confession." The other option for absolution is the "declaration of grace," cited here from *Divine Service, Setting Three* in *LSB*, p. 185: "Almighty God, our heavenly Father, has had mercy upon us and has given His only Son to die for us and for His sake forgives us all our sins. To those who believe on His name He gives power to become the children of God and has promised them His Holy Spirit. He that believes and is baptized shall be saved. Grant this, Lord, unto us all."

   At the time of the Reformation, a dispute arose over "general absolution" in the Church's public liturgy. "The Nürnberg Controversy over Public Absolution" was concerned that it might lead to the rejection of "private confession and absolution." Since then, the Church has balanced this tension between general absolution and the "so-called sacramental confession" in her liturgical life.
8. Norman Nagel, "Introduction," *Lutheran Worship* (Concordia: St. Louis, 1982), 6.
9. Luther Reed, *The Lutheran Liturgy* (Philadelphia: Muhlenberg Press, 1947), 255.
10. *The Liturgy of St. John Chrysostom*, with commentary by Basil Shereghy (Collegeville: Liturgical Press, 1961), 14–15, quoted in Philip Pfatteicher, *Commentary on the Lutheran Book of Worship* (Minneapolis: Augsburg Fortress, 1990), 115.
11. Pfatteicher, *Commentary*, 118.
12. Josef Jungmann, *The Early Liturgy* (University of Notre Dame Press, 1959), 295.
13. Author's translation.
14. Author's translation.

15. For God's glory on earth, see Numbers 14:21 and Isaiah 6:3.
16. See the transfiguration in Luke's Gospel where Moses and Elijah are speaking of His "exodus" which He was about to fulfill in Jerusalem (9:31).
17. Cf. the Ambrosian, Mozarabic, and Celtic rites.
18. See Pfatteicher, *Commentary*, 124.
19. See Pfatteicher, *Commentary*, 125.
20. There are some who would like to change the language from "the feast of victory *for* our God" to "the feast of victory *of* our God." Pfatteicher, *Commentary*, 125, anticipates this by saying: "The celebration is described as 'the feast of victory for our God,' that is to say, a feast of God's victory: it is victory for God that we celebrate and proclaim, the victory over death won by Christ. It is the feast of victory of our God, but it is also a feast *for* God, that is to say, in honor and celebration of his triumph" (*emphasis Pfatteicher*).
21. *Lutheran Worship*, pp. 169 and 144. See Pfatteicher, *Commentary*, 124–25, for a similar analysis.
22. Ulrich Asendorf, trans. by K. D. Schulz, "Viva vox Evangelii: A Necessary Course Correction," in *All Theology Is Christology: Essays in Honor of David P. Scaer* (Fort Wayne: Concordia Theological Seminary Press, 2000), 229.
23. Hughes Oliphant Old, *The Reading and Preaching of the Scriptures in the Worship of the Christian Church* (Grand Rapids: Eerdmans, 1998), 1:186. Although Old comes from a Presbyterian background, and his understanding of "presence" is more reflective of a Calvinist understanding than a Lutheran one, his discussion of "kerygmatic presence" reflects more the understanding of the Early Church fathers than later Reformation distinctions.
24. Old, *Reading and Preaching*, 1:187. Citing John Murray's commentary on Romans (*The Epistle to the Romans* [Grand Rapids: Eerdmans, 1993] 2:58) in connection with Romans 10:14–17, Hughes Old finds the greatest implication for Paul's words in Murray's observation that "Christ is represented as being heard in the Gospel when proclaimed by the sent messengers. The implication is that *Christ speaks in the gospel proclamation.*" *Viva vox Jesu* understands therefore the Word of God as a preached word. See Old, *Reading and Preaching*, 1:187.
25. To give a sense of the time it takes to read Scripture, to read the entire Epistle to the Galatians takes about twenty minutes, and for the Epistle to the Hebrews, around forty minutes.
26. See Arthur A. Just Jr., *Luke 9:51–24:53*, Concordia Commentary (St. Louis: Concordia, 1997), 849–50, and the essay in the festschrift *Mysteria Dei: Essays in Honor of Kurt Marquart* (Concordia Theological Seminary Press, 2000), 115–28, entitled "Eating and Drinking at His Table."
27. AE 53:24.

Chapter 10

1. Isaiah 5:1; Hosea 10:1; Ezekiel 19:10; Psalm 23:5; Revelation 14:15; and John 6:48.
2. Psalm 116:12, 17, 13–14, 19.
3. The preface first appeared in AD 150. According to the principles of interpretation of liturgical texts, we might read back two or three generations and assume that the liturgy used in AD 150 might also have been used in AD 90 when John the evangelist was still alive.

4. See the appendix for a list of all the proper prefaces in *Lutheran Service Book* as an example of the profound theology and sublime poetry of the proper prefaces as part of the Church's eucharistic piety.
5. C. J. Evanson, "The Divine Service," in *Lutheran Worship: History and Practice*, ed. Fred Precht (St. Louis: Concordia, 1993), 420.
6. Frank Senn, *Christian Liturgy: Catholic and Evangelical* (Minneapolis: Fortress, 1997), 85.
7. Luther Reed, *The Lutheran Liturgy* (Philadelphia: Muhlenberg Press, 1947), 313–14.
8. Philip Pfatteicher, *Commentary on the Lutheran Book of Worship* (Minneapolis: Augsburg Fortress, 1990), 161.
9. These comments on Psalm 118 were gleaned from S. Mowinckel, *The Psalms in Israel's Worship* (New York: Abingdon Press, 1962) 1:170ff., particularly pp. 180–182.
10. As cited by Reed, *Lutheran Liturgy*, 314.
11. Pfatteicher, *Commentary*, 162.
12. "And while the Benedictus is being sung, let the bread and cup be elevated according to the customary rite for the benefit of the weak in faith who might be offended if such an obvious change in this rite of the mass were suddenly made" (AE 53:28).
13. Senn, *Christian Liturgy*, 278.
14. G. Wainwright, *Eucharist and Eschatology* (Oxford University Press, 1971), 34 (emphasis Wainwright).
15. Large Catechism, "The Lord's Prayer," 73.
16. Large Catechism, "The Lord's Prayer," 76–80.
17. AE 42:56–57, 58. He also says, "To believe in this same Word is the same as eating the bread" (AE 42:59).
18. AE 43:34–35.
19. SC, p. 22.
20. Excerpts of this section on the Lord's Prayer are from Just, *Luke 9:51–24:53*, 460–71.
21. In the Synoptic Gospels, Jesus' command "Do this in remembrance of Me" is found only in Luke 22:19b. (St. Paul includes those words spoken over both the bread and over the cup in 1 Corinthians 11:24–25.) Luke records Jesus' command spoken *over the bread.* This further suggests that in Luke and Acts the bread can represent the whole meal. As the Church remembers the liturgical action of Christ at the Last Supper, the celebration of the Sacrament may be called "the breaking of the bread."
22. The single cup should be reflected in church practice. When individual cups are used, the unity and fellowship (*koinonia*) of the community is somewhat fractured. If we are to "bear one another's burdens, and so fulfill the law of Christ" (Galatians 6:2), then sharing the common cup is the first step in this burden bearing. Although we must take seriously people's concern for diseases, they are not a serious threat, and studies show that individual cups, touched by the hands, also pose health issues (hands are more likely to pass germs than the mouth). The practice of the common cup was the only practice in liturgical communities until the nineteenth century. The issue of common cup/individual cups should not become a divisive issue in congregations. The concern of some that disease might be spread is so acute, one should

not try to change a congregation's practice from individual to common cup without a long period of catechesis, and even then, perhaps the best solution is to offer both. It is still unfortunate that the common cup, as the sign of the congregation's unity in Christ, is being usurped by the individual cups.

23. Joachim Jeremias, *The Eucharistic Words of Jesus* (London: SCM, 1966), 59–60.
24. John's Gospel is particularly significant in linking Jesus' feeding in the wilderness with the manna miracle, and the discourse on the bread in John 6 contains Jesus' self-designation as "the bread of life."
25. Remember, when Moses, Elijah, and Jesus are conversing on the Mount of Transfiguration, they are discussing Jesus' exodus that He is about to fulfill in Jerusalem, that is, His suffering, death, resurrection, and ascension.
26. The two best representatives of these positions are J. Jeremias, *The Eucharistic Words of Jesus*, 237–55, who supports the "God remembers us" position, and Xavier Léon-Dufour, *Sharing the Eucharistic Bread* (New York: Paulist Press, 1982), 102–16, who supports the position "we remember God."
27. Matthew has "for many" (περὶ πολλῶν; 26:28). Mark has "on behalf of many" (ὑπὲρ πολλῶν; 14:24).
28. In Isaiah 52:15 we see that the Suffering Servant will "sprinkle many nations," and the reference back to the first covenant in Exodus 24 is clear.
29. This is one of the reasons why "closed communion" is practiced among our congregations and has been from the time of the apostles.
30. Parts of this section on the Lord's Supper are taken from Just, *Luke 9:52–24:53*, 819–38.
31. AE 53:28–29. Note that Luther has the Lord's Prayer after the Words of Institution, whereas in our services, the Lord's Prayer precedes them.
32. Reception in the mouth came about when the doctrine of transubstantiation became prominent. If the bread ceases to be bread and only the body of Christ, as transubstantiation teaches, then communicants who received it in their hands would not consume it but take it home to worship the "body of Christ." The most effective way to stop this was to place the host directly in the communicant's mouth.
33. When individual cups are used, plastic disposable cups should be avoided at all costs. The common practice with plastic, disposable cups is to throw them away while they still contain remnants of the wine that was used to communicate the blood of Christ.
34. Pfatteicher, *Commentary*, 188, whose information comes from J. Jungmann, *The Mass of the Roman Rite,* rev. Charles K. Riepe (New York: Benziger, 1959), 485.
35. Cf. AE 38:123, where Luther shows how well he understood the significance of the Agnus Dei for the liturgy: "Particularly the *Agnus Dei*, above all songs, serves well for the sacrament, for it clearly sings about the praises of Christ for having borne our sins and in beautiful, brief words powerfully and sweetly teaches the remembrance of Christ."
36. This collect is from the propers for Maundy Thursday, *LSB: Altar Book*, p. 590.

CHAPTER 11

1. Norman Nagel, "Introduction," *Lutheran Worship* (Concordia: St. Louis, 1982), 6.
2. This paragraph is from Aidan Kavanagh's "Liturgical Structures" class (class notes, Yale Divinity School, fall 1983).
3. See John F. Baldovin, *The Urban Character of Christian Worship* (Rome: Pontifical Institutum Studiorum Orientalum, 1989).
4. This definition is from Kavanagh's "Liturgical Structures" class.
5. This section on the urban liturgy is from Kavanagh's "Liturgical Structures" class. See also Kavanagh, *On Liturgical Theology* (New York: Pueblo Publishing Company, 1984), 57–60, where he gives a detailed description of the urban liturgy.
6. Such urban liturgies, however, may be found in places such as Redeemer Lutheran Church, Bronx, New York, and throughout the world in places such as Rome, Latin America, and Kenya.
7. "Adapt culture to the liturgy rather than liturgy to culture" is Kavanagh's final recommendation in achieving an authentic liturgical style in his *Elements of Rite* (New York: Pueblo Publishing Company, 1982), 103–4.
8. Cf. Galatians 2:11–14, where Peter may have retreated from table fellowship with Gentiles because of his concern for the persecution of zealous Jews against Jewish Christians in Antioch.
9. Luther's protector, Frederick the Wise, was one of the greatest keepers of relics in Germany. Luther tolerated this abuse, but relics in general were part of the meritorious Christianity in need of reform.
10. Nagel, "Introduction," *Lutheran Worship*, 6.
11. Lutherans do not believe in transubstantiation; rather, they confess that bread and wine, body and blood are all present. Following Luther, they say that the body and blood are "in, with, and under" the bread and wine.
12. This section on the medieval period is from Kavanagh's "Liturgical Structures" class.
13. Bryan Spinks, *Luther's Liturgical Criteria and His Reform of the Canon of the Mass* (Bramcote, Nottingham: Grove Books, 1982), 22. Spinks's entire monograph argues that Luther's reforms were governed by the doctrine of justification by grace through faith.
14. AE 53:24.
15. Frank Senn, *Christian Liturgy: Catholic and Evangelical* (Minneapolis: Augsburg, 1997), 303.
16. Senn, *Christian Liturgy*, 304, who cites Roland Bainton.
17. Senn, *Christian Liturgy*, 306–7 (*emphasis mine*).
18. Senn, *Christian Liturgy*, 287.
19. See Richard C. Resch's DVD entitled *Singing the Faith: Living the Lutheran Musical Heritage* (Fort Wayne, IN: Good Shepherd Institute of Pastoral Theology and Sacred Music, Concordia Theological Seminary, 2008).
20. See, for example, Hermann Sasse, *This Is My Body: Luther's Contention for the Real Presence in the Sacrament of the Altar* (Minneapolis: Augsburg, 1959).
21. Matthew Harrison, introduction to *Fight, Work, Pray! Luther on the Lord's Supper and Care for the Needy* (St. Louis: LCMS World Relief and Human Care, 2004), 3.
22. AE 35:57.

23. Sara Bielby and A. A. Just Jr., "Serving Christ by Serving Our Neighbor: Theological and Historical Perspectives on Lutheran Deaconesses," *Issues in Christian Education* 39:1 (Spring 2005): 6–13.
24. For example, Lutheranism in Germany, Sweden, and Latvia, to name a few.
25. Bielby and Just, "Serving Christ by Serving Our Neighbor," 13. In light of Luther's "The Blessed Sacrament of the Holy and True Body of Christ," the last line should read as follows: ". . . where the Pastor feeds these lambs by bringing them into communion with Christ *and his saints* as he comes to them in Word and Sacrament" *(emphasis added)*.
26. SC, p. 31.
27. See AE 35:45–73.
28. AE 35:51.
29. AE 35:53–54, 61–62.
30. AE 53:24.
31. AE 53:25.
32. AE 53:28. In our churches today it is more common to see the elevation of the offering plates than the elevation of the elements. Elevating the elements simply shows the people that these are the gifts of salvation whereby Christ comes in His body and blood to give us forgiveness, life, and salvation.
33. AE 53:28–29.
34. This presentation of Luther's Order of Service paraphrases AE 53:22–30.
35. A restorationist is someone who attempts to implement the practices of some idealized past. An innovator is someone who wants to adapt liturgy to culture.
36. Louis Bouyer, *Eucharist* (South Bend, IN: University of Notre Dame Press, 1968), 392, cited in Senn, *Christian Liturgy*, 303. Bouyer is a Roman Catholic liturgical scholar who grew up as a Lutheran.
37. *Adiaphora* is a technical term to denote "things indifferent," in other words, things not commanded in Holy Scripture.
38. Nagel, "Introduction," *Lutheran Worship*, 6.
39. I am grateful to my colleague Dr. Daniel Reuning for first offering these three positions in his fall 1976 Lutheran Worship class at Concordia Theological Seminary.
40. The favorite passage to cite is the following: "Under the title and excuse of outward adiaphora, things are proposed that are in principle contrary to God's Word, although painted another color. These ceremonies are not to be regarded as adiaphora, in which one is free to do as he wants. They must be avoided as things prohibited by God. In a similar way in such a situation ceremonies should not be regarded as genuine free adiaphora, or matters of indifference. This is because they make a show or pretend that our religion and that of the papists [in citing this same passage, Walther replaced "papists" with "Reformed"] are not far apart in order to avoid persecution, or they pretend that the papist's ceremonies are not at least highly offensive to us. When ceremonies are intended for this purpose, and are required and received (as though through them contrary religions are reconciled and become one body), we cannot regard them as adiaphora. When returning to the papacy and departing from the Gospel's pure doctrine and true religion should happen or gradually follow from such ceremonies, we cannot regard them as adiaphora" (FC SD X 5).
41. FC SD X 10 *(emphasis mine)*.

42. C. F. W. Walther, *Essays for the Church* (St. Louis: Concordia, 1992), 1:197. In *Der Lutheraner* 9:24 (July 19, 1853): 163, Walther was equally emphatic when the liturgy of his church was labeled "Roman Catholic." (Edited translation based on Arthur H. Drevlow, *C. F. W. Walther: The American Luther* [Mankato, MN: Walther Press, 1987]).

    Whenever the Divine Service once again follows the old Evangelical-Lutheran agendas (or church books) it seems that many raise a great cry that it is "Roman Catholic": "Roman Catholic" when the pastor chants "The Lord be with you" and the congregation responds by chanting "and with thy spirit"; "Roman Catholic" when the pastor chants the collect and the blessing and the people respond with a chanted "Amen."

    Even the simplest Christian can respond to this outcry: "Prove to me that this chanting is contrary to the Word of God, then I, too, will call it 'Roman Catholic' and have nothing more to do with it. However, you cannot prove this to me."

    If you insist upon calling every element in the Divine Service "Romish" that has been used by the Roman Catholic Church, it must follow that the reading of the Epistle and Gospel is also "Romish." Indeed, it is mischief to sing or preach in church, for the Roman Church has done this also . . .

    Those who cry out should remember that the Roman Catholic Church possesses every beautiful song of the old orthodox Church. The chants and antiphons and responses were brought into the church long before the false teachings of Rome crept in. This Christian Church since the beginning, even in the Old Testament, has derived great joy from chanting . . . For more than 1700 years orthodox Christians have participated joyfully in the Divine Service. Should we, today, carry on by saying that such joyful participation is "Roman Catholic"? God forbid!

    Therefore, as we continue to hold and to restore our wonderful Divine Services in places where they have been forgotten, let us boldly confess that our worship forms do not unite us with the modern sects or with the Church of Rome; rather, they join us to the one, holy Christian Church that is as old as the world and is built on the foundation of the apostles and prophets.

43. This section on liturgical renewal is a revision of an excerpt from my chapter "Liturgical Renewal in the Parish," in *Lutheran Worship: History and Tradition* (St. Louis: Concordia, 1994), 21–43.

44. These four criteria—utility, simplicity, flexibility, and intimacy—come from James White, *Introduction to Christian Worship* (Nashville: Abingdon, 1980), 94–97, who describes more fully how these criteria can serve as guidelines in renewal of space.

Conclusion

1. This phrase comes from J. Louis Martyn, *Galatians: A New Translation with Introduction and Commentary* (New York: Doubleday, 1998), 482 n. 41.
2. Frank Senn, *New Creation: A Liturgical Worldview* (Minneapolis: Fortress Press, 2000), xiv (emphasis mine).
3. This language of Christ's apocalyptic invasion comes from Martyn, *Galatians*, 97ff.
4. Martyn, *Galatians*, 391–92.
5. This section on Galatians is inspired by L. Martyn's commentary on Galatians. Some of this argument is also included in my chapter, "Christ and the Law in the Life of the Church at Galatia," in *The Law in Holy Scripture: Essays from the Concordia Theological Seminary Symposium*, ed. C. A. Gieschen (St. Louis: Concordia, 2004), 173–87.
6. Norman Nagel, "Introduction," *Lutheran Worship* (St. Louis: Concordia, 1982), 6.

Glossary

Absolution, Holy. The full and free forgiveness announced to a sorrowful sinner by the pastor in God's or Christ's place; follows a private or corporate confession of sins; considered a third sacrament among many Lutherans.

Advent. Latin for "coming"; refers to the four-Sunday season that begins the Church Year and prepares worshipers for Christmas; begins the first Sunday after the feast day of St. Andrew (November 30); a contemplative mood dominates.

Agnus Dei. Latin for "Lamb of God"; designation given to Jesus by John the Baptist (John 1:29); more specifically, refers to the canticle in the Communion liturgy that begins with those words; the first Communion distribution hymn during which the officiants may commune.

alpha and omega. A and Ω, the first and last capital letters of the Greek alphabet; a symbol of eternity or of Christ.

altar. A stone or wooden structure at the center of the chancel from which the Lord's Supper is celebrated; the sacramental focus from which God gives His gifts; the sacrificial focus of the congregation's worship.

antiphon. Greek for "responsive"; refers to a Scripture verse sung before and after a psalm or canticle; sometimes used as congregational responses during a longer psalm sung by the choir; may provide a central theme of the psalm.

apse. Semicircular structure with a half-dome roof in a basilica-style church; often forms the chancel; early basilicas located the bishop's chair in the apse for acoustical purposes.

Baptism, Holy. Sacrament by which the Holy Spirit creates faith through the application of water connected with God's Word.

baptistery. An often elaborately decorated room containing a baptismal font; may also refer to a large pool of water used for baptisms; structured with six or eight sides, symbolizing creation or resurrection.

basilica. Greek for "king's hall"; describes the earliest accepted form of church building; features an apse, transepts, and large nave for the assembly.

Benediction. From the Latin for "[The Lord] bless [you]"; the Aaronic Blessing (Numbers 6:24–26) is commonly used in connection with Holy Communion, while the Apostolic Blessing (2 Corinthians 13:14) is used at other times.

Benedictus. Latin for "Blessed be"; from Zechariah's song in Luke 1; the Gospel Canticle for Matins; particularly appropriate for Advent and Christmas; also may refer to the second part of the Sanctus in the Divine Service ("Blessed is [He who comes]"); the song of the Jerusalem crowd on Palm Sunday (Matthew 21:9).

blessing. An authoritative declaration of God's favor; a verbal formula to set aside objects for religious purposes.

canticle. Latin for "little song"; Scripture texts sung as part of the liturgy.

cantor. Latin for "singer"; refers to a song leader who usually offers unaccompanied music in a liturgy; may refer to a choral leader or minister of music; Lutherans retained this office after the Reformation.

catechesis. Greek for "one under instruction"; refers to organized scriptural and confessional instruction prior to Baptism or confirmation, as well as continuing Christian nurture of the faith through the Word; in the Early Church, this instruction took between three months and three years.

catechumen. Greek for "one under instruction"; denotes young adults or adults undergoing instruction in the Christian faith before Baptism or confirmation.

chancel. Liturgical space around the altar from the rail to the liturgical "east" wall; usually includes the pulpit and the lectern; sometimes called the choir in cathedrals.

Christological. Having to do with the person and work of Jesus Christ, particularly the divine and human natures in the one person of Christ, but also His conception, birth, anointing, obedience, redeeming death, resurrection, ascension, and session at God's right hand on behalf of His Church.

Church. The Body of Christ; the congregation of all the saints called forth by the Holy Spirit from the lost race of humanity that confesses Jesus Christ as Lord and Savior; the people who gather around Word and Sacraments to receive blessings and express gratitude with prayers and praises; the building in which God's guests gather; a worship service.

Church Year. The Church's calendar organized to observe the events in the life of Christ and the Church; sets the theme for each service.

collect. Short prayer.

Communion, Holy. The celebration of Christ's true body and blood under the forms of consecrated bread and wine. Christians eat and drink this Sacrament for the forgiveness of sins and the strengthening of faith; also referred to as the Eucharist, the Lord's Supper, or the Sacrament of the Altar.

Confession (of Sins). The act by which one admits or confesses sin(s) and the guilt of sin.

consecrate. To dedicate to the Lord; to declare holy, as when Jesus' words are spoken over the bread and wine during the celebration of the Lord's Supper.

Creed. From the Latin word *credo*, "I believe"; a summary of what the Church believes; refers to any of the three Ecumenical Creeds used in worship: the Apostles' Creed, often used at baptisms, funerals, and non-Communion services; the Nicene Creed, often used at services with Holy Communion; and the Athanasian Creed, often spoken on Trinity Sunday.

Divine Service. The name of the regular weekly service that includes the celebration of the Lord's Supper; derived from the German *Gottesdienst.*

Epistle. From the Greek word for "letter." In the Divine Service, the Epistle is the second reading, usually drawn from an Epistle in the New Testament.

Eucharist. Greek for "giving thanks"; another name for Holy Communion, the Lord's Supper, or the Sacrament of the Altar; originates from Jesus' giving of thanks over the bread and wine at the institution of this special meal.

Flood Prayer. Luther's baptismal prayer; connects the saving of Noah and his family with the waters of Baptism; follows the imagery in 1 Peter.

font. Large basin or pool, often made of stone, that holds the water for Baptism; smaller wooden fonts may include a metal basin for the water; located either near the chancel or at the church's entrance; serves either as a reminder of the sacramental community into which the baptized is brought or to underscore the act by which God bring believers into His family of faith.

Gloria in Excelsis. Latin for "glory in the highest"; the angel's song (Luke 2); a Hymn of Praise in the Divine Service.

Gloria Patri. Latin for "glory to the Father"; a liturgical text used to conclude a psalm or Introit.

God's Word. The Holy Scriptures; the inspired revelation of God's plan and record of salvation.

Gottesdienst. German for "God's service" or "service of God"; connotes both the Divine Service by which God serves His people through Word and Sacrament and the setting in which worshipers serve God with prayers and praises.

Gradual. A liturgical response, drawn from the Bible, which follows the Old Testament Reading.

Holy Gospel. A reading from one of the first four books of the New Testament as part of the Service of the Word; always contains the words or deeds of Jesus.

host. Latin for "sacrifice or victim"; individual Communion wafers; sometimes embossed with a cross or other symbol; Christ Himself, who serves His gathered guests.

hymn. Song of prayer or praise in stanza form.

Hymn of the Day. Chief hymn of the Divine Service; a hymn specifically selected to reflect the theme of the day, especially the Holy Gospel.

Hymn of Praise. Song following the Introit or Kyrie in the Divine Service; affirms God's actions for the world; the Gloria in Excelsis is traditionally sung.

Introit. Latin for "enter"; psalm verses sung or spoken at the beginning of the Divine Service.

Invocation. From the Latin for "call upon"; the words "In the name of the Father and of the Son and of the Holy Spirit" spoken at the beginning of the service; serves as a reminder of Holy Baptism.

Kyrie eleison. Greek for "Lord, have mercy." The Kyrie is the first prayer of the congregation in the Divine Service; it is a cry for mercy that our Lord and King hear us and help us in our needs and troubles.

liturgy. Greek for "work of the people"; the worship activity of the Divine Service; for Lutherans, the activity also includes God's work through the means of grace and the people's responses of hymns and prayers.

Liturgy of the Lord's Supper. Second main part of the Divine Service, beginning with the Preface.

Liturgy of the Word. First main part of the Divine Service, beginning with the Introit.

Lord's Supper. Another name for Holy Communion, the Sacrament of the Altar, or the Eucharist.

narthex. The gathering space of a church outside the nave; the baptismal font may be located here.

nave. Latin for "ship"; architecturally, the main portion of a church; place in which the assembly offers prayers and songs; early Christians portrayed the church as an ark into which the saved were brought by Baptism.

Nunc Dimittis. Latin for "now let [your servant] depart"; Simeon's Song (Luke 2:29–32); the Post-Communion Canticle after the distribution of the Lord's Supper.

Ordinary. Parts of the service that remain the same each week, for example, the Kyrie and the Sanctus.

Preface. Proclamation of praise and thanksgiving that begins the Service of the Sacrament; concludes with the Proper Preface, which changes according to the Sunday, festival, or season of the Church Year.

Propers. Parts of the service that change according to the Sunday or festival of the Church Year, for example, the Introit and the Scripture readings.

rite. Prescribed liturgical form containing the words (liturgy) and the actions (ceremony), such as a Rite of Baptism or a Rite of Confirmation.

Sabbath. Hebrew for "rest"; the seventh day of creation that God assigned as a day of rest.

Sacrament. From the Greek word "mystery"; a sacred act instituted by God in which God Himself has joined His Word of promise to a visible element and by which He offers, gives, and seals the forgiveness of sins earned by Christ; Holy Baptism and Holy Communion.

Sacrament of the Altar. Sacrament by which the Lord offers His body and blood under the form of consecrated bread and wine for Christians to eat and drink; through such eating and drinking, communicants receive the gifts of the forgiveness of sins and the strengthening of faith; also called Holy Communion, the Eucharist, and the Lord's Supper.

Sanctus. Latin for "holy"; follows the Preface in the Service of the Sacrament; based on Isaiah 6:3 and Matthew 21:9.

seder. Order of service for a Jewish Passover meal.

synagogue. Greek for "place of meeting"; traditional Jewish place for assembly to study, pray, and discuss spiritual, biblical, and community concerns; early Christians met here for worship.

"This Is the Feast." A Hymn of Praise; often used as an alternate to the Gloria in Excelsis for festival days in the Church Year and the Easter season because of its strong resurrection theme.

Triduum. Latin for "three days"; Good Friday, Saturday, and Easter Sunday (traditionally marked from sunset on Maundy Thursday until sunset on the evening of Easter).

Trinity, triune. One true God in three persons: Father, Son, and Holy Spirit.

Word and Sacrament. Lutheran emphasis on the tangible vehicles through which God's Spirit is actively working to produce and nurture faith in

Christ; the preached Word from Scripture as Law and Gospel and the sacraments of Absolution, Baptism, and Communion.

worship. The service to which God calls and gathers His people to give to them the gifts of life and salvation by means of Word and Sacrament.